The Richest Girl In The World

*The Extravagant Life and
Fast Times of Doris Duke*

Stephanie Mansfield

G. P. PUTNAM'S SONS   NEW YORK

For Philip and Andrew

G. P. Putnam's Sons
Publishers Since 1838
200 Madison Avenue
New York, NY 10016

Photograph on endpapers © UPI/Bettmann Newsphotos

Library of Congress Cataloging-in-Publication Data
Mansfield, Stephanie, date.
The richest girl in the world : the extravagant life and fast
times of Doris Duke / Stephanie Mansfield.
p.   cm.
Includes bibliographical references and index.
ISBN 0-399-13672-X (acid-free paper)
1. Duke, Doris, 1912–   . 2. United States—Biography.
3. Celebrities—United States—Biography.   I. Title.
CT275.D8769M36   1992   91-42771 CIP
973.9'092—dc20
[B]

Book design and composition by The Sarabande Press

Printed in the United States of America
3   4   5   6   7   8   9   10

This book is printed on acid-free paper.
∞

Contents

Acknowledgments

RESEARCH FOR THIS BOOK began in April 1989 and is based on interviews with more than 400 people. Many of the documents were obtained through the Freedom of Information Act, and I am grateful to the Justice Department, the FBI, the CIA, and the State Department for their cooperation.

I would like to express my deepest gratitude to the late James H. R. Cromwell who, in lengthy interviews before his death in 1990, spoke on the record for the first time of his former wife, Doris Duke.

My warmest thanks to Barbara Scherer, whose initial enthusiasm and research provided invaluable contacts, insights, and moral support. Also to William Green for his introduction to Duke University and his hospitality in Durham; to historian Robert F. Durden, William King, and Linda McCurdy of Duke's William R. Perkins Library and Bill Irwin and Pat Webb of the Manuscript Department I extend my gratitude.

My editor, George Coleman, and Amanda Urban of International Creative Management deserve much of the credit for keeping this project focused. Andrew Zeller of Putnam deserves special mention, as does Gael Love for her initial assignment to smoke out the reclusive Doris Duke.

My appreciation also to Peter Brooke, Mr. and Mrs. Joseph Castro, Walker Inman, Jr., Leon Amar, Mrs. Edward Macauley, John Reagan ("Tex") McCrary, Franco Rossellini, and members of the Duke-Biddle families for their trust and assistance. To the former butlers, maids, gardeners, and staffers who wished to remain anonymous, my gratitude in providing pieces to the puzzle.

I also wish to thank the following: Cindy Adams, Cleveland Amory, William E. Andersen, Newton Angier, Dr. Jay Arena, Vicki Arnold (Duke University), Bruce Abrams, Brooke Astor, Mrs. Anita Aughey, Helene Arpels, Dr. Lenox Baker, Ann Mueller Baker, Robert Balzar, Cobina Wright Beaudette, Ernie Betz, Pandora Biddle, Alfred S. Branam, Jr., Phil Benson, The Bettman Archives, Paul Blythe, Baron Bohnet, Peter Byrne, Ruth Buchanan, John Butler (U.S. Archives), Joel Biddle, Cobey Black, Earl Blackwell, Elvis Brathwaite (Wide World Photos), J. Carter Brown, Richard Banks, Whitney Balliett, Jayne Bennett, Charlie Borgois (Festival Productions), Father Tim Brown, Taylor Burke, Joe Bushkin, Justice William Brennan, The Bishop Museum, Honolulu, Ernie Byfield, Kathleen and

Denise Cahill, Oatsie Charles, Noel Cunningham-Reid, Michael Cunningham-Reid, Ralph Cobey, Beatrice Coelho, Ralph Cowan, Marajen Chinigo, Robert Cunningham, Bob Colacello, Fred Corriher, Jr., North Carolina Transportation History Corp., George Constable, Louis Cortese, Oreneece Coleman, Eaton and Mary Cromwell, Frank Como, Judy Canter of the *San Francisco Examiner,* Ken Craven (Harry Ransom Humanities Research Center), Deena Clark, Minnie Cushing Coleman, Art Cooper.

Also: Carol Dandereau (*Mansfield News Journal*), Neil Daniels, Susan Davis, Trudy Davis, John Gunther Dean, Kenneth J. DeWitt, Robert Dingwall, Christopher Duffy, A. Biddle Duke, Jr., Anthony Drexel Duke, Angier Biddle Duke (for permission to read the Angier Duke Papers at Duke University), Nicholas Rutgers Duke, Jane Dunn, Dominick Dunne, Tony Duquette, Dorothy Donnagan, Eleanor Tydings Ditzen, Maureen Dougherty, Dr. William Davison, Aimee de Herren, Mark Deren, Jeanne Dixon, Gregg Dodge, Leonard Downie (*The Washington Post*), Katherine Dunham, Reverend Norm Eddy, Sophie Engelhard, Mrs. Charles (Jane) Engelhard, Gerri Engelhart, George Englund, Millicent Fenwick, George L. Ferreira, Douglas Fairbanks, Jr., Ibrahim Farrah, Leonard Feather, Mrs. Jordan Franklin, George Frelinghuysen, Fred Friendly, Lacy Fetting, Tom Forbes (*Newport Daily News*), Cristina Ford, Geraldine Fuller, Ron Gallela, Mary Gamberdella, Luiz Gastal, Ellen Bromfield Geld, Sig and Andre Girgus, Mrs. James Graham, Stephane Grappelli, Fitzhugh Green, Mike Gesing, Jacob and Esther Guyer, Irving Guyer, Virginia Grace, Memphis Green, Lee Graham, Sam Greenspoon, Zsa Zsa Gabor, Mary Hamilton (The Brearley School), Eleanor Hufty, Mary Homi, John Haines (The Library of Congress), Hugh Harter, Stephen Heffner (*Providence Journal*), Betsy Holloway, Marilyn Humphries, Hope Cromwell Hopkins, C. David Heymann, former Governor Richard Hughes, Lawrence Huston, Peggy Ann Huber (Miller), Robert Huffman, Brooke Hayward, Michael Hahn, U.S. Embassy Rome, George Hurrell, Tony Jackson, Eddie Jaffe, Teresa Jeffries (*The London Daily Telegraph*), Ken Johnson, Donald Law, Edmund Kara, Nan Kempner, Richard Kent, Gordon King, Donald Kahn, Stanley Karnow, Julie Kirsh (*The Toronto Sun*), Susan Inman Key, Edward Lansbury, Hugh Lightsey, Bertram Lippincott (Newport Historical Society), Elaine Lorillard, Joe Lubin, Eleanor Lambert, Philip Langdon (The Bel Air Hotel), Charlie Lampach (Time-Life Research), Sarah Tomerlin Lee, Polly Guggenheim Logan, Fran Lebowitz, Doris Lilly, Caroline Latham, Gloria Long, Dolly Lovegreen, Peggy Lyman, Betty McIntosh, James R. McCredie, Director Institute of Fine Arts, Elizabeth McConville, Jeanne McManus, Marian McPartland, Nancy Mallory, Lucy Welch Mazzeo, Boaz Mazor, Dr. Joseph Mirto, Deborah Mitchell, Claude Marchant, Linda Marx, Ruth Montgomery, James Maher, Hope Ridings Miller, Joan Munkacsi, W. Michael Murphy, William Norwich, John Nutt, Patrick Nutt, Sydney Omarr, Scott Olson, Father Peter O'Brien, Ivan Obolensky.

My gratitude to The Palm Beach Historical Society, Angelo Pizzi, Andrea Portago, John Poole, John J. Pullen, Luvie Pearson, Louis Persel, A.I.A., Ned Patterson, John Plant, Samuel Pryor, Olwyn Price, Mrs. R. Stuart Rauch, Jr., Ben Reed, Newport Restoration Foundation, William Rocker (Washington Memorial Library, Macon), Ann Rayburn, Mrs. John Barry (D.D.) Ryan, Lady Reigate (Emily Cross), John Richardson, Severigna Rivera, Mark Renovitch (The Roosevelt Library, Hyde Park), Birney Robert, Tim Ryan (*Honolulu Star Bulletin*), Joseph Radice, Rex Reed, Dee Ray, Patrick Reynolds, Jimmy Reynolds, David Rimmer, Faigi Rosenthal (*New York Daily News*), Barbara Ryan, Martin Ransohoff, Bina Ramani, Annie Ross, Senator Terry Sanford, Phyllis Saretta, Ray Scherer, Arthur M. Schlesinger, Jr., Farol Seretean, Ed Shonk, Helen Sinclair, John Spuches, Mike and Penny Stabile, Hy Steirman, Wallis Sewall, Howard Simons, Leonard Stanley, Mike Stern, Mary Sanford, Geraldine Saunders, Stephen Scott, Hugh Craig Smyth, Lyle Stuart, Liz Stevens, Maralee Stevens, Hope Bromfield Stevens, Phil Strider, Doc Stryker, Cecily Surace (*Los Angeles Times*), Russell Selwyn, Victor Skrebneski, Robin Smyth (*The Observer*), Joan Smyth, Liz Smith, Jean Smith (The Library of Congress), Eilene Slocum, Mr. and Mrs. Joseph Kingsbury-Smith, Susan and Harry Spivak.

Also: Nick Tanasy, Taki Theodoroacopoulos, Fredrika Templeton, Nancy Thompson, Henrietta Wise Thompson, Richard Towill, Roseanna Todd, Charles Trenet, Irene Tirella, John Taylor (The National Archives), Colonel Cloyce Tippett, Ans VanderGoot, Emma Veary, Robert Venturi, Mamie Van Doren, Candace van Alen, Hildy van Roijan, Philip van Rensselaer, Walt Wadlington, Senator John Warner, Arthur Whittaker, Frank and Eleanor Waldrop, George D. Weaver, Ann Werther (*Washington Post* Paris bureau), Denise Winkler, Helen Siegel Wilson, Kitty White, Walter Wright (*The Honolulu Advertiser*).

If history is a scrapbook of extraordinary lives, Doris Duke certainly deserves a place.

Her story is one of money and madness; greed, guilt, envy, and amorality. Her fortune became a passport to decadence, and in the end, bitter isolation. The embarrassment of riches brought her fame and celebrityhood, but her struggle to overcome the burden of her inheritance was constant.

That she survived at all is a miracle. The odds were certainly against her.

Diana Vreeland once said that a woman can neither be too thin or too rich. Doris Duke was the exception.

Stephanie Mansfield
November 1991

Prologue

TATOU, a trendy Manhattan supper club on East Fiftieth Street, once the home of the old Cafe Versailles, was temporarily closed to the public one autumn night in 1991. Outside, a throng of paparazzi and autograph hounds gathered, elbowing one another for a better view. Word had spread that Franco Rossellini was holding a private party for actress Sophia Loren and two hundred of her closest Hollywood friends after a screening at The Museum of Modern Art of Vittorio De Sica's 1961 classic, *Two Women*.

Among the expected guests was the notoriously reclusive tobacco heiress Doris Duke, rumored to be making a rare public appearance.

As the flotilla of limousines pulled up to the curb, the crowd surged forward. Suddenly, from the back of a black stretch emerged a tall, slim, slightly regal figure with wispy, shoulder-length blonde hair. Her thick gold necklace gleamed in the lights, set off by a gold lamé top and leopard-print pants. It was Doris Duke, the last of the poor little rich girls. Her sculpted face was heavily made up, and she seemed startled and slightly bemused. A roar went up from the crowd. She was followed by a smaller, darker, slightly plump woman with a moon-shaped porcelain face: former Philippines First Lady Imelda Marcos. Three years earlier Doris had come to Imelda's rescue, posting the $5 million bail for her friend who had been indicted on federal fraud and racketeering charges and offering her the use of her private $25 million Boeing aircraft.

Doris, Imelda, and their close friend Cristina Ford had just come from Doris' pink and black Park Avenue penthouse where they had enjoyed cocktails together. Now the three women, flanked by security guards, were ushered inside the supper club amid the cheering throng. The high drama of their entrance was not lost on the crowd.

Inside, round tables had been set up for dinner. Imelda, Doris, and Sophia Loren were seated together. Doris and Imelda were side by side. "Doris looked witch-like and particularly weird," said a guest seated across from her. "She was off in another world."

Peter Allen, former husband of Liza Minnelli, had just flown in from a safari trip. At first he was seated between Doris and Imelda but changed his place. "He was afraid of being photographed between them," said one guest. Calvin Klein was there, "walker" Jerry Zipkin, socialite Pat Buckley, fashion designer Carolina Herrera, all dining on chicken breasts, crab cakes with cilantro *roulé,* and double chocolate terrine. Amid the din, conversation was impossible. Ten security guards watched over Doris and Imelda, who were openly affectionate to one another.

R. Couri Hay, columnist and author, noted Doris and Imelda "were happy as two little clams." He made an attempt to chat. As jazz music filled the air, he realized that Doris was nostalgic about the old Cafe Society, days when she would listen to the sounds of long-forgotten bands of the 1930s and 1940s. As the crush of people swarmed around them, Imelda and Doris decided to return to the penthouse.

"Shall we call for the car?" said Imelda.

"My scarf? I've got my scarf," answered Doris.

She moved slowly and carefully out to the door. The sudden flash of strobe lights lit up the Manhattan sidewalk, and for one brief, giddy moment the legendary, enigmatic seventy-nine-year-old Doris Duke was once again the object of intense desire. The closest thing to American royalty.

"My goodness," she said in her breathy, little girl voice. "All these photographers."

The richest girl in the world was ready for her close-up.

Chapter One

The Durham Dukes

IN THE SUMMER OF 1865, Washington Duke trudged down the winding dirt road to his family's farm, three miles east of Durham. He had been walking for days, just released from a Yankee prison in Richmond and paroled in the coastal town of New Bern, 130 miles from home. He rounded the bend and caught his breath. There, in ruins, was the family homestead; the ramshackle buildings collapsed, the crops destroyed, the supplies looted by hell-raising Union soldiers cutting a swath throughout the Carolinas. Duke, a tall, well-built man who had been conscripted by the Confederate Navy two years earlier, slumped to the side of the road, half-starved and heartbroken. He was forty-five, a widower with four children, two blind mules, and a fifty-cent piece in his pocket given to him by a Union soldier in exchange for a now worthless five-dollar Confederate bill.

Under the blistering sun, he surveyed the wreckage; stepping over the splintered wood railings and leaning on a broken-down wagon, he pondered his future. His feet were swollen from the long march and his hands were raw from years of labor in the fields. One of ten children born to Taylor and Dicey Jones Duke, young Wash was raised on a farm, which grew mostly wheat and corn, sometimes tobacco and cotton. Wash Duke would later say he had spent more time behind the plow than any man his age.

He had married at twenty-two, and a son, Sidney, came quickly. But his young bride died shortly after giving birth to a second boy, Brodie, leaving him a widower at twenty-seven. Five years passed and the two boys were cared for by relatives before Duke purchased a tract of land and built a two-story frame house on what would eventually become the family homestead. He decided to marry again. His new wife, Artelia Roney, was one of the prettiest girls in the county. They met when he spied her singing in the local church choir. She bore him a daughter, Mary Elizabeth, and two more sons, Benjamin Newton and James Buchanan. James was born December 23, 1856, and named, in a burst of patriotism by his proud father, after the newly elected Democratic president.

But the hardscrabble life took its toll on the family. In the summer of 1858, typhoid fever swept the county and the eldest boy, Sidney, succumbed to the disease at the age of fourteen. Duke's twenty-nine-year-old wife Artelia, who had nursed her beloved stepson day and night for weeks, also came down with typhoid and died ten days later. The other children escaped the fever. Ben, a delicate child prone to illness, was only three. The youngest boy, James Buchanan, known as Buck, had red hair and was strong and vigorous, although severely pigeon-toed. (Forced to wear heavy, custom-made shoes as a child, Buck later had surgery to correct the deformity.) Motherless at the age of two, with no memory of Artelia's warmth or beauty save for a faded photograph, he would eventually make the family name synonymous with American business moguls Rockefeller and Vanderbilt.

Duke made his way to a small outhouse. He unlatched the door and forced it open. There, in the cramped darkness, he found a quantity of cured tobacco obviously overlooked by the marauding Yankees. Duke quickly reunited with his sons, Ben, then ten, and Buck, nine, whom he had placed in the care of relatives during the war. They beat out the tobacco with hickory sticks and a grain flail, sifted it through a sieve, and packed it in muslin bags, labeling the contents Pro Bono Publico; "For the public good." In the dilapidated wagon, Wash Duke, accompanied by his sons, bartered and sold the salvaged crop, sleeping on the dusty Carolina roadsides at night and existing on corn meal and sweet potatoes.

Until then, cigarette smoking was not a socially acceptable habit (even if Sir Walter Raleigh had considered it healthful), and the tobacco trade around Durham was modest, concentrating mostly on plug tobacco. But things were about to change in the dusty town whose very existence was almost accidental. Only a decade earlier, the North Carolina Railroad had approached a storeowner about locating a station on his land. But the man wanted too much money. A young physician, Dr. Bartlett Durham, stepped in and offered four acres of land for the station. In gratitude, they named the depot Durhamville, later changed to Durham Station, and then simply Durham. By the end of the Civil War, the town—declared a neutral territory—had several hundred occupants and was a lively spot for passing troops, although luxuries were unheard of and "store bought" items were scarce. Soldiers returning home carried the Spanish Flavored Durham Tobacco, and soon the demand increased. Bright leaf tobacco, cured by charcoal instead of wood, had a lighter colored leaf and sweeter taste. When local tobacco merchant John Green adopted the bull logo from a jar of Coleman's Mustard (made in Durham, England) naming his product Bull Durham, it put the town on the map.

The Dukes were industrious farmers and energetic salesmen, especially young Buck. Cock-sure and self-reliant, he was already managing his co-workers by the age of fourteen. They had built a twenty-by-thirty-foot curing building on their land and later moved their operations to a small factory, producing 15,000 pounds of tobacco in 1866, which fetched fifty cents a pound. (Twenty cents of that went to taxes.) By 1869 Wash Duke's son by his first marriage, Brodie, had moved to Durham, producing tobacco under the name "Duke of Durham." Wash, Ben, and Buck (who at eighteen had hurredly finished a stint at Poughkeepsie's Eastman Business College) soon joined forces with Brodie and another young man, George Watts, to form W. Duke, Sons and Company. Six years later, production had risen to 125,000 pounds per year and the operation was centered in a three-story factory on downtown Main Street. It had a false front, a bell tower, and was equipped with a screw-press, which could squeeze the tobacco into plugs or ground it for smoking.

By this time, Washington Duke had sold the farm and moved into Durham, which had become a hurly-burly, Bright Belt boom town; money and women and whiskey were easy to come by and Blackwell's race track was said to be the state's finest. There was a bustling red-light district and even the mayor was arrested for public drunkenness. Like other Southern towns, hundreds of thousands of freed slaves roamed the streets as the pungent smell of tobacco wafted over its shanties. Durham was regarded as coarse and common, not at all like the staid nearby Chapel Hill, which boasted the state university, or even Winston, where a young man named R. J. Reynolds had started his own company selling plug tobacco.

Buck spent his early years on the road, often saving on hotel bills by sleeping upright in the caboose of freight trains. (Later in life, he was said to be unable to comfortably sleep lying down in bed, and would prefer an easy chair, owing to this early rail-riding experience.) He would often relieve the tension of work in the company of relatives and friends. In August of 1880, he wrote to his brother Ben from Memphis, describing a raucous time at Uncle John Duke's in Milan, Tennessee. The letter was typewritten and is one of a handful of correspondence surviving.

> I romped and played with the girls so much I declare I was so tired at night I could not sleep. I aked all over. Old man John was about half stued most of the time and he would join in with me & them and I know if you had been there you would have split your sides laughing at us. It first started by Lida & Mattie putting a little water on me & got me started. I then, you know, wanted to get the best of them so it went from drops to dipperfull & finally ended in bucketfull on top of one & another until we were wet from head to foot . . .

Buck felt great affection for his older brother, whose physical condition prevented him from taking a more active role in drumming up the trade. As Buck wrote, "It does really appear that you have very bad luck, so much sickness, & I think I can't be thankful anough to my maker for giving me such good health." He offered Ben money for a vacation, mainly out of guilt that he had been born with such a robust temperament.

While Ben may have been better educated, it was Buck who was the driving force. He once recalled, "I have succeeded in business, not because I have more natural ability than many people who have not succeeded, but because I have applied myself harder and stuck to it longer. I had confidence in myself. I resolved from the time I was a mere lad to do a big business. I loved business better than anything else. I worked from early morning to late at night. Superior brains are not necessary."

Business was prospering, thanks in part to the new "Bonsack" machine which could turn out twice the number of hand-rolled cigarettes.

Ben had married Sarah Pearson Angier, daughter of storekeeper M. A. Angier. Their sister Mary had also married. The Dukes were expanding their horizons to Europe. On one trip, Wash Duke was allowed to sit in a chair reserved for royalty by claiming to be the Duke of Durham.

In April 1884, Buck Duke made a decision to move to New York. It was a daring idea. Boys from the South rarely moved up north, but Buck, at twenty-seven, was certain that a factory in Manhattan would be a success. He took a two-dollar-a-week furnished room and quickly set up shop in a loft on Rivington Street near the Bowery. A tall, gawky man with a Southern accent as thick as sorghum who was snubbed by the other tobacco lords, he pounded the pavements hawking his new-fangled, machine-made cigarettes.

Duke's nearest competitor was Allen & Ginter, located in Richmond, followed by New York's Kinney Tobacco Company, Rochester's W. S. Kimbell & Company, and Brooklyn's Goodwin & Company. Like John D. Rockefeller, who successfully overran competitors to own ninety percent of the nation's oil, Buck Duke—firing the deadliest shots in what had become a fierce trade war—was after its tobacco. After unsuccessfully attempting to buy out his competitors, he strongarmed them into joining forces, and in January 1890 the American Tobacco Company was formed with assets of $5 million. Buck Duke, one month after his thirty-third birthday, was elected its president.

"I hated to close my desk at night and was eager to get back to it early next morning," he said. "I needed no vacation or time off. No fellow does who is really interested in his work. There ain't a thrill in the world to compare with building up a business or watching it grow before your eyes."

Exclusive use of the Bonsack rolling machine was purchased by the Dukes. Several old tobacco firms were bought or closed, with competitors asked to sign clauses prohibiting them from going back into business. Middlemen and dealers were cut out; tobacco was bought directly from farms. Duke's measures paid off. Profits for the first year were $2.5 million, and the pigeon-toed farmboy had twisted the Bull's tail and cornered the market.

The so-called "Tobacco Trust" did not initially include R. J. Reynolds, who declared, "I don't intend to be swallowed by Duke. If he does, he'll have a bellyache the rest of his life." But the ruthless Duke turned his attention to plug tobacco. In a letter to his brother Ben, Buck wrote that he hoped to "make the Plug Mfgrs hustle like we once did Ciagarette Mfgrs." Duke bought out competitor Drummond and cut the price for his plug dramatically. Next, he took over Lorillard and finally, R. J. Reynolds, although the deal was kept from the public.

By 1900, the Trust boasted 92.7 percent of the cigarette market, 80 percent of snuff, 62 percent of plug, and 59 percent of smoking tobacco.

Buck Duke's insatiable appetite for money and power was fueled by a deep-seated, almost adolescent insecurity. He was a man obsessed. At night, he was known to wander the streets of Manhattan, counting the number of discarded cigarette packs and noting the brands. As a promotional stunt, he offered fifty dollars for anyone turning in the most empties bearing the Duke imprint. He also reinvented himself; giving up his favorite chew for cigars, moving his headquarters to Gramercy Park, and modeling himself on another rags-to-riches mogul, John D. Rockefeller.

Duke had translated his family's assets into American Tobacco Company stock worth $7.5 million and was now scarfing raw oysters at Delmonico's with fellow mogul J. P. Morgan. He built a private stable in Manhattan, traveled to Europe and California, went to the opera, and in 1893, bought three hundred acres of farmland in nearby Somerville, New Jersey, for the requisite country estate. He also took a mistress, Mrs. Lillian McCredy.

His new offices, located at 111 Fifth Avenue, were missing the familiar spitoon as J. B. Duke had taken up expensive La Eleganzia cigars. He was also gaining a reputation as a hard-nosed financier who had no use for books, personal publicity, or sentiment. When salesman Edward Small, who had labored for years as the most energetic salesman, balked at Duke's request to move his family from Atlanta to Cincinnati, he was fired.

Buck Duke, described by one observer as "big, loud and physically violent," was not particularly popular. Bernard Baruch faulted his "rough language. He didn't speak very grammatically." On one occasion, when dashing young Pierre Lorillard left a business meeting at the urging of a spirited group of comrades, Duke was heard to mutter, "I think I'll have to buy me some friends sometime."

Trusts were destroying small businesses and price fixing became common. Elected officials owned blocks of tobacco stock and enacted friendly legislation reducing the tobacco tax. Labor was cheap and there was no income tax. In 1902, there were eight thousand millionaires—including four Dukes—twice as many as there had been at the turn of the century. While the average American family lived on nine hundred dollars a year, the new steel and auto and railroad millionaires were erecting elaborate Newport castles and filigreed Fifth Avenue mansions. They went to Europe and returned with paintings, tapestries, priceless antiques, and French-speaking servants. If they didn't have it, they'd buy it. And while they may have been socially snubbed by more established families, this flotilla of free spenders would usher in a new social order unparalleled in American history.

Back in Durham, Wash Duke, now in his sixties, defended his son's brazen business practices, which were hurting the small, local tobacco growers. The campaign was fueled by zealous preachers and doctors who warned of the dangers of cigarette smoking. Boycotts were organized, and laws prohibiting the sale to minors were enacted by state legislatures, with Kansas banning sales altogether. The term "coffin tacks" had become part of the vernacular. Various diseases were already being attributed to smoking tobacco. (Curiously enough, chewing was more tolerated.)

"Tobacco is the poor man's luxury," Buck said. "Where else can he get so much enjoyment for his five or ten cents?" Unfazed by the criticism, Duke (hit with a variety of lawsuits) hired an army of lawyers and lobbyists and became the country's chief tobacco pusher. He was even indicted by a New York grand jury in 1896 for conspiracy to restrict competition. The charge was a misdemeanor.

Buck Duke could not be stopped. His newly formed American Cigar Company took over the cheroot and little cigar business, buying up the Havana-American Companies factories in Tampa and Key West. Overseas, he formed the British-American Tobacco Company, buying the largest tobacco concern in the country and drawing a hailstorm of disapproval. "It has raised a great howl," he wrote to his father. "They call us the American invaders & are appealing to the people to repel us." After another British tobacco company threatened to open factories in America directly competing with Duke, he backed down and decided to join forces with them.

To celebrate the union, Duke hosted an elaborate dinner in the Charles II dining room of the Carlton Hotel, on the evening of October 7, 1902. His culinary tastes not yet refined, he ordered an associate to "take care of the grub." The men feasted on caviar, blinis, Mignonettes of Sole, three different meats, asparagus, "Neige au Clicquot," and Supreme de Foie Gras, washed down with vintage wines including Moet & Chandon cuvee, 1836. The *Illustrated London Mail* headlined the story, "A Millionaire's Dinner Party" and dutifully reproduced the menu—with a picture of the portly J. B. Duke—printed in gold and bound with white silk.

In the end, he slayed the bull. Duke took over the Durham Tobacco Company, first dissolving his old competitor and reforming the North Carolina company in New Jersey, to a chorus of criticism.

A worried Wash Duke, who once said there were three things he could never understand: "Ee-lec-tricity—the Holy Ghost—and my son Buck," began questioning his overambitious offspring's advertising campaigns, specifically the use of sexually suggestive photographs of women, to sell cigarettes. But Wash's deeper disapproval was reserved for more personal matters: his son's illicit affair with Lillian McCredy. Buck had kept knowledge of his New York mistress from his father, although Ben was aware of the six-year relationship. When Wash Duke learned of the liaison, Buck, by then approaching his forty-eighth birthday and hoping to avoid a family scandal, promised to make an honest woman of his live-in lover.

It would take more than marriage.

A bubbly, socially active forty-two-year-old woman who adored frilly clothes and French novels, Lillian Nanette Fletcher had come to New York from Camden, New Jersey, to train as a singer. She married stockbroker William E. McCredy, but was soon divorced. McCredy accused his wife of infidelity with three men, including a young Cuban, whom she signaled with the lowering of her boudoir blinds.

Soon after meeting her in a hotel lobby, Buck was living with Lillian and her sister in a Manhattan townhouse. He later provided $30,000 for a five-story mansion at 11 West Sixty-eighth Street, off Central Park, and presented his mistress with gifts of diamonds, emeralds, and valuable stocks.

Buck was besotted by Lillian, interrupting important business meetings to see her and riding in open cabs down Fifth Avenue oblivious to the stares. He was also oblivious to the fact that Lillian was simultaneously carrying on an affair with another suitor, Frank T. Huntoon, a dashing man about town who was no financial match for the red-haired, rough-cut Duke. A confirmed bachelor and workaholic who suffered from eczema and had a taste for whiskey, Duke had enjoyed casual sexual flutters with many women, but he managed to avoid any serious commitment and certainly didn't want children. (One historian concludes that the reason Southern men of this era postponed marriage was the availability of black female concubines. In Duke's case, it may have just been his devotion to work.)

Business associates assumed the attraction to Lillian was merely sexual. But at the urging of Wash Duke, Lillian and Buck wed quietly on November 29, 1904, in the home of her aunt in Camden. The story was leaked to the press and appeared on the front page of *The New York Herald*. The following day they sailed on the *Baltic* for a two-month honeymoon to the French and Italian Riviera, where it was unseasonably cold and rainy.

Some weeks later, Ben Duke learned of the impending marriage of his half-brother Brodie to a thirty-seven-year-old Chicago-based tobacco businesswoman, Alice Webb. He fought bitterly with Brodie, trying to dissuade him. Buck interrupted his honeymoon to send cables urging Brodie to get rid of her and hired a battery of lawyers and private detectives to investigate Miss Webb, who was trying to interest Brodie in a real estate scheme. A month after the wedding, Brodie was kidnapped from a Park Avenue hotel and committed to an insane asylum. He had $40,000 in cash and securities on him and had already made out promissory notes to his wife for $15,000. An alcoholic, he had been previously sent to a clinic after drunkenly galloping through the Durham factory astride his favorite horse. But this was more serious. Brodie had been on a month-long bender delirious from alcohol and drugs and could barely remember his wedding ceremony.

After an initial protest, Alice Webb slipped out of town, no doubt having been persuaded by the Duke family. Brodie Duke was released from the asylum and spent the next two months drying out in an Asbury Park, New Jersey, hotel under an assumed name in the care of a physician. Ben Duke threatened criminal action, but settled for a quick divorce. (Three years later, the same Alice Webb was arrested in Chicago for passing bad checks.)

There was no question that Brodie was a failure. Unprofitable cotton dealings he had arranged had become a drain on the family coffers, perhaps more of a sin than his chronic alcoholism, compulsive gambling, or poor taste in women. Brodie, at fifty-eight, was the polar opposite of Buck. His share of the family fortune, once estimated as $3 million, had dwindled to $250,000.

The Dukes of Durham, once known for their strong Methodist background and work ethic, were gradually succumbing to the kind of self-destructive habits that accompany sudden and enormous wealth.

There was such a thing, Buck Duke would learn, as having too much money.

Chapter Two

Tobacco King
in New York

BUCK DUKE'S FOOT HURT.

Since childhood, damp weather had caused it to cramp and swell, and wouldn't you know it would start acting up here on the French Riviera. Lillian had little sympathy. Since leaving New York she was remote and strangely unhappy. Buck wondered why he had agreed to the marriage in the first place, announced when the exuberant Lillian had hundreds of Tiffany-engraved cards sent out to friends stating that the couple would be "at home" after February 1 at 11 West Sixty-eighth Street.

For six weeks they had been at each other's throats. Nothing seemed to please her. The only solace was the Paris edition of the *New York Herald*, which Lillian, in frilly bed jackets, had delivered to her daily by her young maid, Nellie Sands.

While Buck wanted to tour the countryside in open cars despite the weather, Lillian sulked, saying the trips were harmful to her delicate health. They fought bitterly, hurling accusations at each other with increasing venom. Duke wondered how long the charade could continue. He was miserable. In mid-January, he received a cable saying his father was ill. It was the excuse he needed.

"We're going home," he announced.

The couple packed up and sailed to New York, arriving on February 8,

1905. After a week in Durham to visit the ailing Washington Duke, the newlyweds—Buck's own condition growing worse by the day—returned to New York where his foot was operated on. Doctors had diagnosed his ailment as blood poisoning and told him his foot was gangrenous. He was ordered to his third-floor bedroom for six weeks.

Washington Duke was fading. He had suffered attacks of vertigo and in December had fallen in the doorway of a Durham bank and broken his right arm. A month later, he fell again and broke his hip. Buck and Lillian hurried south for Easter, and then later witnessed the patriarch's death at 2 P.M. on May 8. Old man Duke, who had flailed out a small barnful of tobacco to feed his family, told a friend that the only reason he hated to die was "I do not want to leave the boys." He was eighty-five.

In his will, the Durham house and conservatory of music was left to Buck. What was left of Brodie's money had been put into a trust for his family's protection. Money was also left for aging Methodist preachers, the "circuit riders" who had so influenced his early years.

In his lifetime, Wash Duke had given generously to various causes, among them Trinity College in Durham, which immediately commissioned a bronze statue of the bearded patriarch sitting in an armchair. Originally, the college was located 100 miles west of the city. When Trinity announced that it was looking for a more urban location, Wash Duke promised to outbid any competitor by $50,000 on the condition that the school admit women and move to Durham, which it did in 1892. It would become, with Duke's gift of $2.1 million, the richest college in the South Atlantic States. One wag suggested the school motto *Erudito et Religio* be changed to *Erudito et Religio et Cherooto et Cigaretto*.

Now that his father was dead, Buck Duke felt released from his marriage vows. After all, it was his father's idea that he marry, and now Duke felt no obligation to continue the farce. He began looking for a way out.

Knowing Lillian detested the country, he suggested they spend the spring and summer at his property in Somerville, New Jersey. The town was small and rural, a favorite stop for travelers going from New York to Princeton. It seemed a logical spot for a *maison secondaire*. Over 300 workmen were crawling over the estate, laying out gardens and digging ponds, and the construction left mountains of dirt and dust storms over the land. When Duke bought the farm from the Veghte family, he decided to expand and remodel the main house. He hired architects and began construction, putting in heated stables that cost $60,000 alone. (By today's standards, that figure would translate into half a million dollars.) The stalls were separated by cocoa matting rugs and the building was adorned with four murals: "America," showing the Western plains; "Africa," showing two Bedouins crossing the Sahara; "Asia," featuring turbanned hunters approaching a tiger; and "Europe," depicting huntsmen in pink coats.

He built a lavish dining room and new chimneys, throwing out the architects' plans at times in favor of his own ideas. He wanted a fireplace in the parlor, and also in the dining room and library. He installed electric lights and hot water heaters and was one of the first to purchase a telephone. A water filter system purified the supply from a five-acre reservoir on the farm.

By all accounts, the farm was a turn-of-the-century Babylon. "Miles of macadam drives sweep among rolling hills and dales, passing through stately groves and winding around pretty streams, and fern bordered lakes," according to the March 21, 1903, edition of *Town & Country.* "The whole panorama of woodland, rolling valley and winding river now form a landscape scheme that for original design and decorative treatment may find few counterparts." It was open to visitors and tourists, who thronged through its gates.

Duke spent $1 million on the artificial lake alone, crowded with geese, swans, and imported water fowl. There was a race track, carriage house, and ornate greenhouses filled with tropical fruits. "In the palmhouse, the foliage runs riot. The air is laden with the fragrant jessamine, orange blossom and magnolia, mingled with the wild azalea and pond lily; among the trailing vines of moss and tendrils of wild vines swing dainty butterfly orchids," the article continued. There were acres of roses, American Beauty, La France, and Marchal Niel, carnations and spring bulbs, gathered daily for arrangements.

"Mr. Duke has recently collected from abroad bronzes by famous sculptors for the ornamentation of his grounds." There was a lifesize gilt statue of President William McKinley. (One story has it that Duke originally envisioned a cigarette dangling from McKinley's lips, but changed his mind when the artist wanted to charge two dollars more.) Another ornament was the white sandstone fountain imported from Paris that shot water twenty feet in the air. (Duke had an almost pathological obsession with fountains.) There was also a central clock tower and cathedral chimes.

The main house contained eleven bedrooms, six bathrooms. It had a staff of five: housekeeper, cook, waitress, chambermaid, and laundress to run the living quarters alone. The larder was stocked with eggs, meats, canned goods, and all sorts of freshly grown vegetables from the gardens. There were two refrigerators. Often, Duke would show up with half a dozen business associates from the city and boast that his only rule about such get-togethers was that the servants were only entitled to thirty minutes' notice before his arrival for a meal.

Even by Gilded-Age standards, Duke's Farm was outrageously grand; a monument to nouveau American fortunes and a testament to the prevailing envy of the European aristocratic life-style. The land was described as a parallelogram one mile wide and three miles long, bigger than many cities of the day. Duke, the country bumpkin, had created his own feudal town with a faux English feel.

Every Friday night, he motored for three hours along country roads to reach the retreat. Once there, he couldn't relax. He would often be heard admonishing contractors and workmen, Italian immigrants who worked for low pay. (One worker sued Duke after he was hurt in a construction accident only to have the suit thrown out of court.)

There was no question that Duke wanted things his own way. One day, a rug man was laying the carpet under the hearth.

"I want you to bind the carpet," Duke ordered.

"But, sir, in the city they bind the carpet. In the country, they do it like this."

"Well," Duke bellowed, "we want this just as good out here as it would be in the city."

The next day, the carpets were bound.

When he didn't like the way his horses were being treated, he fired his trainer and tore down the stables to build a new one. An early experiment with blooded cattle ended in boredom. He tired of cows and turned to horses. The lighted, half-mile track was replaced shortly after with water-works. He constructed lake after lake, with a fountain in the center. When he tired of an artificial mountain, he leveled it. It was said that 500 men were kept constantly busy rearranging the scenery to suit the owner.

Duke's mistress, Lillian McCredy, had been coming to the farm for years, formerly accompanied by her mother who was now paralyzed and in a sanitarium. Despite her position in New York, she had little authority in Somerville. It was a man's residence, furnished with heavy Victorian furniture and deep-hued Wilton carpets. All those statues of bulls and lions! After the marriage, Lillian demanded that a conservatory on the second floor be made into a sewing room. She also insisted on the construction of large drawers to hold her ever-expanding wardrobe and jewels.

But it wasn't the lack of closet space that annoyed the red-haired Lillian.

It was the presence of Duke's housekeeper, Mary Smith. Her older sister Maggie had come to the farm in 1894, first as the housekeeper and then taking the position of cashier. Two months later, she hired her younger sister Mary to fill her old job. Eventually, Maggie Smith took over as manager of Duke's Farm and the beautiful Mary was dining at night with Duke (leaving the other girls in the kitchen). Duke was generous with the Smith sisters. Mary's salary rose from four to ten dollars a week. There were gifts of jewelry and tobacco stock and on one Christmas, Maggie Smith was presented with a jeweled ring. Both sisters also played the stock market, profiting from their employer's financial advice.

A week before his marriage to Lillian, Buck Duke made it clear that the Smith sisters were in charge of Somerville. He insisted Lillian write to Mary, asking her to lunch. Under duress, Lillian assured the sisters that their positions would remain unchanged and even invited them to the wedding.

Duke might have been happier had he wed Mary instead of Lillian, but men of wealth simply did not marry servants. Bedding a chambermaid was quite common, but wedding one was out of the question.

Lillian grew jealous of the arrangement. "They ate at the table with us," she complained. "They were always around whenever we were. I don't think I ever went out to drive alone with my husband but twice after I was married to him . . . he always took the Smith girls."

By that time, Buck had become a driving enthusiast, purchasing three automobiles and directing his stablemen to start using the blood horses for ordinary farm work. He enjoyed taking Mary on rides around the countryside. After all, their relationship needn't change just because he was a married man. They often stayed up late at night, drinking Duke's imported wine and talking, long after Lillian had gone to bed.

It was Mary who hired the servants and ordered the meals, not Lillian. "I wasn't even permitted to say what I would like to eat," Lillian later recalled. "I asked once, I would like to have some flowers sent in from the green house to the New York house; she informed me they didn't have enough for themselves. I asked on another occasion for some vegetables. I was told they didn't have enough for themselves." (Lillian eventually went around her nemesis, getting the produce directly from the male farm manager.)

Lillian hated Somerville, the one point she and her husband agreed on. "I was very much dissatisfied because she ran to the New York house so much," Buck later said. "I told her I wanted her to go to the farm and stay there—that was the home, and we wanted to build up our home there and she rebelled at it." Finally, Duke threatened to stop paying the bills for the New York house.

"I'll take care of the house myself," Lillian cried.

"I'll shut down the stable," Duke threatened.

"I'll go to a livery stable and hire a team and send you the bill," snapped Lillian.

"I won't pay it," Duke replied.

A new main house had been planned on the grounds of Somerville; a grand, half a million faux chateau designed by noted Philadelphia architect Horace Trumbauer. Buck and Lillian fought over the location, finally agreeing on a spot high on a hill overlooking the Raritan River.

By July, Duke had tired of the battling. He also suspected his wife of adultery. He consulted two lawyers, Junius Parker and Caleb Dula of the firm of W. W. Fuller. It was decided to have private detectives follow Lillian while Duke was in London, suddenly called overseas for a bogus business meeting. (Duke had already relied on espionage as a business weapon. Why wouldn't it be as effective in his own personal life?)

On July 16, Duke sailed for Europe. Lillian wrote him every day, complaining of the noise the steam shovel made at the farm, where work on the new house had begun. Buck had already spent close to $150,000 for grading, terrace work, and steel for the basement floor, but the house would never be completed, the enormous stone foundation still intact today.

From London, Duke wrote to Lillian, telling her to expect him on the *Lucana* steamer, scheduled to dock September 2. When she went to the pier to meet him, Duke was not on the boat. Two days earlier, he had slipped back into the country on a different steamer and gone directly to Ben Duke's Fifth Avenue house in Manhattan.

Ben had recently moved up from Durham with his wife, Sarah, and their two children, Mary and Angier, nicknamed "Angy," who had just graduated from Trinity College and was already making a name for himself as a dashing young bachelor in New York. At twenty-one, he was a reckless rich kid, having blown off his right hand in a hunting accident in North Carolina. Doctors amputated his right arm at the elbow, which didn't stop the young millionaire in his quest for life-threatening activities.

At Ben's house, Buck was joined by Mary Smith. He also managed to hire every one of his wife's maids, including Nellie Sands, installing them in his brother's house. He later admitted that he had hired his wife's servants to spy on Lillian.

The day of his return, Buck filed a divorce suit in New Jersey, naming

"Major" Frank Huntoon—a member of The Old Guard—as the correspondent. The process server went to Lillian's house disguised as a gas inspector and served the papers in her boudoir. The story broke on Sunday, September 3, and *The New York Times* played it prominently on the front page. Huntoon, a tall, weathered man of sixty-seven with a penchant for race tracks, was described as the president of a mineral water company and "a man about town" who lived at the Hotel Wolcott. On the day the story broke, he fled to Southampton. Reporters who knocked on Lillian's front door were told she had no comment. "Mr. Duke's marriage to Mrs. McCredy was a great surprise to his friends," *The Times* commented. "He was then 48 years old and there were few who knew he contemplated matrimony." (The marriage announcement in *The Times* had earlier referred to Duke as a "confirmed bachelor.")

Lillian countersued, saying Duke was a resident of New York, not New Jersey. She then accused her husband of committing adultery with Mary Smith and also of mental cruelty, citing their disastrous honeymoon during which Lillian said she lost twenty pounds. She said Duke forced her to take long journeys in open vehicles, "exposed to rain, hail and snow, and cold over a large part of Italy and France traveling every day, exposing defendant to hunger, and depriving her of sleep often times when defendant was barely able to walk to the vehicle . . . She was affected with pain and sleeplessness, and her nerves and physical health was wrecked."

She also accused Duke of striking her with his crutch, choking and shaking her, leaving black and blue marks on her body. It seems Lillian brought out the beast in Buck. She testified that he routinely called her "vile names such as whore, wench, bitch; and this was likely to occur and did occur almost every night; his habit was to drink large quantities of intoxicating liquors every night, which inflamed his brutal spirit and increased the infliction of wrongs and indignities to which he subjected defendant."

Lastly, she denied the charges of her own adultery, saying through his vast wealth, Duke had "vilified her in the public prints and organized an army of former servants of defendant, and paid witnesses to heap abuse upon her by false testimony to be given in the courts."

Duke vs. Duke went into overtime.

Buck denied hitting Lillian and passionately defended Mary Smith. The newspapers devoured every morsel of the scandal, which became, like the latter-day Trump divorce, juicy fare at breakfast tables from Flatbush to Fifth Avenue. Ben Duke was deeply embarrassed by the publicity, mainly because his wife was making important social inroads with the more established East Coast aristocracy.

After Lillian lost her bid to have the suit thrown out because of lack of jurisdiction, the silver-haired vice chancellor Pitney in Newark began taking testimony. Both Dukes showed up at the hearing, Lillian in a black gown and a flare hat of white velvet trimmed with large black feathers and a small smile on her face. Huntoon sat in the back row. Buck took the stand and said he considered the New Jersey estate to be his permanent residence. The next day, Lillian testified, telling of her marriage and rain-soaked honeymoon and husband's infidelities.

Duke was prepared for a fight. Personal ads allegedly placed by Huntoon in the *Paris Herald* as messages to Lillian were revealed. In them, Huntoon seemed preoccupied with Lillian's cleavage. "Your house pets are well. The bird sings sweetly. I dream every night you will be mine forever. Don't wear low-neck dresses."

And another: "Oh memories that bless and burn! This separation is killing. Please don't wear low-neck dresses. Shall enjoy your home until octopus returns."

Octopus was Huntoon's code name for his rival, Buck Duke.

The courtroom erupted with snickers, and the elderly Vice Chancellor Pitney had to warn photographers they would be punished for taking any pictures during the proceedings.

Lillian portrayed her husband as a bad-tempered brute worth tens of millions of dollars who fraudulently incorporated the American Tobacco Company in New Jersey to escape New York taxes. "He told me when he purchased the property in Jersey," Lillian testified, "that he had to buy property in Jersey on account of the corporation law, taxes or business, something of the kind, and he often expressed a wish that he was not obliged to have that property: that he would like to have had property on the Hudson River."

It was publicly revealed that in March 1903, the "confirmed bachelor" had set up his mistress of eleven years in the Sixty-eighth Street house, staying there three nights a week while keeping a room at the Hoffman House as a cover-up. He had a back, third-floor bedroom and dressing room and kept a pair of horses and carriage at the address. His monogrammed underwear was regularly scrubbed by Lillian's washwoman.

Other details of Buck and Lillian's illicit affair were bared, including the furnishing of the love nest. "Mr. Duke told me to be very particular what I bought—to get the best of everything—and large furniture, so that it could be used in the house on Fifth Avenue and 82nd Street, as he was going to purchase it for me and it was to be our home."

According to Lillian, the plan was to buy Ben's house at 1009 Fifth Avenue, which faces the Metropolitan Museum of Art. Known as "Millionaires' Row," Fifth Avenue had become home to such arrivistes as the Astors and the Vanderbilts. Lillian, more than Buck, wanted to join Ben and Sarah and the New Society.

All the while, her affair with Huntoon continued. Servants said he often brought champagne to the house while Buck was away on business, and he and Lillian would drink and sing in the music room. "Everytime Uncle Buck would go out of town, they would have a seance together, and so he got suspicious," said the wife of one of Duke's nephews.

Buck was spending more and more time visiting the Duke factories in Durham, St. Louis, Louisville, Baltimore, and Richmond. Huntoon was a welcome diversion. Lillian left New York for the White Mountains Prospect House to meet Huntoon. There, she received a letter from Duke proposing marriage. He wanted, the letter stated, to put to rest certain disagreeable "rumors or scandal." He asked her to return home. Two days later, she arrived in New York. Huntoon took the same train, but got off before it reached the station, according to Nellie Sands, who also said Lillian was with Huntoon on the eve of her marriage to Duke. They parted tearfully in Philadelphia. Nellie Sands felt sorry for Lillian. "She was such a foolish woman to throw herself away."

On the honeymoon, Sands passed Huntoon's letters to Lillian, acting as the go-between. Lillian admonished her to be careful, that Duke was a very jealous man. Huntoon resorted to the *Herald* personals, offering to come to Europe to rescue Lillian. Sands also said she passed a letter to Huntoon, who was waiting at the pier when the Dukes returned from their honeymoon.

The divorce was not the only legal battle brewing. The government, anxious to enforce the Sherman Anti-Trust Act, was already gathering evidence against the American Tobacco Company, which now controlled four-fifths of the total domestic tobacco industry, having gobbled up 250 rival companies. Many of them, like R. J. Reynolds ("Sometimes you have to join hands with a fellow to keep him from ruining you."), agreed to keep the deals secret and pretended to operate independently of the Trust. Tensions were mounting, and night riders were destroying barns of tobacco in protest. Duke's elaborately furnished private stables in New York were destroyed by a suspicious fire started from a gasoline explosion in the basement. It took only thirty minutes to gut the West Sixty-sixth Street building. Four horses died. A touring automobile and a number of carriages were also destroyed.

For now, Duke was preoccupied with his domestic problems. Distressed by Nellie Sands's testimony, Lillian feigned illness and stayed away from court. So did Huntoon. A motion for delay was denied. On May 7, 1906, Duke won a divorce decree. Lillian filed an appeal. "I am not yet done with James B. Duke," she declared. "No woman on God's earth ever paid dearer for her wealth than I did. If that had been the only motive of my marriage to Mr. Duke. I suffered humiliations almost beyond belief." She lost the appeal several months later.

In the end, she got nothing.

"The trial was a travesty," she told reporters. "The paid witnesses against me could show no real wrongdoing. Major Huntoon has been a friend of 20 years standing. True, letters and telegrams passed between us. What of that? We are living in a modern age and a wife can no longer be made a prisoner by her husband as Duke sought to make of me."

She called her husband "resourceful, cunning, vain and vindictive . . . He has frequently expressed that he could get anything he wanted, and that what he couldn't get rightfully, he had money enough to purchase."

After the verdict, Lillian dropped another bombshell: her two sisters, Emma Morrison, a widow, and Mrs. Louise Bail, wife of a Reading Railroad official, had spied on her. Years later, Lillian would be vindicated when court papers revealed that Bail was secretly paid $15,000 by Duke for damaging information about Lillian and Huntoon. Bail had, with shrewd foresight, saved incriminating letters from Duke and his lawyer, Junius Parker, and later threatened to expose them. She hounded Duke for years, reminding him of his promise to "take care of her for life." When he refused to pay, Bail filed a lawsuit in 1914 and settled out of court for an additional $7500.

Lillian would also come back to haunt the "Octopus," who had already chosen a poised, petite widow from Atlanta twelve years his junior to be his second wife.

Her name was Nanaline.

"I have met the most beautiful woman in the world," Ben Duke wrote to his brother in the summer of 1906 after becoming acquainted with Nanaline Holt Inman at a posh Lake Toxaway resort in the mountains of North Carolina, the kind of resort where soignée Southern belles rubbed parasols with cigar-smoking moneybags on the loose. Ben, having taken it upon himself to find a more suitable mate for his younger brother, had come to the right spot.

The widow Inman was not only available, but actively husband hunting. Buck Duke—freshly divorced and a fat cat of fifty—was about the biggest catch of the century. Literally.

Chapter Three

The Dollar Princess

THE SAME WEEK Washington Duke was trudging home from the War with a fifty-cent piece in his pocket, the distinguished former Judge Thaddeus Goode Holt was meeting with other town elders in Macon, Georgia, to discuss the state of the South. As a delegate to the Constitutional Convention in 1865, Holt made an impressive sight, arguing passionately in favor of abolishing slavery and offering amnesty for the thousands of disenfranchised citizens. His son Thaddeus G. Holt, Jr., had been a gallant officer in the 10th Confederate Cavalry and returned to Macon to take up residence in the family's home, a Greek-Revival white-columned mansion built in the late 1830s by Judge Holt on the fashionable corner of Orange Street and Georgia Avenue.

Macon was a town of broad, tree-lined streets on the Ocmulgee River and boasted roughly 8,000 citizens. During the latter part of the War, the city became an oasis for homeless Southerners and wounded soldiers. Thaddeus Holt, Jr.—married to dark-haired Florine Russell—had two children, five-year-old Thaddeus III, and two-year-old Florine. A third child, Nannie Lane, was born on September 17, 1869.

While it's tempting to imagine young Nannie peering over the balcony of the Tara-like mansion, wafting in the scent of lilacs and magnolias, waiting for young gentlemen callers to ascend the graceful horseshoe entrance steps to the front porch, the Holt family fell on hard times and the house was sold when Nannie was thirteen. The next year, her older sister Florine died. Her father, records show, died at sea when she was fifteen and her older brother Thaddeus II also died, unmarried.

Florine Russell Holt, proud but penniless, took in boarders and supported her only child by sewing party dresses for well-to-do neighbors. Nannie used to model the pale satin and ribboned gowns before delivering them to their rightful owners, sparking a lifelong passion for fine clothes.

Reared in genteel poverty, she never shook her penchant for thriftiness. (Even years later as the wife of a multimillionaire, she was notoriously stingy.) She inherited her beauty and social graces from her mother, who like other Southern women of the day had groomed Nannie to marry a rich man. Popular with the opposite sex, Nannie was a familiar sight in Macon at military dances, fairs, and summer picnics, and at a two-day competitive drill in 1887, served as one of the sponsors.

"[She] was the prettiest thing you ever saw," an old friend recalled. "And anything she wore looked lovely on her. This was fortunate because the Holts, like many of us, were not as well off as they had been before the war. She had black hair and gray blue eyes and very fair skin. She was an Irish type. And she had charm, of course. Young men fell over themselves falling in love with her."

Educated at The Branham School, she later attended Wesleyan Female College's prep school (class of 1886) for two years as her sister Florine had done before her. Her grandfather had been a trustee and member of the board of the school for many years.

On April 30, 1890, in her mother's living room, Nannie married twenty-seven-year-old cotton buyer William Henry Inman, scion of a prominent Atlanta family. The Inmans, originally from Tennessee, became one of the largest buyers of cotton in the South and had once owned the *Atlanta Journal*. Inman, described in the wedding announcement as "one of Atlanta's most popular and accomplished young gentlemen," had graduated from North Carolina's Davidson College before entering the family business and was considered one of the greatest "catches" of the day. The wedding was small, attended only by a few relatives, and the nineteen-year-old bride was described as "one of the most beautiful and fascinating young ladies that ever lived in Georgia. She has reigned a favorite queen in society since her debut, and no belle ever had more admirers."

The 1900 Atlanta census shows Will Inman, thirty-five (occupation: cotton buyer), living with his wife and his mother-in-law, Florine. The census also reveals that Nannie gave birth to two children, but only one was living, a five-year-old son, Walker Patterson Inman. (The death of her first child remained a mystery. In fact, Nannie never spoke of it. A close friend revealed after her death that the child, a boy, died before its second birthday. According to the friend to whom Nannie confided her secret, "She said, 'I'm afraid I was too young to know how to care for him, and now I have lived to be so old, I realize that no one knew the care of a child in those days like they do now. They don't lose their children.'")

A year later, William Inman became ill and spent three months in Elkin & Cooper's sanitarium. A close friend of the family claims Inman was an alcoholic. In critical condition, Inman returned home and on the afternoon of March 20, 1902, died at the age of thirty-eight. The death certificate on file in Fulton County lists the cause of death as "diabetes."

A much sought after widow, Nannie Lane Holt Inman began traveling north to New York and Newport for shopping trips, and her name soon became linked romantically with several prominent men. She also dropped the rather unsophisticated "Nannie" in favor of the more aristocratic sounding Nanaline, a combination of her names Nannie and Lane.

Several weeks after meeting the tobacco-rich but married Ben Duke at Lake Toxaway, she and her mother Florine moved to Manhattan and set up residence in a suite at the Hotel Webster. That November, Ben and Sarah hosted a dinner party at the Waldorf, and the widow Inman was publicly presented to the unattached MegaBuck Duke, although it seems likely that they had already met. (In fact, Lillian angrily accused Buck of romancing Nanaline prior to his final divorce decree.)

"She [Nanaline] had beautiful things and she wanted beautiful things," an old friend recalled. "She was a beautiful woman. Mr. Duke loved beautiful women, and he fell very much in love with her." Nanaline "had the most delicate hands and feet and body, and she kept it beautiful. She dressed quietly and no one ever took her picture or exploited her in the newspapers at all. She wouldn't have it." Emotionally, she was extremely reserved. "She was not a warm person like Mr. Duke," the friend added.

For Buck and Nanaline, theirs was a mutually satisfying arrangement: she had social entree to the finest drawing rooms on Fifth Avenue and he could bankroll her upwardly mobile life-style. As the widow Inman, Nanaline's tastes had become increasingly refined; she had acquired a healthy appetite for large jewels, imported cars, walk-in closets, Newport in the summer, and *Town & Country* magazine. Although he was said to be able to walk into a room and pick out the most valuable paintings and antiques, Duke was still a roly-poly diamond-in-the rough. A man who smoked two dozen cigars a day and considered business his true mistress, he was fifteen years older than Nanaline and scornful of her high society. But they had one thing in common: both were bent on leaving their past behind.

Duke began to dote on Nanaline, buying her an Italian limousine, diamond necklaces and earrings, and a basket-seated, silk-canopied surrey pulled by two jet black horses. He tried to win her twelve-year-old son Walker's affection by presenting him with a pair of ponies and a pony cart, and that Fourth of July spent thousands of dollars for the most elaborate fireworks display the state had ever seen. Rumors of an engagement circulated when Nanaline and her mother spent more and more time at Somerville, although she plainly preferred Fifth Avenue to the farm. "I'm no picnic girl," she often complained.

The prospect of a Duke-Inman alliance became a topic of discussion.

"It is assumed that with Mrs. Inman's beauty, influence and well-established society record to back him," one newspaper reported, ". . . James B. Duke will be entering the enchanted life of society which so far has been a closed book to the Duke family, even with all its millions."

By the spring of 1907, Buck Duke was shopping for a suitable, garish Manhattan residence. He considered the James Henry Smith mansion at 68th and Fifth and the Edward Holbrook house at Fifth and 52nd, not far from the Rockefeller mansion. He finally settled on the Henry H. Cook estate at Fifth and 78th, which he purchased for $1.25 million as a wedding present for Nanaline. The property sat on one of the most desirable blocks in the city and already boasted the Payne Whitneys (uncle Oliver was one of the original Standard Oil men), the H. H. Rogers, and the Stuyvesant Fish family. There was speculation that Duke would tear down the house and build a new one to surpass in elegance the Ninetieth Street palace of Andrew Carnegie.

"It has long been current gossip that the social ambitions of the president of the Tobacco trust and his bride elect would lead them to settle in close proximity to Fifth Avenue," *The New York Times* reported.

But there was one last obstacle: the first Mrs. Duke. Lillian, who never met a gossip columnist she didn't like, was still convinced that her divorce was a sham, and Duke, anxious to make Nanaline his bride, ordered his lawyers to pay off his ex-wife to buy her silence. Estimates of the settlement ranged from $500,000 to $3 million, but it was sufficient to muzzle Lillian—at least temporarily.

And so, with little fanfare, on July 24, 1907, Nannie Holt, at the age of thirty-eight became the second Mrs. James Buchanan Duke, or as her calling card would state, "Mrs. Duke." In her mind, she was the one and only Mrs. Duke. The wedding was a private ceremony at the Brooklyn home of Mrs. William Stackpole, an old friend of the groom's. Duke and Nanaline had motored to the city from Somerville with Nanaline's sixty-two-year-old mother, thrilled by her daughter's marital coup. Walker Inman reluctantly accompanied his mother, along with a few business associates of Duke's.

Buck's mind was also on his business. Two weeks earlier the government had filed suit against the American Tobacco Company. Criticism of the tobacco magnate grew more vocal as his two-fisted reputation increased. One critic blasted Duke, calling him "as lusty a capitalist as ever reaped shekels from the virgin soil of America's terrain." The climate was so anti-trust that when a relative of Buck bought two delicatessens on Broadway, jittery deli owners feared a "delicatessen trust" was secretly forming with the backing of the giant tobacco concern.

Duke was subpoenaed early in the proceedings, but claimed to be too ill to go to court. Instead, the court came to him. On February 25, 1908, surrounded by a battery of physicians and nurses, Buck Duke gave testimony from his bedside in front of two court stenographers, a government lawyer, and four defense lawyers, including an ex-judge and Junius Parker. Reporters were barred. Propped up in his bed, his head against the pillows, he spoke with candor and gruffness for two hours. He said he bought up the other tobacco companies as investments. His purpose was to make money, not monopolize the market. In May of that year, in a separate legal proceeding, it was revealed that Duke had secretly bought up controlling interest in rival companies, allowing the public to think the firms (including R. J. Reynolds) were still independent of the Tobacco Trust and competition was still alive and well. It was also revealed that Duke and his cronies had set up an elaborate underground network of spies to help them infiltrate competitors during the height of the tobacco wars.

Buck Duke was making more news. He tore down the historic Cook mansion in 1909 to build a new residence. The plans were drawn by Horace Trumbauer, the architect of the robber barons' imposing country estates and townhouses who would design the Stotesburys' massive Philadelphia mansion, Whitemarsh Hall, as well as P.A.B. Widener's "Lynnewood Hall," the largest Georgian residence in the country. Trumbauer was much in demand by the gilded set, and his clients included coal magnate E. J.

Berwind (who commissioned "The Elms" in Newport), and Philadelphia sugar refiner E. C. Knight. It was Knight's Trumbauer-designed Newport mansion "Clarendon Court" which later became the scene of one of the resort's biggest scandals: the von Bulow affair. (It was at Clarendon Court that Claus von Bulow was accused of trying to kill his wife with insulin injections. After the reversal of his conviction, Claus von Bulow gave up his rights to the house.)

Trumbauer, whose motto was bigger is better, was inordinately fond of spending other people's money. When a client once asked for a house of terra cotta rather than the more expensive stone, Trumbauer replied, "Madame, if money bothers you, then I'm not your architect."

For James B. Duke, Trumbauer modeled the grand limestone house after a late-eighteenth-century French country chateau. The three-story structure would take three years to build and earn a *New York Times* headline as the "costliest home" on Fifth Avenue.

At Nanaline's insistence, her husband purchased a box at the Metropolitan Opera for $1250. The Dukes' appearance "excited quite a ripple of interest by her beauty and her jewels," a gossip column reported.

> She and her adoring spouse had as guests Mr. and Mrs. Suffern Tailer and Mrs. Herman Oelrichs; which would seem to indicate that the beauteous Nannie Inman has at last reached the goal of her ambition, and is to be numbered among the "real blue fish," as George Ade calls them, of New York. Mrs. Duke looked exceedingly well; in fact, better than I have ever before seen her in white satin covered with old lace, but her diamonds—well! If the late Mrs. Astor could have seen that tiara and those corsage jewels, I honestly believe the haughty old lady would have been almost envious. I wonder where the adoring Mr. Duke procured these marvelous gems? They shone and sparkled so that even the Italian standees marveled and one asked, "Who is the human lighthouse in the box?"

While Ben and Buck were busy in Manhattan, brother Brodie, at sixty-two, had picked out his fourth wife. This time, his intended was a twenty-three-year-old Durham woman, Wylanta Rochelle. Brodie had known her father, often stopping by the Rochelle house on his way to the factory to talk politics. After a brief courtship, Wylanta went to Washington, D.C., for finishing school. Brodie followed her there and in June, 1910, they obtained a wedding license. The preacher, having been made aware of Brodie's notorious marital history, refused to perform the ceremony. The story made the front pages of the newspapers, and the Duke family once again swung into action trying to stop the marriage. Brodie and Wylanta fled to Camden, New Jersey, where a Justice of the Peace performed the ceremony. When they returned that night to the Ebbitt House in Washington, reporters had staked out the hotel lobby.

"Just say I'm married and supremely happy," Brodie told them.

"When, where, how?" the newsmen shouted.

"None of your business," he snapped, and bolted upstairs.

Six weeks later they returned to Durham where the eccentric Brodie presented his bride with an office building as a wedding gift. By now, Ben and Buck were no longer on speaking terms with Brodie and the brothers remained estranged. Brodie died nine years later at the age of seventy-one, leaving his share of the Duke fortune to the young Wylanta.

The government's anti-trust case, which had dragged on for two years, was appealed to the Supreme Court. In the end, the American Tobacco Company was ruled unlawful and ordered dissolved. The decision was read in the hushed marble Washington courtroom, and the lobby was crowded with senators, representatives, and lobbyists who had created a mob scene in the hall waiting for the decision. Duke, back in Manhattan, heard the news by telephone. The Tobacco King had been dethroned. The tycoon who had broken every rule on his way to the top sat at his desk, silently tearing up slips of paper and letting them drift to the floor. "In England, if a fellow had built up a whale of a business, he'd be knighted," Duke told an intimate. "Here, they want to put him in jail."

A staunch Republican, the lusty capitalist was protected by his political connections, including President William Taft. There would be no jail term. Instead, the government turned to Duke for help in breaking up the tobacco trust. He was the only man who could unravel the tangled web. The other tobacco lords were buoyed by the verdict. Said R. J. Reynolds: "Now, watch me give Buck Duke hell." A few years later, he did just that when a new Reynolds cigarette, "Camel," came on the market and captured the country's attention. In 1916, the American Tobacco Company retaliated with their own wildly popular "Lucky Strike," although Duke's interest in tobacco was gradually replaced by his involvement in overseas ventures and the growing market in hydroelectric power in Canada and North Carolina.

After officially resigning as president of the American Tobacco Company, he became chairman of the British-American Tobacco Company (BAT), a job which required him to live for six months of each year in England. Nanaline was elated. The Dukes were among a flotilla of wealthy Americans fleeing to Europe, hoping to live like lords. After all, they could get more for their money: more social distinction, more servants, more royal elbows to rub. In a white and gold brocade dress, diamond encrusted on the bodice, and a red velvet cape, Nanaline made a stunning entrance as she was presented at the Court of St. James's. She was not accompanied by her bear of a husband, however, who adamantly refused to be seen in public wearing the required purple knee breeches and sent an associate as her escort.

With their separate agendas and travel schedules, it is unlikely that the soignée Nanaline was overjoyed to learn of a pregnancy in early spring, 1912. Her husband had talked of having an heir, but her childbearing days were long behind her. Nanaline would be forty-three when the baby was born. Her husband would be fifty-five. Although society now trumpets the over-forty mother, in 1912 it was considered unusual. It would be more appropriate for the Dukes to be grandparents, not parents. Nanaline's son Walker would be seventeen in August and nearly out of prep school. Buck may have wanted the child to insure his immortality. He also may have wanted an heir as insurance that his growing fortune would not be left to his hapless stepson, with whom he often quarreled bitterly. Duke had earlier offered to legally adopt young Inman and asked if he would consider changing his name to "Duke." The boy refused, saying, "I was born an Inman and that is good enough for me."

Nanaline passionately defended her son, and the two were often united against Duke, which strained the marriage. By all accounts, young Inman was a spoiled, self-indulgent, unpopular Mama's boy who started drinking heavily during adolescence. As a result of having lost her first child, Nanaline was overprotective of her second. "Well, you couldn't like him unless you were his mother," observed a family friend.

Early that summer, the Dukes returned from abroad and went to Newport. (Fortunately, they had not booked passage on the *Titanic,* which sank on its maiden voyage a few weeks later, killing several Newport acquaintances, including John Jacob Astor and George Widener.) Back in New York in the fall, their lease had already expired on a house at Fifth and 80th they had been renting, so they were forced to move into the Trumbauer creation on Seventy-eighth Street while construction was still proceeding.

Late on Friday, November 22, 1912, Nanaline—fretting about the plaster dust and workmen and general upheaval—gave birth to the child, a daughter. They named her Doris. "I have a new niece this morning," Ben Duke wrote to his wife Sarah back in Durham. "Mother and child doing fine and father very happy."

The baby was delivered in the master bedroom on the second floor attended by a fleet of high-priced private physicians and nurses. "No child of royal blood ever came into the world amid more comfortable and luxurious surroundings than the daughter of the Dukes," one newspaper reported. "The magnificent Fifth Avenue mansion was turned into a private hospital; no expense was spared in obtaining the best physicians and nurses, and the baby's layette represented the outlay of a small fortune. The great wish of a millionaire's heart was to be gratified and no preparations were overlooked."

The day-old Doris was described as "a bouncing specimen of babyhood . . . [she] may grow up to be as attractive as her mother."

News reports listed Doris as sole heir to her father's $100 million fortune, calling her "probably the richest mite of humanity in all the world," her nearest competition being W. K. Vanderbilt's son (heir to $60 million), followed by Edward Vinson McLean ($50 million), John Nicholas Brown ($10 million), and John Jacob Astor ($3 million).

A "trophy baby" if there ever was one, Doris was Buck Duke's most prized possession, even though he had wanted a son. Nanaline saw the baby as a social asset, and she and Buck argued over Doris' christening. Naturally, Buck wanted it done in a small church with little pomp and circumstance.

"People ought to know the preacher and the preacher ought to know the people, and 4,000 people are just too many for one church," Buck said.

But Nanaline had decided that the christening would be an elaborate affair, done by the esteemed English minister, Dr. Jowett. When Mrs. Duke called the preacher, he abruptly said he'd send an assistant. Nanaline was livid at the slight, while Buck "just chuckled and chuckled," according to one account.

The proud father showered mother and daughter with the finest money could buy; he bought paintings and tapestries and panels including a few Hoppners and a Gainsborough. Buck also developed an intense fear that someone would try and kidnap his baby, so Doris was guarded around the clock by a battery of nurses and bodyguards, although one electrician who worked at the house, Rudy Felix, was allowed to hold the week-old "Million Dollar Baby" in his burly arms and never forgot the experience.

Almost immediately, letters began arriving at the house on Seventy-eighth Street, begging the Duke baby for money. There were so many letters they had to be bagged and sorted.

Duke was also petrified of germs. He purchased a private Pullman car and named it *Doris* so she could be isolated from the public. As an epidemic of infantile paralysis swept the country, he posted guards about his Newport home, barring strangers and other children from his beachfront. Private nurses were hired to watch for symptoms of the illness among her nannies and other household servants who were constantly examined for any sign of infection.

Duke also found it unsuitable to stay in hotels with his family. In January 1914 he leased a historic London townhouse from Lord Crewe on Curzon Street in Mayfair. The house, with thirty rooms, came complete with a dining room Chippendale set and was considered the most fashionable address in the city. Crewe had apparently been trying to sell the mansion for some time, but no one could afford it. Rumors circulated that Duke would become a tax exile, perhaps with an eye toward a peerage. No doubt Duke felt the climate was not only more conducive to his business but also to raising his daughter, who had already, in the first year of her life, become the subject of inordinate curiosity.

Part of that curiosity was Duke's own obsession with every facet of Baby Doris' welfare. In fact, when his daughter's sleep was disturbed one morning by a wheezing hand organ outside her London window, he went to Switzerland and had a custom-made marble and gold clock built which would awaken his Million Dollar Baby each morning with a chorus of softly increasing chimes and bird sounds. It stood in the hallway outside her door, and at the touch of a button by Doris' nanny, would begin its morning ritual.

But in August 1914, their charmed life was shattered by the outbreak of war. Like other expatriates, Duke found himself stranded in London. He quickly arranged to return to America and once in New York, drove wildly to half a dozen banks, hurredly exchanging cash for gold. He managed to collect $1 million in gold bars and transported it under cover of darkness to Somerville for safekeeping. (When conditions improved, he sheepishly returned the gold to the banks.)

With the introduction a year earlier of the income tax, the Treasury Department was finally aware of the vast fortunes amassed by the robber barons. For the first time, the government publicized a list of the richest men in America. The concept of "millionaires" became a nationwide fascination. Leading the pack was John D. Rockefeller (oil, gas, electric light), followed by Andrew Carnegie (steel), J. P. Morgan (banking), Vincent Astor (real estate), and in ninth place, James B. Duke. (Although extravagance wasn't limited to the top few. The wife of E. T. Stotesbury, a Philadelphia financier, had their forty-room house in Bar Harbor completely rebuilt twice before she was satisfied.)

Ben Duke was reported to be worth $10 million, far less than Buck, but Ben had not been as ruthless, nor as driven as his younger brother. "A prince he is among men," one news story said of Ben. "His splendid character and integrity; his unfailing generosity; his many acts of charity of which the world never knows; his loyalty to the people of the south, who in turn loyally love him and honor him . . . the enviable position he has attained, both socially and commercially among his newfound friends—this and much more proclaim him a shining example of the great man of wealth."

Buck was desperate for the same acceptance, sending J. P. Morgan 2,000 Havana cigars and importing gifts of food from the farm for business associates. His private car *Doris* featured a steady supply of champagne and cigars and was staffed by a private chef whose skill was reknown.

But Buck was not like his brother. Annoyed by the parade of unruly visitors to Duke's Farm, he became increasingly concerned with security. Baby Doris was said to have almost been run over in her carriage while being taken out for a stroll. There were the disguised poachers goggles caught with carloads of English pheasants shot on the grounds. There were also the souvenir and postcard sellers dotting the landscape. Duke finally had three teenage boys arrested for violating a newly instituted town ordinance: selling postcards without a license. After an "automobile party" left empty lunch boxes on the grounds, Buck Duke announced the public would no longer be welcome at his park. He closed the gates to his vast estate for good.

Whether he was keeping the world from his daughter, or keeping his daughter from entering the world, one thing is certain. Duke was obsessed with his only child. "Mr. Duke's whole heart was in Doris," a family friend said. Anxious not to appear to spoil the child, he was giving his daughter twenty-five cents a week in allowance while simultaneously showering her with every conceivable material possession: Ponies, carts, toys, pets. Occasionally, another child would be imported to the cavernous halls of Somerville for an afternoon of play, but this was rare. With Nanaline preoccupied with ladies lunches and bridge games, young Doris—growing increasingly anti-social—spent her time with nannies and nurses in gilded isolation. She had no peers. She was the richest little girl in the world; a flaxen-haired angelic princess locked in a gilded cage.

Her father assumed the role of a glorified Santa Claus; a mythical figure of unending generosity and the only source of warmth. The chauffeur would bring young Doris to Duke's office on Fifth Avenue and she would stand at the door saying, "I'd like to talk to my daddy." An associate would go to Duke and tell him Doris wished to see him. "No matter how weighty the subject under discussion, Mr. Duke would stop right there and go out where Doris was," one associate recalled.

By this time, Ben Duke was increasingly unable to keep up the demands of his work and he turned a large part of his responsibilities over to his free-wheeling son, Angier. Brooding, handsome, and dark-eyed, Angier Buchanan Duke had begun socializing with the Biddles of Philadelphia. Known as one of the First Families of the Quaker City, the Biddles had an illustrious family tree, including the flamboyant statesman-financier Nicholas Biddle who built the country mansion Andalusa. In the Academy of Natural Sciences stands a stuffed moose shot by a Biddle.

A. J. Drexel Biddle was a trustfunder who collected alligators as pets, authored books and was a boxing enthusiast, often challenging visiting pugilists to square off in his living room. The Biddles were everything the Dukes were not; aristocratic, well-bred and wildly popular. Angie Duke was twenty-nine when he met sixteen-year-old Cordelia Biddle on Thanksgiving 1914 at a house party in New Jersey. He was instantly taken with the high-spirited teenager (who would later pen an amusing family memoir, ""My Philadelphia Father," which was filmed as "The Happiest Millionaire") and the two began an affair. Their first child, Angier Biddle Duke, arrived November 30, 1915, seven months after the lavish April wedding ceremony which marked the beginning of a celebrated social alliance between two of the richest families of the day.

In the pre-War era, the monied set had become genuine celebrities, and the public was hungry for details of their gaudy lifestyle made all the more fascinating by their willingness to flaunt it. More than 2,200 wedding guests thronged to Holy Trinity Church in Philadelphia's Rittinhouse Square, many of them arriving on special trains. The gawkers numbered in the thousands and were barely controlled by scores of mounted police. The exuberant crowd rushed the young bride, upsetting the wedding canopy and tearing loose the curtains of her automobile.

Gifts of more than $300,000 were sent, the inventory dutifully revealed by the bridal party. Angie gave his seventeen-year-old wife $150,000 worth of jewelry. A $75,000 pearl necklace came from the groom's parents (who also gave the young couple a starter mansion on Eighty-ninth Street and $1 million in cash). Buck and Nanaline presented Cordelia with a $20,000 diamond bracelet and the Stotesburys weighed in with a diamond and sapphire brooch the size of a dinner roll.

"In splendor, in mere magnitude, in public interest, in the significance of the social world, in the wealth of the families, in the crowds inside and out—in all of these things and more there has been nothing like it in Philadelphia for many years," trilled *The Philadelphia Press*.

At the reception, Ben Duke offered a toast and then made a surprise announcement: his daughter, twenty-eight-year-old Mary Duke, was engaged to marry eighteen-year-old Tony Biddle, brother of the bride. There was a collective gasp, then applause. Could it be? A double alliance? It was *too too* much.

The second Duke-Biddle wedding was set for June, and Nanaline seized the opportunity to host the reception at Somerville. "My aunt was very anxious for me to be married there among the wonderful flowers and the pretty surroundings and, of course, I was delighted," Mary told a social writer. But Nanaline had more than posies on her mind. "Country weddings" were all the rage and the event would give the J. B. Dukes a chance to increase their own social profile among the Philadelphia aristocracy. Indeed, the Durham-born bumpkins were already rewriting history, no doubt aided by Nanaline's penchant for inventing ancestors. In one news clipping, the former tobacco farmers were said to be one of the finest Southern families honored "for their birth, breeding and distinction . . . The Dukes are of English origin, having settled in Virginia during colonial times."

Mary, a sweet tempered girl with huge cocker spaniel eyes, was a regular on the social circuit in Newport and New York. She had a strong singing voice and was an accomplished pianist. She had first laid eyes on Cordelia's brother Tony at a dinner four months earlier while wearing a shimmering white gown and her prized pearl necklace (considered second only to her mother's in all of New York) and was instantly taken with the athletic high school senior seated beside her. "My brother Angier and Cordelia seemed to have fallen in love with each other the moment they met, just as Tony and I did," Mary said.

The summer of 1915 was a turning point for the Dukes. They were now admitted to the inner circles they so slavishly aspired to. With the war's ban on foreign travel, the first thing Ben and Sarah did was lease "Sunshine," the Great Neck, Long Island, Dugmore estate at a cost of $17,000. The bayfront house, formerly rented by Mrs. Cornelius Vanderbilt, was said to be ideal for entertaining, something the Dukes took up with a vengeance.

They also bought a $100,000 Hoppner painting, "Portrait of Mrs. Carey." As for Buck and Nanaline, they planned to return to Newport, renting "Inchiquin," the French Renaissance villa owned by the Livermore family. Four years earlier, they had leased "The Orchard," the elegant French chateau of Colonel George Fearing on Narragansett Avenue but were now ready to move up to Bellevue Avenue.

Of all the glittering watering holes of the day—Tuxedo, Hot Springs, Palm Beach, Saratoga, Bar Harbor—the tiny former trading port and island of Newport was the crown jewel. The oldest seaside resort (it was said to be fashionable even in pre-Revolutionary days), Newport had been the favorite summer idyll of artists and writers before gaining a reputation as the playground of the rich and famous. While Bar Harbor attracted the wealthy from Philadelphia and Boston (The Stotesburys, the A. Atwater Kents, Evalyn Walsh McLean, and the J. P. Morgans), Newport appealed to New Yorkers: the Astors and Vanderbilts, the Lorillards, the Van Alens, the Goelets. Nouveau types like the Tinplate King William Leeds and his stunning wife Nancy, along with the J. B. Dukes, soon learned the ropes; it was said to take four seasons to be accepted into Newport society and hopefuls were advised to rent for the first few seasons before buying. There were two golden rules: Never try to outentertain, outdress, or outjewel the reigning dowagers and never try to steal anyone's husband. Nanaline, even with Buck's coarse manners and scandalous divorce, had the good sense and necessary bank account to wait it out.

With its broad Bellevue Avenue flanked by grand marble "cottages" (The Breakers, owned by the Vanderbilts, boasted seventy rooms), Newport rose from the rocky shoreline like a mythical kingdom. It was an American fairy tale. As writer Julia Ward Howe observed, even the air "made the common breath of life a pleasure." No extravagance was spared in entertaining, which took place from dawn to dark. There were footmen in knee britches. Even the servants had servants. Bathing at the exclusive Bailey's Beach, one might encounter James Van Alen swimming in his white straw hat and monocle, puffing a cigar. There was lawn tennis at the Newport Casino designed by Stanford White. Yachts the size of small hotels bobbed in Newport Harbor. One popular hostess banned anyone from her table who was worth less than $5 million. People routinely spent $200,000 for a costume ball. At one dinner, the center of the table was covered with sand. Guests were given sterling silver shovels and pails and at the signal, dove into the miniature beach to retrieve their favors; genuine rubies, sapphires, emeralds and diamonds.

There was Mrs. Stuyvesant Fish's Mother Goose Ball and the famous "Monkey Dinner" in which one of the guests—a monkey dressed as a prince—drank champagne and climbed the chandelier, pelting party goers with light bulbs. Another dinner was held for 100 dogs in fancy dress. Then there was The Servants Ball, in which wealthy guests arrived dressed as their maids and butlers.

Nancy Leeds (who went on to become the world's richest widow and eventually marry Prince Christopher of Greece) took guests on their yacht over to Rocky Point, where an entire amusement park had been rented out for the evening. Considered vulgar by many of the establishment, Nancy found a mentor in the powerful Mrs. Oliver Belmont, the first girl of her "set" to marry a Vanderbilt. The Leeds entertained lavishly at Rough Point, the gray stone Tudor home built by the Frederick Vanderbilts in 1890 on one of the most spectacular pieces of real estate in all of Newport. Nanaline, already shopping for a suitable "cottage," had set her sights on Rough Point, but the Dukes would have to wait eight long years to occupy the mansion.

In mid-June of 1915, at the start of the summer social season, the second Biddle-Duke extravaganza took place. The stage was Somerville. Guests were transported to the affair by special trains from New York and Philadelphia, and the VIP's (the Stotesburys, the Harrimans, the Drexels, the Charles Scribners, the Van Renssalaers, the Wanamakers) regrouped en masse, loaded down with leather trunks stuffed with feathered and beaded gowns, jewels, china, silver and, of course, the French-speaking servants who were all the rage. Eva Stotesbury employed three secretaries, traveled with her own personal fashion designer and had once organized a $500,000 hunting expedition in order to bag enough alligator skins to fashion her own personal extensive set of luggage.

Somerville was crammed with roses and tall white peonies in huge vases. The marble conservatory had been turned into a chapel, a make-shift altar banked with potted palms and lily-of-the-valley. There was a built-in organ. The bridesmaids wore pink taffeta gowns and carried Leghorn hats filled with pink rambling roses and peonies, which hung from their shoulders by long blue satin streamers.

The reception was held in the oak-panelled living room, but the heavy cloud of cigar smoke drove guests out the French doors to the magnificent gardens beyond. Nanaline and Buck had outdone themselves with their faux-Versailles setting. "Between the big fountains," one report read, "which kept up a rippling obbligato to Frantzen's music . . . [were] two

Louis Seize marquees of white and green, which only needed Marie Antoinette and her court ladies to complete the illusion." Supper tables were arranged on the lawn covered by huge umbrellas and caged turtle doves cooed over the many-tiered wedding cake.

The event marked the first public appearance of Buck and Nanaline's "Million Dollar Baby," Doris, chosen by her cousin to act as the flower girl. A few months shy of her third birthday, Doris wore a white lace dress with a pink sash, white Mary Janes, and a wreath of flowers in her blonde hair. She was a serious child, with a sweet, round face who appears to be pouting in the wedding pictures, no doubt wishing to be somewhere other than center stage. Her expression, even at that age, was one of wariness and echoed her father's squinting air of mistrust. She was uncomfortable with the attention, and her parents were even more uncomfortable having her photographed. It would be years before another photograph of Doris Duke was released to the newspapers, increasingly anxious for even the slightest news of her lifestyle. This demand eventually led to a frenzy of newspaper and magazine articles, with former nurses paid handsomely to reveal the most trivial news of the tobacco king's toddler who, according to reliable sources, ate baby porridge from a 14-carat gold cup.

The family received more unwanted press when a story appeared on the front page of *The New York Times,* saying Cordelia had lost a $30,000 diamond bracelet playing golf on a Long Island course. The jewelry was found by a local teenager, and the next day a scathing *Times* editorial raised the question of "why anybody wore a $30,000 bracelet while playing golf."

But the Biddles were not just *anybody.* They were oblivious to the criticism. As the epitome of nouveau American wealth during the pre-War era, Tony Biddle had seven houses, including the Villa Sarmiento in Palm Beach. Mary was a world-class shopper; after one trip to Europe, she brought back $300,000 worth of clothes, jewelry, and other personal items on which she paid over $77,000 in duty—the largest amount ever collected by Customs from a private individual.

The Dukes occasionally turned to charitable causes to polish their image. Buck announced a rather modest $5,000 gift to establish a children's ward in the Volunteer Hospital at Beekman and Water Streets. The new department would naturally be named The Doris Duke Ward. Meanwhile, Ben gave $100,000 to Wesleyan College, and was continuing to support Trinity College in Durham. Angier Duke had also begun giving to Trinity College, donating $25,000 for a new gymnasium. Despite such generosity, Angie couldn't shake his reputation as a rich, troubled trustfunder. One car wreck on the Bronx Parkway left a pedestrian killed when Angie's car hit a stone wall. His marriage was also in trouble; Cordelia had given birth to Angier and a second son, Anthony, but her husband didn't care for domestic life. Three years after the extravagant wedding, Cordelia filed for divorce. (In fact, both the ballyhooed Biddle-Duke alliances went up in smoke; Mary and Tony who had two children, Nicolas and Mary, would also split. Along with most of their peers, marital failure eventually became a genetic predisposition for both families.)

After the divorce, Angie's reckless behavior increased. In 1922, he was involved in a serious car accident in Southampton. Months later, on his way home from the Kentucky Derby, he fractured his left shoulder when he was crushed between two railroad cars entering the terminal in Cincinnati. (It was never explained what he was doing on the tracks.)

He bought a 76-foot yacht, the *Althea*, and hosted raucous parties frequented by champagne-sipping unattached women and swarthy polo players. On Labor Day weekend, 1923, at 2:30 in the morning, Angie fell off a dingy in Greenwich, Connecticut, and drowned. His body was found six hours later underneath the float. A few months short of his thirty-ninth birthday, he had reportedly struck his head against a piling. During an inquest, it was revealed that the party of three men and three women had eaten dinner at the Indian Harbor Yacht Club and drove to the floating raft to make the short trip in a rowboat to Angie's yacht. The boat capsized, flinging the group into the water. They had been drinking heavily.

Ben and his wife Sarah were distraught, unable to attend their only son's funeral. Sarah suffered a nervous breakdown; Ben never recovered from the shock.

Buck and Nanaline were abroad at the time and unable to go to Durham for the funeral. Cousin Doris, in New York under the care of her French governess, Jenny Renaude, and other servants, did not attend. After all, there were sure to be photographers. Doris, who had shuttled back and forth from Europe with her parents, was secluded in the cavernous East Seventy-eighth Street mansion, which was beginning to feel more and more like a prison every day.

Chapter Four

⤔❧⤕

*Her Heart Belongs
to Daddy*

⤔❧⤕

EDWARD HANSEN HURRIED through Manhattan's Central Park on a crisp
November morning in 1921 and stood before the imposing white marble
house on the corner of Seventy-eighth and Fifth. It was the Duke mansion.
He knew the name from the cigarette ads on the Fifth Avenue buses and
sidewalk kiosks, and now he had been sent by an employment agency for
the position of assistant butler. Hansen, thirty-two and a Swedish immi-
grant, nervously approached the marble steps leading up to the filigreed
iron and glass door flanked by two tall white pillars. Through the glass, he
could see the footman on duty. The heavy door swung open and Hansen
was ushered inside, met by a burly servant.

"George Weston," the man said, extending a hand.

Hansen nodded and looked around. He knew Weston was the majordomo of the Duke house, said to be the most beautiful and most expensive
in all of New York. The front hall looked like a castle, and Weston's clipped
British accent echoed over the marble floor and tapestried walls. Weston
noticed Hansen's apprehension.

"Don't worry," he said with a small smile. "It's no worse here than
anywhere else."

Rounding the corner was Mrs. Duke, in a dark tailored suit and velvet
hat, her trademark string of plump pearls encircling her pale, slender neck.

She was accompanied by her personal maid. Normally, she refrained from addressing the servants, but on this day she stopped.

"What nationality are you?" she asked cooly.

"Swedish," Hansen replied.

Looking up, she fluttered her eyes and said, "All right."

On their way to the back stairs, leading down to the kitchen and servants' quarters, Hansen heard men's voices coming from the drawing room. The voice had a Southern accent. "We have never stated in any manner, shape or form that tob-accah is pure. You buy the tobacco for what it's worth."

Weston took Hansen down to the basement and showed him his bedroom, past the steam-filled laundry room, tiled in white and bustling with activity. At the far end of the hall was the spacious kitchen, vegetables piled high in wicker baskets, meats hanging from hooks, and a cook sharing a cup of tea with two giggling chambermaids, dressed in their starched white morning uniforms.

"Mrs. Duke was a beautiful housekeeper, even though she had so many servants," said Bertha Marshall, a family friend. "She directed everything and kept up with all her accounts. And she did the ones from the office. They got it direct from her, not from any servant, what the expenses were. She knew exactly what the expenses were. She knew exactly the cost of everything."

The thirty-two-room Duke house, modeled after the late-eighteenth-century Maison Labbatiere in Bordeaux, was more a museum than a private home. "It was like living in a tomb," said one of Doris' schoolmates, Lucy Welch Mazzeo. Bertha Marshall recalled that as a child, Doris was not happy in the Seventy-eighth Street house. "She said there was so much marble, she didn't like it. She was born there and they hurried to have the house finished for her birth, but it was an immense and cold house. Mrs. Duke," Marshall added, "loved it."

A tour of the mansion would start in the front hall, decorated (by the infamous Duveen brothers) with priceless works of art, including Raeburn's "English Gentleman in Red Coat," Hoppner's "Miss Charlotte Dennison" and Gainsborough's "Lord Gwyder." There was also statuary: "Girl Playing The Flute" and "La Musique" by Nicholas Coustou. The central staircase was covered in emerald-green carpeting, but guests normally used the small elevator to the right of the stairs, large enough to hold four people. The elevator was said to be quite unique among the Fifth Avenue residences, with its intricate oak paneling and mirrored ceiling.

In the grand foyer was an Isfahan silk palace rug. To the left were the library and dining room (complete with Regency tapestries and Chinese temple jars of the Yung Chang period); to the right, the ballroom and drawing room, furnished with two velvet settees, a large mahogany leather topped table, a grand piano, and a small Oriental rug over pale green carpeting. The walls were painted white and gold, the windows were covered in silk balloon shades and full-length gold damask drapes, which puddled fashionably to the floor. The furniture was Louis XVI. Two five-foot-high urns stood in each corner.

The drawing room opened to the oblong-shaped ballroom, or music room, the largest in the house. It was often used to show movies to young Doris, who giggled over the antics of Charlie Chaplin while being served ice cream in 14-carat gold sherbet cups. There were five chandeliers and an inlaid oak-wood floor and a gallery on the west side of the room seven feet wide for the orchestra.

At formal parties, with perhaps one hundred white-tied and gowned guests, the dancing would begin at 10:30 and last until three in the morning, with Buck Duke (having spent the evening huddled in a corner smoking cigars and talking to business associates) slipping out shortly after midnight to retire to bed, leaving Nanaline twirling with one of her many admirers on the highly polished oak dance floor that had been imported from England.

"Her evening clothes were superb," said Bertha Marshall. "She would be exquisitely dressed."

Buck never said goodnight. Uncomfortable in white tie and tails and at six-two and over 200 pounds, too portly to be much of a dancer, he would simply disappear to his bedroom. Like other members of the gilded set, Buck and Nanaline had separate bedrooms, although there were twin beds in the master bedroom, one of which he occupied on occasion.

The room also had a loveseat, a marble mantel over a fireplace, and a bedside table for the telephone. The bedside lamps were lit every evening by the chambermaids in their black nighttime uniforms, and the windows were dressed in silk drop shades and full-length draperies.

Next to the master bedroom was the boudoir occupied by Doris' French governess, Mademoiselle Jenny Renaud, who was hired several days after Hansen in 1921, when Doris was nine. Exceedingly loyal, Jenny stayed with Doris for thirteen years and became the most beloved female influence in her life. Unlike Nanaline, Jenny was an easygoing, demonstrative woman and endeared herself to the servants by never fussing about the food. She and young Doris "spoke nothing but French all day and night," Hansen said.

Nanaline, on the other hand, was not as adept at languages and did not speak a word of French, which put her at a distinct disadvantage.

Even then, Doris had a hectic schedule, with tutors and special piano teachers hired to come to the house. Hansen was critical of one particular French tutor, "a fussy little bit of a woman. If we knew that Miss Duke had another engagement to go out somewhere and interrupted the class to bring her luncheon a little bit ahead of time, she didn't like it."

There were French lessons at eleven, music lessons at noon. A Steinway grand piano was installed in her sitting room. Young Doris had a reputation for changing tutors with alarming frequency; one year she hired and fired six different piano teachers. Finally, an exasperated Nanaline demanded to know why her daughter kept changing from one instructor to another. Doris looked up and smiled. "Well," she answered, "one has a certain technique and the next one has something else, and you blend it together."

While Doris may not have been inherently gifted, she practiced faithfully, often staying up late at night alone in her sitting room at the keyboard. "She certainly did improve as far as her playing was concerned," said Hansen. "And of course, she had the means to engage the best tutors in the world."

But Doris was reluctant to perform in front of others. Her father, otherwise devoted to her, rarely asked her to play for him, and her mother was usually too busy to lend much support. The only encouragement came from Mademoiselle Renaud, who sat listening for hours to Doris' playing.

Lunch was served at 1 P.M. in her sitting room. Usually, it was just the two of them: Doris and Jenny eating from a moveable table. In the afternoons, Jenny would take Doris to the theater. They had a car and Crocker, the family chauffeur, at their disposal.

The adjoining room was sometimes used by Walker Inman. He was in his twenties now and flew his private plane from his plantation in Georgetown, South Carolina. He would come for a visit in the spring and then another at Christmas. A heavy drinker, Inman would convince the servants to bring him a highball every twenty minutes or so behind his mother's back. "Don't get caught," he'd whisper to Hansen. He also made a habit of using the back stairs instead of the elevator, hoping no one would see him in his inebriated state.

Duke, as was his habit, hired private detectives to investigate Walker's decadent life-style and eventually banned him from the Seventy-eighth Street house. For years, Inman had to wait until Duke was gone to even telephone his mother, which only intensified Nanaline's affection for him.

"She adored her son Walker. He could do no wrong," Dorothy Mahana Macauley, a childhood friend of Doris, said. "I couldn't tell if she adored Doris. It was very hard to tell. She was sort of a cold person."

"Dottie" Mahana was the corn products heiress, who lived just down the block. Doris "didn't really have a happy childhood," she added. "It's awfully hard for an only child, which she was because Walker was years older. And he wasn't around much, almost never."

Doris' bedroom was just in front of the elevator door, with an adjoining sitting room. As a young girl, she had two twin beds and often Jenny would sleep in the room with her. (Later, she bought a Chinese four-poster with a fire-breathing dragon embossed on the canopy.) Scattered on the tabletops were framed photographs (Doris feeding the pigeons in Rome) and a giant dollhouse. A large closet with built-in drawers held her clothes. There were approximately sixty dresses imported from Paris, each one photographed and kept in a catalogue with a sample swatch of the material. Doris would sit on her chaise and look through the catalogue to choose her daily wardrobe, mostly dark blue or gray wool dresses with ruching at the neck.

Just beyond Doris' bedroom was Mrs. Duke's bath, with its sunken marble tub and solid gold hairbrushes and combs. Off the bath was Nanaline's dressing room, a circular, two-storied affair complete with wrought-iron balcony and staircase. Mrs. Duke's maid was in charge of this room with its hundreds of day dresses, evening gowns, and cocktail dresses, many of them in her favorite color: blue. There were gloves to match every outfit, which the maid was expected to keep in order. It was not an easy task. The maid was also required to recall exactly which outfit Mrs. Duke wore to every outing. On one afternoon, no doubt in a rush, Nanaline came home from a party wearing the wrong fur coat. Fortunately, her French maid Germaine had sewn her name inside the right coat, which was of considerably more value than the one Nanaline had worn home.

Her dozens of mink and sable furs (from Frères on Fifth Avenue) and imported Russian laprobes were stored on the second floor of the dressing room and sent to storage in the summer. There were thirty individual wood-paneled closets with brass fixtures and separate rooms for dozens of hats (made of ornate velvet and resting on stands) and a sea of shoes. Nanaline had room for more than 300 pairs of shoes. "They were all satin shoes," according to the butler. "Mrs. Duke had a rather tiny foot." In one corner was the Herring-Hall-Marvin safe to store her sizeable jewelry collection. One evening, Nanaline came home from a bridge game without her $40,000 diamond ring. A Mr. Whitehouse, the husband of a bridge partner, found it on the floor under one of the tables and nervously returned it in person.

"She never seemed to have any vanity about her looks," recalls Bertha Marshall. "If she wanted to go anywhere, she would go in the shortest notice. She didn't take forever to primp and fix up. She was not that kind of woman. She was so immaculately good-looking, she didn't have to do that."

Nanaline was vain, however, about her age. On her 1923 passport application, she listed her birthdate as September 19, 1874. According to Georgia census records, she was born in 1869.

She was also the kind of woman who would sneak a cigarette every so often, risking her husband's wrath. "He didn't like women smoking," Marshall recalled. "We were once in Newport and he said to her, 'You've been smoking!' And she said, 'I can prove it by Bertha Marshall that I haven't been smoking.' She had me in a predicament, because she sure had. The stub had lipstick on it. He would have known it wasn't the servants. I don't know why Mr. Duke was so against it."

Duke's objections were not frivolous; the tobacco tycoon was fully aware of the health risks associated with tobacco, which had nevertheless been the source of his vast fortune—estimated to be $100 million. By 1919, women were openly smoking cigarettes. In fact, advertising slogans like "Reach for a Lucky Instead of a Sweet" were aimed at the female consumer. The war had also caused cigarette consumption to reach an all-time high as the Army and Navy purchased huge quantities to be shipped overseas.

At the end of the hall was the guest room, with a large canopied bed and heavy drapes. Facing noisy Fifth Avenue with its ever-increasing cacophony of automobile horns, it was rarely, if ever, in use. There was also a sitting room for Nanaline, with a large Oriental rug, chairs covered in French brocade, yellow silk balloon shades, priceless jade figurines, and a lifesize, unflattering portrait of Buck Duke. On the far wall was a full-length portrait of Doris in a long sashed dress, painted from a photograph by the English artist DaCosta, who was living in Manhattan for several years in the early 1920s. Nanaline had also posed for the artist and her portrait hung downstairs in the drawing room.

On Nanaline's desk was her mail and messages and on the end tables were her magazines. She had numerous subscriptions, including *Time, Life, Town & Country, House & Garden, Vogue,* and *Harper's Bazaar.* She was also a faithful reader of the *American Journal,* especially the Cholly Knickerbocker society column, which served up choice morsels of society gossip: Who was dining at Sherry's the night before. Who was seen at the Waldorf.

What the Vanderbilts were up to. Who the Prince of Wales was seeing. Nanaline even gossiped about her predecessor, the colorful Lillian Mc-Credy, who had recently made news as the "other woman" in a scandalous divorce case involving former Representative Lafayette Pence of Colorado and his wife Catherine. ("I intend to make Mrs. Duke pay for the honeymoons she has spent with my husband," Catherine Pence told the press. Lillian heatedly defended her honor, saying she had only gone to Pence for legal advice.)

Pullcords in every room were used to signal the maids, and dumbwaiters brought food and drinks to the second floor from the kitchen in the basement. There were imported console tables and a red velvet runner in the long, marble hallway, rolled up in paper and camphor every spring with the other rugs while the Dukes went to Newport. Also in the hallway outside Nanaline's sitting room was a straight-backed chair where Edward would wait for the gentle tinkle of a handbell, the signal that her lunch tray was ready to be picked up.

The house had a back staircase which was used by the servants (and Walker Inman). The female servants were sequestered on the third floor, which held fifteen bedrooms and two bathrooms, one at each end of the hall. The men were housed in the basement: George Weston, the butler, Edward Hansen, his assistant, another footman (several British footmen had come and gone after arguments with Weston), two chauffeurs, and a watchman. A grand total of sixteen servants were needed to run the Seventy-eighth Street house, and it was never dull.

"I was amazed at how such petty jealousies could come into people," Hansen said. "Of course I expected it. Because more or less they are not very educated, most of them."

Hansen eventually took over as head butler when George Weston retired, earning $100 a month including room and board. It was not an easy job. In fact, the tall Swede quit several times, returning to his native country. But after a few weeks he'd receive a letter from Nanaline, begging him to return. He worked for the Dukes for thirty-six years, returning every so often to Sweden. "I had to leave once in a while or I would have gone to the bughouse," he said. "It wasn't always a picnic. Mrs. Duke wasn't exactly too easy to please at times . . . She had a temper, too."

Imitating the other grandes dames on Fifth Avenue, Nanaline was a stickler for protocol. Servants could speak only if spoken to. "She was very haughty that way," said Hansen. One day, a new chauffeur dared to utter, "Good morning Mrs. Duke." His greeting was met with stony silence.

(There is one tale of a certain blueblood matron who rode in her chauffeur-driven limousine for several hours, lost in Manhattan. Rather than speak to the driver to give directions, she sat in proper silence in the backseat.)

Hansen was fond of Buck Duke. He was "a real nice gentleman," he said, recalling how the tobacco king liked to tease the young parlor maids. He also gave the servants bonuses after they had been in his employ for five years, often in the form of British-American Tobacco stock. "He got a great deal of enjoyment out of being generous and kind," said Hansen.

Duke was also a man of habit. In bed every night by 9:30, he woke every morning at 7 A.M. The first thing he did was shave in his bedroom, then go to his dressing room. He was not above wearing the same gray suit for three days in a row without pressing, much to the dismay of his butler, not to mention his wife. Downstairs, servants waited in the pantry for his breakfast to be brought up on the dumbwaiter. It usually consisted of a piece of toast and a cup of hot water.

He left for his offices on Forty-fifth Street and Fifth Avenue every morning at 8:30 A.M. and could not bear tardiness. When an employee arrived at the office thirty minutes late saying he had to go to the dentist, Duke growled, "If I were you, I would rather come and open the office first and then see the dentist later." Every day, Buck Duke would arrive home promptly at five. He would stand at the elevator door, often becoming impatient if the maids were occupying it. He once issued an order banning the servants from using the lift for an entire year.

"Is Mrs. Duke at home?"

"No, sir," Hansen replied, "she is not home."

"Is the baby home?"

"No, sir."

Duke continued to refer to Doris as "the baby," even though she was now an adolescent. Retiring to the sitting room, he would read the newspapers, waiting for Doris. When he finally heard her footsteps, he would go to her room. "He was very fond of Miss Duke," Hansen observed. "Anything she asked him for he would promise to get for her. One year . . . she wanted a harp and she got the harp. If she had asked her father for a million dollars, she would have gotten it."

Doris sent her father love letters. "She had a big influence over him," Bertha Marshall said. "He would take her letter from his pocket, read it, kiss it and put it back in his pocket. He would do that two or three times a day. He really adored her." Marshall also recalled walking into the breakfast room at the Duke mansion, seeing Duke "kissing her and loving her and I said, 'Go as far as you like. Don't bother about us.' He really was devoted to her. And he admired her mind, but she said that she got that mind from him . . . She could sit every evening and not go anywhere and enjoy him as much as she enjoyed any party or anything in the world. She told him all the things that had happened and he just loved that. You see, he hadn't had any of that life. He hadn't had any real home life."

Doris had been presented with a Shetland pony named Patsy. The pony was given a beautiful, elaborately equipped stall in Somerville. One Sunday, at a Methodist Sunday School, there was a discussion of heaven and hell. Doris wanted to know where ponies go when they die. The answer? Ponies don't go anywhere because they don't have souls. A tearful Doris told her father, and then asked, "What are you going to do about it?" Duke immediately had a sign painted and placed at the head of the animal's stall: "Ponies do have souls and Patsy most of all."

By early evening, Nanaline would arrive home from her bridge game. Hansen could always tell if she had won or lost by her mood. The ladies played for money, and Nanaline hated to part with a dime.

Buck and Nanaline's dinner was served every night at 7 P.M. in the dining room. Doris and Jenny had supper brought upstairs to her sitting room.

The Dukes preferred simple food; soup and chicken, although Buck had a weakness for terrapin. "He could eat chicken every day," recalled Hansen, who with the other servants ate in the downstairs dining room. The food for the servants was prepared by the "second cook," and it was heartier fare than what was served upstairs; fresh vegetables, chicken, chops, and fish every Friday.

Every three days, fresh flowers were imported from Somerville and all through the house were humidors. It was reported that Duke smoked twenty-six to thirty stogies a day and stuffed two or three in each pocket. ("Take care, my boy," wrote W. B. Taylor of Winston-Salem's Taylor Bros. Tobacco, "for 24 cigars per day is too much for anyone to smoke, and it will get you.") To accompany his meals, Duke drank copious amounts of champagne (his wine cellar was stocked with over 2,000 bottles), especially at dinner parties which called for an extra cook and twenty-four waiters dressed in velvet coats and britches. As they poured magnums of Moet and served terrapin and pheasant on gold plates, the servants strained to get a glimpse of Mrs. Evalyn Walsh McLean's Hope Diamond and loved to gossip about the jewel's famous curse. "You know, she lost one of her sons, Vinson, in Newport. He was guarded by private detectives. He ran across the road and was killed."

Evelyn, a friend of Nanaline's, once stayed at Seventy-eighth Street for a week while taking another child to a doctor in New York. At the end of her visit, she tipped Hansen a full month's salary. When Nanaline learned of her friend's generosity, she called McLean a fool.

There were other guests: the Vanderbilts, the Livingstons, Lady Mendl, Countess Kotzebue, Mayor Jimmy Walker, who once took the Dukes to a speakeasy.

The room off the dining room, the library or "Oak Room," was rarely used. In fact, the Dukes didn't own enough books to fill the shelves, so they had rows of false books put in. "Reading was too slow for him," Edward Hansen said. "Mr. Duke's idea was always to make more money."

This quest took J. B. Duke to the rivers of North Carolina. He had already experienced hydroelectric power on a small scale back in Somerville, with water pumped from the Raritan River for his fountains and lakes. Now, with his other business interests in the Piedmont region, he began buying land near the rushing waterfalls with an eye toward investing in the newly harnessed form of power, commonly known as "white coal." He bought up acres of land on which to build power plants, and by the early 1920s more than 300 cotton mills were supplied with Duke's Southern Power Company, later known as Duke Power.

Regarded as a man with sharp business acumen and little patience, Duke made enemies among the Southern industrialists in his zeal to become the Piedmont power king. "He merely thought faster, more accurately, and grasped a situation more quickly than most men," said W. S. Lee, a Duke business partner. "And once he had decided, he acted promptly."

"He is not a conversationalist," a reporter wrote after a rare interview with the publicity-shy Duke. "His mind works constantly like a great dynamo in one of his power plants . . . His mind moves with terrific velocity and just crumples up anything that gets in its way."

Duke's pursuit of the dollar was no accident. Motherless at the age of two, he later saw his father go off to war and then as a nine-year-old boy worked day and night selling tobacco, vowing never to be poor. "The pathological quest for money," wrote James Knight, in *For the Love of Money*, "is often closely associated with the maternal image . . . If the individual could find mother for the rest of his years, life would be relieved of many of its uncertainties and misfortunes. It is no small surprise then that man is driven to pursue this mirage and find in money a substitute for mother."

Buck Duke, no doubt, would have deemed that hogwash. In his mind, making money was simply the only thing he knew how to do. Whether it had to do with his own self-worth was of no concern. In short order, he had doubled his fortune to an estimated $350 million. His obsession with hydroelectric power eventually took him to Northern Quebec, Canada, where he spent millions for water rights on the Saguenay River and at two developments, Ile Maligne and Chute à Caron. Duke even went so far as to predict that his "life's ambition," twin power plants being developed at the Grand Discharge of Lake St. John, would be one of "the Seven Wonders of the World."

But it was the booming cotton and textile town of Charlotte near the Catawba River which held his fascination. Duke decided he needed another estate, one befitting the most powerful industrialist in the New South. He chose a white mansion in Charlotte's suburb of Myers Park. The house, designed by local architects Hook & Rogers, had been built in 1915 in the Colonial revival style and belonged to Z. V. Taylor, an officer of Southern Public Utilities. Its closest rival was "Reynolda," the 1,000-acre, 60-room residence in Winston-Salem of former archrival R. J. Reynolds, who had died of pancreatic cancer in 1918.

Duke bought the Myers Park house and surrounding acres in 1920 and spent two years renovating it.

"It was not large and Mrs. Duke wanted to leave it as it was, but Mr. Duke wanted to add on," said Bertha Marshall. "Mr. Duke couldn't see anything but something in the large numbers, the large sizes, and he was large himself. His mind was large. And he built that house over there; nine bedrooms and sixteen servants on the third floor and perfectly enormous rooms."

The house eventually grew to fifty-three rooms, with ornate mouldings and broad porches, formal gardens and garish, oversized fountains. One shot 150 feet in the air and could be seen from fifteen miles away. It was said the entire water pressure of Charlotte went down when Duke's fountain was operating. In winter, children would skate on the frozen fountains. In 1922, the estate became known as Lynnewood, and Nanaline—plagued with her own economic insecurity from her impoverished youth—

complained bitterly of the millions her husband was spending on the Charlotte residence. "Now you just let him alone," her friend Bertha Marshall scolded. "Look at all those beautiful diamonds he has given you. This is his diamond bracelet . . . Let him enjoy himself."

The sixty-four-year-old Duke began walking to his Charlotte offices, with his chauffeur following at a discreet distance down the small city streets, talking with the townspeople. On one occasion, he admired a house and saw a small boy sitting on the steps. "I think I'll buy this house right here," he said. The boy scowled. "You're not gonna buy this house. It's my daddy's."

He showed home movies in the living room, a hobby he had picked up from Evalyn Walsh McLean. He was said to be as happy as a child with the new projection machines. Besides, he liked to show movies after dinner so he wouldn't have to sit around and talk.

Life was simple, and soothing.

"Mr. Duke just loved to come to Charlotte," said Bertha Marshall. "He loved to laugh and he loved to enjoy watching people's grass grow. He would go in and ask them how they grew their dahlias, or whatever. He had not had that part of life."

Charlotte represented a return to his Southern roots and Duke had become sentimental in his older years. Dr. Bennette E. Geer, who ran Judson Mills in Greenville and later became president of Furman University, observed, "He wanted her [Doris] to marry a Southerner. I've always felt that he built that house in Charlotte hoping that Mrs. Duke would come down with Doris and Doris would meet one of the Southern boys." But Nanaline made no secret of her lack of enthusiasm for the industrial town of Charlotte; she loathed it. Charlotte "didn't suit Mrs. Duke," Geer concurred. "She wouldn't stay here. She would come down occasionally, but she wouldn't stay long."

The Dukes traveled to and from North Carolina on board their private Pullman car, *The Doris*. Once owned exclusively by railroad executives, the "p.v.'s" (private varnish) were the most visible status symbol of the day, the corporate jet of the 1920s. Duke, who owned a small rail line in North and South Carolina, the Piedmont and Northern Railroad, began renting private cars and then bought the 80-foot-long *Doris* in 1917 for $38,050 (half a million dollars in today's currency). It had sleeping accommodations for ten, a golden oak humidor, embroidered linens, china, glassware, and was staffed by a waiter and a chef. "I remember the cook, this marvelous colored man," said Dorothy Macauley. "He was the one we liked the most." The car (often the site of Duke's raucous New Year's Eve parties with business associates) was stocked with gin, sherry, champagne, and thousands of Orlando cigars. In one eighteen-month period, revelers consumed 5,000 cigars.

The quiet, well-mannered Doris had briefly attended a kindergarten in the rear of a neighborhood grocery store in Charlotte. "One instruction was not to give her any candy or sweets," the proprietor later recalled. The only thing Doris lacked was playmates. When Evalyn McLean told J. B. Duke that her children played with the offspring of her maid, Duke bellowed, "By George, that is what we are going to do for Doris. I am sick and tired of seeing that child by herself. I know who could play with her. The gardener has a lovely child. She ought to make a real playmate for Doris." Duke carried out the plan. "Nannie Lee was furious with me," Evalyn later wrote. "When she went to Europe with Doris that summer she had to take that playmate child along."

After a succession of private tutors, her first taste of formal education was in New York at the elite Brearley School. Buck and Nanaline enrolled Doris in October 1922. She was a month shy of her tenth birthday. "I sat next to her for a year," said Lucy Welch Mazzeo. "She was terribly bright and always got the best marks. She always wanted to get A's. She would get upset if someone else got a better mark. She wanted to show, I think, that it just wasn't her money."

Picture the scene at the Duke mansion every morning: Jenny Renaude carrying Doris' school books downstairs, then handing them to the first-floor footman who passed them to the butler who passed them to the attendant chauffeur, George Roberts. In good weather, Doris would simply walk to the curb. In the rain, a canopy would be erected so not one rain drop would dampen the girl's head. There would also be a carpet spread over a rubber runner on the marble steps.

The Rolls-Royce would be driven the short blocks to the Brearley School, Doris in the backseat swaddled in an ermine laprobe. In spring and fall, she would often be seen walking to school down Fifth Avenue, her chauffeur driving slowly behind her and two private detectives following at a discreet distance on the sidewalk. The detectives would wait outside until the 2 P.M. dismissal and then escort her home.

Kidnapping children of the wealthy for ransom had become an alarming trend during the 1920s when the crime (prior to the Lindbergh law) was not yet a federal offense. "They had a lot of kidnappings. They were always after rich children," said Lucy Welch Mazzeo.

There were other heiresses at Brearley: Dorothy Mahana, the corn products heiress, and Marion Snowden, an oil heiress, who later became Princess Rospigliosi. But Doris was by far the most notorious. "She was always news," said Macauley. "I don't think you can be—I don't want to say—completely normal, but it does something to you. It was awfully hard on Barbara Hutton, too." Doris Duke "was never even inside a food shop," she added. "She never did things that other girls did."

Almost every weekend, Dottie accompanied Doris to Somerville. The two girls were driven to the farm by the Duke chauffeur. "They had a whole slew of Rolls-Royces painted sort of dark red, and you could stand up in them," said Macauley. "The house was hideous, no question about that. Hideous. When you go in the house, it's like being in a village. Because it goes on and on and on. The architecture changes. There was the indoor tennis court. The indoor swimming pool. The theatre.

"The butler used to bring in huge stacks of letters. I was so impressed. Then Doris looked at me with this funny look and said, 'Open one.' I said I couldn't do that, it was her mail. She insisted. So I started opening the letters. They were either begging letters or threatening letters. From all over the world. Everywhere she turned, people were asking for money."

Isolated from her peers, "The Richest Girl in the World" became something of a freak. During one history lesson, the teacher showed slides of ancient Greek ruins. At the sight of one elegant marble temple, Doris said under her breath, "That looks just like my house."

"She was a smart girl, sardonic and kind of scrawny," recalls Frances Brewster Rauch, a classmate. Doris was neither athletic nor particularly popular. "She would have fit in better if she had been more coordinated," said Rauch.

Nanaline was openly critical of her daughter. Far from the diminutive Southern beauty the newspapers had predicted, Doris was an ugly duckling. A gawky adolescent with a large, rounded chin and wisp-thin pale blonde hair, she was insecure about her appearance. "She was so thin and wore these funny sort of smock dresses, brown oxfords that were supposed to be good for you, white socks, an elastic band holding her hair and these terrible gold specs," said Macauley. "She was miserable about her looks."

Nanaline was unusually strict about Doris' wardrobe. "She would never allow her to have things that other girls had," said Macauley. "I remember when we were at Brearley. I would have something like silk socks. She nearly died over that! She wasn't allowed to have anything like that. She was very plain. She wasn't allowed to do anything dashing or fun like other girls."

Nanaline did allow Doris to show movies every Thursday afternoon in the ballroom of the Seventy-eighth Street house. Classmate Betsy Jennings, whose mother was an Auchincloss, was forbidden to attend these screenings. The reason given was because they were held during the school week, although Mrs. Auchincloss was, in all likelihood, not eager for her daughter to socialize with the nouveau Dukes.

"Doris was terribly interested in music and dance," said Dorothy Mahana. "We used to go to Ned Wavens, a place on Broadway, for dance lessons. All these Broadway people started there. We had these two French governesses. I think we were considered real freaks. We worked so hard, learning tap dancing. It was surprising that Mrs. Duke let her do that. It was very out of character. We just lived for those days."

Was Doris closer to Jenny than to her mother?

"Oh much," said Macauley. "She gave her a better life. Nanaline was a very difficult person. There was no question about it. She was so formal and cold. There was no way of having any kind of communication. And she was busy as a beaver with all her social things. She was on this committee and that," said Macauley.

One relative recalled seeing young Doris run to hug her mother, only to be held at arm's length so as not to muss Nanaline's hair. Later in life, Doris told a friend that she remembered hiding in the Seventy-eighth Street house from Nanaline who, it seemed, was always reprimanding her. "She didn't have a very happy time with her mother," said Macauley.

Nanaline's superiority and aloofness were met with an intense desire on her daughter's part to please—at least superficially. "Doris would always be extremely nice to her mother and conferred a lot with her and had such a great deal of confidence in her," said Edward Hansen. "She wouldn't do anything to displease her mother."

That was left to Walker Inman. He had eloped with the daughter of a Kokomo, Indiana, clergyman, Helene Patton Clarke. "Mr. Duke was at that time disgusted with Walker," recalled Bennette Geer. "The girl was of bad character."

Their divorce suit was a major scandal in Reno. He accused her of infidelity with a vaudeville tenor and bootlegger, one Dapper Dan Collins. She accused him of cruelty. Walker won a divorce settling $75,000 on Clarke. Nanaline was deeply embarrassed by the whole affair and mother and son quarrelled. The next summer, Inman was conspicuously absent from Newport, prompting one columnist to observe, "Can it be possible that Mr. Walker Patterson Inman does not share the pleasures of [Newport] because the presence of Walker would be a tip-off on the number of birthdays Nannie Duke hasn't celebrated?"

After renting for several seasons, the Dukes had finally won acceptance and they made plans to purchase "Rough Point," the Nancy Leeds house with the spectacular ocean view, certainly one of the grandest "cottages" on Bellevue Avenue. The house, originally built by the Frederick Vanderbilts, had been boarded up by Leeds after she left Newport to marry Prince Christopher of Greece. The Dukes gutted the mansion and spent millions on renovations.

"Rough Point" became Nanaline's triumph. Socially, she was embraced by the grandes dames even if her husband was not. "He used to say, 'I like those old ladies in Newport, but I don't want to sit by them every night,'" recalled Bertha Marshall.

Compared to several of the more colorful summer colonists, the Dukes kept a low profile. Nanaline "entertained elaborately when she did entertain at Newport, but she did not really like to entertain," said Marshall. "She enjoyed a card game. I played with her many times and she was a very fine card player. She always played in the afternoon. Every afternoon."

As for her daughter, the demands of social life were met with disdain. "Doris hated Newport. It was pretty stuffy," said one friend.

I. Townsend Burden, whose family owned a house in Newport, remembered Nanaline as extremely austere. "She was a strict old gal. And he [Duke] was a very frightening-looking guy. The way he talked down to you." Doris, he said, was never particularly social. "She was very quiet. She never played tennis or golf. I would say she was very reclusive. She wasn't really interested in anybody. She liked to be by herself."

Nanaline encouraged Doris to seek out friends, especially young Dorothy Fell, daughter of the ultra-rich Mrs. Ogden Mills. Nanaline was "thrilled" to know Mrs. Mills, according to Dottie Macauley.

But Newport was not Doris' style. Even Bailey's Beach, the ultra-elite crescent of sand and its weathered private cabanas held little attraction. "It was perfectly revolting. Still is," said one socialite. "You'd go in and go swimming and there would be some old dead chicken floating by. You see, all the boats went by."

Perhaps even more compelling a subject than the tobacco lord's quest for money was the question of how he would dispose of it all. Duke had already voiced his overwhelming admiration for John D. Rockefeller and Andrew Carnegie, two names closely associated with American philanthropic endeavors.

Already generously supported by most of the Duke-Biddle clan, Trinity College in Durham became the recipient of a $1 million grant from Buck Duke in 1922. Two years later, on December 8, 1924, Duke announced a staggering gift of $40 million to be used for educational purposes in North Carolina, including hospitals, the care of orphans, and aging ministers. Six million was set aside for land and buildings at Trinity College, which Duke had envisioned as a sort of "Harvard of the South." The money represented three-fourths of his holdings in the Southern Power Company. Standing in the living room of the white-columned Myers Park in Charlotte, Duke was surrounded by reporters and business associates when he made the announcement.

That same day in Rochester, New York, George Eastman of Kodak announced his gift of $15 million in Kodak stock for educational purposes.

"I don't believe that a college education does a man much good in business," the gruff Duke said, "except for the personal satisfaction it gives him. But when you have a great community growing like the Carolinas you've got to have five kinds of leaders whose minds are trained. The first is preachers, the second is teachers, the third is lawyers, the fourth is chemists and engineers and the fifth is doctors."

The man who had taken so much from the poor, backward Carolinas was now prepared, perhaps out of guilt, to make restitution. But his gift, unlike that of Eastman's, had strings. The money would be endowed only if Trinity College agreed to change its name to Duke University. The board of trustees voted unanimously to accept the condition.

"Personally, where it comes to that point where Trinity can take the lead in educational circles of the entire South," one alumnus wrote to then-president William Preston Few, "I am inclined to shout with Shakespeare: WHAT'S IN A NAME?"

News of Duke's endowment was greeted with some skepticism by *The New Republic,* which called the $40 million gift an act of "gross philistinism," and went on to speculate whether the family tobacco, "Duke's Mixture," would be inscribed upon the portals. (In truth, historians now note that school president Few may have instigated the name change, working behind the scenes for years with J. B. Duke and his family.) Trinity College was an excellent school, but nothing particularly distinguished to qualify for such enormous bounty. Especially in a backwater town like

Durham! Duke himself had even considered moving the University to Charlotte. There was also speculation on the extent Duke's business interests would be intertwined with the university.

"The motive which has inspired him to provide for the integrity of his companies is probably the same ingenious vanity which is expressed in the designation of 'Duke University,'" *The New Republic* said. "Nevertheless the fact remains that boards of trustees competent to manage multi-million dollar corporations are not competent to exercise anything more than a benevolent quieticism over the education institutions instructed to their care. Their function is to be conservators of established businesses and established educational types. The mission of millionaires in short is to endow prevailing institutions, and the business of their trustees is to perpetuate their trust."

But Duke had a plan; by tying his tobacco and power fortune to a state university, the government would be less willing to impose heavy taxes on his holdings because it would, in effect, be taxing its own institution. It was a brilliant move. The trust would be administered by fifteen trustees, including Nanaline Duke, business associate George Allen, attorney William R. Perkins, Ben's son-in-law Anthony Drexel Biddle, Jr., Edward C. Marshall (Bertha's husband), and Bennette E. Geer.

Returning to Somerville on his private railroad car, Duke issued a statement recommending the university hold on to securities of the Southern Power System as the prime investment for the funds of the endowment.

Three days after his announcement, Duke filed his will in Somerville. Another trust had been created: the Doris Duke Trust. At his death, one-third of his estate would go to the trust, the income to go to his daughter. One third of the principal would be given to Doris when she reached the age of twenty-one, another one-third at the age of twenty-five, and the remainder at the age of thirty.

On February 20, Duke left his farm for Durham aboard the *Doris* to discuss site plans for Duke University. He had chosen the Newport "cottage-maker" Horace Trumbauer to design the university. Trumbauer took as his inspiration the Gothic spires of Oxford and Cambridge, with a chapel tower 240 feet high as the centerpiece. The legendary Boston firm of Frederick Law Olmsted, which had designed Central Park, was entrusted with the landscaping job. Duke's private car sat on the siding in Durham for several days, as the blueprints were unrolled and food and champagne were served in copious quantities.

The original Trinity campus would be enlarged and renamed the East

Campus. New land was purchased several miles away for the West Campus, where Trumbauer's homage to the tobacco king would be built. A large, man-made lake would be featured, along with the Duke signature, a garish fountain. Carloads of stone were shipped in from the North and test walls were erected around the grounds. Luckily, a quarry was located nearby, so the out-of-state stone was scrapped in favor of the native North Carolina rock, which was more suitable and far cheaper.

Just as the name Duke was up for sainthood, an ugly scandal occurred. On the morning of March 9, as Duke descended his marble stairs at East Seventy-eighth Street to his waiting Rolls-Royce, he was met by a process server. Lillian McCredy Duke had, two years earlier, been swindled out of $275,000 in cash and $50,000 in jewels by a Wall Street confidence man, Alfred E. Lindsey. She had failed to recover her losses and had turned to Duke for financial help. He refused. As a last resort, Lillian filed a lawsuit claiming she and Duke were still married.

The story of the first Mrs. Duke "breaking her twenty-year silence" was a bombshell. Lillian based her claim on the fact that she and her husband had never lived in Somerville and therefore the New Jersey courts had no jurisdiction. She also claimed that Duke had been romancing the widow Inman before his divorce became final on May 3, 1906. Nanaline was devastated by the publicity, and kept it from Doris and her young friends while Duke's lawyers swung into action. Many of the Dukes' socially prominent friends were unaware that Buck had been married before. What would happen to Nanaline and Doris if Lillian prevailed?

The Dukes, one story said, "are leaders in the gold-studded sets that divide their time between Newport and Palm Beach. An invalidated divorce might be an outcome both pleasant and profitable to [the first] Mrs. Duke, but it would fall like a tragedy on the multi-millionaire and his family." Depositions were taken; Ben Duke swore that he introduced his brother to the widow Inman in the fall of 1906, after the marriage had broken up. Nanaline was also deposed, and swore to the same chronology.

Lillian began trailing her former husband, even following him to Durham. Duke refused to see her. She became hysterical. Ben MacNeill, a reporter with the *News and Observer*, was sent to Ben Duke's house where Buck was staying. "I never saw a man more scared in my life," MacNeill recalled. "He had been drinking and he took me into the library and brought out a bottle of whiskey. He told me that his first wife had been the most wicked influence in his life, that she was a double-crosser and thoroughly no good. He said several times, 'I wanted a son. She wouldn't give me a son.'"

Duke "cussed a good deal. At other times, he snivelled and tears came to his eyes."

Duke's high-powered legal team was headed by former governor Nathan L. Miller. Lillian's lawyer did not even have stationery with his own letterhead. Oral arguments were held April 9. Miller filed a motion to dismiss. Six weeks later, the motion was granted, upholding Duke's twenty-year-old divorce and ensuring the legality of his second marriage.

Relieved and trying to focus on his work, Duke took a business trip in mid-July. Accompanied by officials of the Aluminum Company of America (ALCOA), Duke boarded the *Doris* for a one-week journey to the Saguenay River in Canada. The ALCOA group had a separate car. On board was Secretary of the Treasury Andrew Mellon.

Mellon and Duke had several discussions about wealth over the course of the week. They talked of the "robber barons'" accomplishments: providing cheap transportation, heating, and power. Duke boasted of his own worth: "providing as much fun out of fifteen cents as buying a package of cigarettes and enjoying them."

While Mellon and the other men feasted on Duke's famous food, the tobacco king himself was limited to a strict diet. Nanaline had insisted that her burly husband shed twenty pounds. Instead of his usual griddle cakes and sausage for breakfast, Duke was limited to "three damn prunes," which he complained bitterly about.

But the diet left him weak, and he had trouble walking. Had he simply worked himself to a state of exhaustion or was it the lack of nourishment? Earlier that summer, he had suffered an almost complete nervous breakdown and was confined to his room and put on a diet of broiled liver and strawberries. "I don't know what in the world got into him to take that diet and just deplete himself," recalled Marion Williams, who had married one of Buck's nephews.

Pernicious anemia was the original diagnosis, later questioned. "Although I never saw Mr. James Buchanan Duke myself, I did see his blood in August, 1925," wrote Dr. George Minot two decades later. Minot disputed the diagnosis of pernicious anemia, saying Duke suffered from "one of those fundamental disorders of blood formation that have commonly been called aregeneratory anemias, conditions that sometimes have been called aplastic anemia." There was another, more serious possibility: leukemia.

In mid-September 1925, as the Dukes were leaving Newport, Buck collapsed. Ben Duke wrote to Sarah, "J.B. came home last Sunday in his private car, arriving here on a special train which brought him all the way from Newport. He had a terrible bad spell just as they were leaving Newport. One of his doctors came down with him. On his arrival here, an invalid's chair met him at the *Doris* and took him to the auto that brought him to his house." Buck asked for his brother as soon as he arrived. Ben found him "dreadfully weak. Nanaline said he hadn't been nearly so well the last week they were in Newport." Duke began experiencing fainting spells two or three times a day, accompanied by severe stomach pains. His physician, Dr. Wylie, told the family that Duke's blood was anemic and that he would die.

After a blood transfusion, Duke rallied. But he was annoyed at having to stay in town and miss his weekend trips to the farm. Lying awake at night, he fretted over business decisions. "Please don't disturb me," he told his nurse, "I'm building a steam plant down South." Ben wrote to his wife, saying the doctors "were stupified" over the case. Nanaline was prepared for the worst as Buck became bedridden, but the family kept his condition secret. "We are not," Ben wrote his wife, "telling folks how sick he is."

Friends of Doris recall being led into the sitting room on the first floor to greet the tobacco lord, who was by then in a wheelchair. The girls would curtsey, as if to a head of state, and shake his hand.

Across town, Lillian Duke was planning a new assault. On September 30, she filed an appeal, aided by a tenacious young female lawyer, Lucille Pugh. In a letter dated October 8, one of Duke's attorneys, H. Bartow Farr, wrote to Forrest Hyde at Duke's office: "I am enclosing some publicity in the Duke case which you may not have seen. This is perhaps the result of Miss Pugh's appearance in the case."

Hyde's reply was succinct. "Notoriety of that kind seems to justify the existence of the gunman."

Whether Duke's lawyers were fantasizing about Lillian's demise is unclear. But they were distressed over the proliferation of news stories, which the family kept from Doris. (In fact, one of her closest friends never knew of the scandal, or that Duke had been previously wed.)

"I have suffered in silence since 1905," Lillian said. She denied her affair with Huntoon and became a favorite interview subject of eager young scribes. "Mrs. Duke still retains vestiges of that queenly beauty that brought men from the highest walks of life to her feet years ago," one interviewer wrote. "Her face is unmarked by wrinkles and there is not even a streak of gray in her titian hair."

Her face was splashed on every Sunday supplement. Most reporters seized upon the rather obvious and dramatic contrast between the first Mrs. Duke's poverty and the unparalleled opulence Nanaline and Doris enjoyed.

In late September, a beleaguered Duke called for George Allen. He was worried that he had not provided enough money to complete all the planned buildings for Duke University and on October 1 a codicil to his will was signed, giving Duke University another $7 million.

By now, Duke was aware that his condition was terminal. His businesses would thrive, and the university was established. His name would live on. In his mind, the only thing troubling him was Doris. They had long talks. Duke certainly would not have wished to appear paranoid, but he did impress upon his daughter the fact that people would be after her for her fortune. He knew she was not prepared for the responsibilities. One story has it that he warned her repeatedly, "Do not trust anyone."

Nanaline sat with Buck every night, shivering under her fur cape as the brisk autumn air wafted through the large windows. Lying in his Louis XV bed, Duke labored to draw a breath. His lungs were filled with mucus; he was literally drowning. "I saw him the last time on the Thursday evening around 6 o'clock," Edward Hansen recalled. "One of the nurses rang for me. She needed some help. So I went up and entered the room. He recognized me, but he said, 'I am in pretty bad shape, Edward.' I said, 'You look pretty good, Mr. Duke.' 'But you can't go by looks,' he said."

Hansen noticed Duke's heart palpitating under his bedclothes. "I think he knew it was hopeless, the way he spoke to me," Hansen added. Doctors came and went. A hush fell over the house. On Friday, he lapsed into a coma. At six o'clock Saturday evening, October 10, 1925, the nurse rang for Edward Hansen once more.

Buck Duke was dead.

Hansen telephoned the New York office, and then the newspapers. A gale, packing winds of 78 miles per hour, brought bitter cold and snow into Manhattan that night as wires and telegrams began arriving from all over the world. It was the coldest October 10 on record.

The next morning *The New York Times* carried the story on page one:

Tobacco King Dies of Pneumonia. Duke was eulogized as "The greatest figure in the American tobacco industry and one of the nation's leading philanthropists."

His wife and twelve-year-old daughter were in a daze, as servants draped black bunting inside the Seventy-eighth Street mansion. Suddenly, everything went dark. "Doris expressed no outward grief at her father's death," said Hansen. "I don't think she fully realized the loss."

On Monday, Duke's massive corpse was removed from the bedroom to the first-floor drawing room where his body lay in an open casket. Next to the coffin was a $1,000 spray of orchids sent by Ben Duke, who had taken ill himself. A fleet of shining black limousines lined up for blocks, as the wealthy business leaders came to pay their respects. (Most of Nanaline's bridge partners stayed away, saying they would rather remember Duke as he was.)

Among the curious crowd gathered to watch the comings and goings was a rather striking, red-haired woman standing on a knoll in Central Park, oblivious to the steady drizzle of the cold October rain. It was Lillian Duke. She had lost her bid to overturn the divorce and was now destitute. At 4 P.M., she watched the solid bronze casket carried down the front steps of the Duke house into a hearse. The body was driven to Penn Station and Buck Duke made his last trip home to Durham.

On October 13, thousands of spectators lined the streets to see James Buchanan Duke for the last time. It was the largest funeral in the history of Durham. Schools were closed and factory business was suspended. Fourteen hundred students of the University formed an honor guard, holding wreaths of flowers while burly members of the football team were chosen as pallbearers to lift the 1,500-pound casket into the Duke Memorial Church. Duke lay in state prior to the procession to Maplewood Cemetery, where he was buried in the family mausoleum next to Brodie and Washington Duke.

In deference to the tobacco tycoon, the cities of Danville, Winston, and Salem suspended cigarette sales for a full ten minutes on the morning of the funeral.

"With Duke's passing," said the trade journal *The Tobacco Leaf,* "there goes out of this world the most remarkable figure that the tobacco trade has ever produced. As Wrigley may have been said to have made the United States a nation of gum chewers, so James B. Duke pioneered in the process of making America a nation of cigarette smokers."

Two weeks later, Duke's will was filed in Somerville. For giving his fellow man a simple five-cent pleasure, he had reaped an estimated $300 million.

Ignoring Henry Ford's observation that "Fortunes tend to self-destruction by destroying those who inherit them," Duke left the bulk of his estate to his twelve-year-old daughter, Doris. The will provided Nanaline with $100,000 a year plus a life interest in the New York house, Rough Point, and Myers Park.

The Doris Duke Trust, with all the power company shares, contained more stock in Duke Power than the Duke Endowment.

Two names were conspicuously absent from Duke's will: Walker Inman and Lillian Duke, who at that moment lay in her rooming house on East Eighty-eighth Street, starving to death. She sank into a coma several days later and died.

News reports noted that the only food in the room were two eggs, although curiously enough her pet Mexican hairless dog Pom-Pom seemed well nourished.

Chapter Five

The Gilded Cage

ON THAT FALL DAY as Buck Duke's body lay in the heavy bronze casket, Doris remained in her room, dressed in black. It was bizarre, people thought, to see such a young girl in this mourning attire. To save money, Nanaline had ordered several of Doris' dresses dyed black by the laundress. For the next few months, Doris wore these recycled mourning clothes to school, with thick black stockings and a black cloche pulled down over her eyes. With her father's death, a portion of her own life—that carefree, over-indulged adolescence—was over. Now, on the brink of becoming a woman and with her own mother so cold and withholding, she was confused, depressed, and utterly alone.

Her heart had belonged to Daddy.

"After her father died, she was a changed person," a classmate recalled. While Buck had taken an active interest in Doris' intellectual development—sitting in the Brearley gallery one afternoon watching his daughter win a spelling bee—Nanaline's only interest was society with a capital S.

"Doris never mingled with the other girls," the classmate said. "Her mother kept her busy doing things with very rich people and foreigners with titles. Café society types. Her mother was awful. If her father had lived longer, she would have been a different person."

The classmate received a letter from Doris sometime later. The stationery was bordered in black. It was mourning paper. "The kind grown ups would use," the classmate recalled.

"She was a sad girl," recalled Virginia Grace, one of Doris' teachers at Brearley who attended Doris' thirteenth birthday party. Miss Grace had received the invitation by messenger, and a car and chauffeur arrived at the appointed hour to bring her to the mansion. The house was covered with roses: pastels, rich deep reds, grandifloras, and tiny tea roses. Doris told her teacher that they had come from the gardens of Somerville. "The farm belongs to me now," she said defiantly. Doris, like her father, had formed a lasting attachment to Duke Farms and had convinced her mother and the lawyers not to sell the property as Duke had directed. It was evident to all that the strained relationship between mother and daughter had worsened with Buck Duke's death. Mrs. Duke, perhaps feeling the burden of single parenthood and resenting her financial dependence on Doris, became even more strict with her daughter.

"During the birthday party, Nanaline took me aside," Miss Grace recalled, "and said she was worried about the company Doris was keeping. I was surprised. I always thought Doris was a quiet girl." But Nanaline pressed the matter, asking the teacher to keep an eye on Doris, saying she was worried about the "fast crowd" and unsavory characters Doris seemed attracted to.

Not surprisingly, the kidnap threats increased. Frustrated reporters tried in vain for any glimpse of the Duke women, shadowed by bodyguards.

In August of 1926, Nanaline booked a modest second-class cabin on the *France* and, with Doris and governess Jenny Renaude, sailed for Europe. (Always penny-pinching, Nanaline waited for the winter rates to go into effect.) As they stood on the deck, Nanaline in black with her trademark string of pearls, her awkward daughter in a loose-fitting brown dress, they watched intently as photographers snapped the more dazzling celebrities. Finally, one of the photographers, not knowing their identity, asked them to also pose. The richest little girl in the world smiled shyly, blushed, and looked up into her mother's face. She did not reply. Nanaline finally consented. Surrounded by a battery of cameras, Doris moved closer to her mother and again smiled her slow, enigmatic smile. The photographers, unaware that the two were anything other than ordinary passengers watching the more glamorous celebrities coming aboard, asked them their names. Mrs. Duke answered, "Oh yes, Mrs. Nanaline H. Duke and my daughter, Doris. Thank you very much."

The photographers were shocked that the two had slipped unnoticed on board ship, and the picture made every newspaper from Newark to New-port Beach.

The fascination with Doris and Nanaline was not unlike the public's hunger for news of Gloria Vanderbilt and her mother.

Nanaline—who was living on her late husband's bequest of $100,000 a year—had been appointed Doris' guardian. By early October, Doris and her governess quietly returned to America in a modest C deck cabin on the *Aquitania*. Nanaline stayed behind in London. The thirteen-year-old heiress was already making plans to sue her mother and other executors of the will over the question of who owned the Seventy-eighth Street house, the art collection, the automobiles, and the private Pullman car.

One clause of the will said the various Duke residences belonged to Nanaline, while another clause stipulated that the real estate be sold and the proceeds divided among the executors. The properties would be sold to the highest bidder unless Doris legally intervened. The suit was filed in New York's Supreme Court in December, with Nanaline named as a defendant, along with George Allen, William R. Perkins, and the trustees. The auction, even with Doris buying the properties with funds provided by the estate, would be "a vain and useless proceeding" since Doris had enough money to outbid any prospective buyer. If the house in New York were advertised for sale, the great unwashed public would be allowed to view the mansion, thus depreciating its value. The lawsuit claimed Doris wanted to buy the property outright, giving her mother a life interest. The trustees (it was known that Nanaline disagreed with Doris and favored selling New York and Somerville) insisted on sticking to Buck Duke's will and said an auction should be held.

On the same day, a similar suit was filed in Rhode Island's Supreme Court, with Doris asking to take possession of the Newport estate, without going through the formality of an auction.

In February 1927, the courts agreed that Doris Duke was the sole owner of the New York house, valued at $1.6 million, as well as Rough Point, with Nanaline retaining the right to reside in both residences until her death. Duke Farms was a separate matter. Although Nanaline was anxious to sell the property, which had fallen into disrepair, and divide the proceeds, Doris insisted that the farm and all its contents (including over 2,000 bottles of imported champagne) was hers and hers alone. By September, the deed to the 2,000-acre property was conveyed from the Duke Farm Company, Inc. to Doris Duke. She was fourteen, sentimental about her father's rolling acres where she had spent so many happy childhood years, and bitter that her mother felt no such attachment. She told Nanaline she wanted to renovate the farm and live there part of the time. A truce was declared: Newport became Nanaline's territory while New Jersey would belong to Doris.

Neither felt any attachment to Charlotte, despite the fact that the Duke Endowment had been created there. Lynnewood, with its fountain which could be seen for miles and its Southern gentility which Nanaline had disdained, was unceremoniously unloaded. So was the *Doris,* the gilded, private $35,000 "rolling palace" resting in the yards of the Pennsylvania Railroad Company. The car, primarily used for business and gin-soaked, cigar-smoked "duck hunting parties" by the late Buck Duke, was expensive to maintain and was sold to Fred Whitman of Western Pacific Railroad. After languishing for years in a Barstow, California, shopping mall, the faded blue car is back in North Carolina and in the process of being restored by a non-profit group of railroad buffs, Duke University having donated $50,000 to the project.

Concentration of the Duke wealth was in electric power projects, real estate, and tobacco. The final accounting of the estate showed, among other holdings, 125,904 shares of Duke Power, 99,433 shares of British-American Tobacco Company, 38,281 shares of Liggett & Myers Tobacco Company, 106,600 shares of R. J. Reynolds Tobacco Corporation, 5,100 shares of American Cigar Company, and 51,236 shares of ALCOA.

Meanwhile, the worldwide search continued for "blood kin" of J. B. Duke, to distribute the $2 million left to lineal descendants. The search resembled a screwball comedy, with dubious claimants scrambling for a share of the Duke millions. With the help of well-worn family Bibles, relatives were located in thirty-eight states and nine foreign countries. Of the 700 who claimed to be relatives, only 167 were considered legitimate, including one feeble seventy-eight-year-old man living on a Missouri farm who was left $12,000. Several nephews were found living in a dilapidated log cabin in the rural mountains of Kentucky. One cousin, a sergeant in the Marine Corps, was located on a small island in the Pacific and presented with a check for $12,000. A schoolteacher in Montana and her brother, a timekeeper on a Cuban banana plantation, had each thought the other dead before letters arrived saying they would split their share.

A ragtag group from Texas, led by a thirty-five-year-old feisty Wichita Falls telephone operator, Mary Elizabeth Duke, tried to convince a Somerville judge that evangelist Reverend Tom Duke—known as "the bully of Georgia" with 108 living descendants—was the illegitimate brother of

Washington Duke and therefore related to the tobacco tycoon. The Texans took their case to court, with one elderly gentleman from the Lone Star State propping his feet on the railing and fiddling with a long pocketknife while testifying. "The best claim of Miss Duke of relationship to James B. it would seem is her genius and capacity for organizing big things, which is an admitted Duke characteristic," a dubious Durham newspaper reported. Duke family lawyers accused the telephone operator of forging records and faking affidavits, and the Dukes of Texas, as they were dubbed, went back to the panhandle penniless. "I want to get back to my pet bull," one of them said, leaving Somerville.

As colorful as these stories were, none could touch Doris Duke's. Newspapers seized on her image as "the wealthiest heiress of her years in the world." One story was headlined simply "Poor Kid," and the prevailing wisdom was that she hadn't the slightest hope of becoming a responsible citizen. She was alternately praised for her simplicity (wearing hand-me-downs from her mother, shopping for penny candy at the local Somerville store) and chided for her self-indulgence. The truth was somewhere in between. While the image of a down-to-earth millionairess in second-hand clothes sold newspapers in the 1920s, so did fantasies of her gilded ease. The fifteen-year-old girl was reported to bathe in colored water splashing from an ancient Italian fountain installed in her bathroom, and wash her hands in an oval basin of amethyst glass inlaid with antique Roman gold. She owned 37 robes especially designed for her "morning travel from her satin and lace Louis XVI bed to her crystal scented sunken pool." Wool robes were imported from Arabia, made, according to one news account, "of a light warmth never to be had from any animal save a particular species of dwarfed camel."

There was more: "Probably there is no bathing pool in the country quite like that of the little Duke heiress. While she bathes, a scented fountain sprinkles into the bath water a fine spray of the chosen scent, while the sun streams in upon the water from high lights where the tinted curtains have been pulled aside."

Doris was said to sniff only the scent of freshly pressed flowers, to be tended by a footman in powdered wig, to eat her supper on $100,000 gold plates and have her satin sheets with a five-inch border of lace sent to Europe to be washed. No one in America could be trusted with such a delicate chore.

Like her fellow "poor little rich girl," Barbara Hutton, the stories usually concluded on a somber note. "The shadow and griefs of common life, like the dust, dirt, flies, germs and noise do not penetrate the $53,000,000 wall of gold that the tobacco king left around his only daughter." But unlike the Woolworth heiress, who inherited the bulk of her father's estate outright, Doris' money was held in two trusts: the first established in 1917 and the second, The Doris Duke Trust, established in 1925 upon her father's death. While she had personal money from both parents, she would not have total control of her famous fortune as Barbara Hutton would.

But despite the millions, the "greatest heiress in the history of the world," as columnist Cholly Knickerbocker (in real life Maury Paul) referred to Doris, was a social dud.

"I remember one coming out party in Newport," said Dorothy Mahana. "We were a pretty horrible set of 15-year-olds. Somebody was coming out and we knew who it was and we wanted to go. We absolutely insisted. It was perfectly unheard of for girls to go to a dance before you came out. We begged, screamed and carried on until Mrs. Duke said, 'All right, but you have to come home at a certain time.' We knew boys from having been up at the beach in the daytime so we went down to the florist on Bellevue Avenue and sent ourselves corsages.

"The boys looked right through us. They didn't even know we were alive. We sat on the stairs leading to the ballroom the whole evening and not one soul came near us or danced with us or anything, so home we went."

Newporters began to gossip about Doris. How she had the nerve to take her maid swimming with her at the private Bailey's Beach. And of course, there was the question of her clothes. "Those who congregate at Bailey's Beach, the most exclusive bathing place in the world," one columnist wrote, "become fed up with accounts of 'the party last night,' and anything as exciting as Doris Duke wearing her mother's old clothes becomes a subject for much sly comment."

One day Doris went bathing in a white swimsuit. When she emerged from the ocean, the dowagers were shocked because the suit was unlined and became transparent when wet. "She was pathetic," one female observer, a former Brearley classmate, recalled.

Tourists thronged down Bellevue Avenue, and tour guides with megaphones pointed out the various "cottages" and their owners. "In this house," a guide would bellow like a circus barker, "lives Doris Duke, the Richest Girl in the World." Crowds would crane their necks in hopes of catching a glimpse of the Tudor mansion and the young, blonde heiress. Often, she would be walking along in a simple tennis dress and no one would recognize the tall, slim girl as she slipped unnoticed through the gates.

"You wouldn't call her pretty," one storekeeper was quoted as saying. "And she has had no boyfriends. Still, she's the kind of girl who would have boyfriends pretty soon even if she didn't have a dollar. Doris doesn't care much for dress. She wears simple things."

She was also one of the only sub-debs who did not make a habit of bringing small dogs to fancy restaurants and checking them along with her coat.

An observer wrote: "Her blue eyes are keen, set deeply beneath a smooth, determined brow. Her firm chin slightly cleft protrudes a trifle, and so the eye observes the chin, perhaps, before noting the well formed and kindly line of the mouth." It was added, "She isn't the kind of a young girl that would invite even from her own friends a too familiar display of enthusiasm or affection."

One intrepid female reporter once drove through the gates and pulled up to Rough Point. A footman in livery opened the car door. The reporter walked brazenly into the house, with rugs, tapestries, and furnishings "one might see on entering Buckingham Palace." The sound of a gramophone playing the latest jazz record wafted through the room. A second liveried footman appeared, a portly, red-faced man with an unperturbed expression. "Who shall I announce to Miss Duke?" he asked. He returned shortly and led the way through a half dozen spacious rooms to a huge room, softly tinted in green and cream, overlooking the ocean. She was soon to go to the Casino to play tennis with Huntington Hartford, heir to the A&P chain store fortune, and Leta Morris, a Newport friend. The reporter asked for an 0interview. "But if I talk, there will be more publicity. And I do not like being singled out from my other friends," she said, in her little girl voice.

"But that is the penalty," the reporter answered, "for being known as the richest girl in the world."

Doris paled. "It appalls me to be so spoken of. It is terrifying."

"But the gods have been so kind to you," the reporter said.

Doris bit her lip and looked puzzled. "I think it is quite dreadful that my name and my picture should be given all this publicity. I am no different from anyone else. Really," she continued, "it is ghastly."

"But I fear it is your life's sentence."

"Oh please be more hopeful," Doris answered in her breathy whisper.

"I am afraid one can't as long as you are so wealthy."

"Well, perhaps one day it won't be so and it won't matter," she said, asking that "nothing be said about me" because "there really is nothing to say."

She just wanted to be alone, adding that she enjoyed tennis, jazz music, swimming, and her friends. She also liked to dance. She and her friend Leta Morris learned clog dancing at Adeline King Robinson's Tuesday dancing classes in the grill room at the Ritz-Carlton, directed by May Leslie, a former Ziegfeld girl. She also liked to drive. Somerville residents described how they had seen the heiress at the wheel of one of her seven automobiles with George Roberts, her personal chauffeur, beside her, burning up the road between Somerville and Morristown.

Everything Doris did was news and her air of mystery only increased the attention. One front page headline screamed: DORIS DUKE, HEIRESS, SPURNS BODYGUARDS IN SALT LAKE VISIT. She had merely gone for a walk alone.

"Everywhere we go, it's the same," her half brother Walker Inman told a reporter. "She gets to see a few sights, go out to dinner a few times and then her identity becomes known."

Doris' sixteenth birthday was celebrated quietly at Somerville, with Nanaline and Walker, who would fly his private plane to New York from his Georgetown, South Carolina, plantation. Armed guards stood at the gates, and motorcycle policemen from Raritan patrolled the estate grounds.

By now, Nanaline was convinced that her daughter was a social disaster. She enrolled her in Fermata, a girls' boarding school in Aiken, South Carolina, which rivaled Farmington and Foxcroft as the finishing school of choice among the well heeled. Dorothy Mahana was also enrolled, and the two girls became roommates with the daughter of an Aiken doctor, Rose-anna Todd. The school, located on the tree-lined Whiskey Road, had been started in 1919 by pianist Joseph Hofmann and his wife Marie. In musical terms, *fermata* means "pause" or "rest," and the school was often mistaken as a home for rest cures. It might just as well have been. "It was a silly school," recalled Mahana. "We learned nothing." Hofmann and his wife had instilled a certain pseudo-English feel to the school, which had 70 boarders and 28 day students, dressed in uniforms of bright green tunics, gray stockings, and bloomers. Fermata (which later burned down in the 1940s) was popular among the daughters of the nouveau riche, and offered classes in table setting, pouring tea, managing a household, and, of course, horseback riding.

Doris, Dorothy, and Roseanna often broke out forbidden bottles of wine and would slide down a rope outside their room to escape the strict confines of the school as well as Doris' private detectives, who were spotted about the campus disguised as gardeners. Doris was neither popular nor athletic (skipping the 5 A.M. lacrosse practices), and wanted to go home. Nanaline refused.

"Mrs. Duke wanted her to see how other girls lived, what they had to do to be tidy in their rooms," Edward Hansen, the family butler, later recalled. "She wrote a letter to her mother and told her she would like to come back because she didn't care for it. But Mrs. Duke thought it would be a good idea to train the child."

To her friends, the image of Doris as the richest girl in the world was a joke. To the rest of the school, it set Doris apart. "There were barriers put in her way because she was Doris Duke," a friend later said. "There was resentment and jealousy." The other girls could be hurtful. "Doris was always a person who wanted to be recognized for herself, not for her wealth."

The students would hang out the windows to see what kind of cars parents drove up in. Being taken out for lunch was a major event. But although Doris waited for her mother, Nanaline visited her daughter only once over the course of two years.

Dottie Mahana became Doris' closest confidante. When Mahana broke her neck in a riding accident and was confined to a hospital in South-ampton, she was visited by Doris, who brought a projector and showed movies on the hospital room ceiling for her friend, who was in traction. Dottie was told she would never walk again. "She's a very good friend when you're in trouble. When the chips are down, she will come across and be there. I will never forget how she came to the hospital to see me."

Dorothy and Roseanna Todd had left Fermata in June 1929 and by December, Doris was sufficiently miserable to convince Nanaline to allow her to quit. She was anxious to attend college. "Why, Doris?" Nanaline cooly told her. "You won't ever have to teach school." Said Mahana, "None of our friends went. It really was terrible. Most of us who were raised that way had a hard time fitting in later."

Nanaline did encourage Doris to become involved with her father's legacy, and enlisted her daughter to represent the Duke family in laying the first cornerstone of the new campus. Amid the booming derricks and buzz of riveters, college officials welcomed Doris to the university. At six in the evening, on June 5, 1928, under cloudy skies, a solemn-looking Doris in cap and gown joined the procession of college officials and North Carolina's governor through the mud and lumber to the stone foundation of the Union Building. President Few made the opening remarks: "Duke University owes its existence to a great Trust established by the late James B. Duke . . .

[who] has set up noble goals for this university and makes wise provisions for its educational administration . . . and who in its founding cherished the beautiful hope to do some permanent good upon this earth."

Doris took the trowel and smoothed the first layer of cement. "Without haste and yet with the same directness which characterized the every act of her father," the *Alumni Register* recorded, "Miss Doris Duke placed the mortar about the corner stone . . . Miss Duke appeared as the gracious daughter of a great benefactor, maintaining a keen interest in the occasion and radiating a gentle dignity befitting the momentous exercise which marked the transition from the old into the new physical surroundings of the University."

As the choir sang "The days of old have dowered us with gifts beyond all praise," Few was grimly assessing their financial situation. Far from being the most well endowed university in the country, Duke was in dire need of money.

"The sad fact . . ." historian and author Robert Durden recently concluded, "was that Few had either sold J. B. Duke an overly ambitious plan or had, despite great intelligence and experience and noble intentions, simply underestimated to J. B. Duke the costs involved in building the type and quality of university that was envisioned."

Few had written a letter to a friend the year before about the proposed medical school: "I am frankly worried. It was just as clear to me the day Mr. Duke died as it is now that we do not have either in hand or in sight sufficient resources to develop the other departments of the University as Mr. Duke expected us to develop them and also support the sort of medical school and hospital that the public expects of us and that all of us want to see here."

Another factor in the lack of fund-raising success was the question of the school's integrity, being so closely joined with the Duke Endowment's business agenda, as well as the rather dubious ghost of J. B. Duke himself. H. L. Mencken in his *American Mercury* reflected that sentiment:

The late Buck Duke's immediate aim in pouring out his millions to transform an obscure Methodist college in a North Carolina mill town into the university which now bears his name was simplicity itself. What he wanted was a Babbit factory—a mill for grinding out go-get-em boys in the wholesale and undeviating fashion in which his Chesterfield plant across the way ground out cigarettes . . . what he had in mind in the long run was Profits . . . for Profits was the only thing he ever came to understand in his sixty-eight years on this planet. For all other purposes, he remained in the end essentially what he was at seventeen, a red-headed, shambling Methodist-jake out of Orange County, North Carolina—which is to say, a sort of peasant out of the Eleventh century, incredibly ignorant, incredibly obtuse, incredibly grasping and picayune.

In 1928, Duke's tuition was raised to $150, less than Vanderbilt's ($227) and those of older endowed universities in the Northeast. Plans were scaled back. A lake and fountains were eliminated. A grandiose tribute to the Duke family was also scrapped in favor of a more modest memorial chapel where the bodies of Washington Duke and his two sons, Buck and Ben (who died in January 1929), would lie in marble sarcophagi. It was gentle, sickly, educated Ben who had been so instrumental in convincing his brother to endow the university. "He had an influence on J.B. to give the money, no doubt about that," said one university official. But the statue eventually erected at Duke was not of Ben but his near illiterate brother, who stands frozen in bronze on the quadrangle, his back to the chapel, a ubiquitous cigar in hand.

Few was convinced that the key to becoming a great university was to build a strong faculty. He embarked on a campaign to recruit the best professors with unheard-of salaries. One leading Harvard psychologist was wooed by telegram with a remarkable offer. The Harvard professor quickly cabled back, "I accept. Where is Durham?"

Plans for the medical school were proceeding, aided by a $300,000 grant from the Rockefeller-funded General Education Board. A former Rhodes Scholar, Dr. Wilbur Cornell Davison, was chosen to head the medical school, which he did for the next thirty-five years.

"I remember the day I walked in and applied for admission," Dr. Lenox Baker recalled. He was then a Duke undergraduate. "I didn't even have an appointment." Another professor took Baker to see Davison. The man said they'd like to have Baker as one of the first medical students. "Davison said, 'If he's good enough for you, he's good enough for us.' I said, 'Does this mean I'm accepted?' He said, 'Yes.' We started to leave and I asked if I should fill out some application forms. He said, 'We don't have any yet. By the way Baker, what are your grades like?' I said, 'I'm on the dean's list.' He said, 'Well excuse me for asking. I should have known that.'"

Dean Davison later became a confidant of Doris. In fact, Davison was the person Duke officials called upon to serve as an intermediary between the school and the benefactor's daughter, who was looked upon by succeeding college officials as a private piggy bank. Davison, roly-poly and down to earth (wardrobe by Sears & Roebuck), became a surrogate father to the heiress. "I think she adored him, and he felt that way about her," said a former associate of Davison's. According to Senator Terry Sanford, former president of Duke, "Davison made friends with virtually everybody. You had to have tremendous respect for him. I'm sure Doris did."

Nanaline was the only female trustee of the Duke Endowment, which now occupied offices at 535 Fifth Avenue in New York. She attended sporadic meetings and was involved in the disbursement of the endowment's funds. She was said to be an astute businesswoman, working closely with her late husband's associates, Endowment chairman George Allen and legal counselor William R. "Judge" Perkins, who had authored the indenture. Perkins and his son Thomas, also an attorney, would increasingly become involved in Doris' activities, watching over her movements as their "ward," and in later years engaging in constant damage control.

Nanaline's energies were also devoted to landing a suitable (i.e., titled) son-in-law for her daughter, whose inheritance was currently estimated at half a billion dollars. "Fortunate indeed," one columnist trilled, "will be the young man who secures the heart and hand of Nannie Duke's daughter."

Winters were spent in Palm Beach, summers in Newport, Southampton or Bar Harbor. It was there, in August of 1929, that Doris Duke first met James Henry Roberts Cromwell, son of the upwardly mobile Eva and Edward Stotesbury. The introduction came through mutual friend Evalyn Walsh McLean, who owned a house in Bar Harbor near the Stotesburys' Wingwood House.

Evalyn McLean, unlike Nanaline, spoiled her children. Her son Vinson had been labeled the "$100 Million Baby" and every Christmas he and his sister Evalyn were treated to a $15,000 party. Every child went home with an expensive toy: trains for the boys and huge dolls for the girls. Ringling Brothers circus came to their house for exclusive command performances. The children had a miniature coach with three tiny horses and were dressed in ermine suits by Worth in Paris. Her husband Ned was an alcoholic, and reportedly gave his pet seal a bottle of whiskey a day. Evalyn's life ambition, she once said, was to die bankrupt. She and Eva Stotesbury had much in common.

"Evalyn was very influential with my mother who was ultra influential with me," Cromwell recalled. In fact, to the day he died, his mother remained the most important woman in Cromwell's life. She was born

Lucrecia Roberts in Chicago, had married Oliver Cromwell, a New York financier and descendant of *the* Oliver Cromwell, and bore three children: Louise, Oliver Eaton, and Jimmy. The Cromwells moved to Washington where Eva became the reigning hostess. But her husband died of a stroke in 1909 and she was left a widow at the age of forty-four. The following year, while crossing the Atlantic with her daughter Louise, Eva met widower Ned Stotesbury and the two immediately fell in love. They married in 1912 at her Washington house on New Hampshire Avenue with President William Taft attending. While Main Line Philadelphians snubbed the Stotesburys and their vulgar display of wealth, they nevertheless became the most notorious party givers of the 1920s. Eva kept detailed scrapbooks with seating charts and information on every dinner she had ever hosted. Her jewelry collection was displayed on neck mannequins on a dressing table. It resembled a jewelry store. Her diamond tiara was reportedly so heavy it gave her a sore neck.

Tireless in her pursuit of social acceptance, Eva Stotesbury was nevertheless charming, good-humored, devoted to her husband (whom she called "Kickapoo"), and more than willing to carry out his desires. "Father was a show-off, not my mother," Jimmy told author Stephen Birmingham. "He was of a generation of men who wanted to show the whole world how important they were . . . His theory was: If you've got it, flaunt it."

Jimmy's relationship with Stotesbury, a man who never read a book or magazine, was somewhat remote. He had been ten when his father had died and never really benefited from a male role model. "He was a mother's boy," said Mary Sanford, who lived next to the Stotesburys in Palm Beach. "His mother just adored him."

Eva, with Evalyn's help, encouraged her son to pursue Doris Duke. "My mother finally invited Doris to be her guest at our house." Wingwood House, said to cost $1 million to build, was a 50-room Georgian colonial mansion with quarters for 30 servants, and a garden room that could easily accommodate 200 dinner guests. It was there, Jimmy recalled, "when I first tried to have an affair with her. That was the purpose of the visit."

Doris was sixteen, socially awkward, inexperienced, and in all likelihood looking forward to disposing of her virginity. Jimmy was sixteen years her senior, tall, athletic, with a slight taint of scandal, having just been divorced from madcap auto heiress Delphine Dodge and losing millions in a Florida land scheme.

Jimmy's taste in women ran to heiresses, show girls, and Cafe Society socialites. "I was a ladies man," he said years later. With the chiseled looks of the Arrow shirt man and the suave, champagne-sipping charm of a playboy on the prowl, he was much in demand. "I was an extremely good-looking man," he said. "I used to have a perfect physique."

During the war, Jimmy was stationed in Paris. There he had met Cobina Wright, a beautiful young society girl who later became a singer, columnist, and close friend of Doris Duke. "Jimmy, tall, laughing, witty, handsome in his Navy uniform, had left most of his consciousness that he was the very rich son of the very very rich Mrs. Stotesbury of Philadelphia at home in the U.S.," Cobina would later write. "I think, for the first time in his eventful life, he had a fine time just being Jimmy and I was all too willing to help him. Our love, wild and emotional, was punctured by frequent quarrels provoked, of all things, by my ridiculing wealth . . . I spent much time scoffing at his description of the snug little home he had left behind him where, at his mother's estate, a panel of buttons in each room fetched everything from the bootblack to a soda jerker. 'That,' said my Jimmy, 'is the way to live.'"

Louise, Jimmy's older sister, acted as a peacemaker between him and Cobina, who described the dark-haired Cromwell girl as "the most thorough exponent of the I-don't-give-a-damn attitude I had ever met. We called her 'The Jazz Girl,' and certainly many of our officers found her merry philosophy a beacon light in time of war and singed their wings at her gay flame." Louise, reputed to be the most beautiful girl in the world, became the mistress of General Pershing and ran a sophisticated "salon" in Paris during the war.

"We had this beautiful apartment in Paris when Louise came over," Jimmy recalled. "I found it. It was on the Seine. It became a visiting place for all the top people at the time of the Treaty of Versailles. All the important French generals and politicians used to come to this apartment to see her. She had enormous charm, my sister, as well as beauty. Beauty and charm and wealth; a pretty good combination."

Eva, who had a volatile relationship with Louise, sent over her friend, Elsa Maxwell, to serve as a chaperone for her daughter. Maxwell played the piano at many a wild Saturday night dance frequented by the American military delegation, which she described as "Louise's blowouts."

Jimmy Cromwell was not unlike Walker Inman, the overindulged son of Nanaline. Just that year, Walker Inman's ex-wife threatened to sue Nanaline for alienation of affection. Helene Clarke told reporters that their marriage had "infuriated" Mrs. Duke. "I wasn't rich or socially prominent enough for her," Helene said. "I was practically driven into signing an agreement to give my husband a divorce for $75,000." Her lawyer claimed that agents working for Mrs. Duke took part in a raid on Helene's former apartment. The publicity surrounding the case evidently caused Nanaline to increase Helene's settlement. A new agreement was signed, giving the Kokomo show girl another lump sum of $54,000 and $750 a month for life. Her attorneys would be paid $25,000 by Inman, and Helene would receive $5,000 in expenses for the Reno divorce. Edward Hansen later recalled the sum being much higher: $150,000 a year for life as long as she did not remarry.

"Mr. Inman would have won the case," said Hansen, "because everything was in his favor. But Mrs. Duke didn't want to read any more about it, so she insisted he give [in] to Helene's demands." Although Nanaline disapproved of playboy Jimmy Cromwell, she was not willing to alienate social queen Eva Stotesbury, who doted on her free-spending son and envisioned a financial windfall with a Duke-Cromwell alliance.

Society, as Elsa Maxwell defined it, "consists of people of common interests who know one another and like to be with one another. It is simply people who prefer to be with their own kind." Although in some circles the Dukes had been ridiculed as tar-heel tobacco folk, in Jimmy's eyes "they had what it took to be socially prominent: plenty of money."

And Bar Harbor was the place to spend it. In *The Last Resorts,* author Cleveland Amory recounts an exchange Mrs. Atwater Kent had with her maid. On one particular dizzying day in the resort, Mrs. Kent was invited to a luncheon, a tea, a cocktail party, and a dinner, which required four elaborate changes of outfit. "Madam," the maid said, "I wouldn't change places with you for a million dollars."

Doris and Jimmy were thrown together constantly. They went swimming at the beach, played tennis, and drank champagne. Doris was amused by his attentions. "Jimmy wasn't the type you'd fall in love with," recalled Mary Sanford. "He didn't have any sex appeal. And he was so much older."

Evalyn Walsh McLean, Jimmy said later, was "the fixer" in the match. But the two couldn't have been more opposite: Jimmy had been surrounded by even more decadence than Doris. Their house in Philadelphia, White-marsh Hall, was crawling with servants and Eva—unlike Nanaline—spent money with a frenzied abandon.

Doris, even with her millions, had been raised in a more austere manner, and was a far cry from the glamour girls Jimmy associated with. As a child, she had worn leg braces to correct her pigeon-toed walk and with her protruding chin and flat chest, she was far from a beauty. In the madcap heiress department, Doris was rather backward compared to the more flamboyant Delphine Dodge or Barbara Hutton. What did the divorced Cromwell see in Doris Duke besides $100 million?

"I found her very attractive," Cromwell said. "She had a beautiful figure. She was tall and I was enough taller not to be embarrassed. She had a soft voice, like a little girl. She had lovely eyes and she was a lovely blonde. She had unusual eyes. Kind of slanted."

Doris appeared to be a lonely, repressed girl. "She was subdued. Doris and her mother did not get along well. I think she thought Doris was too selfish. Too self-centered. She always put herself first."

During that visit to Bar Harbor Jimmy slipped into Doris' boudoir one night after the others had gone to bed. He undressed and climbed under the sheets. His attempts to make love to the sixteen-year-old Doris were unsuccessful.

"She was upset and so was I. It was an awful joke for me. I was pretty successful with the ladies because I was devoted to women and this was surprising to me. I was convinced that Doris was sexless."

Jimmy would later nickname Doris "my Frigidairess," and the two embarked on a rocky, on-again, off-again six-year courtship. Nanaline was worried by Jimmy's obvious pursuit of her daughter and kept Doris on the move, trying to avoid Eva Stotesbury's son. Although friends say he was the aggressor, Cromwell later claimed that the richest girl in the world was pursuing him. "She decided that she was going to marry me and that was that."

Nanaline wasn't alone in her disapproval.

Doris' friends didn't think much of Cromwell or his "unsavory" friends. "He was a real operator," said Dorothy Mahana.

Jimmy was fifteen when his widowed mother Eva married Stotesbury. He had dropped out of University of Pennsylvania's Wharton School of Business to enlist first in the Navy and then the Marines during World War I. In 1917, he fitted out a privately owned motor launch as a submarine chaser and took command. An amateur boxer, he once went three rounds with Tommy Loughran, then light heavyweight champion of the world, and played tennis with Bill Tilden. "For a long time in my life," he once said, "I thought the world was just a nice big pie and I cut myself a slice."

At twenty-four, he had married twenty-one-year-old Delphine Dodge after a two-month courtship in June 1920. The ceremony took place in Detroit, with the reception for 1,000 guests at Rose Terrace, the palatial Grosse Point home of the bride. The wedding itself was held at the

Jefferson Avenue Presbyterian Church, and Delphine was escorted by armed guards watching over her $100,000 pearl necklace (a wedding gift from her father) and a sapphire bracelet from Cromwell, a souvenir from Eva's vast jewelry collection.

The union was seen more as a business merger than a marriage, uniting the two American dynasties of Drexel and Dodge. Delphine was the dark-haired, diminutive, and high-spirited only daughter of Horace Elgin Dodge, the automobile magnate. Her mother Anna gave her $100,000 worth of silver as a wedding present. Following a lavish reception (with armed guards standing over the wedding gifts), and Anna and Eva congratulating each other on such a brilliant match, Jimmy and his bride made their getaway under an archway of roses to the waiting 243-foot Dodge yacht, *The Delphine,* with a crew of sixty which was moored at the foot of the rolling lawns on Lake St. Clair. "It looked like a battleship," Jimmy recalled. They embarked on a year-long honeymoon and were vacationing in Hong Kong when they received word that Delphine's father had died. They did not make it back in time for the funeral.

In 1921, Eva Stotesbury and her husband opened their celebrated 145-room Horace Trumbauer-designed villa, Whitemarsh Hall, in Philadelphia. The house cost more than $3 million and took five years to complete. A reception to introduce Delphine to society was held that October, and guests from the social and banking communities were awed by the Versailles-like surroundings. The palatial mansion (the structure took up almost two and a half acres) boasted forty-five bathrooms, twelve elevators, an indoor gym, swimming pool, squash and tennis courts, and an ice-making plant capable of turning out a ton of ice a day. The house—staffed by forty-five live-in servants—had its own switchboard and operator, a bakery, tailor, barber shop, and movie theater. Seventy gardeners tended the 300 acres of landscaped grounds.

Henry Ford, upon visiting Whitemarsh Hall, was heard to remark, "It is always a great experience to see how the rich live."

Four orchestras played that night; and Eva moved through the guests, it was reported, with a typewritten catalogue of her paintings purchased by the famed dealer Joseph Duveen, who had also supplied the Dukes with many of their ersatz antiques. This gaudy display was eagerly devoured by widow Anna Dodge, who was conservatively worth $40 million and would live at Whitemarsh Hall for nearly a year, recovering from her husband's death. (She would eventually marry a former actor, Hugh Dillman.) Anna herself had come from simple stock and was not warmly received by the snobbish Philadelphians. "My mother simply didn't give a damn," Jimmy later said. "She felt it was her duty to help take care of Anna." That night Anna presented Delphine with her prized $1.5 million pearl necklace once owned by Catherine the Great of Russia.

Jimmy had developed an interest in business and helped arrange the sale of Dodge Brothers for a whopping $146 million.

A daughter, Christine, was born on September 10, 1922. Neither parent bothered to hide their disappointment that the child was a girl. That same year, Jimmy's sister Louise, back from Paris, married a young army general, Douglas MacArthur, at a ceremony held at El Mirasol in Palm Beach. It was her second marriage (her first to Walter Brooks ended in divorce), and Jimmy served as best man. Pershing warned Louise not to go through with the wedding and threatened to have MacArthur, then superintendent of West Point, transferred to the Philippines. Louise and MacArthur returned to West Point after the wedding, where Louise's conduct raised eyebrows. MacArthur's mother was mortified by her daughter-in-law's behavior: riding a bicycle about the grounds and fraternizing with the first classmen. "She was trying to get into the sack with anybody she could," according to one friend.

Pershing, well aware of Louise's promiscuity, had informed his former mistress: "Marrying you would be like buying a book for someone else to read."

Two months after the wedding, MacArthur was indeed posted to the Philippines and there were rumors that Pershing was indeed behind his subordinate's transfer. But Pershing needn't have bothered. The marriage was a disaster, and they divorced in 1929. Louise said of MacArthur, "He is the least likely man I know to succeed." The volatile Louise recalled their joyless marriage. He was standing behind her "looking like Napoleon" with his arms folded when she broke a handmirror over his head. Later, at a crowded Washington cocktail party at the home of Drew Pearson, she physically assaulted her escort who happened to be a major general. "He was sitting on the arm of a wicker chair talking to Liz Whitney and Louise came in and said, 'Let's go.' He said, 'Just a moment, Louise.' She said, 'I said LET'S GO,' and she hauled off and hit him," said one guest. "This poor old man fell off the arm of the chair and rammed the table, covered with whiskey. Jesus, it was funny. So he's scrambling up out of the glassware and whiskey. She said, 'Don't give yourself airs. I've knocked down a four-star general.'"

The first Mrs. MacArthur also would regale Washington dinner parties with tales of the war hero's sexual inadequacies, including holding up her bent pinky finger so as to make it limp and saying, "Doug didn't think his penis was for anything except to pee with."

In 1930, Louise married actor Lionel Atwill, who later starred in many Frankenstein films. The two lived in Hollywood and Washington and were famous for their heavy drinking and decadent parties.

Domestic tranquility was not in the cards for either Louise or Jimmy, who purchased a fifty-acre country estate on Manursing Island near Rye, which had belonged to his family years earlier. He and his bride were reported to be planning to take up residence in "the old Cromwell home." But Jimmy and Delphine were a restless pair, and homemaking held little attraction. They preferred parties, polo matches, champagne, and speedboats. Delphine was the first woman to drive in a race of sweepstakes distance and won the President's Cup—presented by Calvin Coolidge—in 1927. Jimmy was developing a taste for spending the Dodge money. The couple were given an allowance of $200,000 a year and were pressed financially. On several occasions "Mother" Dodge was also called upon to settle Jimmy's gambling debts, to the extent of $100,000 or more.

Jimmy's greatest folly was "Floranada." Envisioned by his ambitious mother as "Jimmy's City," Cromwell went into the real estate business, forming the American-British Improvement Corporation. The winter resort would hopefully become the social capital of America and would rival Biarritz as a mecca for the rich and famous. The tract consisted of 3,600 acres between Palm Beach and Miami. Streets were laid, electric lights put in, a golf course and a clubhouse constructed. It was reported that the deposed king of Greece planned to buy a home there. "Jimmy's City" even had its own seal: an American eagle on one side, a British lion on the other.

Eva Stotesbury and Anna Dodge were listed as social sponsors of the project. But the kings, lords, and financiers who were promised never materialized and the dozens of lots went unsold. Florida land was abruptly devalued, causing a major real estate bust and in May 1926 Floranada collapsed, with a loss of about $6 million to its stockholders.

The following month, Jimmy fled to Europe, where he would spend the summer. Anna and Eva lost $2 million each, plus the $500,000 they reimbursed friends who had invested in the plan. It took two years for process servers, representing angry creditors, to find Jimmy (they eventually staked out his Park Avenue apartment for five weeks) and serve him with papers. During court hearings it was revealed that funds were hastily drawn from the bank on the eve of bankruptcy and the corporation's books were accidentally "drowned" in a Palm Beach canal.

Meanwhile, Cromwell had leased a thirty-three-story hotel apartment house on Park Avenue and Thirty-ninth Street from broker Robert J. Coverdale. Originally dubbed "The Cromwell Arms," the name was changed to the Delmonico Hotel after Jimmy lost control of the corporation. Jimmy and Delphine, who had put up $200,000 for the venture, had signed a lease for the upper three floors. Eva Stotesbury, Louise and Douglas MacArthur, and Anna Dodge were also committed to leasing apartments. Not trusting his business partner, whom he suspected of wrongdoing, Cromwell hired a private detective to tail Coverdale while he went on a hunting trip to British Columbia. "I thought maybe he would do something and I could catch up with him on this dirty deal he put over," said Cromwell. "When I came back, this fellow behaved in a very peculiar way." The detective refused to hand over the secret report to Cromwell. Jimmy later learned that the detective had followed Robert Coverdale into Delphine Dodge's bedroom. According to Jimmy, Anna Dodge paid the detective $50,000 to keep the scandal hushed up.

Jimmy and Delphine officially separated in January 1928. The relationship had deteriorated over the last two years and the animosity between them was evident to all. Jimmy retreated to the Stotesburys' twenty-five-acre Palm Beach estate, El Mirasol, with its forty rooms, forty-car garage, and private zoo with twenty-five monkeys and a flotilla of parrots and parakeets. There he entertained friends like architect Addison Mizner, Tony Biddle, Mrs. William Randolph Hearst and Mrs. Flo Ziegfeld. During one costume party Eva's doting son was dressed, one columnist said, "as Little Lord Fauntleroy and no comments of incongruity were heard."

Four months later, Jimmy went to the Kentucky Derby while Delphine went to Reno, Nevada, to obtain an uncontested divorce. Jimmy was still fighting a flurry of lawsuits over Floranada. Naturally, he went to Eva for help. He was observed kneeling by his mother's bedside, tearfully begging Eva for a loan of $300,000.

During the divorce hearing, it was revealed that Jimmy often made sarcastic remarks about the small allowance provided by Anna Dodge and had grown increasingly indifferent to his wife. Jimmy kept silent about Delphine's promiscuity and heavy drinking. In exchange, Anna Dodge would forever show her appreciation to the son of Eva Stotesbury, a woman she imitated and admired.

The custody of Christine, known as "Cee Cee," was also settled—for the time being. Jimmy relinquished his daughter, agreeing to annual visitation rights from June 15 to September 15, with Delphine retaining custody of the girl the rest of the year. "Mother" Dodge would pay $25,000 a year toward Christine's support and Delphine would pay her French governess, Madame Jubault. Jimmy, although he protested mildly, did not see any reason to contribute to "Cee Cee's" support while she was in her mother's custody.

Anna Dodge did more for Christine than Delphine, who was not comfortable with motherhood. "Delphine, unfortunately, liked to drink," Jimmy said. "And she was pretty dumb. She didn't have much on the ball."

Jimmy took Cee Cee to Newport the summer of 1929, and wrote to Anna Dodge:

Christine is very happy at Newport and is making many little friends of her own age. She has a most comfortable suite at the Muenchinger-King Cottage on Bellevue Avenue [one of only two approved social residences], which consists of a fine big porch, a large sitting room, and two connecting bed-rooms with a bath for her and Madame. The food is splendid and as the Managing Housekeeper was formerly a trained nurse and has taken a great fancy to Christine, she is supplied with the best of everything. She is taking riding lessons for two hours each week at the Walker Riding School and is progressing rapidly because of her fearlessness. She appears extremely smart in her little "horse suit" as she calls it, and looks forward eagerly to her riding lessons.

Jimmy reported that Christine was attending dancing class twice a week at Mrs. Lorillard Spencer's home, and often dined with "the Biddle children."

In December of that year, Delphine married Raymond T. Baker, former director of the United States Mint. They had met in Reno while obtaining divorces from their respective spouses and it was hoped that Baker, many years her senior, would serve as a stabilizing influence on the increasingly self-destructive heiress. In fact, Baker objected to the large allowance Anna Dodge was paying for Christine, and so she reduced it to $10,000 a year, bristling at Jimmy's suggestion that Delphine and Ray were benefiting financially from Anna's generous allowance to Christine.

"I have tried every way to meet the desires of all you children in this matter without much success apparently," an angry Anna Dodge wrote to Jimmy.

On the eve of the greatest period of financial reversals the country would ever know, Edward T. Stotesbury hosted a dinner at the Bar Harbor Club. It was August 1929. "I have today received a letter from my financial adviser telling me I am worth $100 million." Eva was achieving her own life's ambition—spending every cent of it. But by late October, the Stotesbury fortune had sustained heavy losses in the stock market crash, and there were rumors that the super-rich Philadelphia banker was among the greatest casualties of "Black Friday."

"On Friday, the balloon burst," Cobina Wright observed. "We were hurled into space . . . the day our world ended." Wright, who had married William May Wright, awoke one morning a millionaire and "went to bed the same night penniless." Not only was the past gone, she said, but the future was mortgaged. But the crash of Wall Street only enhanced the white-tie gathering Cobina had planned that evening. She called it the Last Party, and the guests included Doris Duke, Clifton Webb, Birdie Vanderbilt, William Paley, and Serge Obolensky.

"By the fountain I stood for a moment with young Doris Duke, so stately, so proud. It's happening to everybody. Could it happen to Doris Duke?"

Luckily, the tobacco business and Duke Power were still thriving. The Dukes weathered the crash, although they did sustain paper losses on stocks. In the chaos that followed, the gilded set saw their world collapse. "Ours was a pinpoint in the world gone mad," Cobina Wright observed. "Quite mad. Ladies offered their fur coats in hotel lobbies for whatever an unknown out-of-towner had in his pocket. Yachts and polo ponies wouldn't bring a ten dollar bill. Long lines around the block waited to get into the pawnbrokers. I saw a woman alight from a custom-built Rolls-Royce that had cost thirty thousand dollars and sell it on Madison Avenue for one hundred and fifty dollars cash . . . Vividly, I remember three envelopes that came to me. One from Jessie Donahue, one from William Paley, one from Doris Duke. Each contained a large check. The messages said the same thing: "You might need a little cash to tide you over. For friendship's sake, don't ever mention this . . . and for friendship's sake I never did mention it." (Cobina Wright's daughter, Cobina Jr., said Paley actually gave her mother a blank check.)

As for the impetuous Jimmy Cromwell, freshly divorced and deeply in debt, he was told by his stepfather that he'd better find another rich wife because he wasn't going to get a dime from Stotesbury.

Chapter Six

Putting on
the Ritz

EMERALD LAWNS WERE being hand clipped, trees strung with Japanese lanterns, swimming pools cleaned for the invasion of midnight dippers, and bed was something you crawled into at the crack of dawn.

Welcome to the Deb Season of 1930.

> DON'T—Try to economize on the music at the dances you give. The young people of today demand two orchestras for continuous dancing. Many debutante parties have been ruined by a mediocre band.
>
> DON'T—Permit your daughter to indulge in spectacular stunts— even in the name of "sweet charity."
>
> DON'T—Fail to keep the Grade C and D debutantes at a safe distance.
>
> DON'T—Think it is helping your daughter socially to have her made a "free ad" for night clubs. Warn her to keep out of the range of press agents' cameras.

Nanaline Duke read that last piece of advice in the society pages with a sigh. There was nowhere her daughter, the most famous heiress in the world, could go without a camera far behind. Even that summer in Europe, she and her daughter had been snapped by a newshound. The picture appeared in a London society magazine, captioned: "Doris Duke and Friend."

Immediately after leaving Fermata at Christmas, Doris accompanied Nanaline to Paris. They took an apartment on the Place des Etats-Unis, while Doris was permitted to sit in on classes at the Sorbonne. Nanaline immersed herself in parties, prospecting for a titled son-in-law. Mrs. Duke's closest friend, Mrs. Rufus Patterson, the wife of one of Buck Duke's former assistants, joined her there and the two women would motor down the Champs Elysées and through the Bois de Boulogne. In late April, classes finished, they took a trip to Spain and then headed home for the start of the summer season.

It was Doris' turn to take her place in society, and a debutante party— that curious tribal rite of American monied maidens—was arranged. Doris would make her debut at Newport during Tennis Week, the last week of August, which was the height of that resort's social season. Suburban debuts were coming into vogue, and country residences were actually the height of chic for a coming out. The guest list would be small—only 600.

The fact was, few people actually knew Doris Duke. "To many of us, she was a little strange," a former Newport playmate recalled. Because she was so aloof, and traveled abroad so often, she was considered a snob by some— dull by others. "I'm sure she left Brearley because it was too much," the Newport woman recalled. "I remember the poor child going down the beach one day while her governess sat there, frustrated. She told my governess, 'We didn't get very far on the 9 times table.'"

Her name had been linked to childhood friend Huntington Hartford (whose socially ambitious mother favored the match more than Hartford himself), as well as to young Sailing Baruch, but these were merely family acquaintances who happened to be boys.

Launching a deb in 1930 was a lavish effort, but the halcyon days of the Roaring Twenties were over. One deb who came out in New York in 1929 immediately after "Black Friday" recalled the somber mood. "A lot of parties got cancelled that winter." Debs even went to work in department stores as sales clerks or models to help their socially prominent families, wiped out by the crash.

Prior to 1930, deb balls with 1,500 guests were commonplace. Banker Otto Kahn paid Enrico Caruso $10,000 to sing two songs at his daughter's debut while Pavlova danced. Another Newport father had a $15,000 ballroom custom built for his daughter—the sarsaparilla heiress—which was torn down the day after the party. The ball was said to cost $35,000—even more than Mrs. Hamilton Rice's annual tennis ball.

The postwar hysteria which had ushered in a new order of social climbing (led by Edward Stotesbury threatening to move Drexel & Co. from Philadelphia unless he and Eva received an invitation to that city's Assembly) had subsided. Still, the debs were an eclectic mix of old blood and new money. In New York, the daughters of Tin Plate kings and robber barons, "butter and egg" men and daughters of pushy Southern belles vied with the offspring of Morgan, Vanderbilt, Whitney, and Roosevelt for bids to the Autumn Ball, the Junior Assemblies, and the Junior League. Only one hundred girls were chosen; the others were also-rans. The average age of the deb was eighteen to nineteen, and the end result was for a girl to meet her future husband.

The parties were populated by fortune hunters, gigolos, and college-age scions of rich families who drank heavily. The desired ratio was one boy and a half to each girl for dinner dances, and two boys to every girl for supper dances. Armed with unending supplies of alcohol and food, the fun seekers were known to smash furniture and glassware. "The girls are a secondary matter," one stag told a reporter. "The object in going to a debut is to get tight at somebody else's expense. Everybody agrees these affairs would be terribly boring if it were not for the liquor. For those that don't drink, they're impossible."

Marriage was the furthest thing from their minds. "So many of us have seen so much marital discord, so many separations, divorces, remarriages in our own families," said one deb, "that we'd rather wait."

Even prominent social voices were beginning to see the deb party as outmoded. Evalyn Walsh McLean remarked that "a big debut is like putting a girl on the auction block." And Cobina Wright, former lover of Jimmy Cromwell and future Hearst columnist, declared that deb parties were "just a lot of nonsense."

Nanaline knew that Newport's Old Guard expected Doris to have a debut, so the party was arranged. Much to Nanaline's delight, the current financial climate had put a damper on extravagant entertaining (even if fathers were cashing in life insurance policies to pay for their daughters' $20,000 debuts), so she cut costs in the name of good taste. That would not have been the case had Buck Duke been throwing the ball.

. . .

But there was a more pressing event that spring: being presented at Buckingham Palace. Every year, only a handful of girls were chosen for that honor and Doris, at seventeen, was among the nine American women (seven of whom were married) selected to curtsy before the king and queen on May 14, 1930. Among the debs were Campbell Soup heiress Charlotte Dorrance, bottle heiress Eleanore Edwards, and Elizabeth Kent, daughter of radio magnate A. Atwater Kent. Barbara Hutton would endure the ritual the following year.

The tobacco heiress had a "tiff" with British police when she tried to park her car at the palace at five o'clock in order to secure her spot in the front of the line. (Debutantes had complained of the long wait to get into the palace and Doris was not about to endure that.) Told to keep driving, she instead ordered her chauffeur to stay put. The police sternly warned her again and she just as sternly told her driver to keep stalling. Finally, he was able to move at a snail's pace along the Mall until six o'clock when Doris seized the first place in the line and held it. The other American debs behind her waited for up to two hours to enter.

For mind-numbing pomp, nothing in America could rival the Court of St. James's. Queen Mary, in her pearl and diamond tiara propped on her silvery gray hair, wore a gown of silver lace chiffon while King George sat in the golden throne beside her, wearing the scarlet uniform of colonel-in-chief of the Coldstream Guards. The military band played "God Save the King," and as Barbara Hutton described it, "The debutante is escorted forward by a series of ushers, her card of introduction handed from one to another until finally it reaches the Lord Chamberlain, who announces her name to Their Majesties. She curtsies, usually badly and with a frozen smile." The King's face "was twisted behind an expression of supreme indifference. He could barely keep his eyes open."

As the daughter of the late president of the British-American Tobacco Company, Doris—wearing a gown with a flowing train and carrying three feathered plumes—felt like royalty herself. But others back home decried the practice of kneeling before a throne. "My daughter is much too democratic for that sort of thing," sniffed one mother. "Half of the girls who are presented don't know what it's all about. Meeting the king and queen is just another cocktail party to them." American ambassador Joseph P. Kennedy would later restrict the number of Americans presented at Buckingham Palace and the practice eventually died out.

·   ·   ·

Nanaline and Doris returned to America that summer, with Doris going to Southampton for a house party at Mrs. Rufus Patterson's during Tennis Week before coming to Newport. "She was so impressed with coming out," said one guest at a luncheon. "She was thrilled to be going down to Long Island where she said there would be people just for me. It was a fairyland to her." Southampton, where cousins Angie Duke and Tony Duke and Cordelia Biddle, now Mrs. T. Markoe Robertson, summered, had a more eclectic crowd than Newport, a resort once described by Elsa Maxwell as "the city of the living dead."

Billed by Cholly Knickerbocker as "the most brilliant event ever given at America's social capital," Doris' debut would take place at the imposing gothic Rough Point. The Dukes hadn't hosted a large party for many years and the servants were bustling with activity. The Tudor residence would be transformed into a fairyland with lights illuminating the grounds of the estate and masses of flowers decorating the house.

But the August 23rd dinner dance (robbed of many important social figures who chose to attend Robert Goelet's ball for 600 at Ochre Court that same night) was not the grand affair many expected. It was, however, excedingly tasteful by Newport standards. It was the third large dance in as many nights, and was preceded by a round of dinner parties. There were only two orchestras in the ballroom: Meyer Davis and Vincent Lopez and his Hotel St. Regis Orchestra, the bands screened by banks of gladioli and palm trees. A supper tent, where the Royal Hungarian Orchestra played, was erected from the main house facing the ocean and huge waves pounded the rocks. The entrance was ringed with foliage and baskets of gladioli. The flowers were provided by Leikens and the "electrical effects" by Bardsley & Riley.

Bronze and blue spotlights lit the gardens and floodlights illuminated the trees. Doris, by now over five feet eight inches tall and nearsighted, received the summer colonists and out-of-town guests (including Evalyn Walsh McLean, Barbara Hutton, the dashing Jimmy Cromwell and his close friend, New York psychiatrist Dr. Richard Hoffmann) under a bower of pink and white lilies. The fireplace in the old mansion was also banked with orchards and lilies.

"It was fantastic," one guest recalled. "There were orchids all over the place. There was also a circus tent and animals in the bushes, all lit beautifully. It made you think you were out on a safari."

Doris, in her long white gloves, had been limping the day before with a tennis injury at the Casino, and her right knee was still bandaged tightly. At midnight, as the others were eating a supper of scrambled eggs, one of the women asked Mrs. Duke where Doris was. Nanaline replied she had sent Doris upstairs to rest. "She came down an hour or two later. Doris was always delicate, or at least her mother said so."

The party lasted until dawn, and just as the sun was coming up, one of the orchestras led the dancers onto the lawn where they formed a long snake dance to the sea.

The next day, as etiquette required, there were hundreds of engraved visiting cards left at the Duke mansion.

Barbara Hutton's debut in the ballroom of the Ritz-Carlton Hotel that December was more elaborate. It was said to cost $35,000 or more and was considered a "brilliant" social event of the season compared to Doris'. Over 2,000 guests—including Doris, Jimmy Cromwell and Douglas Fairbanks, Jr.—danced to four bands: Rudy Vallee's Orchestra, a Russian string ensemble, Howard Lanin's Orchestra, and, of course, Meyer Davis. The room was transformed into a moonlit garden, with $3,000 worth of California-grown eucalyptus sprays alone. The party favors were small jewelry cases filled with unmounted diamonds, emeralds, rubies, and sapphires.

Now that she had made her debut, Doris socialized with more frequency, although not at the chic dinner parties her mother would have liked. The richest girl in the world, it seems, had developed a taste for "slumming it."

"Doris was always hell bent to go to the Cotton Club," said the scion of one prominent Newport family. "She would ask me to take her. I agreed, but she always wore these long chandelier earrings and I told her she cannot go with those long earrings. But we went. I didn't like it. In those days nobody went to Harlem. I thought we would be murdered or something. Doris just loved it. We went several times."

On one trip home their car was hit in the rear by another, and the backseat flipped up, hitting both Doris and her date on the head.

He described Doris as "aloof, in the clouds. She was never a very warm person. She was very elusive. Very much into herself. And she was not physically attractive. I think she felt ill at ease. She was conscious of her looks and I think she felt unhappy about it. The best thing about her were her eyes. They were green and kind of slanted, like a tiger's."

An acquaintance once met Doris on the beach at Antibes. "Tell me something of your life," the person inquired. Doris only smiled, sphinx-like, and declined to answer.

One friend, found her "ill at ease. She was under such stress all the time." Still another observer, Frank Waldrop, former editor of *The Washington*

Herald and later *The Washington Post,* found her "defensive. If she hadn't been Doris Duke, no one would have paid her any attention. She was just a little girl with a lot of money."

As Cole Porter would say, there were the rich and the "rich rich," and certainly she and Barbara Hutton, often seen together, were in the latter category.

One socialite recalled going to Walter Lippmann's on Park Avenue where both "Dee Dee" and "Babs" were guests. "I left the living room to go to the bathroom, and walked down the hall," the woman said. "I opened one door and found Barbara Hutton in bed with a man. I quickly shut it and opened the door across the hall and there was Doris Duke, in bed with another man. They were no angels."

Doris was "extremely aloof, much more aloof than Barbara Hutton," the woman added. "She didn't care what people thought. She did what she felt like doing. She never came out of the bedroom. Neither one of them did."

Both Hutton and Duke—labeled the "gold dust twins"—had experienced emotional loss at an early age. Barbara was four when her mother committed suicide. Her father, Frank Hutton, left the Woolworth heiress an orphan for all practical purposes as she was raised by governesses. Hutton remarried while Barbara was an adolescent, but she felt rejected by both her father and new stepmother. Sent away to boarding schools and left for extended periods with her aunt, Mrs. Jessie Donahue, she told Elsa Maxwell: "I never had a home life."

Both Barbara and Doris, born within one week of one another, had grown up as ugly ducklings. While Barbara was pudgy, Doris was tall and "chinny." As only children, the poor little rich girls lived in gilded isolation and loneliness, increasingly inventing their own reality. For a time, they found a certain solace in one another. "They were friends, but not close friends," recalled Cromwell. While Barbara had been raised by her French governess, Mlle. Germaine "Tiki" Tocquet, Doris had been reared by Mlle. Renaude. Barbara had hated her father. Doris hated her mother. Barbara wrote poetry; Doris played piano. Barbara's court jester, companion, and "spokesman" was her cousin, Jimmy Donahue. Doris relied on half-brother Walker Inman. The loss of her father left Doris with a sense of abandonment, and both Doris and Barbara harbored lifelong feelings of inadequacy.

They were also avid travelers and became transatlantic commuters at an early age, both caught in the revolving doors of the world's finest hotels. Perhaps out of fear of kidnapping, they were constantly on the move. They both had a penchant for eccentric characters and smoke-filled nightclubs.

The Colony Club, the Central Park Casino, Cobina Wright's newly opened Sutton Club, and the members-only roof of the St. Regis Hotel (controlled by the A. J. Drexel Biddles) became favorite haunts.

Private parties, especially those staged in *Vogue* and *Vanity Fair* owner Condé Nast's triplex apartment on upper Park Avenue, were also frequented. They were filled with bootleg liquor and a potpourri of people from the worlds of stage, screen, arts, society, and business including Hedda Hopper, Jimmy Cromwell, Marie Dressler, Clifton Webb, even Mrs. Vanderbilt herself, all duly reported by Maury Paul in his Cholly Knickerbocker column. Paul, who made no secret of his homosexuality, was a flamboyant fixture on the scene. He coined the phrases "glamour girl" and "Cafe Society," and wrote scathingly of the rich and famous, although he was more critical of Hutton than Doris Duke. "He considered Doris a tight-fisted gal," the gossip columnist's biographer Eve Brown observed, "but he had respect for her as smart, uncompromising and unbuyable, and didn't trifle with her. It must have broken Maury's heart to treat her that way."

"It was a strange period in society," Jimmy Cromwell recalled. "There were no strictures on girls anymore. Girls had been more protected and secluded, but when they went to speakeasies it kind of let things down for them. You'd be next to a girl at a bar which of course had never happened before. It was a changed society that was brought about. There was a great deal more freedom for women."

Doris embraced that freedom. Both she and Barbara balked at the special police protection in 1932 following the tragic Lindbergh baby kidnapping.

Barbara, friends said, tried to emulate Doris. Whatever Doris had, Barbara wanted. But Barbara viewed her inheritance as a necessary evil. Barbara squandered it on grand gestures while Doris withheld, burdened by the responsibility and the obligations of such a fortune. Barbara had been told as a child that no one would ever love her for herself alone and she believed it. She entertained lavishly and loved publicity, granting interviews and creating news wherever she went. Her romances were breathlessly reported: Broadway playboy Phil Plant, Italian princes, and finally her first husband, fortune hunter Prince Alexis Mdivani, who had first discovered the young heiress when she was just fifteen.

Doris shunned publicity. She was also, like her mother, gaining a reputation for being stingy, despite her private acts of generosity to friends like Cobina Wright. Doris never carried any money, and friends complained they were often stuck with taxi bills and restaurant tabs when going out with her. She simply had no concept of money.

"I wish I could go into a store and shop for things just as a girl," she lamented.

But Mr. Stotesbury's private nurse, Margaret Konnell, recalled accompanying Doris to shops in Bar Harbor. "Doris would come along and say, 'Meg, loan me five bucks.' So I did a couple of times. She said her secretary would give it back to me. I said, 'You give it to me. The very idea of you going out without a pocketbook or a penny and asking me for money.'"

Doris, in her breathy voice, denied that she was tight with money. "When people know who you are," Doris complained, "the prices usually go up twice as high to start with. People who have money wouldn't have it long if they didn't ask how much things cost and then refuse to buy half of them."

One news report said, "Never knowing the value of money, Doris is one of the smallest tippers among the young social set. Waiters do not fall over each other trying to serve her. One noon, at a smart restaurant, the doorman made two calls for her. She thanked him properly but did not tip him, perhaps never dreaming what a couple of nickels might mean to a doorman."

The story added that New York dressmakers "despair of ever getting her into either the very latest clothes or the most expensive." (Doris claimed she couldn't afford certain styles and made a practice of asking for discounts from designers.) "Whenever she gives a party, the women guests invariably receive corsages of rare, expensive orchids from 'Duke Farms.' However, she seldom wears them herself."

How much of Doris' behavior was a direct reaction to Barbara Hutton's excesses is unclear. But one thing was certain: Doris Duke, whose fortune was four times greater than the Woolworth heiress's, was not an easy touch.

Both girls were pursued by every slick fortune hunter in New York. "All the horrible men at every dance would line up to dance with Doris Duke," said the former Isabella Hardy (Mrs. Edward Watts), a Brearley classmate. "None of the nice people. They were the deadbeats, South American men. Nobody you wanted to know. She was just besieged by these awful men."

Few of the desirable men wanted to be seen with either girl for fear of being labeled a gold digger. "Doris didn't stand a chance with any decent man," said Dorothy Mahana. "But aside from that, she wasn't really attracted to those sort of men. She loved people who were artistic. People who were kooky."

Which explains her attraction to Jimmy Cromwell, who was now living with his mother in the renovated "tea house" at El Mirasol for his winter residence. Summers were spent in Newport. By now, his daughter Christine was staying with Jimmy and his brother Eaton in the resort. Cromwell was bound by his custody agreement to return Christine to Delphine by September 15, 1930. When he failed to do so, Delphine filed suit against Cromwell for custody of their eight-year-old daughter, who was now a pawn in the continuing Dodge-Cromwell spat.

Jimmy accused Delphine of gross neglect of the child. Christine had been put in a school in France and left there while Delphine went on a tour around the world. Christine had then drifted from London to Paris to Cannes to Cairo under the care of her uncle, Delphine's alcoholic brother, Horace Dodge, and had contracted a "tropical disease." (Actually, it was tonsillitis). Jimmy attempted to take Christine to Philadelphia for an operation before Delphine slapped him with a writ of habeas corpus.

The publicity stung Anna Dodge and Eva Stotesbury, who worked feverishly behind the scenes for a resolution. A hearing was set for October 9. The courtroom was jammed with eager spectators hoping to learn of Delphine Dodge Cromwell Baker's myriad failings as a mother. Suddenly, Cromwell bowed to the higher court of his mother and Anna, announcing he was handing over Christine without a fight.

The two dowagers worked out a new agreement for the care of Christine, who was not to be taken out of the country without Jimmy's consent. Christine would still be left in the hands of various nannies and housekeepers by both Jimmy and Delphine, who was now living on the $2 million annual interest from her father's $57 million estate. Tragically, Anna Dodge Dillman was the only one who ever cared for the girl, shuttled from one boarding school to another.

A more serious legal tangle was brewing, this time over the apartment building Cromwell had invested in. Jimmy had convinced Delphine to sign for the leases on the building, but had tried to void the deal after the divorce. Cromwell was sued by an investor, Robert F. Norton, who claimed Jimmy owed him $50,000. (The case was dismissed.) Norton wrote a letter to Eva Stotesbury. "Knowing you to be a lady of great wealth as well as fair-mindedness, wouldn't you or couldn't you spare me dragging this matter through the courts with such a terrible unpleasantness to all concerned by repaying me?" All the time he was representing that his wealthy wife . . . was backing him, he and his wife were living apart and planning a divorce.

Jimmy filed a $250,000 suit against Norton for damaging his reputation.

That same night, he sailed to Europe aboard the *Bremen,* most likely to pursue Doris. They hadn't seen one another since Valentine's Day, when "the fixer" Evalyn Walsh McLean gave a dinner dance in Doris' honor at the Embassy Club in Palm Beach. Doris and Nanaline were houseguests of Evalyn at her Villa Oheka.

While Jimmy was on the Riviera, Doris was entertained in London by prominent hostess Mrs. Charles Cartwright. How Nanaline beamed when Lord Fairhaven twirled Doris, in a simple dress of white satin without jewelry, onto the dance floor. Her daughter spoke French and Italian more fluently than English, and Nanaline envisioned Doris married to at least a count.

Once again, the demands of Duke University interfered with Doris and Nanaline's relentless social schedule. In the spring of 1931, the medical center was scheduled to open and officials were anxious for Doris to attend.

"As we grow in years and have a better understanding of our human life, most of us, I think, come to feel that only those are fortunate who can link their lives with great and undying causes," President Few wrote to Doris. He closed with the information that Duke now had a good football team and invited her to see the games. In one of her few handwritten letters (Doris preferred telegrams), she answered Few's letter and said she was delighted to hear that Duke was progressing so rapidly. (The rest of her correspondence was normally handled by her social secretary or her business manager, William Baldwin.)

While the heiress had little affinity for undying causes, she did attend the medical school opening on April 21, 1931. Much to the university's embarrassment, *Time* magazine duly reported that the heiress "appeared bored and left after a short while."

Dr. Lenox Baker, a medical student, was assigned to escort Doris on a tour of the new facility. "She was a long, lean, leggy 19-year-old girl who hardly opened her mouth. I got the impression she was very shy. She didn't have a lot of self-confidence." The tour ended at a small chapel on the West Campus. "She said, 'This is cute.' Those were the only words she uttered."

The Depression had cast an ominous shadow over the country. Suddenly, the rich who had been so revered and celebrated in the Roaring Twenties were seen, along with their opulent playgrounds and palatial "villas," as an anachronism in the Thrifty Thirties. Newport was especially hard hit, with mansions boarded up and some being sold. Villa Rosa, the home of Mrs.

James B. Haggin, went on the block. So did By-the-Sea owned by J. Beal McLean and Dudley Place, once owned by William K. Vanderbilt. Suddenly, anyone with enough cash could buy their way into the most exclusive resort in the country.

Evalyn Walsh McLean was forced to pawn the Hope Diamond for $37,500 to stop the bank from foreclosing on her mortgage. She also ripped open the back of a chair and grabbed a fistful of jewels that were hidden in the stuffing and pawned them for $50,000. (Evalyn would become a frequent visitor to New York pawnshops over the years, as her fortune dwindled. "Money was our devil," she later wrote of her free-spending days, "but it was not money's fault.")

In Palm Beach, even Eva Stotesbury was put on a budget. Her husband ordered her to spend no more than $50,000 a month on entertainment.

Of all the wealthy Americans, Jimmy's mother and stepfather were singled out for the harshest criticism. A Philadelphia radio commentator even recommended that a bomb be dropped on Whitemarsh Hall, the largest private residence ever built in America. The Stotesburys also heard the rumor that a band of starving citizens had been organized to storm the house and burn it down. Terrified by these threats, Ned and Eva stripped the house of its treasures in June 1932 and closed it down.

Under armed guard, six large furniture vans transferred the Stotesbury furnishings to the Pennsylvania Museum, where they were loaned for an indefinite period of time. Rare antique furniture, paintings, and tapestries (all purchased from Joseph Duveen) went on display with sculptures, rugs, and porcelain. One report said Ned Stotesbury was fed up with the grandeur of Whitemarsh Hall and wanted to live in a less ostentatious manner. The truth was, he could no longer afford such grandeur. The staff of servants, gardeners, and workmen had been cut to the bone—thirty-five chefs, waitresses, butlers, and housemaids were reduced to a "skeleton" force of ten, just enough to keep the cobwebs swept. Six chauffeurs were dismissed, with them the mechanics and car washers. The corps of engineers was trimmed from twenty-five to ten. The nine fountains were turned off. Ned and Eva sailed to Europe on the *Bremen*. "If we never come back, we've had ten wonderful years of it," Eva said.

When the Rolls-Royce carrying the Stotesburys, accompanied by their son, pulled up to the hotel in Cannes, there was Doris Duke's Pierce Arrow. They joined forces with Mrs. Duke for a few weeks vacation. Once again, Doris and Jimmy were thrown together. "We had had a big fight," he said. "I thought she was impossible. But there we were together and we started all over again." Cromwell shook his head. "We'd date and then we'd fight. Mostly because I thought she was selfish. She always wanted to have her own way."

On the Riviera, Doris and Jimmy were joined by Alec Cunningham-Reid and his wife. Cunningham-Reid, known as Bobbie, was a devastatingly handsome Cambridge-educated war hero with black wavy hair and cupid's bow mouth. He had served as secretary to Colonel Wildrid Ashley, former Minister of Transport, and was elected to Parliament as a Conservative from Marylebone. At thirty-seven, Bobbie was a dashing figure whose war-time experiences included piloting his friend the Duke of Windsor over Cologne and across the Rhine where they did some "stunting" 7,000 feet up, ending in a spin over the spire of Cologne Cathedral. Bobbie developed a taste for heiresses early on. He romanced Beatrice Byrne, the elevator heiress, and eventually followed her to Bar Harbor. Their secret engagement was broken after an argument with Beatrice's father. Heartsick, she followed Cunningham-Reid to England, but he was already wooing another heiress, Ruth Mary Ashley, his former boss's daughter and one of the richest women in England. (Her grandfather, Sir Ernest Cassel, had left an estate of six million pounds.) Beatrice Byrne, suffering a nervous breakdown, went to Switzerland and plunged to her death, falling into an Alpine stream.

In 1927, Bobbie and Ruth Mary were married in a lavish ceremony while a noisy crowd of spectators waited outside. The sight of the handsome groom was said to elicit high-pitched feminine squeals and more than one woman fainted. Her family (one daughter had already married Lord Mountbatten) vehemently opposed the' match, but Bobbie's persistent charm was irresistible to women. Men considered him a social-climbing scoundrel. "He tried to buy his way into several clubs in London," said one associate. "But he was not very popular. He was actually blackballed from several private clubs."

Cromwell and Cunningham-Reid were remarkably similar. While Jimmy had begun courting Doris when she was sixteen, Bobbie had begun ro-mancing the tall, auburn-haired Ruth Ashley when she was barely eigh-teen. She was married at twenty-one, and first son Michael was born the following year and second son Noel was born in 1930. Indefatigable trav-elers, the Cunningham-Reids were familiar faces at all the poshest resorts—St. Moritz, Monte Carlo, the Riviera—and among their friends were the Aga Khan and the Crown Prince of Sweden. Christmases were spent in Klosters, Switzerland, and Ruth Mary's estate, Six Mile Bottom, became the best known shooting lodge in England. Bobbie also raised eyebrows when he put in a private cinema in the rear of their London townhouse.

Both Jimmy and Bobbie, who had begun dipping into his wife's bank account, were veteran heiress-hunters. "We did run around together and it was a nice friendship," Cromwell later said.

Doris, in the meantime, had fled New York after published reports stated that she was engaged to thirty-six-year-old New York state Senator Elmer Quinn, once secretary to former Tammany Hall leader George Olvany. Quinn had been elected to fill the seat Jimmy Walker vacated when he became mayor. He and Doris had met several years earlier on Long Island. The engagement was heatedly denied by Nanaline who said Doris had never met Quinn. A statement was released by her secretary, Marian Paschal: "Miss Duke knows nothing of this supposed engagement. She does not care to talk about it. There have been many rumors. She will say nothing now."

It was said that Doris was forbidden to see any young or eligible man a second time. "She wasn't very successful with men," said Eleanor Waldrop, wife of the *Washington Herald* editor. "She didn't trust men."

Nanaline had also hired private detective Max Krone to act as a "love spy." It was Krone's job to weed out the more obvious fortune hunters among Doris' suitors. (She was said to get at least one proposal a week.) The detective's assignment to protect the Duke millions from obvious poachers drew him a regular monthly fee from family lawyers.

Doris' chauffeur-driven car was equipped with an unusual safety device, one which playboy baronet Sir Christopher Sykes became familiar with. One evening on the Riviera, Sykes accompanied Doris home from a party. When he leaned over to try and kiss her, she pressed a secret button on the floor of the car. Suddenly, the dashboard lit up with red lights and a siren wailed. A similar red flashing light pulsated on the rear bumper, alerting the trailing car of detectives, which pulled up to the limousine and screeched to a halt. Armed guards physically removed the baronet from the car and he was made to trudge home on the deserted road in the dark.

In St. Moritz, later that year, the titled foreigners did not find her tactics very amusing and "decided to chastise Doris socially for her treatment last summer of the young Englishman who admittedly became too amorous of his attention to the Duke heiress," as Cholly Knickerbocker reported. "So Doris goes on her placid way, having her skiing lessons in the morning and mild bobsledding exercise in the afternoon. With 'Nannie' Duke always close at hand to see that no 'objectionables' manage to strike up an acquaintance with the 'dollar princess.' I can think of nothing sillier than Mrs. Duke keeping Doris away from New York this winter owing to her objections to—there! I almost mentioned the divorced club-fellow's name."

The name Maury Paul wouldn't mention was Jimmy Cromwell, now vice president of the Peerless Motor Car Company of Cleveland. "He had this terrible reputation, so that made him more attractive," recalled Dorothy Mahana. "He had a lot of fascinating friends. Disreputable and terribly interesting. He was always running around with famous people. He was glamour for Doris. She never knew anything but these dreary younger boys. They were not very interesting. He introduced her to all sorts of glamorous people."

Eleanor Waldrop recalled Jimmy's considerable charm. "You wanted to know him because you felt he was 'in' on everything because his mother was such a big personality."

"He put himself out," recalled Frank Waldrop. "If he were talking to you, he'd look you right in the eye. He'd be very earnest and tell you that, by George, that's a good idea. The first thing you knew, you'd gotten taken in." Jimmy also "had ambition. He wanted to be noticed."

The Stotesburys had returned from Europe and reopened Whitemarsh Hall. Much to Ned Stotesbury's dismay, Jimmy had become an ardent New Dealer. The playboy turned social rebel had in February 1933 written a book, *The Voice of Young America,* which was published by Charles Scribner's Sons, and offered a cure for the Depression. The irony of Cromwell's quick-change act, from a playboy to a socially conscious voice of his generation, was not lost on Cafe Society types who found Cromwell's latest venture rather odd. But Jimmy basked in the attention. In Palm Beach, at a meeting of the Current Events Club, he announced that the Constitution was antiquated. The country belonged to the people. "All those who disagree with this sentiment will please raise their hands," requested the author. A sea of perfectly manicured hands shot into the air. "Ah," said the suave Jimmy, "it is not with me that you so disagree, but with Abraham Lincoln."

The women were said to be deeply offended. Eva sat in the front row, proud as a peacock.

That June, she threw open Whitemarsh Hall for another speech. Jimmy, tall, tanned and thirty-six, spoke to the 500 members of the Republican Women of Philadelphia. While the women strolled in and out of the game room in the west wing of the house overlooking the wide sweep of White-marsh Valley, Eva talked about her favorite subject: Jimmy.

"Mr. Stotesbury is a strong Republican-Conservative, but Jimmy startled us one day by turning Democratic. It was during Al Smith's presidential campaign. He's been a Democrat or liberal ever since. He is thoroughly sincere and very ardent about his beliefs."

Young Christine Cromwell clapped enthusiastically as her father told the crowd, "The youth of this country is fed up to the teeth with lies, evasions and hypocrisy; with half-baked and futile efforts of reformers trying to spread perfume on a cesspool of graft and corruption." He called for the repeal of the Eighteenth Amendment, recognition of Soviet Russia, and government ownership of all public utilities and transportation systems. He suggested birth control and sterilization as a means of population control.

Among the rich, the anti-Roosevelt faction was so strong that when Elsa Maxwell threw her Pet Hates Party, inviting guests to come as the one person they most disliked, there were more Franklins and Eleanors than anyone else.

Jimmy began to lecture, and became avidly interested in public service. From El Mirasol, he began a correspondence with Senator Robert Owen, a former banker from Oklahoma. Jimmy sent him his brochure on inflation. "I had my pamphlet copyrighted," he wrote Owen, "in order that I might control its use and make certain that it should appear under the proper auspices where it would do the most good." Seized with a patriotic fervor, Jimmy was convinced he could save the economy. He wrote to Owen, "To find a person in Washington as well informed about monetary affairs as you are is like finding an oasis in a desert."

As for Roosevelt, who took office in January 1933, he never considered Cromwell as anything other than a dilettante, although he did value the young man's social connections, especially to the rich-rich. Frank Murphy, who would become a Supreme Court Justice, was already courting Crom-well and strongly suggested that a Cromwell-Duke marriage would be politically correct. Roosevelt even prodded Jimmy to make Doris his bride. "He liked the idea very much of my marrying Doris," Cromwell recalled. "In other words, that fortune would be in the service of the Roosevelt regime."

Stories about Cromwell's playboy antics and partying did little to advance his reputation as a serious politician. He won headlines for introduc-ing the plebian hot dog at a blue-blooded social function and offered his sure-fire recipe for a successful party: "Keep it simple, keep it alive, concentrate it all in one big room and break it up shortly after 4 A.M."

A frequent guest was Elsa Maxwell, whom Jimmy was especially fond of. "Most rich people are the poorest people I know," Maxwell later wrote. "Guilt complexes stemming from the way they made, married or inherited their money warp their normal outlets of warmth and vitality. I brought to them a capacity for friendship and gaiety that offered escape from plush-lined boredom, casual sex without passion and excessive gambling without excitement . . . I had imagination and they had money, a fair exchange of the commodity possessed by each side in great abundance."

But Maxwell did not enjoy the company of Doris Duke. She described the tobacco heiress thus: "She stands five feet ten in bare feet, is unhappy, shuns people and pinches pennies. She talks in jerky, almost inaudible sentences, wears sixteen-dollar dresses . . . which look like sixteen-dollar dresses, walks awkwardly . . . as if mistrusting her ability to cross the floor . . . and has the appetite of a farm hand and the manners of a shy child."

In June 1933 Barbara Hutton, armed with a prenuptial agreement, forty couture outfits, and two dozen hats, married Prince Alexis Mdivani in Paris. Over 200 reporters jammed into the press section for the civil ceremony while a mob formed outside. Hutton gave her husband a string of polo ponies. He gave her a priceless jade necklace, which she purchased. The couple went to India for a honeymoon. He was unfaithful on the honeymoon and chided her about her weight: "You're too fat." Thus began the fanatical dieting which would ruin her health. They returned from Europe in time to celebrate her twenty-first birthday on November 14. Held at her Fifth Avenue home, the party featured Chinese dancers and acrobats, cossack sword dancers, and a balalaika band. Doris Duke said she didn't care for "all the hubbub of it."

The flamboyance of the party and the utter disregard for the sober times brought unwelcome publicity for Barbara, who flaunted her wealth with abandon as the Depression deepened. While Doris had been voted "the best behaved Deb of 1933," Barbara was increasingly seen as a self-indulgent wastrel. Hutton, said Elsa Maxwell, "was too young to understand that ostentatious princesses were offensive to the grim temper of the times."

And grim they were. As the breadlines increased, one newspaper head-line screamed: KIDNAPPING FEAR GRIPS BLUEBLOODS. It was datelined Newport and reported that a wave of kidnapping terror had swept the resort, leaving some of the biggest names in the social register in a virtual state of siege in their palatial homes. Extra private detectives were sent from New York and Boston to guard families who had received extortion letters, including Nanaline and Doris, as well as Countess Szechenyi (formerly Gladys Vanderbilt), Mrs. Truman Saunders, and Mrs. Goadby Loew. Armed motorcycle escorts were seen accompanying them to Bailey's Beach.

During the height of this kidnapping wave, Doris decided to go west, and traveled incognito, first to Salt Lake City, then to Reno to see Walker Inman, and finally to Los Angeles where she was entertained by Edgar and Ruth Selwyn and Marion Davies, who hosted dinners in Doris' honor. (Marion, of course, was the comely actress who had become William Randolph Hearst's mistress. She and Doris would become friends.)

The trip ended in San Francisco where Doris and Walker attended a California-U.S.C. football game. It was duly reported that the fabulously wealthy heiress was compelled to take a "simple" room at the Hotel St. Francis because everything else was booked.

She was forced to leave the city when news of her visit leaked out. "$50,000,000 Duke Heiress Leaves Coast as Identity Becomes Known" was front-page news. Before their hasty retreat, Walker Inman spoke to the press, saying how hard it was becoming for Doris to remain anonymous. "When word gets out that she's in town it's like telling gangsters, 'Here's a lot of money. Come and get it.'

"Cranks are the principal annoyance. Mail comes in by the bagful with all sorts of requests because she is supposed to have so much money." Inman added, "Doris knows where every dollar of her money is and what it is doing."

Asked if he had trouble keeping suitors away, Walker Inman smiled. "No, not so much. The average eligible suitor doesn't want to appear to be a fortune hunter."

The idea of poor Doris (as well as Barbara Hutton) being taken by a swindler became a popular romantic theme. RKO even released a romantic comedy starring Miriam Hopkins called *The Richest Girl in the World*. The plot concerned a poor heiress who invented various ways to insure that men would love her for herself and not her money. As a friend of Doris' confided, "Someday Doris will meet a chap who doesn't know who she is and this will probably be the beginning of her big romance. If she is convinced that he doesn't know her identity, she will believe that he loves her for herself alone."

A week after Barbara Hutton's twenty-first birthday, Doris celebrated her own. She would come into one-third of her $30 million inheritance (down from the reported $53 million prior to the stock market crash), and the first chunk was estimated at $10 million. The news appeared prominently in *The New York Times* along with the fact that no celebration was planned.

"I do not believe in parties during times like these," Nanaline sternly announced. When curious reporters asked Mrs. Duke about the money her daughter would inherit, she seemed taken aback. "After all, Doris is only a child," she said (referring to her twenty-one-year-old daughter!). "Whatever money she has had or will have has made absolutely no difference in her life. How has she been equipped to handle this fortune? How could any child be equipped?"

As throngs of curious autograph seekers and photographers swarmed around at the Seventy-eighth Street house to get a glimpse of the heiress, armed guards struggled to keep the crowd at bay. Early in the afternoon, Nanaline and Doris—in her tortoise-shell sunglasses—hurried to a waiting limousine and fled to Somerville. The previous day, reporters had camped out at Duke Farms, and one resourceful newshound got an exclusive interview with one of the household staff, and, flanked by two 150-pound Great Danes, he called Doris an average girl with a taste for movie magazines. He also said Doris liked to fly, but is not a pilot. "The kid has her feet on the earth."

"Attaining her majority" was less a matter of celebration than of persecution. "And if she has not much more privacy than a movie star, it is probably because she has become the star of a living movie plot," *Newsweek* magazine commented. Doris, who enjoyed sticking her tongue out at pesky photographers, denied rumors that she was planning to live abroad, "unless people go on asking me as many foolish questions as they have tried to ask me today."

She did say in a radio interview that she found Europeans less intrusive than Americans. "Over there, no one ever asks you how much money you have or where you live or where you buy your clothes or any of those personal things. My mother and I live like everyone else. I have no particular talent. I've never been engaged to anyone in my life."

Nanaline echoed the sentiment that Doris was nothing special. "She is no genius," said the heiress's mother.

And while she quietly enlisted young socialites in New York to befriend her daughter, Nanaline was aware of the fact that Doris was a self-absorbed eccentric and a bore. "She has a lot of friends," Mrs. Duke gamely ventured. "They are all very sensible and well brought up, to my way of thinking."

A week later, a small formal dinner party was held in New York at the Duke mansion. Guests included Barbara Hutton and Mdivani; Lady

Mendl, the former Elsie de Wolfe, in full-length sable coat; Prince Serge Obolensky, and the jolly, rotund Elsa Maxwell in black chiffon and velvet. As society columnist Nancy Randolph wrote, "The only visible sign of festivity about the marble pile was the light which blazed through the double glass doors of the 78th Street entrance, where guests were admitted by footmen in dress livery, decked with shining buttons embossed with a large 'D.'"

Nanaline gave Doris a diamond tiara as a birthday present. The only other gift she asked for was an accordion. Nanaline was taken aback by the request, but had one purchased at the nearest music store. "At first, Mrs. Duke probably was flabbergasted by the idea of having an accordion player in the family," Maury Paul wrote. "Then she probably decided it would relieve the monotony of her marble halls . . . to have Doris wandering about wheezing out 'Stormy Weather' . . . on the durn thing." Paul, no doubt snickering with satisfaction, dubbed Doris Duke society's "richest accordion player."

The country was not only fixated on the mythical—almost fictional— Doris Duke. There was the custody battle for little Gloria Morgan Vanderbilt and the arrest of Bruno Hauptmann for the Lindbergh kidnapping. Another brutal kidnapping also made the news. Brooke Hart, the young son of a California merchant, was abducted, hit over the head with a brick and thrown into the San Francisco Bay. A week after Doris' twenty-first birthday, the two accused killers were lynched in San Jose by an angry mob of one hundred men who smashed their way into the county jail after a two-hour battle to seize the pair. California's governor, James Rolph, announced that he would pardon anyone arrested in the lynchings, which he deemed "a fine lesson to the whole nation . . . There will be less kidnapping in the country now. They made a good job of it."

But extortion threats increased. Doris—said to be a self-exiled prisoner at Somerville—and Nanaline were understandably petrified. In the spring of 1934, a desperate seventeen-year-old Newark boy named Thomas Layden was indicted for threatening to bomb Duke Farms. He had sent a series of threatening letters through the mail, including one that read: "I just want to tell you that I planted a bomb on your estate. It will go off at 3 P.M. Saturday, May 26 unless you pay $3,000." The letter designated the spot where the money was to be dropped. Layden also threatened to blow up a Newark power station. He was arrested by officers that same day and held on $25,000 bail.

Kidnapping the queen of England would have been easier than snatching Doris Duke. Somerville employed more guards than servants, and electrical alarm systems were installed in each room. She seldom told anybody but her mother where she was going. She put out false information about her whereabouts: when she was reported at Duke Farms, she was usually at the New York house and vice versa. She began using fictitious names.

Doris had been appointed to the board of trustees of the Duke Endowment and in December, she attended the ninth anniversary of the endowment's establishment held in Greenville, South Carolina. "I'm having a wonderful visit," she said. "Enjoying every minute of it. I hope that I may come back again." Doris, a sort of Lady Bountiful in blonde waves, spent nearly an hour visiting youngsters at the Shriner's Hospital for Crippled Children, a recipient of Duke Foundation funds. As Doris was leaving, the children stood up and gave a hearty cheer to the benefactress. "Such lovely children," Doris told Nanaline. "I enjoyed my visit with them ever so much."

She began a program of quietly donating money to various charities, including the Musicians Emergency Fund and a home for unwed mothers in New York. Her fund, Independent Aid, Inc., was headed by personal secretary and companion Marian Paschal. Doris' charitable works were kept out of the press, including the $100,000 bailout of the First Methodist Church in Charlotte, North Carolina.

Doris was, at twenty-one, still shy and soft spoken, although she was appearing less awkward and more self-assured. On New Year's Eve at the Mayfair Club, she was approached by photographers. Witnesses said she held her table card (No. 20) for fifteen minutes in front of her face. After a cameraman pleaded with her, saying he got a bonus if they got her picture and, after all, they could use the money, she lowered the sign and let the men click away. Many believed that Doris actually loved the attention. "Doris liked being important," Cromwell said. "I think she rather enjoyed being famous in a way."

(It must have been amusing when immigration officials in Mexico failed to recognize the heiress, arriving as a guest of old family friend Ambassador Josephus Daniels, and solemnly insisted on examining her credentials to make certain she had enough money to avoid becoming a public charge.)

Cromwell's attentions to Doris did not go unnoticed, although Maury Paul dismissed the rumors of a romance. "There is no disputing the fact that Jimmie finds Doris most attractive. But then—who doesn't? . . . The matchmakers are all wet this time."

What neither Paul nor anyone realized was that while Nanaline was frantically weeding out the obvious fortune hunters, the supposedly super-rich Jimmy Cromwell was running out of money and looking for a marital investment. "I think the Stotesbury fortune was disappearing fast," one mutual friend recalled. "He began following Doris."

He was invited to Rough Point where, during the summer of 1934, they were frequently seen at Bailey's Beach. "Doris is reigning in her palace on Bellevue Avenue and Jimmie is ringing the doorbell every day," one columnist noted. They also attended the Carnera-Baer boxing match and the Central Park Casino, although Jimmy was quoted as saying he and Doris were "just good friends." In early July, Doris was a houseguest at White-marsh Hall and Jimmy hosted a dinner dance for her. "The rumor that we are engaged is pretty silly in view of the fact that I've only seen her twice in two years," Jimmy told reporters.

Cromwell later said that his mother Eva had instigated the romance. He never loved Doris. Said Frank Waldrop: "I think he loved the idea of her. Of sporting her like a ring. 'Look what I got.'"

Doris Duke had become not only the richest, but the most famous woman in America. She was the toast of Cafe Society: famous for being famous. That fall, it made news when Doris attended the Flemington, New Jersey, courtroom where Bruno Hauptmann went on trial for the Lindbergh kidnapping. She and wealthy heiress Dorothy Fell and her mother, Mrs. Ogden Mills, sat in the back of the courtroom listening to the proceedings.

While Barbara Hutton had spent $25,000 celebrating her twenty-second birthday for 150 guests in Paris, Doris had managed to make a lengthy motor trip through Europe without putting a dent in the $30,000 letter of credit arranged for the tour. And while Barbara was getting ready to shed Mdivani as her first husband, having married him to get away from her family, Doris was about to declare her own independence.

That no one approved of Cromwell made him all the more attractive to Doris. Nanaline was against the match and so was attorney Thomas Perkins. "He was a very nice man," said Jimmy. "A very efficient man, but most of the time we were at sword's point. I think as far as Perkins was concerned, he looked at me and figured I could be worse."

Cromwell, who was now billed as an advertising executive, was right. There was no doubt that Doris, who recently had purchased a Bellanca Skyrocket 450-horsepower prop plane, would have a difficult time finding a suitable mate. And since she and her mother were disagreeing most of the time, it was unlikely she would wed a titled foreigner. (One story making the rounds was that King Zog of Albania sent an emissary to see Nanaline about the possibility of Doris becoming the queen of his cash-starved nation. Doris absolutely refused.)

Jimmy was simply the only alternative. Besides, with all that Stotesbury money it was obvious he didn't need Doris'. But there was one last stumbling block.

"Dr. Richard Hoffmann, Doris and I were all close friends," Jimmy said. "He was all for the marriage. He shared my ambition and he felt this was a great thing for Doris and me—an ideal match. I told him about this [sex problem]. He said, 'Don't worry. I'll talk to her.'"

Doris had spent the fall of 1934 in Hollywood escorted by Harry Crocker, son of the famous San Francisco banker. She even began to contemplate a career in films, which Nanaline—no longer her legal guardian—strongly disapproved of. When she returned home, nursing a cold, she and Cromwell agreed to marry. Doris was anxious for her freedom and Cromwell was simply the easiest escape route.

"Doris was in a hurry to get married," Jimmy recalled. "She wanted to get away from home. She was very anxious to be independent."

Chapter Seven

Diamond Jim

FOR HER TWENTY-SECOND BIRTHDAY, Jimmy Cromwell did not present Doris with a string of pearls from Cartier or a diamond tiara. He cleverly presented the girl who had everything with two Siamese kittens.

Manhattan veterinarian Dr. Louis Camuti was called down to Somerville to tend to the animals. The vet found Doris Duke, at twenty-two, "an attractive, slim young lady dressed in dungarees. On the way to the main house, she took me through the greenhouse, where she grew orchids by the thousands. As she sat there with her legs tossed over the arm of the chair and we talked about the cats and how she should be taking care of them, she asked if I would like to see the estate. I leaped at the chance and she ordered a car brought around." Settling in behind the wheel, Doris turned to her visitor and said, "There's just one thing I want to tell you. The dogs may resent it if you get too close to me or touch me. If you keep that in mind, everything will be fine."

Then, she called out and "three of the biggest Great Danes I'd ever seen came bounding across the lawn and leaped into the back seat of the car. I froze. Just the thought that if I made a move that they didn't like they might rip me apart made me break out in a cold sweat. She started the motor and we were off on what seemed like the longest trip of my life, though it actually took less than an hour. Throughout the entire tour, the dogs kept licking the back of my head but I still didn't move. Miss Duke didn't seem to notice what was going on, and she kept rattling away about this or that building on her property."

As soon as he got back to the house, Camuti went into the bathroom to wash. He hadn't thought Doris was aware of his predicament until he heard a knock on the door. "Her hand reached in, holding a large bath towel for me."

That fall, Doris had been sued by a young Raritan woman who claimed the Great Danes attacked her while walking on a public road at the entrance of the estate, leaving deep gashes on her body and her left arm paralyzed. She asked for $30,000. Doris managed to dodge the sheriff for months, but was finally served with the papers. In court papers, she said the woman was trespassing and that the 150-pound Great Danes were gentle. Eventually, the suit was settled out of court.

In February of 1935, Doris Duke left her estate and the Great Danes long enough to splash alone in the cool-blue ocean at the Roney Plaza Cabana Club in Miami Beach while bodyguards hovered nearby, perspiring in their blue serge suits. She wore a tomato-red woolen tank suit that was three seasons old. As she emerged from the water, toweled off, and sank into a beach chair wearing her tortoise-shell sunglasses, a reporter and a photographer approached her, asking if she were Miss Duke. She denied it, saying she knew no one by that name. Then she lit a cigarette and lifted her dark glasses. "I came down on the train, just like any other girl would. I spent the day in a beauty parlor. A lot of girls do that. See, I had my hair waved. This is the second time I've been out of my room. I have no plans for this evening." The photographer asked her to pose. She turned steely. "No. Photographers are a phobia with me. I don't like to see my face any more than I have to."

(Several months earlier, she had taken a bus from Maine to Boston after her plane was fogged in. Three guards from the airline were assigned to accompany her. When she reached Boston, the flashbulbs exploded in her face and she buried her head inside a black and white checked sportcoat and ran to her waiting limousine.)

"It seems to me that I would be very bad copy. I never do anything. I am not allowed to," she said wistfully, shading her eyes from the South Florida sun. "Maybe it would be news if you told them I strutted down the beach in black and white ostrich feathers."

She denied buying fifty dresses in New York the week before and said she was leaving for Jamaica the next day. She neglected to add "New York." The following day she flew back to Long Island on a private plane and Cromwell joined her, traveling from Palm Beach with his mother.

The marriage plans had been kept secret. Dr. Richard Hoffmann had even arranged for the license to be issued without Doris appearing at the Municipal Building as required by law. Hoffmann had made his appeal in writing, saying, "This is to certify that Miss Duke has been under my care for some time for nervous trouble, and it would seriously jeopardize her nervous system to subject her to the strain of publicity that a premature announcement would entail. I therefore plead for your cooperation and beg your consideration to issue a marriage license to her, avoiding the usual channels."

Eva Stotesbury had spent the previous night coaching her son on his best honeymoon behavior. Under no circumstances, Eva said, should the topic of money be raised unless Doris first brought it up. It was Eva who had nurtured the romance, despite Nanaline's objections to Jimmy's age and notoriety, and she was determined that nothing go wrong. In fact, Eva knew that Nanaline had warned her daughter never to see Jimmy again after that first meeting in 1929. Eva's campaign to win Doris for her son was almost over.

At 10:30 A.M. on February 13, Supreme Court Justice Burt Jay Humphrey arrived at the Duke mansion on Seventy-eighth Street to perform the ceremony. He had never met the couple. Jimmy, thirty-eight, and Doris, twenty-two, in a simple blue crepe dress and hat, were married in the spacious, heavily draped downstairs library in front of a roaring fire. The ceremony lasted five minutes and the word "obey" was omitted from the vows. Doris was given away by Walker, who had arrived from California the week before. Jimmy's older brother Eaton was best man. Attended by an expressionless Nanaline, Dr. Hoffmann (described as "the Duke family physician"), Doris' secretary Marian Paschal, Eva Stotesbury, the elderly Supreme Court Justice Norman S. Dike, and Duke family attorney and trustee William Perkins, the bride and groom were toasted by a glass of champagne and then hurried off in Doris' Rolls-Royce to board the ocean liner *Conti di Savoia*. Just before her departure, Doris turned to her mother. She leaned down and planted a perfunctory peck on Nanaline's cheek. "Bye, Ma," she said frostily.

Two private chauffeurs, one piloting the Rolls, and the other a Minerva, Doris' personal maid Catherine Walsh, and about a dozen suitcases (half a dozen trunks had been sent to the bridal suite the day before) accompanied the couple to Pier 59 at the foot of West Nineteenth Street. They arrived at the dock, laughing and running arm in arm minutes before the noon sailing, Doris in a squirrel coat and large hat.

As the couple's identity became known on the ship, they were chased by reporters. At the request of Scripps-Howard publisher Roy Howard, a pal of Jimmy's who just "happened" to be on board the ship, the newlyweds posed for a picture. Jimmy looked relaxed; Doris was radiant. For the first time, photographers captured her wide, beaming grin.

As the photo session continued, however, her expression changed and before long she fled to her cabin, leaving Jimmy behind. He was triumphant, basking in the attention and telling reporters his bride was too nervous to leave her room. He said he met Doris in Bar Harbor in 1929, and "then it began." Cromwell admitted the marriage was "sudden," but that neither one of them believed in engagements. "Was it love at first sight?" a reporter shouted. The dapper Cromwell lit a cigarette, laughed, and turning to the suite entrance, answered, "It certainly was."

In the midst of all the excitement, Jimmy found time to send a telegram to Senator Robert Owen in Washington. Owen had become a financial mentor and the two had organized The Sound Money League. "Dear Senator," Cromwell wrote. "I am sure you will be glad to learn that Doris Duke and I were married at her home this morning with only the members of our immediate families present. Due to her dread of publicity I promised her that I would not discuss our plans with any of my friends which is the reason that I had not told you before. We have sailed on the *Conti di Savoia* for the Orient where we will be gone until the summer, so keep the good ship Sound Money League afloat until I can get back and help you. Sincerely, Jim Cromwell."

The senator replied by radiogram: "My blessings on your union with Doris. May God bless you both with great happiness."

The marriage took New York and Palm Beach by surprise, and news of the sudden nuptials between the Golden Boy and the Richest Girl in the World spread quickly. It was the height of the Depression and the Stotesbury-Duke union captured the imagination of the entire country, if not the world. A certain segment took delight in the fact that Doris—unlike Barbara Hutton—had passed up the temptation of a foreign title. "The gold of our own Duke stays where it was made—right here," one patriotic reporter commented.

The wedding also gave Cromwell a welcome boost to his political career. "We got tremendous publicity when she and I were married. That's considered something that you need in order to be successful in politics."

But first he planned a long sojourn. It was Jimmy who mapped out their honeymoon tour: the Mediterranean, Egypt, Baghdad, India, Siam, Java, China, Japan, and the Philippines, ending in Hawaii. They would go by air and by sea, by mule and by yacht, by rickshaw and by elephant. The trip would last over twenty-four months.

Their first night on board ship, as Doris slipped into her negligee, Jimmy could stand it no longer. He sat on the bed, lit a cigarette, and coolly said, "Doris, just what might I expect my annual income to be?"

Eva had warned him, but he couldn't resist. Doris' face grew beet red, and she evicted him from her room. Jimmy spent the evening at the bar.

The next day, Cromwell received word that his check to Cook's to cover the initial honeymoon expenses had bounced. Doris hastily wired her business manager, William Baldwin, who covered the check and would begin wiring additional funds as needed. She financed the entire honeymoon, and it was the price she paid for her freedom.

Several days out at sea, Doris and Jimmy bickered constantly. During one argument, Doris angrily kicked her husband in the shins. Jimmy kicked her back.

"We didn't have a honeymoon. We had a sourmoon," Cromwell later admitted. "We knew it all the time. We were America's darlings, roaming all around the world in a completely false position. It was a tragedy, really. We were the opposite of what we were supposed to be."

Despite Dr. Hoffmann's intervention, Jimmy was still unable to enjoy sex with Doris. "I was as patient as I could be and tried hard to go halfway," Jimmy said. "Make it easier for her if I could. But it was very simple. She was frigid."

The latest pictures of the honeymooners appeared in American newspapers. They showed the couple bundled up side by side in deck chairs, a sullen-faced Doris, head buried in a book, with a dejected-looking Cromwell beside her. The other passengers reported the couple kept to their suite for most of the voyage and did not socialize.

The first stop was Monte Carlo. The honeymooners strode ashore on February 21 clad in berets and exuding, it was reported, "an almost royal incognito" while touring the principality. Earlier, Doris had wired her former school chum Dorothy Mahana, who was staying in Monte Carlo at the time. She met the Cromwells that evening for dinner and dancing at a nightclub. She observed the tension between them. "I could see things were not going well. Doris seemed unhappy. I was alone with her for a second and she just shook her head."

"I think her whole life would have been different if she hadn't married Jimmy," Mahana reflected. "He got her into a world she wasn't ready for and couldn't cope with."

During their arguments, according to Jimmy, his Frigidairess never showed emotion. She never cried. "She was very self-contained." Physically he found his bride attractive. "She had a beautiful body. If she had been a normal female, we would never have had any problem."

Cromwell wondered if Doris was simply not interested in men.

"She had this French governess and I did assume that this governess had tremendous influence with Doris. I suspected the governess was 'double-gaited' and the governess' outlook on life may have transferred to Doris. She may have been the one who was responsible for Doris maybe preferring women's company to men. I think Doris got started off on the wrong foot."

Jimmy wired his mother from the ship. "My mother knew we weren't getting along on the honeymoon. She was very upset. Doris and I realized we had to make the best of it. We were both upset, but we tried to put a good face on it. There was nothing we could. We were stuck."

The next stop was Naples, where Jimmy enjoyed the first of many extramarital affairs. "I said I was going to see a friend." He met the woman, a former girlfriend who was an American actress, at her hotel and the two made passionate love that afternoon. "I told her what was going on. She thought I was dreadful. But I was getting pretty desperate."

By early March, the Cromwells reached Bombay, and in the next few weeks headed down the Ganges. Both Jimmy and Doris contracted ptomaine poisoning in Agra where they had visited the Taj Mahal. It was reported that when Doris Duke laid eyes on the Mogul temple, she said, "I want one of those." So she hired a Delhi architect to draw up plans and had tessellated windows and doors custom built for later shipment to the States. Carved windows and doors were inlaid with jade, agate, malachite, lapis lazuli, and mother-of-pearl. Each door took six men three months to make.

Meanwhile, back in Palm Beach, socialites snickered. It was rumored that the Cromwells would add a Mogul-inspired wing to Jimmy's house. Pundits dubbed it "the Garaj Mahal."

Because train travel was so grueling and Doris' health so delicate, she hired a private railroad car. In New Delhi, they were entertained by the viceroy and were guests of Field Marshall Sir Philip Chetwode, commander-in-chief of India. The Cromwells then took a 500-mile detour to Wardha where Mahatma Gandhi granted them an audience.

They took shelter from the burning sun under a tree in the orchard in front of Gandhi's house. He was presiding at a conference nearby, but took time to see the American couple. After greeting Doris and Jimmy under the tree, Gandhi took them to a tiny, unfurnished room. "He was a very interesting man," Cromwell recalled. "We got into an argument about economic theories. I spent an hour or two with him. Doris sat there and listened. She agreed with me. It was the highlight of our visit to India."

While Doris sat on the floor of the barren hut listening, the outspoken Jimmy and "the Holy One," also seated on the floor, discussed the machine age and their different philosophies on life. It was not known what Gandhi, clad in his loin cloth and emaciated from fasting, his eyes blinking behind his spectacles, thought of the American heiress or her talkative husband, but he was very much opposed to the use of tobacco. In fact, he once declined to autograph a silver cigarette case for a United Press correspondent until the owner promised to use it only as a card case.

The meeting ended abruptly when an associate interrupted and said Gandhi was needed. Doris was deeply impressed by Gandhi, especially his views on the emancipation of Indian women. "I had talked to a Messiah, comparable to Confucius, Buddha, Christ or Mohammed," she later said.

Like Barbara Hutton, Doris was smitten with India and the various Indian mystics she met. She and Jimmy went north, heading for the foothills of the Himalayas, in search of the mythical Shangri-la. The next month, they sailed to Singapore on the Sultan of Jaipur's yacht. News dispatches revealed that Doris was spending five days in a Singapore hospital, resting from "the fatigue of her honeymoon travels."

Once discharged from the hospital, Doris went on a shopping spree. She spent $5,000 in a matter of hours, buying clothing, Chinese-style satin brocade pajamas, two-century-old Chinese ivory carvings, lingerie, and jewelry, and ordered more items to be delivered to her in Hong Kong.

She was determined that she was going to make good on the marriage," Cromwell recalled. "I said the whole marriage was a monstrosity."

Meanwhile, the world waited breathlessly for any news of the Cromwells. Jimmy called in reporters and announced, "We are enjoying every minute of our honeymoon."

They flew over Mount Everest to Calcutta and by May 5 they had reached Bangkok, lugging $20,000 worth of ancient rugs, described by their exasperated valet as "not fit for hanging over my telephone booth." If there was to be no sex on the honeymoon, the couple made up for it by going shopping. Already loaded down with curios, they hit the streets for more souvenir buying, which would eventually total more than $300,000. Tiles and jade, a five-foot bronze monkey, and a marble sunken bathtub, the type used by Indian mogul harems, were ordered. Doris, whose childhood deprivation was suddenly reversed by the spending habits of Jimmy, bought a huge ruby for herself, set in a heavy gold chain.

It was rumored that the Cromwells would cut their honeymoon short and return to New York because of Jimmy's so-called "pressing" business matters, lawsuits still pending from his disastrous real estate deals, but they continued on, flying over the Yangtze River. In Shanghai, caught by an army of newsmen, Doris jokingly suggested a new organization: The International Privacy League, of which she would be president.

She also chartered a private yacht, the *Sea Belle,* to take her and Jimmy from Bali to the Philippines. It was entirely refitted for the trip. In July they arrived in Manila where the honeymooners were invited to tea by Mrs. Arthur Rubinstein, wife of the pianist, and were entertained by red-haired Frank Murphy, high commissioner who would later become governor of Michigan and one of Jimmy's strongest political supporters.

Cromwell, tanned and fit, announced that he must be back in America by the fall. "There are a lot of things needing our attention, particularly the Roosevelt regime," Cromwell said. "Something must be done about it and people with money are the only ones who can check the present collapse into chaos."

On August 22, with their valet and maid, the Cromwells sailed from Japan aboard the *Tatsuda Maru* on the final lap of their 18,000-mile honeymoon.

Their arrival in Hawaii was eagerly anticipated by island reporters, anxious for a glimpse of the glamorous couple. It was expected to create even more of a sensation than the recent honeymoon visit of Barbara Hutton, who had shed Mdivani to wed Danish Count Court Haugwitz-Reventlow.

As the ship came into Honolulu Harbor, Jimmy told one reporter, "That American soil looks swell and we are glad to see it," even though Hawaii was still only a territory and had yet to achieve statehood. Doris, who was becoming an expert in dodging photographers, stole down a passageway, climbed down a ship ladder, and made her getaway to shore in a private launch, while on the top deck, Jimmy chatted away to unsuspecting reporters.

Doris was met by her secretary Marian Paschal, who had sailed from California to join her, and was whisked to a lavish suite at the Royal

Hawaiian Hotel. "Marian was a very stout person, really much too fat, but she had an attractive personality," Cromwell said. "I liked her very much. She was a few years older than Doris and she got a salary of some kind."

A group of reporters hovered outside the door. Angry over missing a shot of Doris, they offered a compromise. One photographer would snap the picture and they would leave. "How about that, dear?" Cromwell called. Doris was busy reading a letter and eating a piece of fruit. The letter had come from "Moms," she explained.

Doris finally agreed to the deal. "But you mustn't get my feet in," she said. Giggling nervously, she stood in her bare feet. Back home in New York, Doris' name was making news when a bizarre extortion plot was revealed. It seems some enterprising extortionists had pasted a photo of Doris' head onto a nude photograph and demanded $25,000 for its suppression. Along with the doctored photo was a typewritten letter: "Miss Duke, the pictures and stories of your former lover, it will go places where it will do the most harm." The letter had been turned over to police.

Hawaii was not only a paradise, it was an escape from the paparazzi and the cranks. Doris instantly fell in love with the territory, mainly because she enjoyed such freedom. It was said that when Doris rode down the street, people noticed the car, not the driver. By now, she began to relax. Cromwell said he was able to enjoy sex with Doris six months after the wedding. "I did have love affairs with her on Hawaii" said Cromwell. "It became bearable for her."

Doris was fascinated with the Hawaiians and their culture. "She liked dark people," Cromwell said with a laugh. She began taking hula lessons from dancer Odetta Bray. "Doris worked very hard at it. She had a tendency, being so tall, to be awkward," said her husband.

The Cromwells rented the modest Harry Hayward beachfront cottage on Black Point Road and on a trip to the city pound adopted a stray dog, naming him Curbstone. They discussed buying land and building a house. But Doris and Jimmy were miles apart emotionally and physically. "We certainly had everything that should make a couple happy," Cromwell reflected. "It was not to be."

In late September, Cromwell went home to his mother while his bride remained in Hawaii. "We didn't know where we were going to live," he said, "and we didn't know what was going to happen." In Philadelphia, Jimmy went to Whitemarsh Hall and complained bitterly about Doris. As was the case with Delphine Dodge, he was being supported by Doris with an allowance of $10,000 a month. During this interlude, he went to Washington, New York, and finally Somerville, where he wrote to Anna Dodge. "There is really no reason for me to see you as I have nothing new to report, but it is a real pleasure to talk to you, to hear about old friends and to reminisce about the many joys and sorrows we have shared together. Curiously enough, my 'original' two mothers still seem to be about the only people in this world to whom I can 'squawk' with any safety, comfort or certainty of sympathetic comprehension!'"

Doris spent her days on the beach at Waikiki, surrounded by virile young Hawaiian beach boys diving for coins from the fishing boats. "There was a club where all the beach boys hung out. She loved the beach boys and would bring them to her place. They would sing these dirty songs. They were dirty but fun. 'Kiss me my darling, a looa laya ee la,'" said Betty McIntosh, the former Betty McDonald who was a cub reporter for the Honolulu *Advertiser*.

In her yellow bathing suit, Doris was a familiar figure, surfing in the sapphire-blue water. The ocean, she said later, became a fetish. Dropping her Garbo-like mask, she found peace in the simple pleasures of island life. "She was completely relaxed with the Hawaiians, singing and dancing," said McIntosh. "They had a way of making you relax. They were so easygoing. She didn't have to put on any show and they really weren't looking at her for money. It didn't matter to them. I think it was really a sanctuary for her."

McIntosh saw Doris frequently on the island. "Her eyes were very cold. Very strange eyes. I always thought she was holding back a lot and would never let herself go. She had a kind of chiseled beauty, but it was her eyes that I remember more than anything. Cold blue gray, set far apart."

A month later, Cromwell returned to Hawaii. Doris met the ship in a motor boat and took Jimmy directly to Waikiki Beach. She was anxious to show off her new surfing skills. Unfortunately, she fell off mid-wave and tumbled into shore, the sixty-pound surfboard smacking her on the head. The wound required several stitches, and was international news.

Both Doris and Jimmy had befriended Duke Kahanamoku, Olympic swimming champion and sheriff of Honolulu, who was reported to be one of the last full-blooded Hawaiians. At six foot three inches, Duke was a looming figure who had already played minor roles as Polynesian chiefs in Hollywood films. Considered the greatest swimmer of his time, he won the 100-meter freestyle race in the 1912 and 1920 Olympics and introduced the flutter kick, which he had developed while surfboarding on the island. Duke and his brothers, Sergeant, Sam, and David, were trustworthy and loyal, and would become confidants of Doris. In late December, Sam took

Doris and Jimmy to the Big Island where the two men climbed the top of Mauna Loa. Doris wanted to go but dropped out at the last minute, staying behind with Sam's sister to hike in the park.

On December 28, with forty trunks, the Cromwells finally sailed home together. They arrived in Los Angeles and were met by Louise's son Walter Brooks and a group of friends. Doris, unwilling to embrace Jimmy's extended family, peered down and said, "Not more nephews?" They took a suite at the Hollywood Roosevelt Hotel and spent New Year's Eve with Louise and her new husband, actor Lionel Atwill. Catching up on the gossip, they discussed the scandalous Delphine Dodge, who had given birth to a second daughter, Anna Ray. Delphine was involved in an affair with married import agent Timothy Godde. She and Ray Baker had been planning a Reno divorce when Baker died of a massive heart attack in Washington. At the same time, Mrs. Godde threatened to sue Delphine for alienation of affection until Anna Dodge stepped in and offered the wronged wife a handsome sum. Anna was by now officially separated from second husband Hugh Dillman, whom she had discovered in bed with one of the handsome young male crew members on the yacht *Delphine*.

Several months later, Delphine Dodge married for the third time, becoming Mrs. Timothy Godde and leaving her daughter Christine in the care of her grandmother. "Delphine was horrid to Cee Cee," said one family member. "She used to tell horror stories of neglect and abuse." Guilty over his own absence, Jimmy suggested he and Doris take her. Doris was insanely jealous of the spirited Delphine and she and Jimmy argued. Jimmy couldn't understand Doris' resistance. The subject of Christine was dropped.

Later that week, the Cromwells were joined by Elizabeth Knox, Jimmy's private secretary who had formerly worked for Eva Stotesbury. "Knoxie," as she was known, would also begin working for Doris. The group flew back East on Walker Inman's private plane.

The next month, the jet-setting couple turned up in Detroit. They had come to pick up Jimmy's new $15,000 Cadillac.

Author Ruth Montgomery, then Ruth Shick, was a cub reporter for *The Detroit Times*. "I was new, and the city editor told me Doris Duke was in Detroit with her husband. He told me to go interview her. Of course, I knew she had been the richest girl in the world and I was fascinated. I didn't even know she didn't give interviews. I went over to the Book Cadillac Hotel. It was the finest hotel at that time in the city." Shick went to the house phone and asked for the Cromwells' suite. "As luck would have it, Doris answered.

I explained who I was. She said, 'You know I never give interviews,' and slammed down the phone."

A bellboy tipped off the reporter with Doris' room number. She went to the door and knocked. No one answered. Then, she noticed a waiter coming down the hall carrying a large breakfast tray. She managed to sneak into the room behind the tray.

"Doris was seated at a table, waiting for breakfast. She had her hair done up in big rollers and was wearing a full-length mink coat and galoshes. In a soft little voice, Doris said, 'It's very cold in here.' I announced who I was and she said, 'Can't we have breakfast in peace?' So I went and sat on the sofa. In the meekest tone of voice, I finally said, 'Can't I say anything?' Jimmy started laughing. He said, 'Sure, what do you wanna know?' I asked why they were in Detroit. He said they were here to pick up a specially designed Cadillac trimmed in brass. They said they had gone to a movie the night before, *Stella Dallas*."

The next day *The Detroit Times* featured Ruth's story with a banner headline: DORIS DUKE GIVES FIRST EXCLUSIVE INTERVIEW. (Montgomery ran into Duke in the 1950s, when Cobina Wright invited her to a party. "During the evening I told her who I was. She laughed her head off.")

A week later, the Cromwells flew to Palm Beach for Ned Stotesbury's eighty-seventh birthday party at El Mirasol, the most coveted invitation of the social season. Ned was still a spry man with a neatly trimmed white mustache. Although his wife had lost her crown as the queen of Palm Beach to younger, more energetic hostesses, the Stotesburys were still very much on the scene. Invitations were issued to 350 of their closest friends. "Uncle Stote" banged his Civil War drum and the band played his favorite tune: "Yes, We Have No Bananas." On one such birthday, Eva Stotesbury wore a gingham dress with her famous string of pearls. "Pearls in the daytime?" a friend queried. "Yes, my dear," Eva replied. "I used to feel that way too. But that was before I had the pearls."

Jimmy and Doris occupied the small, remodeled "tea house" on the Stotesbury estate, which he had named Malmaison. With Doris' expected arrival, armed guards were placed at the gate, and Eva began referring to the tile-decorated teahouse as the "Honeymoon Cottage." The Cromwells arrived separately. Friends were curious to see how the two were getting along. Most had heard the rumors of the disastrous honeymoon. From all accounts, Jimmy and Doris put on a brave face. "The lovely Doris Duke is obviously very happy in her new role as Mrs. Cromwell, and judging from the radiant appearance of this couple theirs is one of the modern marriages which is slated to last," a *Palm Beach Life* society correspondent observed.

Coincidentally, Cobina Wright was appearing at the Jardin Bijou in her series of "artistic evenings" with Mario Braggiotti on the piano. Doris was said to be extremely taken with the handsome jazz pianist.

The Cromwells' lack of sympathy was not lost on their friends. As Elsa Maxwell put it, "What Doris lacks, Jimmy possesses. He could, and did, spend a fortune; she thinks twice before agreeing to buy a ticket to a charity ball."

Cobina Wright, Jr., a friend of Christine Cromwell, recalled visiting the Stotesbury estate in Florida. "Doris used to drive this old rattletrap car to go shopping in West Palm Beach. One day she came back with a nightgown which she converted into an evening gown. She had the maid take off the flowers. She said it was a bargain."

Cobina knew that Jimmy was more social than his wife. "One night we were supposed to go to a formal dinner party. We sat outside and suddenly, Doris saw the fires across the lake from the Seminole Indians. Jimmy wanted to go to the dinner." An argument ensued. Jimmy, already dressed, pleaded with his wife. "What shall I tell our hostess?" Doris shot back, "I don't care what you tell her. I don't want to go."

Doris and Cobina drove across the bridge and spent the evening at the Seminole reservation. "They did these fire dances. We watched them. I loved Doris. She was exotic-looking. I thought she was wonderful. But if I'd been the hostess of that dinner party, I wouldn't have thought so."

Elsa Maxwell went on: "Doris is silent, at best monosyllabic; he can—and does—talk for hours. She is never certain of what she or anyone else should do in a given situation; he is never in doubt about anything and feels sure he could cure the ills of this republic if given half a chance."

Washington insiders, however, considered Mr. Doris Duke a lightweight. "Jimmy was a striver," Frank Waldrop said. "He was never a serious figure. He wanted to be in on things and never knew that he wasn't."

In a letter to Duke University President William Few, Dr. Martin Rehfuss, a family friend of the Stotesburys, sent along two of Jimmy's monetary pamphlets. "I know you will be convinced, as I always have been, that there is a lot more to Jim than any of the newspapers have ever pointed out. Jim has always been more or less a victim of circumstances. He possesses a great deal of the charm of his mother and there is no one that I have ever met who quite equals her . . . I have always felt if he could get in the right atmosphere and enlisted in the right sort of cause, his many contacts, his personality . . . might be utilized for greater purposes." That purpose was Duke University. Rehfuss hinted that Cromwell would be ripe for a position on the board and would then be able to harness his wife's millions for the benefit of the school.

Jimmy did encourage Doris to spend more time in Durham. That April, Doris and Marion Paschall took a battered car from Somerville and arrived on campus in disguise. Wearing beat-up clothes and sunglasses, she called herself "Mrs. Hooper." For two days, the daughter of the University's benefactor went about unrecognized, happily attending classes and eating in the cafeteria. When her identity was finally revealed, she fled the campus, returning to Washington, where she met Cromwell at the Shoreham Hotel.

Jimmy was busy scheduling meetings with politicians and generally making a nuisance of himself. He was supposedly working on a new banking bill to be introduced into the next session of Congress. He tried to see Marvin H. McIntyre, assistant secretary to the president, with no luck. Two weeks later, Cromwell wrote a rambling, eleven-page letter to President Franklin D. Roosevelt suggesting ways "to raise the standard of living of the great American working masses. May I assure you that unlike some others in our privileged class I fully appreciate your high ideals . . . ," Jimmy's letter concluded.

Roosevelt was of the opinion that the poor were not getting a fair break and that the Great Depression was a result of the sins of big business. Jimmy wholeheartedly agreed.

McIntyre enlisted New Deal Treasury Department legal advisor Herman Oliphant to draft a response. "The whole approach and concrete suggestions you make are interesting, although there would probably be a number of practical aspects that would present difficulties requiring careful consideration." Roosevelt signed the letter and suggested meeting with Cromwell to "talk over the whole matter."

In a confidential memo to McIntyre, Roosevelt ordered his men to humor Doris Duke's husband. He suggested Cromwell "have a good long talk with Governor Marriner Eccles. Tell Eccles to listen to all of his ideas and treat him very nicely even if he does not agree with him."

(Eccles was a non-conformist Utah banker who had been appointed Governor of the Federal Reserve Board by Roosevelt and would be a key figure in the 1939 Banking Act.)

Jimmy's only hope was to form a political base in New Jersey. Duke Farms would become his headquarters. Painters, carpenters, and decorators were called in by the Cromwells to remodel the mansion and that spring, they moved in.

On June 4, Doris threw a party at Duke Farms to celebrate Jimmy's thirty-ninth birthday. Guards stood at the four entrances to the estate and guests were required to show their invitations. Cars blocked the other driveways and Doris' Great Danes patrolled the grounds. Inside the mansion, guests (including Dorothy Mahana, the Joel Hubers from Philadelphia, Louise Atwill) were treated to a Hawaiian-inspired show, featuring hula dancers and singers. Table tennis, a movie theater, and a swimming pool where bathing suits of every size were provided kept the guests occupied.

At the end of August, Doris and Jimmy went to Newport where Nanaline hosted a dinner in their honor. Ned and Eva Stotesbury were said to be in Baden-Baden, taking the cure. Hawaii was the main topic of conversation. Doris had decided to purchase a four and one half acre plot of land for $100,000 in the residential section of Black Point near Diamond Head. It was considered one of the finest pieces of property on the island and had been owned by Honolulu businessman Ernest H. Wodehouse. (He had paid $16,000 for the land in 1900.)

Plans were announced for a palatial Persian-inspired home and building contracts were awarded to several Honolulu firms. Marion Sims Wyeth, of the firm Wyeth and King, was hired as the architect.

In the meantime, Jimmy took over more and more responsibility at Duke Farms, where the groundskeepers were told to see "Mr. Cromwell" for their orders. When Dr. Camuti, the veterinarian, sent his bill for $385 covering seven house calls and an X-ray for one of the Siamese cats, he received a curt letter from Elizabeth Knox, saying that a New York osteopath had come to Somerville, treated *both* Mr. and Mrs. Cromwell for $25 a visit. "A week later I received a letter from Cromwell himself which held little charm," Camuti said. Jimmy haggled over the bill, accusing the vet of overcharging Doris. Cromwell grudgingly paid $285. When Doris learned of the argument, she promptly sent a check for the extra $100.

More importantly, Jimmy convinced Doris to donate $50,000 to the Democratic campaign fund, money which would ensure an important political appointment by Roosevelt. Another contribution of $5,000 was made in the name of Elizabeth Knox to the local Democratic campaign. Jimmy began calling Roosevelt "the most charming person I think I ever met."

The day after the presidential election, Cromwell wrote to the White

House again, anxious to set up a meeting with Marriner Eccles.

"Doris and I still cannot believe it is true!" Jimmy said of Roosevelt's victory. The letter was in Cromwell's usual exuberant style.

Dear Mr. President and Mrs. Roosevelt. May we add our congratulations to the many thousands? We hope that the example of the tolerance and magnanimity which we so admire in you both, combined with the fate of stewing in the juice of their own vituperation, will serve to teach our compeers a new and much needed sense of responsibility towards their less fortunate fellow citizens and the welfare of the Nation. We are happy in the anticipation of the success of your efforts to achieve, in the next four years, "a more abundant life" for all the people, and we want you to know that we are always ready to aid you in this great task, to the best of our abilities . . . cordially yours, Doris & Jimmy.

Roosevelt replied: "Dear Doris and Jimmy. Thank you for that grand letter. It is heartening to know as I face these next four years that I can depend upon the understanding loyalty of friends like you."

But it wasn't Cromwell's loyalty the president needed; it was Doris' fortune. There were rumors that Jimmy would be appointed the next governor of Hawaii, but Cromwell already had his eye on a Senate seat.

That fall, the Cromwells entertained again in New York, throwing a dinner dance for 500 with the Sanfords. Mrs. Laddie Sanford gave a dinner beforehand at the Sanford townhouse on East Seventy-second Street. The wealthy Stephen "Laddie" Sanford was an international polo player and heir to a carpet fortune, who had married the former actress Mary Duncan and been dropped from the social register. Nevertheless, Mary Sanford became one of the leading members of Cafe Society in New York and Palm Beach.

"Doris' mother got her and me to give the party together," Mary Sanford recalled. "Nanaline wanted her to be more social and have more relationships. She didn't think Doris had much fun. She wanted her to get out more. But Doris didn't want to put the effort into it. She didn't care enough about people."

Hundreds of orchids and palm trees were brought from Somerville for the event. (Doris' hobby for developing rare orchids had gotten out of control. There were 5,000 plants of one species alone in the 14-room greenhouse which currently bulged with over 20,000 plants. It was said to be the largest private collection of orchids in the country. The ever-thrifty Doris began selling the surplus to Manhattan florists for a small profit.)

For the party, Mary and Doris agreed on the joint guest list with one exception: Doris refused to invite Mrs. William Randolph Hearst. While in California, Doris had become enamored with actress Marion Davies, Hearst's bubbly blonde mistress. Said Mary Sanford: "Mrs. Hearst was a friend of mine. She got quite upset about it. But Doris didn't give a damn."

Chapter Eight

Restless
Romancers

WHILE DORIS DISGUISED HER identity by traveling under the name of her secretary, Marian Paschal, photographers recognized her in the Los Angeles airport as she arrived that December enroute to Hawaii to oversee construction of her new home. In San Francisco, she was met by Sam Kahanamoku, and the two boarded the Japanese ship, the *Asama Maru*. Sam was Doris' age, and would become her closest advisor. She was anxious to return to the island, which publisher Roy Howard had dubbed the American Riviera. Young bluebloods were making Hawaii their playground of choice: railroad heir George Vanderbilt, tinplate heir Henry Topping, Pennsylvania steel magnate G. Barton Singer, Jr., and Fleischmann yeast heir Christian Holmes of California, whose wife was known as the society woman who paid off the mortgage on gossip columnist Maury Paul's country home.

The islanders welcomed the wealthy *malihinis* and viewed their reckless spending with amusement. Lavish cottages sprung up near Diamond Head, and the area became known as "Millionaire's Row." Vast numbers of Depression-era dollars were spent on private zoos, tropical gardens, aviaries, and glassed-in aquariums for walls. The Holmeses outdid them all by buying their own tiny island, Coconut Island, and erecting a pleasure palace.

What Doris had in mind was not a vacation home: it was a fortress. She and Jimmy named their soon-to-be-erected house Hale Kapu (Hale is house, Kapu means keep out). It was widely interpreted as Forbidden House, although further research shows the name may have come from its inspiration: the Persian home of Ali Kapu in Isfahan. Later, Doris dubbed the house Shangri-la, named for the mythical Himalayan kingdom where no one ever grows old, taken from one of her favorite movies, *Lost Horizon*.

Doris realized she would need special permits for the house she wanted. When her request for a swimming pool and seawall on the beach was refused by the Harbor Board of Honolulu, she threatened to sell the land and build a palace in Palm Beach instead. Over nine hundred cases of Delhi marble were sitting in crates on nearby docks as the squabble continued.

But Hawaii could not afford to lose the wealthy Doris Duke as a resident. Pressure was put on island officials to relent. Cromwell even enlisted Roosevelt to draft a letter of support. A compromise was reached: Doris purchased an additional one-third acre of land with a rock pool already on it.

In an uncharacteristic gesture, Doris invited the press to her rented home. She served cocktails and sat on the sofa while reporters fired a barrage of questions. She said she never would have built the house in Palm Beach, and held no grudge against the Harbor Board. "I certainly didn't mean to be asking for any special privilege," she said.

But privilege was Doris' birthright. While she may have disdained publicity, she enjoyed wielding the power her money afforded her. With her trademark smoked sunglasses and penchant for pseudonyms, she garnered more publicity than if she had merely gone about as other young women. But she was not like other women. An independent, headstrong girl of obscene wealth with exotic tastes, she embarked on a willful campaign to take—never be taken.

A week later, after sunny afternoons on the broad stretch of Waikiki Beach surfing with the Kahanamokus, her spirits were buoyed. She was considered one of the best female surfers on the island. Outside Hawaii, surfing was considered an oddball activity, not unlike logrolling or alligator wrestling. Heiresses on surfboards were eccentrics and Doris was about as eccentric as they came. She was also developing a somewhat split personality: on one hand she could be gregarious like her father. At other times, she was cold and aloof like her mother.

In her eagerness to please local officials, she paid a well-publicized visit to the ghetto areas behind the waterfront warehouses in Honolulu where local children were starving. "I don't believe there is the acute misery here that you will find, for instance, in crowded New York districts," she said. "But I intend to investigate conditions to see if I can offer any help to the fine work being done."

Society, Doris pronounced, "is definitely out."

This was not only a slap at Nanaline, but a defense of Barbara Hutton who had been dropped from the Social Register presumably for attracting too much notoriety. Hutton had renounced her American citizenship and was in the process of divorcing her second husband, Count Reventlow, with whom she had had a son, Lance. Doris' own husband was back in Palm Beach ostensibly finishing his book, *In Defense of Capitalism,* to be published by Simon & Schuster. Ironically, marrying an American was seen as such a patriotic gesture, but in reality Jimmy behaved with the same callowness foreign fortune hunters did when they snared young American heiresses. His behavior on the honeymoon, a trip he later categorized as "grotesque," was typical of that. In fact, prior to the wedding, he was romancing Ruth Treglown, a beautiful young woman who later wed public relations man Steve Hannagan. At Whitemarsh Hall one evening, he said to Ruth, "Listen honey, I'd give anything in the world if we could get married, but neither one of us has any money."

Not unlike royalty, the Cromwells led separate lives. They were seldom in the same city, and traveled constantly, covering 500,000 miles in the first two years of their marriage. The globetrotting was an opiate for their boredom and lack of companionship. Although Jimmy would have liked a family, Doris did not want a child. Still, in a perverse way they needed each other. Jimmy, of course, was politically ambitious and needed Doris' financial backing. The heiress needed a husband to protect her from cranks and unwelcome suitors and to give her a certain status as an independent woman. Besides, the dashing Jimmy Cromwell knew all the fascinating people. As a pair, they were much in demand. "Few couples in the world are more discussed today than the Cromwells," one columnist noted. "In fact, had it not been for the romance of the Duke and Duchess of Windsor, they probably would be better known than any other couple, with the possible exception of the Lindberghs."

Jimmy's extramarital affairs were well known. He was not discreet in his womanizing. "I had affairs with very attractive ladies," Cromwell said later. "Most were actresses. Doris knew, but she didn't care."

They spent the Christmas holidays apart. Jimmy, vacationing in Palm Beach, told reporters that the rumor of his being offered the job of governor general of Hawaii was just that—a rumor. "I have no desire to go into politics. The one thing I want to do now is get this book finished and to my publishers." Jimmy had hired Hugo Czerwonky, a young engineering graduate and writer to "co-author" the book. Hugo did much of the writing, as Jimmy was too busy enjoying the social scene at El Mirasol, soaking up the sun and Moet Chandon, entertaining Frank Murphy, governor-elect of Michigan. It left little time for his daughter, fourteen-year-old Christine Cromwell, who was staying across town with Anna Dodge.

Prodded by Eva to keep up appearances, Jimmy took the Clipper to Hawaii. He was met by Doris and Sam Kahanamoku at the Pan American base. By now, the twenty-five-year-old heiress was referring to her forty-year-old, rather pompous husband as "the Pope." They occupied separate bedrooms in the Hayward house—Doris on the first floor, Jimmy on the second.

In early March, the Cromwells returned to the mainland and drove straight to the San Simeon estate of, William Randolph Hearst, where they were joined by Laddie and Mary Sanford. "I spent a great deal of time there," Jimmy later said. "The old man was very fond of me."

Marion Davies, Hearst's mistress, had enlisted Mary and Doris as bridesmaids for the wedding of Mary Grace, the daughter of her cook, to the rather elderly editor of the *Hearst Evening Journal*, William Curley. The week before, a seamstress—sent by Marion—had shown up on the Santa Barbara tennis court where Mary was playing to take her measurements for the white organza bridesmaid dresses, provided by Hearst. Neither Mary nor Doris knew the bride. "There were so many odd things happening," Mary Sanford recalled. "If you thought it might be fun, you joined in. There was nothing else for us to do."

Marion, affectionately called "Daisy," adored celebrities and surrounded herself with amusing personalities. Unlike others who were tongue-tied in Doris' presence, Marion breached the distance by the sheer force of her personality. She also drank, smoked, and like Garbo and Dietrich, wore trousers. Doris found her the epitome of sophistication. Hearst had purchased Cosmopolitan Studios to make Marion a star, and as his mistress, she was considered rather scandalous, which made her all the more attractive to Doris. Dorothy Parker, spying Marion's dressing room at Metro, which resembled a small cathedral and was adorned with a statue of a virgin, penned the following:

Upon my honor, I saw a Madonna
sitting alone in a niche.
Above the door of the glamorous whore
of a prominent son of a bitch.

The walls of Hearst's museum-like Spanish castle, La Cuesta Encantada (the Enchanted Hill) were hung with seventeenth-century Flemish tapestries. In fact, San Simeon made Duke Farms look like a bungalow. There were 350,000 acres, and guests were likely to spot American buffalo, giraffes, zebras, camels, and ostriches roaming the grounds. Hearst's private zoo featured lions, tigers, panthers, and chimpanzees.

On one occasion, Hearst urgently telephoned an associate saying he had seen a picture of a castle in Scotland and he wanted it shipped, stone by stone, to California. Weeks went by. He called the associate back, asking if the castle had been bought. The man replied that it had not. "Why not?" bellowed the publisher. "Because," said the associate, "you already owned it when I called."

Jimmy had become intimate with the Hollywood set through his sister, Louise Atwill, and San Simeon was the place to mingle with the stars. On any given weekend you might run into Anita Loos, Elinor Glyn (responsible for crowning Clara Bow "the It Girl"), Charlie Chaplin, John Gilbert, Ben Hecht, Dorothy Parker, Joe Kennedy, Gloria Swanson, Gloria Morgan Vanderbilt, Sr. (whom Doris admired), Lloyd Pantages of the Los Angeles theater family, and Harry Crocker, who had befriended Doris before her marriage and was now employed as Hearst's private secretary. Jack Hearst, the publisher's son, was a crony of Cromwell's. No one was allowed to bring their own personal maid or valet to San Simeon—individual servants were assigned to guests once they arrived. Guests were told to assemble in the great hall twenty minutes before dinner for cocktails. Hearst forbade his guests to bring their own liquor, which led to massive smuggling of bootleg bottles.

"He never drank," said Mary Sanford. "And he never wanted anybody to drink, but he'd give us a little bit. I learned how to drink up there."

After the wedding weekend at San Simeon, Doris and Jimmy left. She returned to Hawaii while he flew East, prompting then-gossip columnist Ed Sullivan to report that the Cromwells had finally separated. Jimmy denied the report, and made plans to accompany Doris to the coronation of King George VI of Great Britain, perhaps the grandest royal spectacle of the twentieth century. As prominent socially inclined Americans, they were naturally on the guest list.

Jimmy was making no secret of his political aspirations, but the idea of Doris as a hostess in the nation's capital was ludicrous. That month, Jimmy hosted a dinner in New York for Manuel Quezon, president of the Philippines. It seemed Doris had developed an aversion to the ballroom and crammed eighty guests into the library, a room designed for five bridge tables. Doris sat on the floor.

That May, after signing a lease to rent the Hayward home in Hawaii later that year, they sailed for Europe, attending the May 12 coronation. "There was a marvelous parade," Cromwell said. "It was the last display of the might of the British Empire. It was just a spectacle to watch. We had seats adjoining the Royal Family." The coronation was followed by a dizzying round of parties and balls, culminating in the Queen's Ball at Buckingham Palace. Barbara Hutton was there. So was Alec Cunningham-Reid, the British playboy who was in the process of divorcing his first wife, Ruth Mary Clarisse. They had been separated for two years, and court hearings revealed that both were heavy gamblers and that Cunningham-Reid had regularly been drawing 20,000 pounds at a time from his wife's bank account.

Not only had Mrs. Cunningham-Reid paid for her own honeymoon, but Alec also withdrew 36,000 pounds to reimburse himself for money he spent on presents for his wife, including her trousseau. He claimed she was "bored by finance." He sat next to his mother during the divorce proceedings, stroking her hand, calling her "darling." After four days of hearings, he agreed to accept 100,000 pounds outright and a sum of 10,000 pounds a year for life. He also got the Mayfair house and their aptly named motor yacht, the *Lizard*.

The Cunningham-Reid divorce was a major scandal, and so filled with tales of lust and greed that the Communist Party put out a pamphlet decrying capitalism ("How The Rich Live") using examples from the divorce trial.

Cunningham-Reid was also investing in the film business with Douglas Fairbanks, Jr., who had just purchased the old Worton Hall Studios. With the promise of putting his wife's money into the venture he was put on the board, but did no work, according to Fairbanks. His political career was also showing signs of neglect. Since October 1936, it was revealed that he had voted in only 49 divisions out of a total of 431. Calls for his resignation went unheeded, and in the words of one insider, Cunningham-Reid "managed to fill the pockets of the people who wanted to oust him."

The handsome member of Parliament already had his eye on Doris Duke, and when they met again the attraction was mutual. Blinded by his charm, she dismissed warnings by friends that he was nothing but a cad and a fortune hunter.

Doris left London with Jimmy, first going to Paris, then Algiers where she shopped for treasures for her Hawaiian home. The Cromwells were then invited to Moscow as guests of Ambassador and Mrs. Joseph Davies. (She was Barbara Hutton's aunt, the former Marjorie Merriweather Post.) As the Nord express rolled toward Moscow, Jimmy anxiously wondered about the new paradise of the proletariat. At Negarole, on the Soviet frontier, they changed trains, climbing aboard one of the old Czarist sleepers. It was clean and comfortable and the porters were polite. The following day, June 10, a gleaming sedan waited at the Moscow train station to take them to their hotel. "They found me very interesting as Doris' husband," he recalled. "She signified everything they didn't approve of—great concentrations of wealth going from generation to generation."

At the time, the Stalinist regime was in the process of wiping out the aristocracy and the bourgeoisie. There were mass executions and reports of terrorism. Four days after their arrival, while Doris sat in a car, Jimmy began snapping pictures of government buildings. He was promptly arrested by a plainclothes detective and detained in the ancient-looking National Hotel for several hours before Ambassador Davies bailed him out. Said Jimmy, "Doris thought it was very amusing. She was laughing."

The Cromwells met briefly with Joseph Stalin. Jimmy gave the Soviet leader a copy of *In Defense of Capitalism*. "I said, 'I think you'll be interested in the opposing point of view and I know you are thoroughly familiar with us.' And he nodded. He knew all about it."

On their return to the States, Cromwell went to Washington and astonished the Agriculture Committee of the Senate by offering a three-point plan to save capitalism, which included his suggestion for negative interest. (The government, Jimmy said, should loan money to investors and pay them interest of six percent for the privilege.) One headline said "Senators Dazed By Plan." He was critical of Stalin, and denounced the fascist dictatorships in Italy and Germany. On August 5, Jimmy gave a speech to the Rotary Club of New York. Several days later, he met reporters in the Duke mansion to talk about his economic theories. "Some of us," he said, "have a larger income than we can spend. But what are we to do with it? We don't want to leave it lying idle in bank vaults."

Jimmy's idea was to spend it. "Doris told me, 'What do you want to make more money for? I've got too much now.'" He convinced his wife to donate $1 million to the Birth Control League and encouraged her to build a swimming pool on the Somerville estate for poor children, a plan which resulted in favorable press for the Cromwells, although the pool was never constructed. "Possessors of great fortunes like my wife or the Rockefellers should relinquish about one-third of them, but not for government uses," Cromwell told newsmen. "These sums should endow colleges, build orphanages, erect hospitals."

Meanwhile, Duke University began courting Jimmy, hoping to lure the lightweight economist to various seminars at the school and ultimately to interest his wife in parting with a portion of her fortune. Jimmy was also responsible for a sizeable donation to Princeton University. The purpose of the grant was to embark on a study of the state tax system.

Cromwell became known as a soft touch. He joined the Somerset Hospital board of trustees and established the unusual reputation of attending every meeting. The Raritan Savings Bank tapped him as a board member, and he rescued the Somerville Fourth of July celebration by financing the fireworks display. "This is Cromwell out at Duke Farms," became a familiar telephone salutation to needy groups. He provided the Somerville Rescue Squad with badly needed equipment and became an honorary member of the Hillsborough Fire Company.

While Jimmy took his daughter Christine to Hawaii for a brief visit, Doris stayed behind in Somerville. A week later, she narrowly escaped a freak accident at Newark Airport when the car in which she and Marion Paschall were riding was nearly hit by an airplane landing on the field. According to the chauffeur, the swooping plane came within two feet of the car. Doris, in the backseat, screamed hysterically.

In traveling to meet Jimmy in Hawaii, Doris boarded the Philippine Clipper in Alameda, one of twelve passengers. Flying was then considered a reckless form of travel. Not many brave souls took to the skies, and those who did had their names duly printed in the newspaper. Doris became one of the first female passengers to fly the huge Clippers across the Pacific. The trip from California took twenty-two and one half hours, and passengers were provided with dining tables, set with fine linen and china, as well as beds.

When she arrived, Jimmy greeted her with a present of a custom-built

Packard convertible. On the dash board of the huge black car was a plaque with the inscription: "Bring 'Em Back Alive."

Jimmy told Doris they needed a yacht. She agreed. He commissioned Westlawn Associates to design a 58-foot cruising pleasure craft, outfitted with every known safety and comfort feature. Named the *Kailani Lahi Lahi,* the boat would be used to cruise the islands and also meet incoming steamers to take guests to their estate. ("Lahi Lahi" was the Hawaiian name given to Doris by Duke Kahanamoku. Loosely translated, it meant "soft as the wind.") The sleek tan and cream colored yacht, gleaming with teak and chrome, was outfitted with a pair of 250 horsepower Scripps motors at a total cost of over $50,000, making it the most expensive boat of its size ever built. The yacht was launched on September 8 at the Consolidated Shipbuilding Corporation in the Bronx. Displaying the blue and white pennant of the New York Yacht Club, the super craft slipped into the Harlem River while onlookers toasted with champagne. But suddenly the cheering stopped. Ten feet from shore, the boat became mired in the silt and the ceremony came to an abrupt end amid disappointed boos from the crowd. Hours later, it was finally towed loose. The sight of the gleaming, expensive yacht stuck in the mud was a fitting metaphor for the Cromwells' marriage.

A month later, Doris and Jimmy returned from Honolulu leaving Christine behind. The girl had formed a tentative friendship with her celebrated stepmother. "She was very fond of Doris and Doris of her," said Cromwell. "Doris felt Christine was a fellow sufferer." Like Doris and Nanaline, Christine and Delphine fought endlessly. The young girl also found her globetrotting father remote and uncaring. "My relationship with Christine was always disappointing to me. She was awfully lazy and not a bit bright. She never felt I loved her, which was true," Cromwell later admitted. Doris and Jimmy enrolled Christine in the Punahou School and announced plans to "commute" between New Jersey and Hawaii.

That fall, Doris wore a bright red dinner dress and diamond bracelets to Mrs. Vincent Astor's party for the Musicians Emergency Fund at the St. Regis Hotel. Attended by Vanderbilts, Whitneys, and Roosevelt cousins, the white-tie event marked her first appearance of the 1937–38 social season. She even entered the fox trot contest, while Jimmy sat brooding at a ringside table.

Despite Doris' $50,000 donation to Roosevelt, Cromwell's political career was stalled. The campaign contribution "pleased the President no end and impressed him and was very impressive to me. I think it showed that Doris was going to use her fortune to help me," Cromwell said, growing impatient for results. On October 16, on Duke Farms stationery, he wrote to Roosevelt's secretary, Marvin McIntyre. "I should like to have 10 or perhaps 15 minutes of his time in order to point out certain errors in his recent fireside chat which, in my opinion have laid him wide open to attack from his opponents. Naturally, I am in no roaring rush but I do feel that the sooner the President could see me the better it would be for those of us who remain his friends and admirers . . . Doris would like to come along with me as she still has a mighty big yen for the Boss."

FDR sent word he would see the Cromwells.

"He invited us down to the White House. And we had cocktails with him. He was very pleasant, and Doris took a great liking to him," Jimmy recalled.

A week later, Cromwell appeared at the Poor Richard Club in Philadelphia accompanied by his mother, Eva Stotesbury, who also addressed the group, saying she knew very little of finance. "The best and only profitable transaction I ever completed was to marry my dear husband." Ned Stotesbury, sitting in the front row, laughed and nodded. Doris was noticeably absent.

In November, Governor-elect A. Harry Moore announced that Jimmy was one of five persons being considered as his successor in the United States Senate. (Jimmy had convinced Doris to contribute $5,000 to Moore's gubernatorial campaign.)

The press pursued the story, but insiders knew the truth: Cromwell would be strung along merely to drain the Duke coffers. Jimmy openly courted Moore and Mayor Frank Hague of Jersey City, a roughhewn arrogant politico who turned to Moore at his first Somerville visit and growled, "Boy, what a place for a clambake."

The Hague Machine was considered the country's most corrupt. Graft was rampant and nowhere in the country was a political ring more blatant in its defiance of law and order than in New Jersey. A former janitor, Hague was first elected mayor of Jersey City in 1918 and was the undisputed boss of the state. He didn't particularly like Roosevelt and hated the pinkos and reds.

That November, Doris inherited the next chunk of her legacy, estimated at $10 to $18 million. Jimmy, acting as his wife's spokesman, told reporters, "Yes, she knows it's a lot of money but she is kind of young yet to decide what she is going to do with it."

The night before her birthday, while workmen put the final touches on the $1 million "Shangri-la," Jimmy was heard on the radio saying "wealthy persons are no longer building magnificent palaces or accumulating fortunes to leave monuments of themselves in the form of endowments to universities, but prefer to use the money and our best efforts to bring a greater measure of comfort, decency and security into the lives of our less fortunate fellow citizens."

Jimmy then ordered Doris to accompany Eleanor Roosevelt to a West Virginia homestead to visit 500 refugee miners. She reluctantly agreed. They motored in a White House car from Washington through the countryside. Doris, accompanied by Marian Paschal, donned a full-length Russian mink coat and English walking shoes to visit the Tygart Valley Co-Operative and wound up signing autographs for the poor children who thought she was a movie star. In a statement which would later be echoed by President John F. Kennedy, Mrs. Roosevelt told the miners, "I'm not interested in what I am doing for you, but in what you are doing for yourselves." The unfortunate workers were awed by the sight of the First Lady and the twenty-five-year-old heiress driving past their dilapidated shacks.

That night they were scheduled to attend a square dance. While the energetic First Lady joined in the dancing, Doris sulked in the corner, declining all requests. "It's been a hard day," she complained. "And after all, this is the first time I've ever seen a square dance."

The following day, they drove to Pennsylvania to inspect another homestead project where their car got stuck in the mud. Doris, supremely bored by the whole trip, didn't say a word. By now, the First Lady and Doris weren't speaking to one another. That afternoon, Doris boarded an airplane for Newark while Eleanor Roosevelt took the train to New York.

The trip was a disaster. Rather than lend credence to Cromwell's interest in public service, it only confirmed Roosevelt's suspicion that they were both dilettantes. After all, wearing a full-length mink coat to greet the poor was considered in poor taste by Eleanor Roosevelt, who found Doris lacking in maturity, if not in sensitivity.

Cromwell's name was immediately dropped from consideration for the New Jersey Senate seat, which went to Frank Hague's right hand man.

Months later, the First Lady confirmed that the much publicized trip had been a failure. She thought that Doris, while a good sport, was a spoiled young woman who did not have the slightest understanding needed to appreciate people born out of her surroundings. "I did not invite her to accompany me," the First Lady said in a moment of candor. "I was asked to do so. I believe her husband was very anxious to have her go . . . She saw everything that met the eye, but what the things she saw meant to her in the way of human need is a question I cannot answer . . . I honestly don't know how much of what she saw meant anything to her." While Mrs. Roosevelt had left one impoverished home with a heavy heart, she could see it failed to impress Doris, a spoiled, sheltered woman who had no time for politics.

Immediately after the trip, Doris showed up at the Cotton Club for an evening of revelry. There, she met dancer "Bojangles" Bill Robinson. Doris told him her secret ambition was to be able to dance like him, and asked to be given lessons every afternoon at 1 P.M. That week, her Duesenberg towncar pulled to the club at Broadway and Forty-eighth Street. The front and back doors of the building were locked while the heiress was inside. Not even delivery men were admitted. That was Doris' dictum.

Taking her hand, Robinson would lead her through the steps for two hours each day. Lessons from the well-known dancer were quite a coup, and he had previously consented to coach only Eleanor Powell, Fred Astaire, and Shirley Temple. What Doris lacked in natural talent, she made up for in enthusiasm. Robinson hoped to continue the lessons, although Doris abruptly ended them when the press learned of the arrangement. She had actually mastered the Suzy Q, Truckin', and several other Cotton Club routines. The dancing lessons made headlines: HEIRESS OFF TO BUFFALO and WEALTHIEST GIRL GETS LESSONS IN HOOFING FROM NEGRO DANCER.

Doris was revelling in her independence. She and Marian boarded the *Bremen* in early 1938, first stopping in Paris for a brief rendezvous with Alec Cunningham-Reid and then on to Persia, Damascus, and Egypt. Doris and Alec were already the subject of international gossip. It seemed that at a recent Palm Beach party, Doris and the Member of Parliament disappeared together for several hours. The brief encounter had culminated with a quick sexual liaison, and Doris was by now infatuated with "Bobbie."

Jimmy stayed in Washington, where he testified before the House Ways and Means Committee, suggesting that the present tax system be junked. He wanted to help less fortunate citizens by doing away with individual and corporate income tax, and revising estate and gift taxes.

"Everytime something like this is proposed, they say it is in the interest of somebody else," one congressman said.

Cromwell also produced a short film, *Of Men and Money,* and continued pestering Roosevelt, wanting to screen it for him. He talked of buying his own newspaper. "I don't think they took him too seriously," said Hope Ridings Miller, then a Washington society editor. "People liked him, but I don't think people had a great deal of respect for him."

Early in March, he left on the *Rex* to join Doris in Cairo. The group later chartered a plane and flew to Turkey, Iraq, and Greece. The press dubbed the Cromwells "The Restless Romancers."

That spring, Jimmy's world would change drastically. Reputed to be the heir to the famous Stotesbury fortune, Jimmy was cut out of his stepfather's will after Stotesbury died at the age of ninety. The Dukes were stunned. Stotesbury left his estate to ten heirs, including the children of his first wife. Eva was bequeathed only a small portion of her husband's mythical estate, which had steadily eroded in the last years. Estimated at $75 million at the time of his death, the estate turned out to be a fraction of that, less than $9 million. (Three years later, after inheritance taxes, the estate had shrunk to $4 million.) The Stotesburys had, in record time, managed to go through one of the largest American fortunes ever amassed.

The will left $1,000 to the chauffeur and $2,500 to butler Henry Sprague, who was immediately hired by Jimmy to work at Duke Farms. The other servants were let go. Whitemarsh Hall was closed, as was El Mirasol and the Bar Harbor house, Wingwood. Eva began selling off most of their property. Their $100,000 yacht, the *Nedeva*, was sold for a fraction of its value. A $6,500 car was sold at auction for $290. The Stotesbury sculpture collection was donated to the Philadelphia Museum of Art, and Eva moved to Washington, where her friend Anna Dodge allowed her to live in her spacious Foxhall Road home, rent free. Anna, at Jimmy's request, also loaned Eva money. Despite her circumstances, Eva put on a brave front and few realized she was broke. Her last hope was Jimmy's career. She began giving parties and her son was heavily promoted.

"She wanted me to be a Senator and thought I would have a very good career," said Cromwell.

Jimmy—at forty—was losing his hair and good looks. He decided to have a face-lift, the first of several. The work was done by Gloria Bristol in New York. Both Cromwells were patients of Gloria Bristol Limited "skin specialists" at 745 Fifth Avenue. When reporters learned of the procedure, Gloria insisted that she had only done a "face peel" to remove bags under the eyes.

As a temporary salve, Governor Moore appointed Cromwell to the New Jersey Commission on Tax Law Revision. Doris was appointed to the board of the State Department of Institutions and Agencies.

Doris initially approached the position with enthusiasm, visiting four institutions the first day. Although it was a non-salaried position, it was the first job she had ever held in her life.

But the attraction didn't last long. Lured by the glamour of Marion Davies and Cobina Wright, Doris became increasingly fascinated with Hollywood. She was approached by Edgar Selwyn and given a screen test at MGM. (That spring, her friend Liz Whitney had tested for the role of Scarlett O'Hara in the upcoming *Gone With The Wind*, a film whose major financial backer happened to be Liz's husband, John Hay "Jock" Whitney.)

Although not classically beautiful, Doris—"The Duchess of Somerville," as she was often referred to—had a sleek, angular body which epitomized the chic 1930s look, although her height would have been a liability.

Doris was serious about a career in Hollywood. She called Warner Brothers photographer George Hurrell, who was known to take stunning black-and-white head shots of movie queens.

"She came down from Santa Barbara. I thought she was a very charming girl, although not too sophisticated. She was a strong-willed gal, but very gentle. She had on a black dress. It was all dirty, as if she had been playing with her dogs. I thought to myself, 'You certainly are an old shoe, even if you are rich.' She wanted to be glamorous. I shot her at Warner Brothers Studio. I had to do it on a Saturday. She must have wanted it badly."

Hurrell said her chances of becoming an actress were slim. "She was much too stiff before a camera."

Doris became a frequent visitor at the beachhouse owned by Marion Davies and rented by Douglas Fairbanks, Jr., David Niven (a close friend of Barbara Hutton's), Roland Young, and Robert Benchley. The tenants had jokingly named the house Cirrhosis-by-the-Sea. Errol Flynn was a frequent guest, and Doris was attracted by his impudent charm and the fact that he was so unabashed about his spending habits. "My difficulty," he once said, "is trying to reconcile my gross habits with my net income."

Doris and Errol became an item for a short time, and their affair ended with a mutual affection. Flynn liked to tease Doris about her wealth and rivalry for "poor little rich girl" title with Barbara Hutton. On one occasion, he walked into her dining room, spied a garish chandelier and said, "Doris, what are you doing with one of Barbara's earrings?"

Her foray into Hollywood was evidence that Doris Duke—up to now a prisoner of her fortune—was breaking out. While her husband was growing more serious, she was growing more frivolous. As one columnist wondered, "His playboy days are over: are Doris's about to begin?"

"Shangri-la", the Cromwell estate, made news as the first private home on Hawaii to cost $1 million. More than 150 men worked for over a year before the house was completed, excavating four and a half acres of black lava on the promontory known as Kaalawai. Cromwell jokingly called it the DDWA: Doris Duke Works Administration.

"It was a production beyond belief," said Leonard Stanley, who as a boy watched the construction. "It reminded me of the building of the Pyramids, with native boys carrying buckets of water to the workers." Warehouses, overseers' shacks, kitchens, and restrooms sprung up with a sentry stationed at the top of the road barring the curious. The excavation site was said to be large enough to hold the entire city hall.

The rigs and scaffolding could be spotted from miles out at sea. "It's like the palace of a vagabond king at the crossroads of the world," one reporter said. "In wandering around the world, the famous couple brought Chinese granite for the courtyard, marble from India, cement from Japan, with coral slabs from Hawaii."

"It was," said Stanley, "like Ali Baba and the Forty Thieves."

Doris herself described the house later in a magazine article. "The idea of building a Near Eastern house in Honolulu must seem fantastic to many. But precisely at the time I fell in love with Hawaii and decided I could never live anywhere else, a Mogul-inspired bedroom and bathroom planned for another house was being completed for me in India so there was nothing to do but have it shipped to Hawaii and build a house around it."

The driveway was white crushed coral, surrounded by an emerald lawn and immaculate palm trees. Doris also insisted on a coconut grove, but was too impatient for them to grow. She arranged to purchase an entire fully grown coconut grove near the heart of the city and had it transplanted, tree by tree.

Two immense stone camels guarded the entrance. There were enormous grills with stained-glass sections through which light filtered like a jewel, throwing off hues of shimmering lavender, pink, and green. The living room featured a 21-foot glass door controlled by electricity, an eleventh-century Moorish mantelpiece once owned by William Randolph Hearst, and a transverse oak floor brought piece by piece from a sixteenth-century French chateau. Doris' bedroom had a stream running through it and was set between her own private garden and a larger tropical garden, built around a lily pond.

Like a true Oriental princess, she would have her own aviary amid the terraced gardens, ponds, and fountains.

The bathrooms were fitted with priceless jade and white marble and special fish fountains. "The largest room in the house was her bathroom," one friend recalled. "She said she's always lived with big bedrooms and small bathrooms and she wanted a house with big bathrooms and small bedrooms."

The music room was supplied with several thousand gramophone records kept in air-conditioned vaults. The 100-foot swimming pool boasted a $35,000 hydraulic lift diving board. "She was a good swimmer," said Cromwell, "better than me. And she was brave. A good diver. She realized she was an awkward type of girl. She tried very hard to take lessons of all kinds that would improve her grace and posture. That was one of her most admirable features. She always tried to improve herself."

She began taking diving lessons from local "water clown" Johnny Gomez, who would become an employee and a confidant. There were lockers filled with surfboards, canoes, and outriggers. Plus tennis courts and a real soda fountain. The dining room had aquarium walls: fish floated by seemingly suspended in midair.

A guest room for Christine was fashioned entirely from an Indian temple: it was cold and massive and architecturally correct.

The grounds were lavishly landscaped and a caretaker's house was built for David Kahanamoku and his wife, who would work on the estate. Florence Hayward helped decorate Shangri-la, filled with priceless antiques and artifacts.

"The house was quite a thing in those days," said Betty McIntosh, a former reporter. "The living room looked out over the ocean. The furniture was modern—slabs of wood with fishnet. There was a stream that went through the house with sand and it went through her bedroom. There was also a little library, maybe a couple of shelves with very simple things—*Alice in Wonderland*. Stuff like that."

Amid the outrageous spending were reports of her picayune sense of thrift. When the house opened in 1938, Doris had purchased an antique lamp from Florence Hayward for her bedroom. Doris tired of it, and four years later, while lunching, said she wanted to return the lamp. "Why don't you take it back and give me a credit?" she cooly suggested.

One evening, she called the Hayward house and asked to speak to Florence. Doris had not been told that Florence's husband had just died. The person taking the call said Mrs. Hayward couldn't speak to anyone.

"This is Doris Duke," the heiress said sternly. "I want to speak to Mrs. Hayward immediately." It was then explained that Mr. Hayward had just passed away. Doris was insistent. "I'm sorry about that, but if you don't put her on the phone immediately, I'm going to cancel every single order I have with her."

She also became enamored of the Haywards' housekeeper, Louisa Jackson, and made her an offer she couldn't refuse. Louisa had been a second mother to Florence's daughter Ann, but left to work for Doris at Shangri-la. "Doris fell in love with her and wanted her to manage the estate," Ann Hayward Rayburn said. "Doris told Louisa, for the rest of your life, you will have no worries."

Whatever Doris wanted, she got.

Said Cromwell: "I don't think money ever worried her at all. For example, I suggested building a breakwater and making a little harbor and it would cost $250,000. I thought that was an awful lot of money. She said, 'Well we need it and I've got it. I'll just wire the foundation to send the money.' And that's what happened."

Construction of the breakwater, seawall, and swimming pool was temporarily halted by the Harbor Board after it was learned that the Cromwells had failed to apply for a permit. By that time, however, the construction was ninety percent completed (including the building up of a natural lava dike). Doris built a right of way so the public would still have access to her beach.

The Cromwells then went shopping for a ranch. They sailed the islands on their yacht, looking for several hundred acres to farm in an experimental agriculture project. They finally found a plot and Doris began growing her own vegetables.

She also was anxious to get to England to see Cunningham-Reid. Under the guise of another shopping trip, she boarded the *Queen Mary* and returned to Europe. "It seems almost incredible that there can be a square inch of space left in the comparatively small house for another bit of bric-a-brac, after the months and months Doris has spent scouring Europe and the Far East for furnishings and knickknacks," gossip writer Nancy Randolph observed. By now, her methods were well known. "There is no record of anyone's ever outdriving a bargain with the very rich Mrs. James H. R. Cromwell."

"She was a real miser in the sense that she was convinced that shopkeepers raised their prices when they heard her name," said fashion publicist Eleanor Lambert. "She splurged on antiques. And she had fabulous taste." She also took advantage of those who had fallen on hard times.

That fall, she bought a complete set of Queen Anne silver from a former well-to-do Park Avenue man who had gone bankrupt.

Few took advantage of Doris. "She didn't like being 'stuck' just because she was rich," said Cromwell. "She resented that. She was very guarded about being stuck for a higher price than would be normal."

"We were shopping on Madison Avenue," said Lambert. "As we walked into a store she said, 'Be sure not to mention my name in any of the shops.' I asked why. She said, 'Because they'll raise the prices.' I said that the prices are right on the tags in all of the places we're going. 'Oh no,' she said. 'They'll want to charge me more.' It was a fixation."

Doris began hoarding her treasures. Lambert said she and Doris used to frequent the same antiques dealer. "He had a shop way over on Third Avenue in the old antique district. He had the most wonderful things, all piled up. He was selling the most wonderful bed. It was absolutely enchanting. It had a canopy of Chippendale scrolls and a beautiful carved monkey on top. I was absolutely mad about this piece and I think he wanted $340. So a few days later I had scraped the money together and called him. He said he was sorry, but that he had sold it for a better price to a collector. He said it was Doris Duke." Years later, Lambert asked Duke about the bed, saying it had broken her heart when it was sold. She described it in detail, asking Doris where it was. The heiress gave Lambert a blank look and sighed. "Oh I don't know. It's in a warehouse somewhere."

Her whims were also well known. Doris was paying $10,000 in insurance and maintenance to a Somerville, New Jersey, garage where her father's 1910 Peerless was stored. She used it twice a year to ride around the estate. "We never know when she will use it," the garage owner said, "so we wash it every day."

Meanwhile, she was becoming friendlier with decorators, artists and jazz musicians while Jimmy courted Frank Hague and the local politicos. Jack Monroe, a homosexual musician, was one of many amusing characters Doris surrounded herself with. She was attracted to gays, for their style and artistic talents. "A lot of them seemed to have that tendency," said Lambert. "They didn't fawn over her. And they were not very demanding."

Monroe was often asked to come down to Somerville from New York to play at the house. "She invited me down to her place in New Jersey," he said. "She played the piano and loved to hear me play the piano. When I first went down there, Jimmy was there, although he was fading out of the picture."

Chapter Nine

∽∾∽

Lahi Lahi

∽∾∽

BY NOW, it was common knowledge among the social set in Honolulu that Doris Duke and the great swimming champion Duke Kahanamoku were an item. With his jet black hair, full lips, and lean six-three body, he was a striking figure and the biggest celebrity on the island. Doris was enchanted with him. That the story never got out is a testament to just how isolated the American territory was before the jet age. But among the well-to-do families on the island, Doris and Duke were a scandal.

"We were invited to go to Hawaii on a statehood mission," said Eleanor Davies Tydings, the wife of Senator Millard Tydings of Maryland, chairman of the Statehood Committee. They were given a party in Honolulu by Princess Liliuokalani, one of the remaining members of the deposed royal family. "The princess was beautiful and just enormous. She was witty and fascinating. She gave a party for us and anybody who was anybody was there." Doris was not invited. "She wasn't there then. She had left. Been run out. She was living with the great swimmer Duke Kahanamoku and the scandal was he was black. The princess was just horrified. Shocked. She thought Doris was the pits. And so did all the other people. In those days, you didn't pal around with black men. When she was with him, she never saw anybody. And nobody wanted to have anything to do with her."

Even then, Shangri-la was well guarded. Said Eleanor, "Nobody ever went in and nobody ever came out. She was there with Duke and that was it."

Doris did emerge briefly one day to win first prize in the Pualini Topping outrigger race. Her partner was Sam Kahanamoku, Duke's younger brother. The two paddled 200 yards, ending at the Royal Hawaiian Hotel. Doris arrived at the race on her yacht, and swam to the starting place. Immediately after the race, she swam back to the yacht and headed home.

Her sense of isolation, rooted in her lonely childhood and dysfunctional relationship with her mother, deepened. Money became her only security. As James A. Knight wrote in *For the Love of Money*, "Even if he possesses wealth, the penny pincher dreads having it known. He is obsessed by the fear of being robbed or envied and becomes compulsively secretive and miserly."

In truth, Doris had no conception of love or money. She lived in her own world, governed by ever increasing demands for privacy. She was suspicious of everyone. "The compulsive nonspender forms poor relationships with other people," Knight observed, "probably because he unconsciously fears that they will deprive him of his money. The descending scale of warmth, scope and frequency of human contacts starts with the conservative spender and ends with the miser, who is often hermit-like."

Her sense of "thrift," something of a religion for Nanaline, was ingrained. Now, it was up to Doris to "protect" her father's fortune. Deprived of his companionship at such a tender age, the "disturbed relationship" distorted her perception of both money and men. She became adept at dangling money in front of them and then withdrawing the offer. Deeply conflicted over the issue, she was capable of splurging thousands on a Persian rug which her dogs would urinate on while chastising an underling for putting too much postage on a letter.

That March, freelance photographer Martin Munkacsi went to Hawaii to shoot the million-dollar pleasure palace Shangri-la for *Life* magazine. Amid the priceless splendor, Munkacsi captured the sun-burnished couple. Afterward, Doris visited the well-known photographer in his Tudor City studio in New York. "I remember Doris coming to the studio," recalled his wife, Helen Munkacsi Sinclair, who was then the photographer's assistant. "She wanted a camera wholesale."

No one was more aware of Doris' pathological fear of parting with money than Duke University. Requests had been made for funding with no success. Doris did agree, however, to attend their centennial ceremony in the spring of 1939. On the eve of the trip, Doris spent a few days in

Manhattan, enjoying the nightlife. She showed up at Fefe's Monte Carlo with the Duke of Sutherland. Decked out in large circular diamond earrings, she stayed at the club until 1:30 in the morning and ran into Barbara Hutton. The two were not speaking. Doris made no secret of her contempt for Barbara's compulsive spending and insatiable need for publicity. It made Doris livid when people compared the two, often lumping them together as the pathetic poor little rich girls. "Mrs. Cromwell and the countess were separated by one table; once or twice the countess turned her large warm blue eyes on Mrs. Cromwell," one columnist reported. "The Duke heiress, however, just sat with her slant eyes concentrated on her plate and it was difficult to tell if she took a little peek at the countess."

Most people knew that Doris' marriage was a sham. The gossip about their estrangement was so persistent, Eva Stotesbury was forced to make a formal announcement: "I would like at this time to publicly contradict the foolish rumors that Jimmy and Doris are not happy," the dowager told reporters. "They are divinely happy."

The truth was evident to all who witnessed the Cromwells' trip to Durham that June. Doris and Jimmy bickered openly. She was impatient to leave. Durham at that time was dry, and there was nowhere to get a drink. The Cromwells left before the end of the three-day celebration. Afterwards, President Few wrote to Doris and hinted at his disappointment in her behavior. He implored her to visit the campus again and to bring any friends, if she wanted. "I wish that you might take [your father's] place in sharing with us the satisfactions that have come, and more and more I think will come, out of what he has done here for the good of mankind."

Doris did agree to donate her father's desk to the university, and loaned them portraits of Washington and Ben Duke, but she had no intention of carrying on the altruistic tradition of the family. In fact, it would be ten years before Doris Duke would again set foot on the campus bearing her family's name.

Cromwell had his own agenda. In a meeting with political boss Frank Hague, Jimmy promised to come up with $300,000 of Doris' money in exchange for the senatorial nomination.

Chip Robert, the smooth-talking Democratic National chairman and his beautiful, blonde, sharp-tongued wife Evie began courting the Cromwells. (Evie even went so far as to name Doris godmother to her baby, Alice. Doris never laid eyes on the child, who lived in a house with a nanny while the Roberts lived in a suite at the Mayflower Hotel.)

"Evie was a glutton for publicity. She wanted to be talked about," recalled

Eleanor Tydings. Naturally, Evie flaunted her burgeoning friendship with Doris Duke. But the heiress had no intention of becoming the wife of a Senator.

Eleanor Tydings recalled meeting Doris at the home of Evie's mother, Mrs. Howard Walker. "The Walkers were giving a big brawl in a big house way out on Massachusetts Avenue. I went to the ladies' room and saw Jackie Martin and Doris. Jackie was a photographer. She was a lovely girl and everyone loved her. Doris was giving Jackie hell because Jackie was hired to be there to take photographs of the guests. Jackie was a gentle, well-born girl, much better born than Duke. I walked in and heard this harangue. Doris was bawling out this poor child until she was almost in tears, she was calling her a cheap little slut who had no business taking her photograph. 'What the hell was she doing there anyway?' She called her everything in the book. I never heard anything like it. I interrupted and said, 'That will do from you, Doris Duke. You can just shut up now. You can't talk to this girl like that. She was asked to be here and she's earning her living. You've never been able to earn a nickel in your life.' I gave her hell with a capital H and she shut up. She was a big, tall girl, but I wasn't afraid."

That June, Jimmy threw himself a birthday party at Somerville complete with fireworks and a dance band, while police with riot sticks kept gate crashers at bay. Even the invited guests had a hard time finding their way up the mile-long drive. Actress Gloria Swanson, a friend of Jimmy's, drove past the mansion and out another gate before a motorcycle officer was assigned to escort the movie star to the house.

Doris was more aloof than usual and left for Hawaii several weeks later. Jane Dunn, a nurse who was working at Queen's Hospital that summer, recalled the heiress being admitted under a cloak of secrecy. "It was a very private thing, very hush hush," said Dunn. "She came in and took a private room on the gynecological ward. She wasn't on the maternity floor. We all felt sympathetic. She just retreated into this room and that was that. She had all private nurses, no hospital help was involved. What was unusual about it was that it was so hush hush."

Dunn said Doris' reputation was that of a rather loose young woman with a preference for Hawaiian men. "It was common knowledge. She went with beach boys. People talked about it."

Later that summer, Doris was scheduled to go abroad with Jimmy. She and Marian Paschal booked passage on a liner and traveled together. Jimmy met them in London. Alec Cunningham-Reid had just divorced his wife hoping to make Doris Duke his next lawfully wedded bank account.

There was a brief detour to Scotland for a grouse hunting trip with the Sanfords. Doris and Marian spent most of the time in their room. Mary Sanford recalled: "She had this close relationship with Marian. They liked to stay inside a lot and order in great things of food. They led a very close life together."

Jimmy went to the Netherlands to visit the exiled Kaiser Wilhelm II and was there the night Hitler invaded Poland. "I said to the Kaiser, 'This is a completely untried army. It will take them six months to get to Warsaw.' The old man snorted. He said, 'The German army still has my general staff and that is the best general staff in the world. We'll be in Warsaw in six weeks.'"

Cromwell left the dinner table. "It was after 2 A.M. I paced the floor and thought, 'God, how I wish I could get this piece of news to the President.'" He quickly called the Belgian ambassador and made plans to leave Europe now that war had broken out.

He met Doris and Marian in Deauville and they drove hurriedly to Italy. At the border, they had to abandon their car and fourteen pieces of luggage. Left with one bag and a gas mask each, the three made their way to Genoa to board the Italian liner *Rex* two minutes before it sailed. They paid $2,000 for a two-room suite with a bath, twice the normal rate. Doris and Marian shared a room together.

Back in Washington, Jimmy went to the White House where he first met advisor and lawyer Tommy "the Cork" Corcoran. "When we walked in, Roosevelt said, 'Here comes super spy.' So everybody laughed. I mean, how in the world could you get information like that? What was I doing with Kaiser Wilhelm the night the war broke out? I mean, who would ever suspect that the husband of Doris Duke would be a Roosevelt spy?"

The Cromwells threw two lavish parties in rapid succession. The first was a birthday party for Peggy Anne Huber, the daughter of Jimmy's friend Joel Huber from Philadelphia. Peggy was Christine Cromwell's best friend.

Doris saw to every detail of the party, held on the roof of the Bellevue Stratford Hotel. A roadside hamburger stand and a black woman dressed as a "Mammy" behind the grill lent the Depression-era bash a certain plebian touch. Doris wanted to show Nanaline and Eva that she too was a hostess in her own right.

Peggy Anne had been in a car accident several weeks earlier on her way home from a Princeton football game and Doris had invited her to recuperate at Somerville. "She was very kind," Huber recalled. "I remember she had a lot of records. There were also Hawaiian people playing music. Whenever

I rang a bell, a servant would arrive. She never had any men servants, only women. Doris always wore slacks a lot, and in those days, women didn't."

To save money on bobby pins, Doris rolled her hair up in toilet paper, Peggy Anne recalled.

Buoyed by her newfound talent for entertaining, Doris threw herself a birthday party at the Manhattan mansion. It was the first large celebration in years at the house, and workers scurried about for days covering the grand staircase with white asters and chrysanthemums.

More than 500 invited guests and 200 gate crashers elbowed through the vast iron doors. It was an eclectic group: tart-tongued actress Tallulah Bankhead, comedian Georgie Jessel, Mrs. Cornelius Vanderbilt, Liz Whitney, Barbara Hutton (with rumored fiancé Bobby Sweeny), Condé Nast (who had hosted a dinner earlier for the Cromwells at his Park Avenue home), Jack Hemingway, Clare Boothe Luce (who Jimmy had a brief fling with before her marriage to Henry Luce), Brenda Frazier with Peter Arno and Shipwreck Kelly, Mona Williams, Betty Furness, Mimi Topping, Frank Murphy (now Attorney General), Postmaster General and Mrs. James Farley, and Gertrude Lawrence.

As a birthday present, Jimmy hired Bill "Bojangles" Robinson to dance for the guests. Cromwell tried to get Doris to join in but she refused, preferring to watch, a regal blonde in her gold and white grecian-inspired gown.

Bars were set up in the wide hallway and it was so crowded people could hardly pass. Nanaline hired a special electrician to stand guard in the basement, making sure the electrical system was not overloaded by the lights.

The party was a smash, said to outshine Brenda Frazier's debut, and Doris' unorthodox menu of corned beef hash and hamburgers earned her comparisons to Elsa Maxwell and her champagne-dispensing cow, not to mention Lady Mendl's performing elephants.

Compared to Barbara Hutton, who frequently called herself the most hated girl in America, Doris was overcoming her shyness with her new-found social life and her patriotic choice of an American husband. She could do no wrong.

In Washington, Roosevelt met with Frank Hague, and the two decided to give the Cromwells a diplomatic post. They were just the sort of celebrity couple who could best represent America's interests. The job of Minister to

Canada was offered to Jimmy and he accepted. It would be a springboard to the Senate and give him the political exposure he needed. The post had been vacant for two years and the staff was more than able to carry on official business with Jimmy as a figurehead.

Unknown to Hague and Roosevelt, Doris was planning to divorce Cromwell. In truth, he was costing her too much money. A compulsive spender, Jimmy was dissatisfied with his $10,000 a month allowance and proposed a plan to organize "Cromwell & Company." The business would have a paid-in capital of $7 million to be provided by Doris—$2 million in cash and $5 million in securities. The company would have a board of directors with Jimmy as president. He would take a salary of $50,000 and $39,000 a year in dividends. He would also be provided with a car and a private plane, all tax deductible. Doris' financial advisor, William Baldwin, and lawyer Tom Perkins (William Perkins' son) were taken aback by Jimmy's plan to get his hands on his wife's fortune. His constant demands were intolerable. Her advisors had been against the marriage in the first place, and now they were openly critical of Jimmy.

Just as Roosevelt was announcing Cromwell's appointment to Canada, Doris flew to Washington and confronted Jimmy at his mother's Foxhall Road house. She asked for a divorce.

Jimmy was shocked. "I couldn't believe it. I thought this embassy in Canada was a terrific thing. It was an extremely important post and I felt tremendously honored and I hadn't any idea that Doris was unhappy and wanted a divorce. She had pursued me so hard and all of a sudden she changed. Maybe she was secretly in love with Cunningham-Reid."

Jimmy was right. Doris was in love with the British MP and planned to make him her second husband. Cromwell's political ambitions were financially draining and his love of publicity was infuriating.

Pundits had a field day with news of the Canadian appointment. "The truth about Jimmy Cromwell," wrote Joe Alsop, "is that he is an amiable, probably rather high-minded young man with a rich mother, an immensely rich wife and a tremendous lot of money which he is willing to shell out to powerful political personages . . . Financially, he is the fattest cat of his time, and Ottawa is his reward for being so fat."

Westbrook Pegler weighed in with a stinging parody. Jimmy was thinly disguised as "Dummy Spelvin," a dim-witted playboy who never paid his bills and let his wife pick up the check. "A big dummy who got married to a rich queen," Spelvin was described as a saloon habitué who won his diplomatic post by contributing to the campaign chest. "I wouldn't say a thing against Mr. Cromwell," another columnist opined, "except that if he were a little better equipped he could acceptably peddle peanuts."

That week, the couple attended the $100-a-plate Jackson Day dinner in Washington. The event, with hundreds of lobbyists and legislators, was held at the Mayflower Hotel. Doris, Liz Whitney, and Mrs. Franklin Roosevelt II, the former Ethel du Pont, were seated together in front of the president and all three young women could not disguise their boredom. Doris was decked out in furs and diamonds and was about to be nominated to her own post: the 1940 Best Dressed list. (She was fourth on the list, after the Duchess of Windsor, The Duchess of Kent, and Madame Patino, wife of the tinplate heir. Barbara Hutton was a distant ninth.)

To keep up appearances and avoid unnecessary scandal, Doris reluctantly agreed to accompany Cromwell to Canada. Perhaps, in some sadistic way, her behavior would force him to agree to a divorce.

On Tuesday afternoon, January 23, she and Jimmy arrived at Ottawa's Union Station and were greeted by the fur-hatted Prime Minister Mackenzie King. It was one of the biggest crowds ever to turn out for such an event. In the sub-zero weather Doris, her lips a dark crimson, wore a $30,000 fur coat and carried an expensive alligator bag. As Jimmy shook hands jovially, Doris stared ahead, her expression one of anger, her feline eyes registering nothing but disgust at her husband. Jimmy was elated at having been made Envoy Extraordinary and Minister Plenipotentiary of the United States to Canada, his rather wordy official title.

Doris thought the whole thing was a sick joke.

They were escorted through the station where a handful of Royal Canadian Mounted Police held back the crowd.

"Welcome to Ottawa," one man cried, and a cheer went up. Newsmen swarmed the couple, asking one question after another.

They were driven to the white marble American legation, which faced the Canadian Houses of Parliament. Then they were taken to "Lornado," the modest ten-acre official residence overlooking the Ottawa River. Earlier in the week, a housekeeper, butler, chauffeur, and maid from Somerville had arrived to set up the house. (The housekeeper had called to say the beds were too short, so the Cromwells had their own custom-made eight-foot beds shipped to Ottawa.)

As newsmen arrived to interview the new minister and his megabucks wife, Doris slipped out to a waiting car and disappeared. Cromwell, explaining her absence, told reporters she had gone shopping "for ashtrays."

Her indifference was painfully obvious and word began circulating that she would not take part in the role of minister's wife. "Keeping up appearances" was not her style. She hated the house, with its dull peach-colored curtains hanging in the gray-walled drawing room, its chairs upholstered in drab yellow and beige.

"Mrs. Cromwell is very concerned with her home," Jimmy allowed. "She likes to have everything just so."

So did Cromwell. His official file bulged with personal correspondence to the State Department, mostly concerning grading the lawn, using manure from the nearby Royal Canadian Mounted Police stables as fertilizer, and haggling over the cost of restoring the living room mantel. He asked for additional gardeners to be employed and requested an "air attaché" to be assigned to Ottawa, and even demanded a special plane from the War Department to shuttle the Cromwells back to New York. "A fairly large one," he specified.

Ten days after their arrival, Doris left Ottawa. Cunningham-Reid had been in New York, waiting for her to join him. They were spotted together at nightclubs, neither bothering to hide their affair.

Word spread in diplomatic circles that the Cromwell appointment was a disaster. Doris failed to hire a social secretary, and attended only three social engagements. The Belgian ambassador arranged a dinner party for the Cromwells. Doris was on a skiing trip, and wired her regrets: "The skiing is too good."

When the Minister of Transport asked Mrs. Cromwell how she liked the city, she quipped, "All I've seen of Ottawa so far is a haze of cigarette smoke through cocktail glasses."

"She made it obvious she was bored and didn't like it," Cromwell recalled. "She was a very aloof and indifferent hostess. I think she thought I saddled her with responsibility. She should have been delighted at her age to become an ambassador. She didn't try. I guess she thought being rich was enough."

One female reporter in Canada met Doris and found she had something in common with the tobacco heiress: her height. "I looked right into the eyes of Mrs. Cromwell . . . and I am five feet ten inches tall. I realized here was one of the chief reasons why most people who meet her are at a disadvantage . . . We compared the size of our shoes and she bemoaned with me the difficulty of being able to get anything but sturdy low-heeled oxfords in the upper-bracket sizes, despite the fact that she was wearing very smart, high-heeled pumps. She is a bit homesick, this tall, shy and very gracious person. Most tall girls are scared to death and it sometimes makes them a bit defiant, and a bit awkward."

There was no question that Doris was defiant.

On March 3, the Cromwells, accompanied by Roseanna Todd, Doris' old roommate, made a visit to the mining region of Val d'Or. "I had been staying with her in Ottawa. She did not plan to be a political hostess," said Todd, who was aware of the lack of sympathy between Cromwell and his young wife. "I went to Val d'Or with them to watch the dogsled races. Jimmy always wanted her to support him and say the right thing."

He urged Doris to speak before a crowd of 10,000 eager spectators. "When she got up to present the crown to the lady who had won, she was supposed to make a speech over the radio," said Todd. "Instead, she stood up and said, 'Hi, Ma. It was a great fight, but we won.'"

Cromwell was furious. A week later, Roosevelt sent a memo to his secretary, asking for a meeting with the newly appointed minister. Before his return to Washington, Cromwell made a scheduled appearance at a joint luncheon of the Canadian and Empire Clubs of Toronto. He had written a speech, declaring his support for the Allies and called the isolationists "cynically-minded and short-sighted."

The speech ignited an international scandal. There was a war on and diplomats were barred from making such inflammatory statements. While his sentiments were echoed by other prominent Americans, Jimmy's speech led to public cries for his dismissal.

That Cromwell was unfit for the diplomatic post was evident. Many felt the speech was merely a publicity stunt. Others speculated that Roosevelt—looking for a way to get into the war—used Cromwell. (Jimmy denied reports that the president had personally approved the speech.)

Cromwell said, years later, he believed that Roosevelt and Secretary of State Cordell Hull did endorse the speech, "but not directly. I deliberately kept them from reading it, because I knew they wouldn't permit me to deliver it. I had to do it strictly on my own. Roosevelt believed that democracy would come to an end, that Hitler would come out on top of the world unless we got into the war in time to save the British and save the democratic form of government in England. He really believed that Hitler would win."

In New Jersey, political boss Frank Hague was elated. The speech had raised Cromwell's profile. A deal was now in the making: Cromwell would resign from his post and run for the Senate from New Jersey.

But the news was overshadowed by an unconfirmed report from New York that Doris Duke was pregnant. Reporters in Ottawa called the Legation for comment. After confronting Doris, Cromwell enlisted his secretary Frank Anderson to confirm that he and his wife were expecting a child. Doris had not bothered to tell him the news herself. While newspapers gleefully trumpeted stories of the "richest baby in the world," Cromwell managed to hide his outrage.

Cromwell believed the child was not his.

Doris' well-planned attack against Jimmy escalated.

In a final showdown, she told him to divorce her. After all, he had ample grounds now that she was pregnant with another man's child.

The couple's belongings were packed and they left Ottawa, privately agreeing to a separation. The question of the child's custody and financial support would be settled later. After a five-year battle of wills, they were both exhausted.

On May 21, Jimmy was unopposed in the primary, thanks to Hague. On June 4, he celebrated his birthday with a party on the roof of the St. Regis Hotel. Doris arrived with Marian Paschal, both wearing black dresses and orchids. Louise Atwill was the life of the party. Jimmy, for the first time in his life, looked pale and drawn. Where would he get the $300,000 that Mayor Hague had demanded?

The next morning, Doris and Marian left for Hawaii. On the *Lurline,* Doris registered under an assumed name and remained secluded with Marian in her suite for the entire voyage.

Compulsive non-spenders are known to be vulnerable to "confidence" men. Just as Doris was shedding one fortune hunter, she was pathologically embarking on a relationship with another.

Since the outbreak of the war, British citizens were restricted in their travel. But Alec Cunningham-Reid had returned to England with a plan. He had convinced Doris to put up thousands of dollars to help refugee British children. Doris had already given $25,000 to the Red Cross for children's relief.

Doris' offer to help British children was made through her friend, Ambassador Joseph Kennedy. She specifically asked that Cunningham-Reid make all the arrangements. The darkly handsome MP declared himself a representative of the Children's Overseas Reception Board and armed with special visas for himself, his mother, Agnes Kingscote, and two sons, Michael, twelve, and Noel, ten, the MP left his country in its darkest hour, bound for Hawaii.

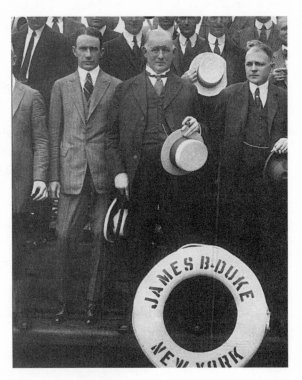

Above, James Buchanan Duke as a young man embarking on a career in tobacco, and right, as a millionaire on board a ship named for him. UPI/ Bettman Newsphotos; Manuscript Dept., William R. Perkins Library, Duke University

The Tobacco Tycoon and his Million Dollar Baby, "the richest mite of humanity in all the world." Kidnapping threats were routine. Manuscript Dept., William R. Perkins Library, Duke University

The Dukes' elaborate marble and gilt East 78th Street mansion, designed by Horace Trumbauer. A price tag designed to outdo Andrew Carnegie. Alfred S. Branum, Jr.

Rough Point, the Dukes' Newport "cottage" that once belonged to the Vanderbilts, was gothic, rambling, and haunted by ghosts of the past. UPI/Bettmann Newsphotos

The first Mrs. Duke, Lillian McCreedy. She steadfastly denied charges of infidelity. UPI/Bettmann Newsphotos

Three heiresses: Dorothy Mahana, Dorothy Fell, and Doris at Bailey's Beach, Newport. Smart and sardonic, Doris was "miserable about her looks." Courtesy Dorothy Mahana Macauley

Doris in London in 1931, well-chaperoned by her mother, Nanaline (left), and the Honorable Lady Bingham. Mother and daughter would have a strained relationship. The Illustrated London News Picture Library

Aloof, Doris shunned publicity and popularized the recluse's favorite accessory: sunglasses. UPI/Bettmann Newsphotos

Lounging on the Lido in Venice, fending off foreign fortune hunters. Cecil Beaton Photograph courtesy of Sotheby's London

Doris trying to dodge a photographer at a New York nightclub. Paparazzi got bonuses for shots of the heiress. UPI/Bettmann Newsphotos

Jimmy Cromwell, Golden Boy of the Depression and great dame hunter, began wooing Doris when she was a teenager. AP/Wide World Photos

The Cromwells fending off the ocean chill on the first leg of their year-long honeymoon in 1935. Doris became frosty when Jimmy's check bounced and she was left with the bills. AP/Wide World Photos

Doris accompanies Eleanor Roosevelt to a miners' homestead in 1937. The First Lady found the tobacco heiress to be spoiled and insensitive.
UPI/Bettmann Newsphotos

Beleaguered British Member of Parliament Alec Cunningham-Reid, after a Honolulu idyll with Doris, returning to face his angry constituents in war-torn London.
UPI/Bettmann Newsphotos

*Doris and Jimmy with Jack
Hearst, son of William Randolph,
attending a burlesque ball at the
Waldorf-Astoria.* UPI/Bettmann
Newsphotos

*Marian Paschal, Doris' secretary and
closest female companion, served as a
confidante and business advisor.
Their friendship sparked rumors
among the monied set.* AP/Wide
World Photos

*Friend David Niven at a
Santa Barbara dinner
party held in her honor.*
AP/Wide World Photos

Shangri-la, the ornate Indo-Persian palace constructed on Diamond Head, named for the mythical kingdom where no one grows old. Bishop Museum Archives; UPI/Bettmann Newsphotos

Duke Kahanamoku, Olympic swimming champion and Hawaiian celebrity, maintained an intimate friendship with Doris that raised eyebrows on the island. Tai Sing Loo/ Bishop Museum Archives

"Doris," said actor Brian Aherne, "had the most beautiful legs in the world." UPI/Bettmann Newsphotos

Doris, a surfer and expert at outrigger canoeing, was a familiar figure on Waikiki Beach. UPI/Bettmann Newsphotos

Left, Doris christens the Liberty Ship James B. Duke. *The Cromwells were also at war.* Manuscript Dept., William R. Perkins Library, Duke University. *Above, a forlorn Doris says farewell to her British MP lover from her monogrammed limousine. It would spark an international scandal.* UPI/Bettmann Newsphotos

Errol was in like Flynn with the heiress in 1941. UPI/Bettmann Newsphotos

Doris weds Husband #2, Porfirio Rubirosa, in 1947. He smoked a cigarette during the ceremony and later fainted in her arms.
AP/Wide World Photos

Doris and Rubi night-clubbing at El Morocco in New York. The marriage had lasted less than a year, but the romance continued.
AP/Wide World Photos

The Bebop Error: Doris and jazz pianist Joey Castro in 1953. She later called their stormy affair "a bad habit." UPI/Bettmann Newsphotos

Hollywood set designer Eduardo Tirella became a trusted friend. He was crushed under her car days before leaving her employ. Providence Journal—Bulletin Photo; UPI/Bettmann Newsphotos

Doris, decorator Leon Amar, and Jacqueline Onassis aboard Aristotle's yacht, the Christina. Jackie was drawn to money; Doris welcomed her attention. Leon Amar

At right, a well-preserved Doris at sixty. Skrebneski

Sister Doris singing with the Angelic Gospel Choir in 1972. Providence Journal—Bulletin Photo

The legendary Martha Graham "kept Doris moving." They are showered with paper hearts at a 1978 birthday party for Studio 54 owner Steve Rubell. Ron Galella

"I'm not a recluse, I'm a loose wreck."
The heiress at the 1981 Newport Jazz
Festival. UPI/Bettmann Newsphotos

Chandi Heffner, former Hare Krishna, mak-
ing an entrance with her future adoptive
mother, Doris Duke. WWD/ Eric Weiss

Socialite Jerry Zipkin, Doris, and a glum-looking Henry Kissinger at Malcolm Forbes'
New Jersey estate. Ron Galella

Doris won headlines by putting up $5 million in bail for former Philippine First Lady Imelda Marcos. A grateful Imelda plants an affectionate kiss on the heiress, whom she called "the Statue of Liberty." Dennis Oda

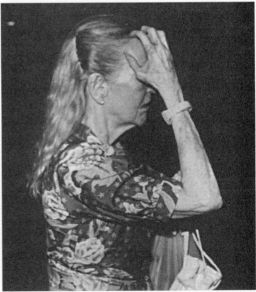

Doris visiting Ferdinand Marcos. She would try to heal the deposed Philippine president. Tim Ryan/ Gamma-Liaison

Doris had evicted Jimmy from Duke Farms and he needed a New Jersey residence. He convinced Eva to lease Boxwood Manor, a 200-acre estate in Silver Lake. Mrs. Stotesbury was not in the best financial situation; Whitemarsh Hall was up for sale and both she and her son desperately needed money. Eva sold Malmaison, her son's house on the El Mirasol estate, for $165,000. The house had been unoccupied for several months and the spider monkeys and exotic birds had been sent to Shangri-la. (Another portion of the estate was bought by Herbert Pulitzer.) She also began hocking her famous jewelry to pay for her son's campaign and ultimately came up with the needed $300,000.

Jimmy began actively campaigning for the Senate and made plans to attend the Democratic National Convention in Chicago on July 15.

Doris was tormented by thoughts that Cromwell would somehow get custody of her child. She couldn't bear the thought of being tied to him. Although her physician had warned her against physical exertion in her condition, on the morning of July 11—while Cunningham-Reid was flying to her side—she went to her favorite spot on Waikiki Beach and surfed for several hours in the pounding waves.

That afternoon, back at Shangri-la, she began bleeding and went into premature labor. She was rushed to Queens Hospital, where she gave birth to a three-pound baby girl. She named the baby Arden. Twenty-four hours later, the child died, its tiny lungs unable to sustain life. Doris was released from the hospital and suffered a minor breakdown. Bobbie was soon by her side.

Reporters desperately tried to reach Cromwell, but he was at a Sante Fe dude ranch. When he finally learned of the death of the child, he telephoned Doris. According to Jimmy, she told him if he came to Hawaii, she would refuse to see him.

"Everybody naturally assumed she was pregnant by me. I knew it wasn't me," Cromwell said.

Rebuked by his wife, Jimmy attended the Democratic Convention, standing on the platform next to Roosevelt, who had been nominated for an unprecedented third term. Jimmy said later that Doris' refusal to allow him to come to Hawaii cost him his political career.

"It made me look hard-hearted and ambitious," he recalled. "It was very inappropriate for a candidate of the U.S. Senate."

For one brief shining month, Doris Duke found romantic love on Hawaii with Cunningham-Reid. He remained with her, much to the discomfort of his constituents back home. Supposedly, Doris and the MP were working out details on the refugee program, but it was only an excuse. His two sons were the only British children Doris was interested in evacuating.

"I remember Doris had these amazing sloe eyes. Almost Oriental. She really was stunning," recalled Noel Cunningham-Reid. "She didn't really want to spend time with two boys. I remember Marian Paschal who looked after us. She was a huge lady. My brother, Michael, looked far more like my father. Doris was very fond of Michael. I was tolerated."

About his father, Noel later commented:

"The subject of his love life could go into some volumes. Women were like bees around the honey pot."

Doris' Hawaiian friends didn't like Cunningham-Reid. In fact, Johnny Gomez was instantly suspicious of the British MP's motives. Calls for the truant Cunningham-Reid to return home grew louder. Jimmy was trying to salvage his own political future. "It was an international scandal when it came out about Doris and Cunningham-Reid. She came back and ruined my career."

The second week of September, Doris returned to New Jersey. "Bobbie" flew to New York, and they were seen frequently. Gossip columnist Dorothy Kilgallen, quoting "Honolulu intimates," said Doris and Jimmy would make their split public "any day now . . . The official reason will be 'incompatibility.'"

Cromwell was frantic. Hague, aware that his candidate was no longer funded by the Duke millions, abruptly withdrew his support. For two weeks, he refused to see Cromwell or even return his phone calls. "My whole organization actually turned up their toes and quit," Cromwell recalled.

According to documents from Roosevelt's Hyde Park Library, Jimmy wired Roosevelt's secretary, Stephen Early, and begged for the president to intervene. In a confidential memo, Early informed the president of Cromwell's concerns: "Jimmy Cromwell phoned me from New Jersey this morning and said as follows: 'Please tell the president that Mayor Hague and his Jersey City machine, for reasons unknown to me, are sabotaging me and my campaign. I don't know why . . . Up to now, everything seemed all right and the chances for the whole Democratic ticket in the state appeared very bright.'" Cromwell had reached the limit to finance his own campaign and desperately needed funds from the state machine. Roosevelt told Early to have an intermediary phone Hague. Roosevelt could not afford to alienate the powerful boss, and Cromwell was cast aside.

By now, Doris was flaunting her affair with Cunningham-Reid, who was living at Duke Farms. Michael and Noel were enrolled at nearby Law-renceville School.

The first week of October, columnist Walter Winchell reported that the Cromwells would divorce immediately after the November 5 election. That week, Doris and Alec, in a chauffeur-driven limousine, screeched into La Guardia airport. After a tearful farewell, Doris' car sped away. Reporters swarmed around the beleaguered British MP, asking whether it was true he and Doris Duke were romantically involved. "I have no statement to make in that connection," he said.

Back in London, he faced an angry constituency, and was branded "The Most Hated Man in Britain" for his sojourn in Hawaii. When his colleagues demanded his resignation, he refused and subsequently became an Independent.

Barely a week before his own election, Jimmy tried to salvage his own image. On the subject of divorce, "It's up to Mrs. Cromwell to verify or deny the information," he muttered. "I have nothing to say about the matter."

For once, he was speechless.

On Tuesday, November 5, as Doris secretly boarded a plane for Califor-nia, the voters of New Jersey rejected Cromwell's bid for the Senate.

Reporters met up with Doris in California as she boarded an ocean liner for Honolulu. Doris told newsmen, "It's very simple. I've separated from my husband. It's a permanent separation. I have no plans for the future." She added, with a slight smile, that it was "a great pity" her husband had lost the election "for he worked so hard."

"That was one of the astounding things about Doris," said Jimmy. "She came back and made that remark without being able to realize that she alone was responsible. That's how far she was from reality. She was so ignorant of life that she didn't realize she had done it. That's being pretty damned ignorant."

Following his defeat, Cromwell tried to see Roosevelt in Washington but was rebuffed. He then went to Palm Beach with his mother, the only woman he ever truly loved.

In subsequent years, "the Golden Boy" faded from the public eye. He abandoned politics, married twice more (fathering a second daughter), and was remembered as the dashing playboy with a taste for rich women.

Delphine Dodge died as a result of her chronic alcoholism at the age of forty-five. Christine ("Cee Cee") Cromwell met a more tragic end.

The Dodge heiress who had been the subject of such a bitter custody dispute eloped in 1941 at the age of eighteen. She eventually had six husbands and was estranged from her family. She deserted her own children and was continually thwarted in her attempts to get her hands on a portion of the $57 million Dodge fortune, held for her in trust. The sorely neglected and emotionally unstable child of Delphine and Jimmy grew into an obese, suicidal woman addicted to Percodan, sleeping pills, and booze. After years of drug and alcohol abuse, she died in 1989 of congestive heart failure in a hotel on the Mexican border. "Cee Cee" was virtually penniless, having borrowed against her inheritance for decades.

Years later, in a letter to Anna Dodge, Cromwell (deeply in debt to his former mother-in-law) wrote that he hadn't had "a decent break of luck since I parted company with Doris in 1940." He portrayed himself as a victim of circumstances, frustrated in his attempt to become financially independent after marrying two of the richest women of his time. "Fate has decreed I will never be a financial success no matter how mightily I may strive," he lamented. "In retrospect mine has been a really weird life in that I have always been connected with great fortunes, Stotesbury, Dodge and Duke, but never, in all the years of my adult life, have I ever had any substantial amount of capital of my own."

Cromwell died, at the age of ninety-three, in 1990. His obituary was headlined: "Former Husband of Richest Girl in the World."

In shedding Cromwell, Doris seized her independence. At twenty-eight, she no longer chafed under the protective bit of her mother, her middle-aged husband, or stuffy legal protectors. Worth over $300 million, she would run her own life. One columnist noted that "she could probably buy and sell Barbara (Hutton) this very minute." Like Barbara, she was an emotionally scarred woman who lived for pleasure and excitement. She had been told by doctors that she could not have any more children.

After Cunningham-Reid's departure, she hosted a reception for the friends of the Honolulu Academy of Arts. Guests were awestruck by the opulence of Shangri-la. "Don't miss the monkeys and the birds over in the cages when you first walk in," Doris smiled. "I have hundreds of cats too, but they're probably around the back of the house. They're rather timid."

For the first time in years, Doris seemed confident. She had learned to cook. She had gained a little weight and found comfort in her friends. In 1941, she spent time in Santa Barbara, entertaining Errol Flynn, which she knew would make Cunningham-Reid insanely jealous. Flynn was Doris' kind of man: bisexual, promiscuous, and not above asking Doris for money. His whole life was once described as a trespass against good taste, which appealed to Doris Duke.

Flynn was rumored to be a Nazi spy, and was not only courting Doris but also Axel Wenner Gren, the Swedish creator of the Electrolux industries, who was said to be the richest man in the world. (His home on Hog Island, near Nassau, was coincidentally named Shangri-la.) Separated from his wife, actress Lili Damita, Flynn was filming *They Died With Their Boots On*. He believed in reincarnation, which Doris became fascinated with. (She told friends that she and Duke Kahanamoku had been lovers in a previous life.)

Doris was fascinated by the bizarre, which led her to Hollywood.

"It is true that from the time it became the Motion Picture Capital of the World, shady characters descended on boomtown Hollywood like swarms of moths drawn to a searchlight," wrote Kenneth Anger. "Two-bit gangsters, leggers', pushers, hard-sell swindlers, blackmailers, burglars, gross and petty extortionists, all manner of ultra kinky sex freaks, dummy stock speculators, crank cultists, dollar astrologists, fake mediums and epicene evangelists, phony healers, crooked fortune tellers and parasitic 'psycho-analysts.' All of them fluttered graspingly about the edges of the charmed circle."

Various schemes to get her to invest in films were frowned upon by the law firm of Perkins and Daniels, who were still engaged in damage control, not to mention ironing out a financial settlement with Jimmy Cromwell.

Doris often made her Hawaiian house available to celebrities as a retreat. One of them was Clare Boothe Luce, who stayed at Shangri-la on her way back from the Philippines where she had interviewed General Douglas MacArthur for *Life* magazine. In mid-October, Clare—recovering from a fever she had picked up in Manila—and Doris were together at Shangri-la, and the wife of Henry Luce convinced the heiress that she should pursue a career in writing.

That fall, Doris went to New York to visit her mother. The government had begun restricting travel to and from Hawaii as war with Japan became a threat. On Sunday, December 7, 1941, that threat became a reality as Pearl Harbor, just a short distance from Doris' Diamond Head home, was bombed repeatedly by Japanese planes.

Doris had a reservation on the Clipper for Hawaii the next day, but all travel was canceled. She spent the day at a suite in the Hampshire House trying to contact Sam Kahanamoku, but the phone lines were dead.

That night, in an anxious state, Doris drove to the Luces' home in Greenwich, Connecticut, and waited for Clare. She finally returned home, having just done a radio program in New York. She was met in the driveway by an anxious Doris, obviously in an agitated state.

Amid the reports of death and destruction, Doris Duke's concern was not for the tragic loss of life. "You and Harry know everything, Clare. Tell me, did they destroy my swimming pool?"

When the United States Navy requested wealthy Americans in Hawaii to donate their boats to help patrol the waters of the islands, owners were told they would be reimbursed by the Maritime Commission. Many offered to give their pleasure crafts to the war effort outright. There was one notable exception: Doris Duke. After her yacht, the *Kailani Lahi Lahi,* was taken by the Navy, officers were shocked to receive a letter from Doris' business office demanding $35,000 for the boat. The price did not include payment for her "sport fishing outfits." Shortly afterward the Navy rejected Doris' "offer" and told her to relinquish the boat. Because she did not want the expense of keeping her home open on the island, she offered Shangri-la to the government. They refused. The house was too grand for the government to maintain, but they did make use of the Olympic-sized swimming pool as a facility for the officers.

As the war in the Pacific raged on, Doris was homeless. She made a stab at working as a research assistant at the University of North Carolina, but when word leaked to the press that she and Marian Paschal were living at the Carolina Inn, she fled Chapel Hill and returned to New York.

Tax troubles with the township of Hillsborough had prevented her from living at Somerville. The local government wanted $13 million in tax on her estimated $220-million income during 1940 and 1941. Doris claimed Hawaii as her legal residence, although her driver's license listed her only residence as New Jersey. In January 1942, she went to court in Somerville to fight the tax. Her lawyer was William J. Brennan, future Supreme Court Justice. Doris told the court why she preferred Hawaii to any other place. "I feel good there. I love to be out of doors. I feel better there than in the United States. It's the sort of life I like."

Wearing a black snood over her blonde hair, she said she often signed papers without reading them and didn't know whether she paid property taxes in Hawaii. Suffering from a slight cold, she sniffed from an inhalator every few minutes as she said she had no idea how many rooms were in her Somerville home or how much money she had in the bank. Her tax returns were prepared by Mr. Baldwin and she never looked at them.

Doris lost the first round when the court ordered her to pay $364,000 in taxes. She appealed the case.

That November, she celebrated her thirtieth birthday and received the last installment of her father's legacy, estimated at $17 million.

With Cromwell and the state of New Jersey both demanding money, and Hawaii no longer an option, she and Tom Perkins decided the best thing for her to do would be to move to Reno and file for divorce. She would make Nevada her legal residence.

On a warm July night, a boxcar with sawdust on the floor and fitted with horse stalls pulled up to the Somerville station. Groom Bob Hannon led a German shepherd and three saddle horses up the ramp, followed by a shiny Packard automobile. News soon broke that the heiress (accompanied by Marian Paschal and Walker Inman) were Reno bound.

The law required her to establish a six-week residence before she could file for divorce. (Other states required at least one year; some required up to three years' residency.)

In September, one week before her residency requirement was fulfilled, Jimmy—in a preemptive strike—sued for a limited divorce in New Jersey. The charge was desertion, and Cromwell's petition asked for a "bed and board" divorce. Under the law, a limited divorce would protect his interest in her real estate if she died before him. It would also forbid either from remarrying.

Doris was furious. What's more, Jimmy had resorted to blackmail; he threatened to give lectures about their marriage and contemplated writing a tell-all book. She did not back down. A month later, in a secret proceeding, Doris filed for divorce against Jimmy, citing his constant demands for money as "extreme cruelty." She said Jimmy would only agree to a divorce in return for a property settlement of $7 million.

Friends said Nanaline Duke urged her daughter to give Jimmy what he wanted, but Doris was stubborn. "Why should I?" she kept repeating.

Cromwell denied asking for $7 million. He petitioned the New Jersey courts to issue an injunction against her suit. The restraining order barred her from seeking a divorce "anywhere on earth" but in New Jersey and also prohibited her from enlisting in the armed services. (Doris was anxious to get overseas to see Cunningham-Reid and had considered the possibility of joining the Red Cross. Their affair had caused quite a stir in London. He was involved in a fistfight in the corridor of the House of Lords with a colleague, Oliver Locker-Lampson, who accused the handsome M.P. of beachcombing in Hawaii while London was in flames.)

The Cromwell divorce was front-page news. There were charges and countercharges and private detectives and enough intrigue to keep even the most voracious tabloid reader satisfied.

On December 21, Doris won her Reno divorce by default. She threw a champagne party that evening. "It's a thrilling Christmas present," she said. Jimmy had ignored her Reno proceeding and she had ignored his New Jersey suit. The question of whether she was still Mrs. James Cromwell was open to debate.

In a desperate attempt to win a settlement, Jimmy threatened to reveal to the press "the real reason" his and Doris' marriage ended and hinted he would call Dr. Richard Hoffmann to testify, presumably as to the nature of the Cromwells' sexless union.

Chapter Ten

Million Dollar Stud

ON THE FIFTY-SEVENTH FLOOR of a building in Rockefeller Center, in the private offices of the Duke Foundation, sat a mysterious, dark-suited, gray-haired eminence often referred to as the "Old Man of the Mountain." His name was William Lee Baldwin, business manager of Doris Duke and guardian of her many millions.

For months, he and Duke family lawyer Thomas Perkins had been trying to come to a settlement with Jimmy Cromwell. Baldwin was furious at the notion of giving him another dime. Ever since Cromwell had wed Doris in 1935, he had been bleeding them dry. First it was the honeymoon, Baldwin recalled. They weren't on the ship three days before Cromwell informed his bride he was broke. Then the check for Cook's bounced and the honeymooners were told they would not be allowed to leave the ship at Cherbourg unless the bill was settled. For the next four years, Cromwell was paid a monthly allowance of $10,000 by Baldwin. There were other payments, including $100,000 to cover gambling debts. Doris also loaned him $300,000 to settle judgments stemming from the aborted Floranada land scheme. Baldwin and Perkins had warned Doris against marrying Jimmy, but she had been adamant. Now the ageing business manager felt a certain pity for the young woman.

The $7 million "Cromwell & Company" plan was out of the question. But it might be in the Duke interest, Baldwin and Perkins agreed, to pay off Cromwell with a small sum to keep him quiet.

Sol Rosenblatt, Jimmy's lawyer, arrived at the Duke offices one afternoon with a new proposal: Cromwell had lowered his demand to $1 million cash. Baldwin, who had previously recommended a settlement, suddenly grew testy. Newspaper stories said Jimmy threatened to reveal the "dark family secret" that had marred his marital life. Baldwin stared across the massive oak desk at Rosenblatt. "Five hundred thousand. And that's our final offer."

Rosenblatt became flustered. It was a pitiful sum. An outrage. Cromwell's attorney left in a huff.

Baldwin and Perkins both knew Doris' Nevada divorce was shaky, and her brief champagne celebration at the Riverside Bar—a Reno tradition—may have been premature. Cromwell—bitter over his Senate loss—would prove a formidable opponent to the Duke forces in what the press had already dubbed the "Battle of the Century."

Rather than stay in Reno, Doris was anxious to join her friends, including Errol Flynn, in Santa Barbara. Gas rationing had all but eliminated such pleasure trips, but Doris was not to be denied. Marian concocted a story about her sick mother in California and the two procured an emergency allotment of seventy-five gallons. They drove to the Santa Barbara Biltmore where they stayed for ten days. (The story eventually got out, and the Reno Rationing Board was not amused.)

Upon her return that spring of 1944 Doris followed the advice of her lawyers and accepted the summons for Cromwell's New Jersey divorce action. In a public display of defiance, she grabbed the papers and clasped her hands overhead like a prize fighter. With her blonde hair tumbling about her shoulders and her face and arms well tanned, the heiress looked ready for battle. Cromwell had taken a phony hotel room in Newark months earlier in hopes of convincing the court that he was a resident of New Jersey. (In fact, Jimmy was living in Washington with Eva at the 2300 Foxhall Road house belonging to Anna Dodge.)

Doris was too infatuated with Alec Cunningham-Reid to let Jimmy stand in the way.

He and Doris had made a spirited pair. In fact, Cunningham-Reid, a year shy of fifty, could barely keep up with the young heiress, already bored with the hijinks of Paris and London.

"Doris always struck me as being someone who would try anything," said Noel Cunningham-Reid. "She was always looking for a new experience. The pace of life was more than he could bear. I got the impression she was very keen to marry him, but he felt life with her would be too demanding." Her fortune, which had been such an aphrodisiac at first, now became an obstacle. Said Noel Cunningham-Reid, "It would have been all the problems that come with the money itself. It makes the relationship difficult."

That Doris was selfish was an undisputed fact. She also had a hot temper and was prone to hurl the nearest moveable object when angered. Lacking the fundamental emotional make-up to sustain any relationship, she was demanding, petulant, and spoiled.

Noel recalled that in early 1944, his father came to Duke Farms to see Doris. "There was a huge verbal battle. The subject of the fight was, 'Are you going to marry me or what?' He said, 'No,' and hurriedly dispatched. That may have been the last time they saw each other."

Cromwell's uncontested suit for a limited divorce was heard in a packed Elizabeth, New Jersey, courtroom that spring.

He told the judge that when his valet went to retrieve his clothes at Somerville in June of 1940, he was made to wait several hours because an errant member of Parliament was occupying his bedroom.

Eva Stotesbury gave a blistering deposition, revealing that Doris had first encountered Cunningham-Reid in early 1936 at a Palm Beach dinner party. She said then forty-one-year-old Cunningham-Reid and the twenty-three-year-old Doris disappeared together for several hours. By the time they returned, all the guests were gone. His wife had become hysterical and rebuked them both for their behavior. (She left him on December 2 of that year, and they subsequently divorced.)

In January 1940, when Doris attended the Jackson Day Dinner in Washington she was "so rude to my son and his distinguished guests, and so contemptuous of the whole affair, that he asked her the cause of her extraordinary behaviour. She thereupon told him that it was because she had been bored by the speeches. She also said that she decided she no longer loved him and wanted a divorce," Eva recalled.

On February 14, 1940, according to Eva, Doris told Jimmy she was pregnant and demanded complete custody of the child, saying Jimmy must promise never to attempt to see it. Unless he agreed, she would refuse to finance his campaign. (He declined to sign a custody agreement, knowing the child would be his financial trump card.)

Eva detailed Doris' frequent dates with men other than her husband. Ironically, the name Eva mentioned was not Errol Flynn but Jack Monroe, the piano-playing bon vivant who fluttered among the rich and famous. Monroe—like the latter-day Jerry Zipkin—was an amusing "walker," often escorting wealthy socialites like Doris and Liz Whitney to various night-clubs while in more intimate surroundings was said to prefer the company of men.

Cromwell himself recounted the death of the baby in July 1940 and his appeals to Doris to allow him to come to Hawaii for the sake of his Senate campaign. Marion Paschal had told him it was not necessary for him to come. "Doris doesn't want you." Cromwell said he didn't care what Doris wanted. "Paschie said, 'I'm sorry if you do this. The door to Doris' home will be closed in your face and she will refuse to see you in the hospital. If you want the rest of the world to know your wife is trying to get a divorce—you'll come and find you will not be allowed in either the house or the hospital.'"

Cromwell, trim and tan in a beige lightweight suit, testified for three hours. Her claims of Nevada residency were a fraud, he said. A Manhattan doorman was paid by Cromwell's attorneys to testify that he had seen Doris visiting her mother's Seventy-eighth Street house while she was supposedly residing in Reno.

Doris' friends begged her to give in and pay Cromwell. She refused. "He got under her skin in an ugly sort of way," one friend recalled. "She came away hating him." Nanaline was mortified, but even she could not convince her daughter to give in to his demands. The only thing for Doris to do was leave the country.

Because of the scandal, the State Department refused to issue the heiress a passport. The only way she could secure passage overseas was with some branch of the service. She approached the Red Cross, but was turned down. Whether Doris longed to see her British MP, as gossips suggested, or simply wanted to escape from Cromwell and the headlines, she was desperate to get to Europe. For once, Perkins and Baldwin agreed on her course of action.

On May 10, the New Jersey court ruled in Cromwell's favor, declaring that Doris Duke was not a bona fide resident of Reno and had perpetrated a fraud on the judicial system. The divorce was not legal. She was still a married woman. Perkins, ignoring the New Jersey ruling, immediately took steps to have the Reno divorce upheld, and filed an unusual amendment in that court.

The following day, in a private arrangement with the War Department, Doris Duke was enlisted as a trainee with the United Seaman Service. Established in 1942, the USS was a small volunteer group which set up hotels and headquarters for merchant seamen. Mrs. Kermit Roosevelt had turned over her Oyster Bay, Long Island, estate to the USS as a training center, and Doris spent the next several weeks there boating on the Sound and playing poker with the sailors.

The job was good for her image. So was a rare interview she granted to a female reporter in New York. "If you're going to live, you have to be part of life," Doris said. She was portrayed as earnest and unassuming. "I couldn't live with myself if I didn't do something real to help in this war. For a long time, I had wanted to take up some kind of war work, but it isn't easy to find the right spot. People are always skeptical of me, you know. It's hard to convince them that I'm in earnest." Bumping over the Long Island roads in a station wagon, Doris drove out to the USS rest home. "I decided that of all the war services, the United Seaman's Service needed help the most."

For the first time, the tobacco heiress publicly hinted at her hermetically sealed life.

"This may sound funny," she said in her breathy, little girl voice, "but I honestly believe that I'm happier now than I've ever been in my life. I feel that I'm doing something worthwhile, earning the right to be friends with a lot of swell, interesting people that I've somehow missed before. I've discovered, I guess, that it's fun to work."

In late September, she sailed from New York for Cairo and took up her duties at the Egyptian Club in Alexandria. By all accounts, she worked hard at the job, entertaining the sailors and making wire recordings for them to send home. "For the first time in her life she was doing something for real people. Everybody adored her," said one friend.

Cairo was a bustling crossroads and center of social activity, with ex-royals, soldiers, and polo-playing British officers at the Gezira Sporting Club. There were rumors that the dashing Captain Cunningham-Reid had been spotted in Cairo, but their affair had already ended.

A young female ambulance driver Cunningham-Reid had seduced months earlier in London was now carrying his child. Angela Williams was a tall, dark-haired daughter of a British naval officer, half Bobbie's age. On the night of October 27 at a Marylebone political reception, the MP announced that he and Williams had been married for some weeks but delayed the official ceremony because of the war. Five months later a son was born.

By now, Doris had already transferred her affections to a young British officer she had met in Cairo. He had fallen in love with her without knowing of her wealth or notoriety. To Doris' few close friends, he was a mystery man, and the love of her life. "I just knew that this was at long last a decent fellow," said one intimate. "She was really in love with him."

It took centuries to produce them. It took years to collect them, a fortune to amass them under one roof, it took four men five weeks to uncrate them, and on a crisp autumn day in 1944, only a few hours to unload them. That day, the Stotesbury collection of art and furnishings went on the block at Freemans' auction house in Philadelphia. Eva's Louis XV tapestries and English paintings, her famous gold plate service, her fingerbowls and antiques were snapped up by curious bidders, eager to secure a memento of the fabulous Whitemarsh Hall, which was now an empty relic of pre-Depression wealth and luxury. Like the J. B. Dukes, the Whitneys, and the Rockefellers, the Stotesburys' opulent life-style was gone forever.

The eighty-year-old Eva was in frail health. Jimmy said Doris was to blame, but others believed her sudden reversal of fortune was the cause. She put on a brave face, complaining about the servant problem, but the truth was Eva Stotesbury had squandered nearly every dime of her husband's money. Whitemarsh Hall had been sold to the Pennsylvania Salt Manufacturing Company as a research laboratory. Its eight-foot-high, 10,222-foot-long steel fence was donated to the War Department as scrap metal. For the next two years, the suburban Philadelphia mansion which had been the scene of such gay, Gatsby-esque balls would serve as a drafty cavernous warehouse.

While Manhattan waited for the air raid that never came, ninety loads of masterpieces were packed up and hauled from the Metropolitan Museum of Art in New York and taken in secret to the old Stotesbury estate, while neighbors wondered why floodlights flashed nightly in the curtainless windows and armed guards patrolled the borders.

In November 1944 Eva's and Jimmy's hopes of getting their hands on the Duke fortune collapsed when Doris' Nevada divorce was upheld by Judge William McKnight, who accused Cromwell of fraud, deception, and extortion. "Aided and abetted by his mother" the judge observed, Cromwell presented "a pathetic picture of how far greed for money can carry one down."

It was the final blow. Eva died several months later.

Doris also suffered from the scandal. Along with Gloria Vanderbilt, Sr., and her sister Thelma Lady Furness, Barbara Hutton, and Jock Whitney, her name was dropped from the New York Social Register, a rite of passage for maverick bluebloods. To the world, she welcomed the ostracism and wore it as a badge of honor. Her break from Cromwell and the stuffy social scene her mother and Eva had so adored led to a heady period of adventure. She was thirty-two, unable to bear children, freshly divorced, and financially independent. She was also developing a feminist conscious. She would never again define herself through a man.

"While he called her a 'Frigidairess,' I think there was something wrong with Cromwell and not Doris," said radio and television personality Tex McCrary. A tall, strapping Texan and former newspaperman, Tex had met Doris at the Stork Club and struck up an intimate friendship. He frequently saw her at Jock Whitney's tennis court on Thirty-eighth Street. "I know how she felt about him. She called him the Pope because he wore these little hats to cover his bald spot. She said it had been an arranged marriage. The two mothers had gotten together. She used the French phrase: marriage of convenience.

"I had a great deal of fun with her," he said. "It was pure, glorious sex. It was the best I've ever known because afterwards we talked and we talked and we talked. She talked about things I didn't understand. She enjoyed knowing something I didn't know. She never did anything if she didn't know everything about it. She had an insatiable, healthy curiosity and a need to create. We continued the affair for years. I can say I loved her.

"Sex with Doris was a joy. It was wild and wonderful. In the hay, she had sort of a line. She'd ask, 'Tell me Texas, what gives you pleasure?'"

By 1944, Tex was a photographic officer and chief public relations officer for the Mediterranean Allied Air Force. He met up with Doris again in Europe.

"She was in love with a man she had met in Cairo," McCrary recalled. "He was the only good man she ever loved. She built a villa in Alexandria and a rest home for American Merchant Seaman in order to be with him. He was with the British Armed Forces out of Cairo in the Desert War. Henderson. That's the name I remember. And then the war moved on to Salerno."

Anxious to get to Italy to join Henderson, she befriended a number of officers with the Office of Strategic Services, the precursor to the CIA. Joining the OSS was a fashionable way to go to war. "She made friends with anyone she needed. People were fascinated by her," said one observer.

Doris had a strong ally in General William J. "Wild Bill" Donovan, wartime head of the OSS. "Donovan adored her," said McCrary.

Without the usual paperwork and mandatory security check, Doris used her connections to join the OSS. She was hired at a base salary of $2,000. Ironically, a press release issued by the United Seaman Service said the OSS had "offered" the heiress a position. Nothing could be further from the truth. According to recently declassified CIA documents, her appointment in January 1945 caused a near revolt among American officers who were livid over the special treatment given the heiress who chose as her code name "Daisy," the curvaceous blonde made famous by Al Capp's "Li'l Abner" comic strip, and coincidentally the nickname given to Marion Davies.

On Saturday, January 6, 1945, Doris flew to Italy aboard a special B-25.

McCrary, then in charge of photo reconnaissance, received a cable from General Donovan, saying "Duke arriving 0400 hours. Campino B-25. Meet expedite. Signed Donovan." McCrary had no idea which member of royalty this might be. "Jock Whitney and I were living in a tent in Caserta and we roared with laughter because Cairo was full of unemployed royalty and Campino was a mud strip in the shadow of Vesuvius in back of Naples. How the hell do you meet a Duke properly? Jock said 'Get an ambulance.' Because it would go through the chug holes, and it's dry. So we got the ambulance, drove out and waited. A B-25 comes in. The co-pilot gets out first, then the rest of the crew. Suddenly, this long pair of legs dangles out from the bomb door. I assume it's the captain. He came over and saluted smartly and I said, 'Where's the Duke?' She flipped her hood back and it was Doris. I said, 'For Christ sweet sake, what are you doing here?'"

Doris blurted out the whole story as she and Tex walked to the waiting ambulance. She told him she was in love, and the man was in Italy. "'He's here and I want to be here,' she said. I don't know how she met him. I said, 'Get your skinny blonde ass back on that plane. I'm sending you back to Corsica.'"

Instead, she reported for OSS duty at Caserta on Wednesday, January 10.

The same day, a memo was dispatched from Cairo to the Secretary of State. The subject was "Daisy."

Common gossip Cairo that subject has personal interest in reaching London and she went to Italy on OSS basis as first easy lesson on how to get London despite British refusal of Visa. Strongly recommend Washington take steps to frustrate this if true for good of our agency which is given full credit at Cairo cocktail parties for employment plus special plush plane to Naples.

Two weeks later, while "Daisy" and Henderson were together at an Air Force hospital, the OSS Cairo office wired Caserta:

Department states that it was with the greatest reluctance they allowed her to go to Cairo, that they know she is trying to get to London eventually. Agreement with her and War Shipping was that if she terminated her services with Seaman Service in Cairo, she would return to the US. Department also upset because it believes publicity in US is inevitable within a week or so.

The memo went on to say that the State Department "may cancel Cromwell's passport."

OSS internal memos indicate that on February 4, 1945, the State Department was insisting that Daisy follow the standard procedures. "If she desires to enter our employ, she must await security check and return to Washington for training, instruction and indoctrination before final approval."

Word eventually leaked out that Doris was in Italy when Eleanor Roosevelt and Special Assistant to the President Harry Hopkins arrived on a tour. Hopkins was furious at Doris' hijinks. At a press conference, cartoonist Bill Mauldin said, "You know, Mrs. Roosevelt, we are the forgotten front out here. Why can't you get the President to send replacements?" Hopkins snorted, "I don't know why you call yourself the forgotten front. You have the richest girl in the world out here."

Doris' cover had been blown. In March, without returning to Washington, she received her security clearance. The whole affair was highly unorthodox. Said Lawrence R. Houston, assistant chief of OSS Cairo. "You're damn right it was unusual. We were sore as hell. Some people saw all this pile of money and were impressed. [But] she didn't do a damned thing."

Having been installed in an Air Force Hospital, Doris spent her days making taped recordings for the wounded soldiers for them to send home to their local radio stations, and giving piano lessons. Three weeks after arriving in Italy, the mysterious British officer, Captain Henderson, was killed in action. Doris received word at the hospital, and broke down. Said McCrary: "I never met him, but obviously she was crazy about him."

Doris wanted to go home to America. But Tex McCrary convinced her to stay. He sent a cable to William Hearst's son, Bill. "How would you like to have a correspondent helping Mike Chinigo cover Italy for the rest of the war? I promise you he will know everything I know as fast as I know it and will never turn in an expense account." A cable came back: "Hire him."

McCrary wired back, "It ain't a he, it's a she."

Joseph Kingsbury-Smith, Paris-based European general manager of International News Service, received a phone call from Mike Chinigo, then manager of the INS bureau in Rome. "He told me that she'd come into the office and said that she would like to have a job. He was intrigued by the fact that it was Doris Duke." Although she had no experience as a journalist, Chinigo hired her as his Girl Friday. He first suggested a salary of $100 a week, which Kingsbury-Smith vetoed. "I said, 'Don't be ridiculous. She doesn't need the money.' So it was finally settled that she'd get $25 a week."

Doris worked in the Rome office as a secretary under Chinigo, who was also in the employ of the OSS. Said Kingsbury-Smith, "She finally went out and did some reporting and wrote some stories which he edited. In fact he told me one time that most of it needed rewriting." The INS received a spate of publicity by hiring Doris. Her first dispatch appeared in American newspapers on February 18: "Doris Duke Finds Widow of Il Duce Happy in Exile." ("She still is the bourgeoise housewife she always was.") A second dispatch April 5: "Doris Duke Finds Squalor in Rome." The story consisted of Doris visiting soup kitchens and the Rome race track. "The faces are coarse and the hands rough . . . Underneath mink and sable coats many still wear their dirty work dresses." In her next dispatch, she went to Cinecitta, Italy's Hollywood, which was used for housing children.

"She was not a natural journalistic writer. But he [Chinigo] seemed to enjoy it very much," said Kingsbury-Smith. "He liked the idea of having a celebrity at the office."

Doris wore a scarf on her head and old slacks to work, having bicycled from her modest apartment in the middle-class section of the city on Via Lima. For the first time, she was living without the usual battery of servants and secretaries, attended only by a personal maid. She credited Clare Boothe Luce as her inspiration and ink-stained mentor, and told friends her job was the toughest and most satisfying of her life. Her ambition was always to do something on her own. To prove to Cromwell, her mother, and the rest of the world that she was more than a bankbook. "I feel definitely drawn to journalism as a means of self expression," she was quoted as saying. "At one point, I thought I'd use a nom de plume, but I reconsidered, because life is complicated enough as it is."

Said Kingsbury-Smith: "The other interesting thing is, she came up to London when I was on a visit. And my wife and I got to know her and had her to dinner a couple of times. And then she asked my wife Eileen to go shopping with her and one of the interesting things was the discovery that she was very, very tight with money. For example, when they would take a taxi to go to antique shops, she insisted that the taxi driver was entitled to only what was on the meter, not any tip. On one occasion, when they got out of a cab in the center of London, and had given the driver the exact amount, he got out and started running after Doris. Eileen quickly interceded and passed him something and he left. But she [Doris] just ignored it completely."

Eileen Kingsbury-Smith recalled: "She was scared to death to lose a dollar. Her whole attitude was that somebody was out to get her."

But if Doris had a pathological fear of being taken advantage of by taxi drivers, she did not appear to be afraid of much else. Her once-frail constitution and nervous state so fiercely guarded by Nanaline gave way to a lust for physical danger. Like other women who were attracted to the European front, Doris became an excitement junkie. "She was fearless," said *Stars and Stripes* correspondent Louis Cortese.

"I used to say I never wanted to be run over from behind. I wanted to die in a head-on crash," said Tex McCrary. "And she said, 'Me too.' And that was her." Perhaps the loss of Henderson had left her with a death wish of her own. "Any goddamn crazy idea I had, she would go along with," said McCrary. "I'd say, 'Okay. Anybody want to go?' No hands would go up. Suddenly, she'd stick her hand up and then everybody had to go. She was never afraid. Never."

The War Department had initially refused to grant her request for credentials as a war correspondent. But she sweated it out, attending briefings for Mitchell bomber missions and visiting various installations in Italy. Her fellow correspondents thought her a dilettante and a lightweight. Just another one of Hearst's "debutramps" looking for a kick. "We more or less laughed at her," said Mike Stern, a *Fawcett* magazine scribe and then head of the American Press Association in Rome. "We felt superior to her. We kind of victimized her. She was just a very rich, unhappy kid. But Mike [Chinigo] thought she was a helluva sweet girl."

Female war correspondents were a rarity in 1945. In fact, there were very few women willing to risk such an assignment. "I think she was very brave to demand her rights," said Chinigo's widow, Marajen, who met Doris a decade later. "She was going to stay in Europe and work. I admired her for it."

She also had an active love life. There was a brief romance with writer

Charles MacArthur, husband of actress Helen Hayes. In Austria, she met up with handsome British actor Brian Aherne, then married to actress Joan Fontaine. Tall, good-looking, and a friend of Errol Flynn and David Niven, Aherne was ten years Doris' senior. The actor had gone to Europe with a touring company of *The Barretts of Wimpole Street,* and they performed before packed houses of G.I.s. The acting company was following the advancing Army and eventually, in February 1945, ended up trapped in Northern Italy near the Austrian border. Doris was also there. She and Aherne's group were holed up at the same hotel where they had a brief encounter which lasted for three days. "He found her very sexy and very amusing," a mutual friend recalled. "And he said she had the most beautiful legs in the world."

Doris' maverick behavior did not endear her to the press corps. Especially when she was invited by General George S. Patton to join him behind the Russian lines.

"Old Blood and Guts" had just completed one of the most brilliant campaigns in military history, cutting a swath through France, relieving Bastogne, and capturing more than three quarters of a million Nazi soldiers. The legendary commander of the Third Army with his token riding crop was being hailed as the greatest military genius since Lee and Jackson. After meeting the Russians in Lintz in a rowdy, glass-smashing rite and drinking the commander under the table, the American four-star general was invited by Soviet Marshal Feodor Tolbukhin to a celebration at his headquarters, located in a chateau near the Czech border formerly belonging to Emperor Francis Joseph of Austria.

On the morning of May 14, four days after the war in Europe had ended, Doris was in Lintz, waiting for a plane to take her back to Italy. "She and I were at the airport. She wore a pantsuit and was very tall and striking, with grayish green eyes," said John J. Pullen, then a young Army officer. Patton's plane landed. Doris walked over to the command car.

"Daisy, what are you doing here?"

"Why Georgie, how are you?"

She climbed into his car and sped away as her fellow reporters grumbled, "Georgie?" She later explained, "I was just doing what any good newspaperwoman would have done."

She and "Georgie" had met a decade earlier in Hawaii while he was an Army lieutenant colonel stationed there. A wealthy man, Patton enjoyed hunting and yachting and had formed his own polo team. Friends in

Honolulu recalled that a starstruck Doris had once made him a gift of polo ponies.

Although Patton was married (and reportedly had one mistress already) it was not out of the question for him to take time for a brief liaison. "Patton would go for someone like her in a minute," said Coy Eklund, an assistant on Patton's staff at the time. "He was socially conscious. He had a lot of well-to-do friends. He liked the celebrities. And Doris was somebody."

Patton was certainly Doris' type. At six feet tall, he had the lean, hard body of a much younger man. Said Eklund: "He was clearly the preeminent hero. He was tall and erect and military. A swashbuckler in cavalry boots, all spit and polish. He played the role beautifully." And as McCrary observed, "Daisy liked older men. She was in love with her father."

As the car drove slowly down the road to the chateau, Patton noticed that it had actually been swept for their arrival, as soldiers lined the fifteen-mile course. He described meeting the Russians in his diary:

> They certainly put on a tremendous show . . . they had soldiers with a sort of shoe-blackening arrangement to clean our boots. They had a great many women retainers who did everything except wipe your face. They did go to the extent of spraying your head with perfume.

After a few rounds of vodka and a fevered dance by a Moscow-imported showgirl, the toasts began. The Russian general stood and drank to President Truman. More vodka was poured. Patton stood and toasted Joseph Stalin. Another round of vodka. Patton fumbled with one of the medals on his chest and announced that he would like to present it to the dancer as a token of esteem for heroic Soviet womanhood.

A tipsy Tolbukhin ("a very inferior man [who] sweated profusely at all time," according to Patton's diary) wanted to do likewise. Looking around the room, he spied the tall, blonde tobacco heiress and in a flowery speech, complimented American working women and their long hours in war plants. He pinned the medal on Doris' chest amid the clinking of glasses. Then he took her face and kissed her on both cheeks. She smirked, embarrassed by the attention. Patton watched the gesture, then stood up and gently took Daisy's face in his strong hands, and slowly kissed her, first one side, then the other.

Flushed with vodka and the Allied victory, Patton was larger than life and Doris was swept off her feet by this virile, colorful man who attacked life with an uncensored J. B. Duke-like profanity. (He once said his greatest ambition was to meet Rommel in a personal tank battle, just the two of them, squared off in a duel to the death.)

The party continued and Doris and Patton were together that day. McCrary later said she spent four days with him near the Russian front. For an excitement junkie, remaining with Patton in the days following his heroic march would certainly have appeal.

"I'll put it this way," said Coy Eklund. "It would be conducive to celebrating."

(Patton, not surprisingly, makes no mention of Doris in his published diaries.)

Meanwhile, officers of General Mark W. Clark's 5th Army had been looking frantically for the heiress. She finally returned to the Hotel Weinzinger in Linz where the commanding officer of the 65th Division, U.S. Major General Stanley E. Reinhart, had turned over his plush suite in the hotel to her.

Days later, says Tex McCrary, "I got a signal from Patton's people and I went and picked her up. There was some difficulty getting her back to Italy, as radio communication was poor." Finally, a P-38 fighter plane was dispatched and she flew back in the front cockpit.

A month later, while on a short leave, McCrary married model Jinx Falkenburg in New York. (They later won fame with their radio and TV show, "Tex and Jinx.") They had told few people of their plans, and when word leaked out McCrary received a one-line cable from Doris: "How about me?"

"That's the only message that I ever had from Doris in writing that made me know how she felt," McCrary later said. "'How about me? Signed Daisy.' I would say that is the only pitiful, pathetic, cry-baby thing she ever said to anybody in her whole life and it got to me."

Despite their passionate lovemaking, McCrary knew that he and Doris would never marry. As she once told him, "Texas, American men have no talent for being married to a rich woman."

"And," said McCrary, "she was right. Clare Luce knew how I had felt about Doris. She said, 'Look, McCrary, whoever marries the Duke becomes the Duchess.'"

He was known in the boîtes of Paris as "Big Boy," this dapper, mahogany-skinned, slightly bow-legged polo player from the Dominican Republic. His jet black nappy hair had been straightened, and he wore it slicked back in a shiny helmet. His wide nose had also reportedly been altered by plastic surgery. Some people said he was a mulatto and that his Negroid features made him look rather like a monkey, but men and women both found the charismatic Porfirio Rubirosa armed with a fatal charm.

He was a rogue and a ranchero and said to be in a permanent state of erection. It wasn't his sexual prowess that made "Rubi" so irresistible to the fair sex. It was his utter devotion to women. Like his friends Aly Khan, Errol Flynn, and Alec Cunningham-Reid, his powers of seduction were legendary. "He is all male," actress Zsa Zsa Gabor once wrote. "Whether he talks with you, dances with you, walks with you, you know he is a man, thinking only of you and always of you as a woman to be taken and possessed and kept away from other men because, being so feminine and desirable, you are their natural prey."

His sexual technique was widely discussed and his penis was allegedly neither hard nor soft, but suspended in a state of retarded ejaculation. "Toujours prêt," as the French say. The technical word is "priapic." Doris later used another description. "It was always numb," she confided to a friend. His penis was also of such proportion that waiters in Parisian restaurants began referring to the giant peppermills as "Rubirosas." Jimmy Cromwell had another name for him: "Rubber Hosa."

There was also an aura of danger. The son of a Dominican general, Rubirosa's family moved to Europe when he was young, and he was raised in Paris, attending a boys school where he had an undistinguished academic career. Rather puny, he took up boxing as a sport. He began drinking and womanizing at an early age, and when his family returned to Santo Domingo, they were not as wealthy as they once had been. He studied law, but when his father died, he was recruited into the army by General Rafael Trujillo, the country's newly elected president and strongman.

Rubi was sent to Trujillo's tailor and gunsmith. He took up polo. With his polished European ways, he was an asset to the roughhewn dictator who named him his aide-de-camp. He soon caught the eye of Trujillo's sixteen-year-old daughter, Flor de Oro (flower of gold). Since the family's financial reversal, Rubi thought of little else but money. He was desperate to marry a rich girl, and Flor de Oro was the richest in the country.

Over Trujillo's objections, his daughter and Rubi were wed in 1932. But the dictator's early disapproval gave way to a sort of machismo admiration. Trujillo had a long list of unsavory jobs to be carried out and this new son-in-law could be useful. One of them involved political assassination.

In 1935, according to confidential State Department documents, Rubi traveled to Manhattan carrying a suitcase containing $7,000 in cash and arranged to have his cousin, Chi Chi de La Fuentes Rubirosa, carry out a political assassination. The target was former Dominican minister Dr. Angel Morales, a Trujillo political enemy living in exile in New York. But the gunman botched the job, shooting Morales' roommate Sergio Bencosme in the back. Morales and Bencosme were planning to return to Santo Domingo as candidates for president and vice president, respectively. They had the backing of the Du Ponts who had made substantial loans to the country that Trujillo had neglected to repay. There were rumors that arms and ammunition were being shipped to the Dominican Republic by the Du Ponts by way of Mexico to aid in the overthrow of Trujillo.

Chi Chi was eventually indicted, but not before he had been spirited back to the Dominican Republic, having been made a lieutenant in the Army by a grateful Trujillo. When he demanded to be made a captain and threatened to talk, Rubi's cousin was mysteriously killed.

Rubi was then sent to Berlin as the third secretary of legation. In 1936, he was transferred to Paris where his indiscretions with other women were more than Flor could bear. She obtained a divorce and Rubi was relieved of his diplomatic duties, although allowed to keep his diplomatic passport.

Pressed for money, he tried various schemes, but mostly relied on the generosity of wealthy women who were happy to pay for his services. He met a jeweler who had fled Spain when the Civil War broke out. The man asked Rubi to go to Madrid to retrieve part of the store's inventory that had been left behind. Another refugee named Johnny Kohane drove the car. He was returning to Madrid to retrieve $160,000 in securities. When Rubi came back, there was no sign of Kohane. Rubi concocted a wild story about being savagely attacked on the road by snipers, but their car showed not a single bullet hole. When Rubi handed over the jewelry, there were several pieces missing, valued at $183,000.

Trujillo, however, had not lost admiration for his former son-in-law and Rubi was named Dominican Chargé d'Affaires. During the war, he made money selling visas to wealthy Jews. In 1942, he married French actress Danielle Darrieux, the highest salaried movie star in France and a known Nazi sympathizer.

According to documents released by the CIA, Rubirosa's name appears on a list of Nazi intelligence agents with the following description: "Dominican. Abwehr agent, formerly Dominican Chargé d'Affaires at Vichy: was at

Lisbon in June 1942 when there were indications that the Germans were trying to expedite his return to Vichy: at the end of December appears to have been refused permission by the frontier authorities to leave France: age 35: height 175 cm: slim, oval face, dark curly hair, thick lips, clean shaven."

Immediately after the liberation of Paris, Rubi and Danielle were riding in a car when a gunman connected with the French Resistance opened fire. Three bullets hit Rubi in the kidney, but he later recovered. (Gossips suggested the gunman was a jealous husband of one of Rubi's conquests, but in reality, the bullets were meant for Danielle.)

He was transferred to Rome when the Foreign Office refused to allow any diplomat to remain in Paris who had represented his country in Vichy. Danielle, between films, accompanied him. The day after Rubi and Danielle arrived in Rome, a journalist showed up at the hotel suite to interview the French film star. The reporter was Doris Duke.

Doris and Rubi were instantly taken with each other. She adored blacks, and Rubi was considerably dark-skinned. Both were adventurers and pleasure seekers, and not overly bright. It is likely that Rubi was blinded by dollar signs. "The ambition of most men is to make money," he later confessed. "Mine is to spend it."

Soon after their meeting, Rubi did acquire a small plane, and suddenly had $500,000 to invest in a coffee growing scheme.

Whether it was true that Doris offered him a cool million to divorce the actress and marry her, the rumor was fueled in Cafe Society circles by Rubi's well-known taste for cash and Doris' legendary purchasing power. Ironically, while Doris was paranoid about being taken by taxi drivers, she was evidently willing to pay for Rubi's companionship.

Rubi, once described as "eleven inches long and thick as a beer can," more than satisfied Doris. There was also no question of children; Rubi was sterile, and Doris had been already told by doctors after her only child died that she would never be able to conceive, having only one ovary.

Rubi's testicles were also said to be oversized, a result of having had the mumps as a child. (That might also account for the sterility.)

He was three inches shorter than she, and properly adoring. While other women may have found his constant fawning unusual—having a match lit before the cigarette was out of the case—Doris found him immensely charming.

She gave him gifts; a sapphire-studded gold cigarette case. He gave her diamond earrings and a gold ruby-studded compact. (Doris' friend Dorothy

Mahana would later recall that it was the only time any man had ever given Doris such an expensive gift.)

"Rubi made her happy," recalled Mike Stern who ran into Rubirosa and Doris at the Aquasanta Golf Club in Rome in the beginning of 1946. The club, frequented by the Aga Khan and King Leopold of Belgium, was a meeting place for the wealthy set. There was Doris on the putting green with Rubi. "They got along beautifully. He came to Rome to be with her. He followed her more than she followed him."

Her employment with the OSS had been officially terminated. She needed a job in order to stay in Europe. Three former *Stars and Stripes* correspondents also were reluctant to go home, so they launched an English language tabloid: *The Rome Daily American.*

One of them, Jack Begone, had known Doris through the INS. They asked her for backing. She agreed, loaning them a total of $40,000 and naming herself "society editor."

(The arrangement, like many of Doris' pet projects, later soured. She wanted Mike Chinigo to run the paper, but Louis Cortese refused to hire him, regarding the INS bureau chief as "rather slippery." Doris threatened to call the loan and Cortese told her she was free to do so. Doris was bluffing. The loan was not called, but relations were strained. Shortly afterward, she sold her stock to another investor, Langdon Thorne, Jr. Said Cortese, "I think her reputation was for picking up people and dropping them at will. I was in shock over it. I never saw her again. It just ended. Very cold, very surgical.")

She continued to write for INS, but her battlefield enthusiasm had given way to post-war ennui. She returned to Paris in March of 1946 where she wrote dispatches complaining of no coffee at the Ritz and the absence of fashionable women, then went to London and wrote about skyrocketing prices of antiques.

There, she was assigned to cover the investiture ceremony for knighthoods and military decorations at Buckingham Palace. Eileen Kingsbury-Smith accompanied her.

"When I picked her up to go to Buckingham Palace, she had her hair done up in toilet paper. The way 'Topsy' did it, the little black girl in the books. Instead of rollers, she'd twist her hair around a piece of johnny paper. Before it started, we had to go to the ladies' room to get the paper out of her hair." (The following year, Doris' hair-care methods earned her the dubious distinction of being chosen one of the "Ten Worst Tressed Ladies" in America.)

Eileen also accompanied Doris to antique stores in London. Doris had already gained a reputation for driving a hard bargain, and she was disliked by many of the dealers. At one store, the two women went upstairs to browse. When they tried to leave by the same door, it was locked. "We had been bounced," Eileen laughed. "We had to leave by the fire escape."

Often, Eileen paid for taxi fares and lunch when it became clear that Doris never carried any cash. Although she was known for small bursts of generosity, she did not strike Eileen as anything but terminally selfish. "There was no largesse at any time."

The two women discussed antiques. "I remember she adored the Oriental things. The Dresden china was too sugary. She said, 'You'll tire of that soon.' She also made some curious remark about something exotic in her background. About being Oriental or something."

Eileen did not think much of Rubirosa. "He was a dreadful creature. When he danced with a woman, it was like paper to a wall. He did everything but make love on the dance floor."

But Doris had made up her mind. He was the best that money could buy. A rogue and a liar and a womanizer, he was simply irresistible. More importantly, every woman in her set wanted him. Which made him, in Doris' eyes, all the more desirable.

The State Department was appalled at Doris' choice of companions. They refused to allow Doris to stay in Europe and threatened to cancel her passport. She was, they believed, harming American prestige by being seen with unsavory characters, Rubirosa chief among them.

That summer of 1946, Doris returned to America after two years abroad and visited Nanaline in Newport. Their estrangement had blossomed into open hostility. In the words of one friend, "They hated each other."

"My father was running the estate then," said Gordon King, Jr. His mother, Cornelia, was Nanaline's personal maid, and his uncle George Gordon King was the head gardener. Each summer, it took twelve men to tend the grounds of Rough Point, which was opened for a three-month period.

The logistics of running such a white elephant were extraordinary. In the damp, Newport winter, the furnaces were stoked by Gordon King, Sr., who slept in the coal room on bitter nights when the gale winds would clock at 30 mph. There were hundreds of panes of leaded glass, and windows had to be latched against the wind and rain. Said King: "Mrs. Duke wanted to open the house for a few days at Christmas which was like reconditioning the *Queen Mary* for a two-day sail." It would take several men two weeks to get the temperature of the house to a comfortable 55 degrees. Often, Nanaline would not make her plans known or change them at the last minute. If she did arrive, fresh flowers, difficult to grow in the estate greenhouses during winter, were trucked in from Boston. "Thirty dozen cut flowers would arrive. And they all had to be a certain color. Money was never an object. They would never give somebody a 50-cent raise, but they would spend money on flowers without thinking about it."

Every summer, it took four weeks to open Rough Point and two weeks to shut it down. Extra servants were brought from Manhattan and Somerville. Nanaline "was basically a recluse at that point," said King. "She entertained almost not at all. She took her breakfast in the first floor sitting room, and then you would not see her." The ballroom end of the house was closed off, and she lived in a few rooms. Every Monday and Thursday, the flowers—mostly her favorite gardenias and orchids—were changed. "As many as twelve dozen cut flowers, and two dozen potted plants," King recalled. There were potted palms, ten feet tall, on rollers. "My father would start at nine in the morning. It had to be completed by 10:30 A.M. because it had to be quiet when Mrs. Duke came downstairs."

The flower beds bloomed constantly. They were planted at their peak and then replaced before even one petal drooped or their color faded. There were never any flowers growing or dying. For Mrs. Duke, there was only perfection. "The flowers never wilted," King said, "the colors never changed." Two men were stationed at a particular spot in the driveway where the morning sun hit the petunia beds. "Two people had to be there between seven and nine in the morning to handpick those beds so there were no dead petunias if Mrs. Duke went out in the morning. She'd look at these beds of flowers and go absolutely berserk if there was anything wrong."

At this seaside "cottage" ringed by formal gardens, strangely enough there wasn't a piece of outdoor furniture. "No one even walked on the lawn. There wasn't even a path to the gardens. It was all inside the house," said King.

Nanaline's lunch consisted of a small portion of lemon sole, boiled broccoli, a cup of tea, and a piece of dry toast. In the next room, the servants would consume standing rib roast, Yorkshire pudding, five different vegetables, freshly baked bread, and two apple pies. "There were these huge, huge lunches," said King, now a successful restaurateur. "It was unbelievable.

The pantries were stuffed to overflowing with food. Her lunch would cost one dollar and the servants would be eating $50 worth of lunch every day of the week."

King's mother washed the delicate lace and silk hand linens in the morning. "Everything was worn for a minute and then thrown away. Everything was replaced and changed all the time." As for the servants, "They had no insurance or benefits. You were fired in a minute," said King. "You could work on the estate for 30 years and if you made a mistake, you could be fired on a Friday and left with nothing. It was very paternalistic." Despite the lack of security, the servants enjoyed a warm camaraderie and the usual Upstairs-Downstairs sense of superiority over their employers. "I guess the assumption on the part of working people was the Dukes must be happy because they're not working," reflected King. "I'm sure my family was a hundred times more happy."

After two years in Europe, Doris returned to Rough Point and found it suffocating. After a few days on the estate, she was anxious to leave and inspect her home in Honolulu. Her marital status had now become a national joke. Her Nevada divorce was recognized in every state but New Jersey, where Jimmy had won his decree for a limited divorce that entitled him to half her property if she died before him and barred either one from remarrying. Eva had willed her money to her grandchildren and two secretaries, which sparked a bitter public family feud over the Stotesbury estate, now a paltry $3 million. Jimmy was living on a $12,000-a-year trust fund, hardly enough to keep him in seltzer water, let alone Dom Perignon. But he decided to end the battle with Doris and filed for an absolute divorce in New Jersey.

After a five-year absence, Doris flew to Hawaii with eleven pieces of luggage and was met by Duke Kahanamoku. It was an emotional reunion, and Doris was keenly interested in how the island had changed during the War.

But she was restless that vacation, and longed to return to Rubi. Her experience in Europe had changed her; she was anxious to go abroad.

Carmel Snow, the slim, white-haired, flamboyant editor of *Harper's Bazaar,* had met Doris in Paris at one of Mary Louise Bousquet's Thursday soirees attended by artists and intellectuals and taken her under her wing. Carmel was hoping that Doris would work for the magazine, perhaps as Paris editor Bousquet's assistant. Women's magazines often tried to lure debutantes to their mastheads. Barbara Hutton, of course, was much more beautiful than Doris, but her famous name would lend a certain cachet to the fashion magazine, which was aware of the publicity value. "I'm sure Carmel was dressing her. She must have been intrigued by Doris' wealth," said Snow's niece, Nancy Thompson, who also edited the magazine at one time. "I don't think Doris contributed anything but a certain glamor."

Doris arrived at the *Harper's Bazaar* offices in New York one day in a huge beaver coat. "She was speechless," recalled a former editor, Sarah Tomerlin Lee. "Carmel said, 'She's going to share your office.' She was so shy. It was miserable for her. In meetings, she never made a remark or asked a question. All we knew was that she wanted to be in the fashion world." Carmel Snow became her mentor. "Carmel was a rascal," said Lee. "She was a heavy drinker and could be outrageous. She always wore pillbox hats, and had luminous skin. Doris was rather dumpy. Without vitality. She was almost mute, and seemed extremely sad to me."

She was also defensive. When Doris visited a fur shop in Manhattan that month the saleswoman tried to interest her in a $35,000 sable coat. "Who do you think I am," Doris snapped, "Barbara Hutton?"

Carmel Snow arranged for Doris to return to Europe as a correspondent for *Harper's*. In March 1947, she arrived in Paris where the postwar glamor and nightlife proved a heady tonic to her depression. "It was as if the world was starting all over again," recalled Eileen Kingsbury-Smith.

By now, Rubi and Doris were a couple, seen in the chicest bistros and gambling casinos and often traveling to the French Riviera where they kept adjoining suites at the Grand Hotel at Cap d'Antibes. Rubi was an attentive lover.

At one resort, the couple ran into British leading man Stewart Granger and producer Mike Todd. "Doris was a tall, good-looking woman and to my amazement, very nice," Granger later recalled. "I thought she would be spoilt rotten and be an arrogant, rude bitch, but she was nothing of the kind. Spoilt, yes. Who wouldn't be with all those millions and all those potential husbands hovering round flattering her. Poor Ruby was in there really pitching. She used to keep him waiting around at all hours to take her to lunch or dinner, and both Mike and I were amazed that any man would stand for it." When Granger and Todd invited Doris to dinner, she accepted "and as we left for a swim we gave Rubirosa, who had been eyeing us balefully during our conversation, a cheery salute. Poor man. With us it was all fun. With him it was business."

They took her to a small bistro. Wrote Granger, "As we both flirted with her outrageously, we realized that she was rather naive and could be swept off her feet quite easily. She just couldn't make up her mind which of us she wanted. She had never been treated in this cavalier way before and it intrigued her."

Several days later, Todd and Granger were seated at breakfast. They asked Rubi to join them. "We apologized for our behavior and swore we wouldn't interfere with his romance any more." Then the two men asked Rubi the secret of his sexual performance with women.

"Simple," the Latin lover told them. "A lot of whiskey. After a certain amount of whiskey it becomes numb. It functions. I feel nothing, but the ladies do." Rubi had also experimented with marijuana and morphine.

By June, his divorce from Danielle Darrieux was final and gossips speculated on the possibility of a Duke-Rubirosa match.

President Trujillo was anxious for the union. If the political opposition was backed by the Du Pont fortune, his regime would have access to the Duke money. In retrospect, could Rubi have been carrying out another "dirty job" for Trujillo?

Said Doris Lilly, gossip columnist, author (*How to Marry a Millionaire*), and later a paramour of Rubirosa's, "Doris Duke was a physically ugly woman. How could she think he would marry her and stay? The only reason he married her was the money, and he was able to get it."

Like Eileen Kingsbury-Smith, Carmel Snow had been disturbed by Doris' infatuation with Rubi. In Paris for the collections, she tried to keep Doris busy with magazine work. One Friday afternoon, Carmel—in her deep, throaty voice—told Doris they would be photographing the next morning.

According to Carmel Snow's autobiography, Doris suddenly said she was getting married that day at the Dominican Legation.

Doris had told no one, not even her mother. Carmel swung into action. She was afraid that Doris would lose her citizenship if they were married at the Legation, technically on Dominican soil. "It was nearly five o'clock on Friday afternoon and I barely had time to get hold of our French lawyer. He said, 'This wedding mustn't go on unless the girl is represented by counsel.' He got on the phone to America and received his instructions."

On the afternoon of September 1, Rubi, in a dark striped suit, and Doris, wearing a green taffeta ankle-length Dior dress chosen by Carmel Snow, a huge artificial rose corsage at the bust, and a chic green hat, drove to the Dominican consulate where hordes of reporters were already waiting.

They had invited only a handful of guests, including the Kingsbury-Smiths, Carmel Snow, and French race-car driver Jean Pierre Wimille.

Champagne was poured and the guests began drinking. Rubi downed two highballs of whiskey in short order.

"There were a lot of people walking in and out of the rooms," said Eileen. "It was all very last minute. Doris was very happy. Rubi looked relaxed and nonchalant. Like we'd all gone out to lunch together. They didn't take care of their guests very well. They were both very self-centered people."

"They looked like adolescent lovers," Joseph Kingsbury-Smith recalled.

But Rubi's mood changed when two men carrying briefcases arrived. They were lawyers from the law firm Coudert bearing a prenuptial agreement for the groom to sign. The document stated that Rubi, in marrying Doris, renounced any claim to the Duke fortune.

"His face was quite a picture when the two lawyers walked in. He looked like one of those fierce black Miura bulls about to charge a red cape," recalled one guest. "I've never seen anyone madder. But he signed. There wasn't much else he could do."

The ceremony began, presided over by Dominican consul general Dr. Salvadore Paradas. Rubi was so upset he smoked a cigarette, then ground it out to place a modest band of rubies around Doris' finger. One wag later reported, "He refused the blindfold but accepted the cigarette."

Doris gave her husband a thick gold wedding band, and observers couldn't help but notice its resemblance to a tiny handcuff.

After the ceremony, Rubi—by now intoxicated—either fainted or collapsed. Later, Doris told friends, "Big boy passed out in my arms."

"He probably fainted," said Eileen, "at the thought of not getting all that money."

There was a brief Riviera honeymoon, where they stayed at the Eden Roc Hotel. Rubi, by now recovered, was so furious at Doris for the prenuptial agreement that he supposedly, according to Eleanor Tydings, refused to have sex with her on the honeymoon. Doris was suitably contrite and, to make amends, bought him a house in Paris as a wedding gift.

Located at 46 rue de Bellechasse on the Left Bank, the mansion had belonged to Princess Chavchavadze, another American heiress. It was a seventeenth-century, three-story house behind an enormous white wall, and appeared to be a fortress. Doris paid $100,000 for the property, then hired decorator Henri Samuel at a cost of half a million dollars. An avid boxer, Rubi wanted an indoor boxing ring set up. Inlaid marble and rosewood paneling, silk tufted ceilings, and shelves for Rubi's polo trophies were also installed as well as a mechanical bull in the courtyard, where

Doris—in tiny short-shorts—could be seen riding the fake hobbyhorse by amused neighbors.

The marriage was rocky from the start.

At a Paris dinner party given by Aly Khan at Maxim's shortly after the wedding, guests couldn't help notice Doris' anger as her husband twirled other women onto the dance floor. "She was very jealous when Rubi began dancing with someone else," recalled Helene Arpels, who later opened a designer shoe salon in New York. "She was watching him *very* closely."

Doris loved jazz music, and filled the house with an assortment of band members. She and Rubi quarreled over these sessions. When they fought, Doris would simply leave the house and move into a hotel on the Avenue George V, where she kept a suite.

One evening, they took Rubi's nephew to an indoor polo game. As the story goes, Rubi spent more time at the bar with a shapely blonde than watching the match. When Doris angrily confronted him in the car going home, there was a vicious argument capped off with an exchange of blows as Rubi tried to keep control of the steering wheel.

Doris, of course, had good reason to be jealous. Rubi was incapable of fidelity, and was bored with marital life. His nightclubbing was an Olympic event, and he would often arrive home in the wee hours with a flotilla of South American friends wanting food and drink. Rubi was a heavy drinker, and could be violent.

When he drank, Zsa Zsa Gabor later recalled, "He was a planet in an orbit of his own, a belligerent, dangerous, reckless man."

One afternoon, Doris had a fever of 102. Dr. Manuel Pastoriza, a friend of Rubi's, came by the house. He diagnosed her ailment as influenza and suggested she be given a dose of sulfa. Rubi offered to go to the pharmacy. On the way, they passed the Tabou, a lively nightclub, and decided to go in for a drink. He lost track of time, carousing with friends. At 5 A.M. Doris was still waiting for the medication, her fever raging.

There were other tales of neglect. While on vacation in the south of France, Doris asked Rubi to buy a pack of cigarettes. When he emerged from the elevator in the lobby, he ran into French restaurant owner Manouche, an old lover. She invited him to have a drink with her. Three days later, Rubi returned with the cigarettes.

(Manouche was later interviewed by Alice-Leone Moats for her book, *The Million Dollar Studs*. She confirmed Rubi's incredible staying power and described his sexual organ as "long and pointed and it hurt . . . It was nothing for ce cher Rubi to take on two or three women in a night. By late at night, when he was good and drunk, he didn't give a damn what kind of legs were opening.")

As a reward for wedding the tobacco heiress, Trujillo offered Rubi the job of ambassador to Argentina. He was flattered by the appointment and made plans to leave Paris. But the U.S. government had disapproved of Doris' choice of husband and declined to issue her a diplomatic visa.

On November 27, a harried Doris arrived in New York for a bitter showdown with Baldwin and Tom Perkins. In an emotional meeting, she was informed of Rubi's past, his role in the murder of Bencosme, the jewel heists, and his many indiscretions. The more Rubi was revealed as a cad and a liar, the more Doris wanted him.

Of all the women ever taken to the cleaners, none went more willingly than Doris Duke. The fact is, she was hynotized by Rubi. She immediately purchased a plane for him, a B-25 bomber. It would be a surprise.

In mid-December, she flew to Buenos Aires to join her husband. The servants had come from Paris, and Doris' furniture and china were flown down in a specially chartered plane.

Rubi and Doris were an instant hit on the social circuit. The plane was refurbished and outfitted with a lavish kitchen. Nicknamed "La Ganza," it could comfortably seat ten and they often flew to Rio, piloted by Colonel Cloyce Tippett, who later wed Liz Whitney.

Rubi was enjoying his new financial status immensely. He even gave the dictator's wife, Eva Peron, a $1,500 donation for a charity. (It is highly likely Evita was among Rubi's conquests in Argentina.) Evita was grateful, saying it was the first time a diplomat had shown interest in her charitable affairs. One rival ambassador was not impressed. He called it "the first time in recorded history that a pimp ever gave money to a harlot."

Rubi and Doris fought constantly. She returned to New York while Rubi flew back to Paris, carrying his usual suitcases full of cash. Gossip writer Dorothy Kilgallen reported that the marriage was over. Doris put on a brave face and left for Hawaii, saying her husband hoped to join her.

But Trujillo had already taken steps to replace Rubi as ambassador after one of his romantic trysts led to an international scandal. It seems a wealthy society woman (married, of course) became infatuated with Rubi after sampling his technique. He decided to flee to Paris. But the woman soon followed. He left, and went to Rome where he met up with his first wife, Flor de Oro, and was spotted in nightclubs with her.

Doris heard the news and immediately left Hawaii, hoping to win her husband back. On July 21, she reached New York and boarded an ocean liner, telling reporters she was ill "and terribly upset." She arrived in Cherbourg on July 28, and was met by Rubi.

They reconciled. Doris even sent for her three German shepherds who were immediately flown to Paris. Soon, the two were bickering again.

"She got this craze for jazz music," Rubi was quoted as saying. "All day she practiced the piano and she got this piano professor, a girl. She wanted to study so much she invited this girl to move into the house with us. I didn't like this . . . So there were fights."

The on-again, off-again romance was also marred by Rubi's inability to control Doris' money. Twice, Doris asked Baldwin for checks in the amount of $250,000. The best she could come up with were two checks for $50,000 each, in addition to her regular income. Rubi tried to interest her in buying a fleet of cargo ships, but this idea was vetoed by her lawyers who discovered he wanted to transport arms from one Latin-American republic to another.

On September 9, Rubi's $50,000 B-25 crash-landed in a New Jersey swamp while attempting to land.

Later that month, according to Zsa Zsa Gabor, after another one of Rubi's indiscretions, he came home to find Doris unconscious, having reportedly tried to cut her wrists. "He later told me there was blood all over the apartment," author Doris Lilly recalled. "I think she thought he'd belong to her. He was another possession. She paid for him. She thought he was hers. But Rubi was a real whore."

Under a pseudonym, Doris entered "Chianciano," the famed rest cure resort in Italy to recover. Two weeks later, still shaky, she secretly flew to New York and immediately telephoned Tom Perkins. She was finally willing to shed Rubi, giving him $25,000 a year for life unless he remarried.

Unknown to only a few friends and her lawyers, she left for Reno. The dark circles under her eyes gave credence to brother Walker Inman's later statement that she was "pretty well broken up." The divorce was granted October 27, seventy-two hours after her arrival. "Little things kept building up. It just didn't work out," is how she put it. "We just couldn't make a go of it. And now," she smiled, "I'm Doris Duke again."

Asked if she was still the richest girl in the world, she replied, "I don't know. I was once called that. I don't know exactly what my status is now."

That Rubi and Doris parted friends was obvious. They continued their love affair for two years, much to her business manager's dismay. There were fights and reconciliations, the two unable to get each other out of their systems. Free from the bonds of marriage, Doris eventually took his philandering in stride.

"Marriage does something to a love affair," Rubi once philosophized, "takes something delightful out of it. There is a piquancy about love, when two people know they can leave each other, that never exists inside the circle of a wedding ring."

Doris—whose name was linked to MGM newsreel commentator Jay Sims—would appear at the Rue de Bellechasse house without warning, often showing up at odd hours. On one visit, Doris arrived while Tina Onassis, wife of the Greek shipping magnate, was in the house. Tina was hurried out of the garden exit by Victor the butler.

When Rubi was injured in a polo accident in Egypt, Doris flew to his bedside. Some even believed that the couple had secretly rewed in Paris.

Once, she made Rubi a gift of a handpainted necktie picturing a nude woman. "I thought you'd like this," she remarked dryly. "You're so fond of naked girls."

Chapter Eleven

Pal Joey

BY THE EARLY 1950s, the richest girl in the world had become one of the richest women in the world. Although she complained bitterly that her father had tied up her money in various trusts, her business manager had invested shrewdly and her fortune was steadily increasing. She owned almost fifty percent of the shares in Duke Power Company alone, worth an estimated $400 million. Her money was also invested in real estate, West Virginia coal mines, and treasury bills.

She decided to change the name of her tax-exempt charitable organization from Independent Aid, Inc. to the Doris Duke Foundation. She set up a Manhattan office, and Marian Paschal screened the steady pilgrimage of beggars, from University presidents to homeless women. The sheer volume of correspondence was overwhelming, and filled an entire wall of file cabinets. In 1952, Doris revealed that since her inheritance she had given away $2.6 million in grants, a rather small sum given her estimated $600 million fortune. Only one gift—$250,000—was made to Duke University. Other recipients were the Center for Self-Supporting Women and Students of New York (which received $307,000), The New School, American Friends Service Committee, Planned Parenthood, and New York's Institute of Fine Arts.

Doris' distrust of people led to confusion among her employees, as she often hired rival "investigators" to seek out worthy causes. Indeed, her global network of private investigators began to rival that of her late father's.

Reverend Norm Eddy recalled how the heiress funded his Narcotics Rehabilitation Program in East Harlem in the 1950s. At the time, most hospitals would not accept heroin addicts for treatment. "Over the course of several weeks," the pastor recalled, "two visitors came to the church separately, a man and a woman. They were both employed by some unknown foundation to find out what organization was doing the best work with addiction. They came independently of each other. It seemed somewhat mysterious." Months later, the woman called Eddy and accused him of being in cahoots with the man. "It seems Doris Duke had hired two separate researchers, not telling either one that the other existed, but telling each that the one who found the best information would get a hefty bonus."

Pitting employees against one another for mythical bonuses became a favorite sport for the heiress, well acquainted with the nature of greed. Like the fictional John Beresford Tipton of the popular television show "The Millionaire," Doris' anonymous gifts often took unusual forms: she once wrote out instructions for a donation to a West Coast university on a scrap of paper while on a camel trip in the Far East and had it delivered by a scruffy messenger.

While her nemesis Barbara Hutton showered money on friends and lovers, hoping to buy affection, Doris parceled out grants and "loans" (mostly in the form of stock) as a power play.

Behind her back, she was ridiculed by the very people who benefited from her generosity. In a confidential letter written by one would-be recipient, one executive said the best way to soften up Marian Paschal was to buy her a few drinks, and that she and Doris were neophytes. "Both gals are evidently restless and romantic and are under the impression they delve deep into American life by making occasional visits to boys' clubs, slums and settlements."

After Marian's death in the early 1950s, Doris hired May McFarland as executive secretary for her Foundation, located at 41 East Fifty-seventh Street. "She was a delightful woman," recalled Reverend Eddy. "Very realistic, very warm, with a quiet sense of humor. She kept saying, 'I'm only a servant. I do what Miss Duke tells me to.' But I had a hunch she was listened to."

Once a year, Eddy would go to the Foundation office for his check. (He would receive $10,000 a year for five years.) "You got the strong impression that Doris Duke lived in a world of her own and never met the people she gave money to."

Doris' personal largesse was directed to artists and musicians who had special access to the heiress. After all, they could show her piano riffs and flatter her ego. One of them was "Bricktop," the celebrated black entertainer and nightclub owner whose protégés included Josephine Baker, Mabel Mercer, and Duke Ellington. Doris had met Bricktop in Paris at her club "Chez Bricktop" on Rue Pigalle. Dee Dee—along with the Duke of Windsor and Cole Porter—would drink at Bricktop's until the wee hours, listening to Django Reinhardt and Stephane Grappelli. With her signature red hair and cigar, Bricktop would often hit up Doris for a loan. With the heiress' backing, Bricktop opened a cafe in Mexico City in 1944. Five years later, she returned to Europe and opened another club on the Via Veneto in Rome.

Doris was infatuated with black jazz musicians and appalled at the discrimination against them. She helped singer Lena Horne get an apartment in New York and once was reportedly banned from Newport's Bailey's Beach for inviting a black musician friend for a swim.

"I think she's been very good to some musicians," said Charlie Bourgeois, jazz aficionado and New York publicist. "She's done a lot of this anonymously. She has a good heart."

Many of her loans were never repaid. Sometimes, in a pique, Doris would try to recoup the funds. One recipient, black Atlanta-born pianist Mary Lou Williams, was bailed out on several occasions. In gratitude, Williams composed a sultry song, "Miss D.D." The friendship was strained, however, and Doris reportedly asked that her loan be repaid. Years later in 1973, when Doris showed up at the Cafe Carlyle to hear the pianist, Williams turned her back on the heiress and wouldn't speak to her.

It was Doris' money and notoriety, not her talent, which was her entrée into the jazz scene. She wouldn't have been welcomed "if she hadn't been born into the position she was," said singer Annie Ross, who once entertained Rubirosa at the Rue de Bellechasse house. "She would love to be in the jazz world. She truly loved it. She was a devotee."

One of her favorite haunts in Los Angeles was the Mocambo where in 1950, she often went to hear jazz pianist Joey Castro. Doris had first met Joey in Honolulu at a concert. Johnny Gomez, Doris' caretaker, invited the swarthy young Castro back to Shangri-la with his trio for a midnight supper and swim.

Born in 1927, Castro was a Spanish-Mexican son of a steel mill laborer, who began playing piano at the age of fifteen. Darkly handsome and highly amusing, Castro was brimming with raw talent. That first night at Shangri-la, Doris took to him immediately.

"I started talking to her about music. The new wave was coming in— Charlie Parker, Dizzy Gillespie. She didn't know anything about it," Castro recalled. "A few days later Sam Kahanamoku arranged for my group to come up to the house and surprise her. We were playing as she walked down the stairs. She was tickled to death. And then we sat up all night talking. That's when she approached me about tutoring her. And I told her I wouldn't tutor her for money, I'd just like to do it."

Doris went to Los Angeles and when she returned to Hawaii, left a message for Joey giving her name as her housekeeper, Louisa Jackson. It was the same name she used to book airline reservations.

"I knew it was her. She didn't think I'd return the call, she told me later. She thought I was young and busy and met so many people." He said he was not aware of who her father was or how many millions she had. "I started going to the house every day. I'd give her music assignments I thought would help her."

The lunches soon turned into dinners. Since there weren't many clubs in Honolulu, the all-night jam sessions at Shangri-la became more and more frequent with Doris paying the musicians what they would have earned at a club. She would often bring Joey with her as she jetted from Honolulu to the mainland.

In Somerville, there were jam sessions with singer Pearl Bailey, Tony Martinez, and pianist Joe Bushkin, who had played in Benny Goodman's band, and was a friend of Doris'. "Whenever I appeared, she always showed up," recalled Bushkin. "She had a wonderful theatre in Somerville with recording equipment. There was good champagne and she'd put records on and ask what I thought of the saxophone or piano player. It was always very laid back. She was never the grande dame of Cafe Society."

Castro recalled spending evenings in the theater at the farm, watching home movies of Buck Duke and his only daughter in a horse-drawn carriage. Said Castro: "Her father was her hero for all time."

On one visit to the Duke mansion in Manhattan, Castro arrived at the appointed hour and was promptly shown to the basement. "They didn't know me. They took me downstairs where the servants were."

The mistake was discovered and Castro was taken upstairs. "It was a lonely place. Just the mother lived there. I saw her walking down the hall, but I didn't say anything. We did have lunch together later. Doris introduced me and said, 'Here's my piano teacher.' Mrs. Duke—we called her Mama Duke—couldn't have been nicer."

While in New York, Castro said Doris was hospitalized for appendicitis. When she returned to Hawaii "it all seemed to fall into place. She asked me to come to Hawaii with her. That's when it all started."

Doris and Joey embarked on a love affair. Fifteen years her junior, he had none of the polish Rubirosa had. Castro was rough around the edges: a hard-drinking, hot-headed young man who was also said to be sexually well endowed.

For their frequent trips to Los Angeles, Doris took a two-bedroom suite with a piano at the Bel Air Hotel, and Joey, for appearances, took an apartment nearby. "We'd have dinner right there. Her maid cooked on a little stove."

Doris had long been infatuated with Hollywood and it was there that she began to lead a schizophrenic life. With her more swanky, social friends, like *Los Angeles Herald Examiner* society columnist Cobina Wright and actor Gilbert Roland, she frequented star-studded parties and expensive restaurants. Then, later at night she would take off her diamonds and Madame Gres designer dresses and go slumming with Joey. He referred to her as "my chick," and the two were often overheard speaking in be-bop lingo.

Photographer Wallis Sewall was an occasional escort of the more proper Doris. "I dated her several times. We went to Arthur Rubinstein's. I found her a charming person, if a bit of a recluse. She was very cool, and very difficult to get to know. She put a wall around herself."

Sewall said Doris loved to dance. "She told me her mother would never let her take dancing lessons. She also said she hated when Nanaline called her name. It was never for affection, only for a reprimand. She'd run when her name was called."

Sewall did a photo shoot of the heiress free of charge. "I knew she'd never have one otherwise. Doris was suspicious of everybody."

Writer Ruth Montgomery, the former reporter who had barged in on the young Doris and Jimmy Cromwell years earlier in Detroit, ran into the heiress in Hollywood. "Cobina had a party for me. Edgar Bergen and Janet Gaynor were there and also Doris Duke. I was wearing an Elizabeth Arden dress. It was the only one I ever owned. It was open at the neck. Doris came up to me and said, 'Now Liz knew what she was doing. This is supposed to be tied.'"

An eclectic group of hangers-on began congregating in her suite: black dancer Katherine Dunham, pianist Mario Braggioti, Lloyd Pantages, the homosexual son of the theater magnate, and Joey Castro. "I didn't have much respect for Joe," said a friend of Doris. "I think he was looking for a fast buck. He used her to advance his own career."

"Doris was an introvert, and kind of horsey-looking," observed longtime Bel Air Hotel concierge Philip Langdon. "She didn't entertain much, but she had her Hawaiian friend Johnny Gomez there all the time." With Marian Paschal dead and half-brother Walker Inman having suffered a heart attack, Gomez filled a certain void. "He was beach bum. He was really her gopher," said Langdon.

Doris occupied rooms 150, 151, and 152 on the south end of the grounds, overlooking a flower-filled patio with a fountain. Rubirosa was a frequent visitor to the hotel, and according to Langdon, Doris paid all his hotel bills.

Another frequent visitor was Eleanor Hufty, psychic and "colorist." She had met Doris through L. Ron Hubbard, the founder of Dianetics. "But she didn't like him, neither did I," said Hufty. With financial backing from Doris, Barbara Hutton, and Marion Davies, Hufty founded something called The Unifying Research Institute in Los Angeles.

"We were trying to resolve personal weaknesses," Hufty recalled. "Doris was dominantly afraid, which always makes a person withdrawn. She was alone. Period."

Hufty would come to the Bel Air Hotel once or twice a week, and charge for her services. "Often, a clairvoyant would go with me to look at the auras. There are certain colors, certain images that occur in aura. A shape moving. Or actions. Sequence of color."

The sessions lasted two hours. "I knew her on a very intimate level. She worked at it. Doris was a gal who never left a stone unturned. She had a pretty high brain radiation. She always wanted to do more, to be more. To be better. That was her basic drive." The child of a hypercritical mother, Doris—especially after two failed marriages—"wanted to experience the passion of doing something well."

Hufty recalled that Doris would lapse into French during the sessions and recount painful experiences. The most traumatic was her father's death. "Suddenly, everything was dyed black. It was the pain of separation. As a female, she was searching for her father. Always."

The death of her child in 1940 was another trauma. "She kept saying, 'Arden loved me.'" (Another intimate recalled that Doris had tried to "heal" the dead child by placing her hands on the baby, but hospital personnel would not let her touch the corpse. "She always felt that something was taken from her," a friend recalled.)

She talked of Nanaline ("not too affectionately") and her rival Barbara Hutton, who was spiraling out of control on drugs and alcohol. "They were not very close. Doris felt very sorry for her. If anyone was ever exploited it was Barbara Hutton." She also talked of Duke Kahanamoku. "She said he was a great kahuna (high priest). He would stand on the shore facing the ocean and chant, and fish would come in. He performed strange and unusual things." Doris then would softly recall the Hawaiian name Kahanamoku had given her: Lahi Lahi. Doris would refer to herself as a kahuna. "If I'm a witch," she told one friend, "I'm a good witch."

But Hufty also saw a darker side of Doris. "If a person didn't fall in line with her wishes, she was disgusted. She didn't like it. Once she jumped against someone, she was adamant in her refusal to understand. There was not much forgiveness in her."

Her relationships tended to be fleeting, and often ended abruptly. "When her interests changed, her friends changed."

She was obsessed with youth, which led her to seek out unsavory faith healers and gurus. Through buxom blonde actress and singer Marilyn Maxwell, she met up with a former circus performer who called himself Yogi Lakshmanasandra Rao. Doris would invite him to the Bel Air hotel, or she would visit him in his shabby Hollywood apartment.

Doris and her yogi would sit in the lotus position, chanting in Sanskrit. He called her Gita. With his long hair and gray streaked beard, he bore a close resemblance to Rasputin, the mad monk of Russia. One witness recalled the following exchange:

"It is not Gita's fault that she has so much money," the yogi told an assembled group.

"No," said Doris a little sadly. "It was my father who made all of it. I just inherited it."

She learned to breathe properly, and gave up red meat in favor of rice and grains. To clear her sinuses and improve her complexion, she also learned to perform *neti,* an exercise that required her to insert a waxed cord up one nostril and bring it out of the mouth.

Doris rewarded him generously. One morning, in long flowing robes, he showed up at a Hollywood bank with a check from Doris for $800. The banker, bemused, asked to meet her. The yogi said he was having her to lunch at his apartment that day. The banker accompanied the Hindu to his apartment where he indeed met up with the famous heiress.

"Gita, will you please tell Mr. Robbins that the check you gave me is good?" Doris assured him it was. "And how many zeros could I have added after the amount?" the yogi persisted. "Until you ran off the paper," laughed Doris.

After bringing him to Somerville and buying a $6,000 tractor for his alleged orphan home back in India, Doris introduced the yogi to Barbara Hutton, then in the process of divorcing her fourth husband, Prince Igor Troubetzkoy. Rail-thin and in poor health, Hutton was convinced she was going to die of some mysterious ailment.

Doris invited Barbara to Shangri-la. The Woolworth heiress later said Doris insisted on two rules: no men and no bacon. The warning had come from her guru. Barbara began consulting Doris' yogi. According to biographer C. David Heymann, Barbara signed up for fifty one-hour sessions with the yogi at a cost of $1,000 per visit.

By November 1952, the yogi eventually sailed for Europe. News reports said he left with three blank checks—all signed by Doris Duke.

She also befriended an elderly Hawaiian woman, Nana Veary, who was a Science of Mind practitioner and medium at séances held at the home of Daddy Bray, a famous kahuna. Odetta Bray, his niece, was a friend and hula teacher of Doris'. Doris and Veary traveled to Seattle for séances with a medium. They also went to Paris, India, Thailand, London, and New York, meditating in cars and planes and trains. Veary would often warn Doris of unknown dangers ahead, and the two would change their itinerary at the drop of a hat.

Doris started wearing wigs as a disguise. "She had very thin, baby hair," said Sewall. "When I did a photographic sitting with her, I had a hairstylist come over. We got her into wearing wigs. She'd travel to Hawaii under an assumed name, wearing a wig. She was insecure about her looks. But she had the most exquisite jewelry of anyone I'd ever seen."

Cobina arranged an evening with British actor George Sanders and Wallis Sewall. "Cobina, George Sanders, Doris and I went to a party at Romanoffs," said Sewall. "George ended up taking her home."

George Sanders and Doris Duke had much in common. Both played the piano and sang, both were jaded sophisticates and both notorious cheapskates. "There's no greater aphrodisiac than money," the actor was fond of saying. Married to actress Zsa Zsa Gabor at the time, Sanders (who would later commit suicide saying he was "bored") had a brief love affair with Doris, according to Gabor. Perhaps he was hoping to marry her. Gabor was alerted to the liaison during a party hosted by Doris and Cobina Wright.

When Doris spotted Sanders, she draped her arms seductively around his neck and said, "That was quite a singing lesson we had yesterday."

"I was consumed with jealousy," Gabor recalled. "I could compete with any woman on equal terms—I could match myself beauty for beauty, sex appeal for sex appeal, against any woman—but I could not compete with the richest woman in the world."

Gabor vowed to get even with Sanders and the heiress by declaring that she would sleep with the great love of Doris' life, Porfirio Rubirosa, at the first opportunity. (The actress kept her word, and the tempestuous romantic triangle of Sanders, Rubi, and the Hungarian spitfire occupied many a newspaper headline several years later.)

It was clear that "Rube," as Doris called him, was not out of her life. Not only did Doris pay for his hotel bills, she continued to finance his bizarre hobbies, including a famed treasure hunt for sunken pirate gold off the coast of Santo Domingo, which cost Doris a quarter of a million dollars and ended in disaster.

As the captain of one of the best polo teams in Europe, Ciboa La Pampa, Rubi was a fixture at Deauville where he won the World's Championship, with Doris watching. In Honolulu, they often wound up in the kitchen, laughing and cooking beans and rice together.

"Doris would give us 24 hours notice before she arrived, and often Rubi came with her," recalled one of the men employed at Somerville. "He was well mannered. He would often stop in at the greenhouse while out riding his horse and have a soda. He would sit and talk to the other men. He was a very cordial guy."

On the cusp of forty, with two notorious divorces and an increasingly decadent life-style, Doris became the object of satire. One of the more embarrassing incidents involved her father's university. The college published a humor magazine, *Duke 'n' Duchess*, which featured a series on the fictional Buchanan Littleworth, his sexually promiscuous daughter Diane, and her Latin American playboy, and the school Littleworth University, which had been generously endowed by the roughhewn papa. The story hit a nerve. Duke University had always treated Doris with kid gloves, anxious for her support. When the offending issue hit the dorms, it was immediately yanked by nervous college officials. Copies were rounded up and destroyed. The editor resigned and the magazine itself ceased publication. (It is not certain that Doris saw the satire, but several sources later cited the crude joke as a possible source of Doris' disdain for the university which bore her father's name.)

Doris also became the butt of jokes over her proposal to raise perfumed pigs on Duke Farms. She asked Hillsborough Township to change its sanitary code so she could build a $50,000 piggery on the estate to complement her dairy and orchid greenhouses. She proposed erecting a concrete motel for 25,000 pigs. Individual atomizers would spray the pigs with a perfumed deodorizer. The local government gave her permission, provided no garbage was trucked in for their feed. The hogs would be raised on a grain and corn diet. Oh yes, the motel would be air conditioned. One wag noted, "If your apartment has been unbearably hot this summer, you can console yourself with the thought that your ham sandwich is comfortable."

Local townpeople were puzzled. "She's got everything beautiful in the world," one woman remarked. "Now what can she want with all those hogs?"

The newspaper headlines continued to link her and Barbara Hutton: "Our Richest Unhappiest Girls." In one nightclub act, as described by Heymann, female impersonators performed a hilarious skit featuring Dee Dee and Babs. The two heiresses take a car trip up the California coast. At a rest stop, Babs goes into the ladies' room. She returns and Doris says she too has to go. "Is it sanitary?" Dee Dee asks. "Clean as a whistle," the Hutton character replied. "Only there's no toilet paper."

Doris wrings her hands. "Oh dear, what will I do?" "You should have said something earlier, Dee Dee," says Barbara, looking through her bag. "If I'd known, I would have saved you a traveler's check. I just used my last one."

In truth, Doris was appalled by Hutton's obscene spending habits. After one visit to Shangri-la, Hutton tipped majordomo Johnny Gomez by buying him a flawless diamond ring. "This upset Doris," said Wallis Sewall. "Doris never gave Johnny anything. Barbara said, 'Doris is so cheap. All that money she's got.'"

By June 1952, Doris finally went public with Joey Castro, bringing him to a lavish party she threw at Cobina's. Doris wore a striking black and white dress, her neck and arms covered in diamonds.

Castro recalled the night:

"Doris had all these drummers from Haiti, they all spoke French. She took this whole troupe and had a party on the lawn with all these torches. I'll never forget it. They all danced up and down. Doris had my little group playing there in case someone saw us and liked us, we'd get a break. Charlie Chaplin, Keenan Wynn, Robert Ryan and Gilbert Roland were there. They used to call him 'Amigo.'"

Chaplin took the microphone and improvised a hilarious opera. "He was speaking this language that no one recognized. Everyone had their mouths open watching this performance." Chaplin invited Joe and Doris to his house the following weekend.

"She envied Joe," a friend recalled. "She would have given up all the money to have the talent he had."

On New Year's Eve, she took Castro to a party at the Mocambo given by Texas oilman Telvis Morrow. It was another star-studded affair, with Edith Piaf serenading the guests, including Joan Crawford with Caesar Romero, Lana Turner and Lex Barker, Dorothy Lamour, Greer Garson, Peggy Lee, Marion Davies and her husband Horace Brown, and, of course, gossip columnist Louella Parsons. Five private detectives guarded the several millions worth of jewelry dangling from the women's ears and necks.

Joey was getting bored with sneaking out of the Bel Air Hotel at night, and suggested to Doris that she buy a house.

One afternoon at the Bel Air, Doris ran into actress Gloria Swanson who greeted the heiress with a bit of news. "Dahlling, you'll never guess where I'm going to be staying tomorrow. Falcon's Lair." Doris was intrigued. "Oh, I've always wanted to see that home." Swanson said, "I'll get Bob Balzar to invite you to tea."

The Spanish-Italian white stucco house with a red tile roof had once been home to Rudolph Valentino. Perched atop a mountain in fashionable Benedict Canyon, the house had a clear view down to Cary Grant's home. With its wrought-iron fence around the driveway and a fountain in the courtyard, it was a symbol of the opulent, romantic Golden Years of Hollywood. It was also said to be haunted. Millicent Rogers, the Standard Oil heiress, had rented the house for three months but left after only one night, telling friends she saw the ghost of Valentino stalking through the halls.

After his death, the house was sold several times. Virginia Hill, the former girlfriend of mobster Bugsy Siegel, was one tenant. So was actress Ann Harding. In the forties, the house was sold to San Francisco restaurateur Gypsy Buys. It now belonged to wine authority and writer Bob Balzar.

"The house was very secluded and very private," recalled Lee Graham, Cobina Wright's assistant. "There were rumors it was haunted. They used to hold séances up there. People claimed to have seen Valentino. He came one night and supposedly said the movies they were making were not as good as they used to be."

Doris was driven up to the house for tea with Balzar and Swanson. She fell in love with the house. The following day, Johnny Gomez called Balzar and told him Miss Duke wanted to buy Falcon's Lair. Gomez named an amount. It was considerably less than the house was worth. Balzar refused to sell. Doris increased the offer by $10,000. Immediately after the papers were signed, an anxious buyer offered twice what Doris had paid for it. "She stole it from me," laughed Balzar.

Decorator Tony Duquette, the last protégé of the great Elsie de Wolfe Mendl, was hired to decorate the house.

"To my horror, they put polka dot wallpaper in the living room," said Balzar. The ceiling and walls were covered in ostrich feathers. The separate guest house was refurbished for Joe's use, and dubbed the Playhouse.

"She liked the idea of having Valentino's house," said Castro.

She also liked the idea of having Joe in residence, and his musician cronies on call for late-night jazz sessions.

"It really was 'Pal Joey' come to life," said Leonard Stanley, Duquette's assistant at the time. "She was crazy about him, no doubt."

"I used to make her laugh a lot," said Castro. "I remember once in Manhattan there was a cab strike and we had sent the chauffeur home after the theater. We had gone to the Latin Quarter. I said, 'How are we gonna get home?' Then I saw this big truck with newspapers on the back. I said to the driver, 'Here's twenty bucks. Can you take us to 78th and Fifth?' We rode on the back of that thing. We were all dressed up in tuxedos and long dress. She was tickled to death. We laughed all the way. She loved things like that."

Joe knew Doris' main problem with music was her performance anxiety. "I'd hire people to come over and play with her who were shyer than she was. Late at night, if she'd had a couple of drinks, she'd start singing the blues. I couldn't tell if she had a good voice, she was hoarse from the shyness."

Castro told Doris it would be a good idea if she played with a band. Then he suggested the unthinkable, that they find a place where no one knew her. Castro would choose sidemen who would not talk to the press. Joe's older brother Paul could play bass and his fiancée, Darlene, could accompany them. An old Army buddy, Phil Benson, would be perfect for the saxophone.

In April 1954, Doris left for Spain. When reporters asked why she was going, she said, "For the ride." And what a joyride it was. She and Joe met up in Barcelona with Claude Marchant, a young black dancer with Katherine Dunham's group. Marchant invited Doris to work out with his troupe. "It was great," Castro said. "The weather was marvelous. We lived in a hotel and she went to dance rehearsal every day. We had a piano. They'd rehearse everyday on the top floor, where we wouldn't bother anyone."

Phil Benson was taken to a Barcelona bar where an elegantly dressed woman sat at a table. "She was extremely shy and vulnerable. Joe introduced her as his girlfriend Dorshka and said she was a dancer. The first thing I thought was that she was a little bit old for Joe. She was not beautiful, but had presence. I could tell she was a cultivated woman."

She and Joe seemed an odd pair. Said Benson: "Joe was such an exuberant, open, generous and volatile person. She had a certain placidity. He was this violent young Mexican American and she was a sophisticated Waspish woman. But Joe was crazy about her. He asked me if I liked her. I said, 'She's terrific. Are you gonna marry her?'

"He said it again. 'It's important to me. Do you like her?' I said she's a marvelous woman. He then told me she was really Doris Duke. I said, 'Who's Doris Duke?' He said, 'She's the richest girl in the world.' He wanted to know if I really liked her before he told me who she was. I guess I passed the test."

Paul Castro's twenty-year-old fiancée, Darlene, also came to Barcelona. "I was so impressed. We met in Barcelona. Doris was sitting there in a black V-cut dress with a string of black opals the size of marbles, and a tight fitting skull cap hat with a black bow. I thought, 'This is really high society.'"

Darlene, also known as Dolly, recalled the various hangers-on, including a man named Pedro. "Doris was not a very good judge of people. This Spanish guy Pedro glommed onto Doris. She thought he could do no wrong. He groveled. From the moment I saw him, I thought he was a con artist."

Doris instructed Pedro to begin purchasing items for Falcon's Lair. Crates of antiques and collectibles arrived weekly back in Hollywood. "She bought all these antique lamps. He packed them up and shipped them. Later, I found out she never saw them again."

While Doris and Joe went to Seville, Paul and Dolly flew to Switzerland to find a location for the group to play and Phil Benson did the same in Greece.

Dolly and Paul immediately found a dance hall in Geneva, the Paladium, willing to book Castro's group. Doris' Italian maid Paola took all the instruments on a train from Rome. She also found an apartment for Doris and Joe on the lake, and put her name on the lease. The rest of the band checked into a hotel.

Claude Marchant and his dancers were a colorful, noisy group. He had appeared with Lena Horne in the 1943 *Stormy Weather.* "Style was very important to Doris. You had to do things with a flair," recalled Benson. "Nothing would surprise me about either Joe or Doris. During this period, there were no rules."

The Paladium wanted publicity shots of the band. Dolly filled in for Doris in those pictures, wearing the long, straight black wig the heiress had brought over for her debut.

Awaiting the start of their engagement, Doris took the group to St. Moritz for Christmas, where they occupied several suites at the Palace Hotel.

"Everything was always first class," said Benson. "Doris introduced me to King Farouk. Gregory Peck was there."

As snow dusted the mountains, the group celebrated Christmas Eve together. "Doris gave us all presents," Dolly recalled. "She gave me ski pants and two cashmere sweaters. But I felt badly. There wasn't that much under the tree for Doris. I kept thinking, why should I feel sorry for her? She has everything. I realized what a shallow life the woman had. She didn't have the ability to find something that satisfied her."

Back in Geneva, the group opened at the Paladium. Castro was particularly energetic on the vibes while Doris, wearing her black wig, nervously played the piano riffs on tunes like "Take the A Train" and "City Jam Blues."

Said Benson: "She was scared to death, but she tried not to let anyone know."

To calm her nerves, she began drinking, Joe said. "She was trying to act in her twenties," said Dolly. "She was trying to keep up with Joe."

On New Year's Day 1954, the group had a day off. Doris was lying in bed with an international newspaper. Suddenly her eyes glanced at a headline: RUBI AND BARBARA HUTTON WED.

How could it be? Doris knew they had met each other, but Barbara was a frail, bedridden woman. And so much older looking! She threw the paper on the floor in disgust.

(Hutton biographers reported that Barbara, at the urging of her step aunt Marjorie Post Davies, called her "close friend" Doris to find out if Rubi was suitable husband material. Rubi supposedly received a rave recommendation from the tobacco heiress. In fact, Hutton lied to her aunt. She never made the call.)

Doris grew more and more depressed as the day progressed. She called these periods "black ass." Her mood turned darker, and Joe knew enough to leave her alone. But he was sufficiently worried about Doris' emotional state to call Dolly and ask her to go over and stay with the heiress.

"I went to the apartment," recalled Dolly, "and Doris was very upset. She was using all these obscenities. She was just furious. She said Barbara had betrayed her. She was a 'fucking goddam bitch' and he [Rubi] was a 'fucking bastard.' She called Barbara a cunt. I was appalled. Here was this woman of the world."

Dolly sat across from the bed. "She wanted to talk to a woman. The bottom line was, she was hurt. Nobody bothered to tell her.

"She was drinking booze. She kept pouring it in a glass over ice. It was early afternoon. I was there for a long time." She told Dolly that Barbara Hutton had always been jealous of her. "He was the love of her life and she stole him. She said, 'We could never get along, but I still love the man.'"

In her alcoholic daze, Doris "reverted back to childhood." Her voice grew more breathy and girlish. "She told me her father was a tobacco farmer and they were so poor they couldn't afford shoes for her. She went barefoot as a child. She said they were dirt poor. They came into money suddenly, and she didn't have anyone to guide her. I assumed both her parents were dead."

She also gave a version of the loss of her child in 1940. "She told me she had been riding in Hawaii and the horse reared and threw her off. It was an accident. She lost the baby because of that. She told me she couldn't have any more children."

Rubi was Hutton's fifth husband. She was his fourth wife. Although he had been romancing Zsa Zsa Gabor, Rubi was in need of money. By December 1953, after Trujillo had abruptly ended his diplomatic service (Rubi had caused an international scandal by being named as "the other man" in two divorce suits), he knew his only course of action was to marry another American heiress. Hutton reportedly offered the "ding dong daddy from Santo Domingo," as *Time* magazine dubbed him, $1 million. After the wedding, Rubi was restored as Trujillo's minister to Paris. But the ink was barely dry on the prenuptial agreement before Rubi resumed his affair with Gabor. Seventy-three days later, the Woolworth heiress and the Stud of the Century officially separated.

"Never again will I marry a woman of wealth," Rubi declared. Of course, he didn't need to. By then, the last of the big dame-hunters had secured a string of polo ponies, the Paris mansion from Doris, a plane from Barbara, and $1 million in cash.

He seemed defensive, wondering why he was always being named as "the other man," and why he should be criticized for making "the mistake of loving and marrying heiresses . . . I've become a fad, like mah-jongg or miniature golf."

Rubi wasn't the only man to bring out the checkbook in Doris. "She was generous to a fault with people she liked. Mostly men," recalled Benson. He and Castro charged clothes to Doris: crocodile shoes, custom-made suits. "Money was never a problem, if we needed something, we got it. Joe and I used to go out and buy Italian ties. I really built up my wardrobe at that time." His brush with the super-rich "really changed my life. I learned what money could buy."

When they needed petty cash, Doris went to the bank and withdrew $25,000 at a time. Joe enjoyed flaunting the power that Doris' money provided. One morning, he called for all the bellboys in the hotel to meet in the lobby. He gave them each a $10 bill. "Now when I snap my fingers, I want to see action," he barked to the employees.

"Joe made money fun," Benson said. They ran up a sizeable bill at the hotel, ordering room service (mostly champagne and lobster). When the hotel manager demanded a partial payment, Joe went to Doris for a check, which he presented at the front desk. "What is this, a joke?" the manager said, eyeing the signature of Doris Duke. He demanded to be paid in cash. Joe drove to the bank and returned with heavy canvas sacks overflowing with pounds of coins. Said Benson: "They were Swiss francs. He came back with $3,000 worth of coins and dumped them on the desk."

Although Joe was running up enormous tabs around town, one item on his expenses—$1 for postage stamps—finally caused an outburst. "Doris flipped," recalled Dolly. "She accused him of taking advantage of her. The booze bills were so extravagant. But she was more upset by the $1 worth of stamps."

At the end of their stay, the landlord presented a bill for damages: broken dishes, glasses, and furniture. "They got into it hot and heavy," said Benson. "There were complaints from neighbors. They had lovers' spats." Benson described their passion as "mixing two potent fluids. They were as opposite as opposite could be."

As news of Hutton's wedding to Rubirosa reached Europe, reporters finally tracked down the tobacco heiress in Geneva.

"We left town in a hurry," said Benson.

Doris booked a flight to Rome under the name Dolly Strayhorn. At Geneva's Cointrin Airport they tried to dodge reporters and Benson hurled a bottle of Courvoisier at a photographer who recognized Doris despite her wig.

In Rome, one of their first stops was Bricktop's. Joe took to the stage and played piano, which annoyed Doris. Said Benson, "Doris was quite jealous, she didn't like people paying attention to him. She wanted to own him."

In Rome, they were met by paid associates of Doris. "Everywhere we went, we were met by people in her inner circle. Their job was to keep Doris from being imposed on by the world. She was constantly pursued. Everybody wanted to get next to Doris. It was the magic of money," said Benson, who seems to have known this first-hand.

That same week, the French singer Charles Trenet announced his "engagement" to Doris Duke. He claimed he was a friend of Rubi's and that they would honeymoon with Rubi and Barbara in Palm Beach. The whole thing was a cruel hoax, perpetrated by Trenet's manager. She had never met him.

In Rome, Joe, Doris and Phil haunted nightclubs, bars, and expensive restaurants. Castro and Benson would tell stories of their impoverished backgrounds. "She wanted to be connected with us," Benson recalled. "She would tell that story of her childhood, of not having shoes."

After several weeks, Doris became bored. She had also drawn the unwanted attention of reporters and photographers. Said Benson: "She never stayed in one place too long."

When the group disbanded, Doris and Joe flew back to Los Angeles where they took up residence once again at Falcon's Lair.

It was then that her periods of depression worsened. While Doris stayed isolated in her room, Castro became impatient and would often leave to see his musician friends.

The tension between them usually involved the subject of money. "I used to get mad and tell her all the money was her father's. I never minced words. I said, 'What's so great about it being yours? Don't you know how many people got cancer out of cigarettes?' She'd say, 'No he went into Duke Power.'"

She gave Castro an allowance. "Doris wanted him when she wanted him. Other times, she would treat him like shit. He grew to depend on her. In the beginning, the attraction was money. But then it deepened. Sometimes he'd cry. He was really quite desperate," said Benson.

Because he was Doris' companion, Joe began turning down job offers. Angry and frustrated, he became more and more belligerent. His career was going nowhere. Doris was supposed to be helping him.

One afternoon, Doris asked George Hurrell to come up to Falcon's Lair to take a portrait of Joey. Hurrell described the scene:

"He was pretty violent the day I saw them at the house. He was yelling and screaming at her all during the sequence. She ran out to the kitchen. I could hear them yelling and cursing. I thought he was going to cut her throat. He had a vicious temper. I don't know what the hell they were fighting about."

The "old shoe" whom Hurrell had photographed in 1939 had undergone a remarkable change. "She wore a lot of eye make up. She began to look ghoulish. She was trying to restore her looks for Castro."

Hurrell believed Doris was deeply insecure. "It was always this search to find people who loved her for herself alone."

Joe and Doris often dropped in at the Morocco Supper Club owned by jazz musician Dorothy Donnagan. She recalled that Joe Castro was "neurotic and volatile."

"I remember after one falling out, Joey Castro came in crying. He said he lost Doris Duke. He wanted to know how to get her back."

The fights were always followed by tearful reconciliations. Often, Doris would try to placate Castro by taking him to Europe and the Far East. Sometimes they were accompanied on these trips by Nana Veary, faith healers, and herbalists, who Castro said would give the couple "treatments."

And, of course, she was also always on the lookout for a bargain. Said Castro: "In India, she'd buy a priceless ruby. It would be considered an antique so she wouldn't have to pay duty on it."

Castro also said Doris made a side trip to Paris to remove two antique outdoor glass wall sconces she had bought for Rubirosa's house on the Rue de Bellechasse. "She never forgot them," Castro said. "They were hers and she wanted them."

Russell Selwyn, son of Edgar and Ruth Selwyn, tells a similar tale of Doris' remarkable memory for purchases. "My mother and Doris went on trips together. On one they bought Persian and Moroccan artifacts including several valuable chests my mother bought." When Doris learned that Ruth Selwyn had died, she immediately came to the house and wanted to buy the trunks.

"She did not want to pay what they were worth," Russell recalled. He turned her down.

Castro said Doris experimented with drugs, including Dexedrine and LSD. "It was supervised by a doctor, a friend of Peggy Lee's. I drove her home afterwards. She was in bed. She said she had talked to my brother, who was dead. She talked about Arden liking her so much. She went into all that kind of thing. She felt very good about it."

(Cary Grant, her neighbor and former husband of Barbara Hutton, would also experiment with the hallucinogenic.)

She became friendly with Cyd Charisse's ex-husband Nico, and backed his Hollywood dance studio. (In gratitude, he furnished the heiress with a private room for her ballet rehearsals.)

As eccentric as Doris was becoming in her relationship with Castro, her half-brother Walker Inman—also a trustee of the Duke Endowment—had become involved with an attractive young nurse from a lower class background, Georgia Polin. "She had nothing. She was nobody," Edward Hansen, the family butler, recalled. "But she was very devoted to him and faithful. She travelled with him in his private plane everywhere." Inman's health was failing. "He'd had a colostomy, and he was very embarrassed by it," said a family member. "It had changed his way of living. He was an alcoholic, and used pills. Georgia tried her best to keep him straight. She had some hard times with him."

Nanaline gave Georgia a diamond bar pin, a diamond encrusted bracelet, and a diamond wrist watch.

"Whether she approved of the marriage, she couldn't do anything about it," Hansen said. "Because her son was a rather stubborn boy himself and you couldn't do anything about him."

(Georgia and Joe Castro got along well, he said. "'What are we doing here? We're from the other side of the road,' she used to tell me.")

On March 24, 1951, Georgia and Walker were married. A year later, Georgia gave birth to a son, Walker, Jr.

In Georgetown, South Carolina, on September 19, 1954, Inman died suddenly at the age of sixty. Under the terms of his will, half of his fortune was left to his wife. There was considerable gossip about the "mysterious circumstances" surrounding Inman's death, and foul play was suspected.

Six months later, the coroner called for an inquest into the circumstances of Inman's death. Although his body had been cremated, an autopsy had been performed. The inquest revealed that Inman died from an overdose of Seconal, a probable suicide.

A year later, Georgia Polin died of a heart ailment, and their orphaned son was sent to live with relatives in South Carolina.

Nanaline had lost all interest in her family and her days in Newport were lonely ones. That summer the winds of Hurricane Edna battered the Newport coast relentlessly and the phone and power lines were down. A terrified Nanaline huddled in her bedroom, the sound of shattering glass echoing through the drafty halls of Rough Point. She feared for her life.

The following day, Mrs. Duke and the servants packed up and left Newport, vowing never to return. The house where the flowers dared not wilt was unceremoniously boarded up, and the furnishings carted away and sold. Rather than return to the vast New York mansion, Nanaline took refuge in a New York hospital for an indefinite stay.

Her daughter was also becoming more isolated.

"Doris had a falling out with the Kahanamokus," recalled Ann Rayburn, who had lost her "second mother," Louisa Jackson, to Doris, who had hired the maid away years earlier. "They were in Los Angeles. Doris called and said, 'I expect you for dinner.' They said they couldn't make it, they had other plans. Doris said unless they came to her home, 'Don't expect the friendship to go any further.'" The Hawaiian friends, so loyal for years, became estranged. Said Rayburn: "The Kahanamokus didn't want to be dictated to."

As strong-willed as Doris had become, there was one man who was her match: Pulitzer-Prize-winning novelist Louis Bromfield. He was sixteen years her senior with a rather brusque manner. Born in Mansfield, Ohio, Bromfield had attended the Cornell School of Agriculture at Columbia University before becoming a writer, returning to Ohio and buying Malabar Farm. With its woods, ponds, streams, and wildlife, the farm became a mecca for the celebrity friends Bromfield had cultivated: Joan Fontaine, Kay Francis, gossip columnist Inez Robb, Jimmy Cagney, Lauren Bacall, and Humphrey Bogart, who were married at Malabar Farm.

"She had read his books and contacted him," said David Rimmer, the son of Bromfield's secretary. In a 1948 *Life* article, Bromfield was described as "the only farmer in America who has written two dozen books, won a Pulitzer Prize and habitually has breakfast in bed."

After the death of his wife and the sudden demise of his trusted companion George Hawkins, Bromfield was a lonely man and a heavy drinker. He and Doris were both keenly interested in the environment. In the fall of 1955, she went to Malabar Farm.

"She was very much like Bromfield himself," said one of the writer's friends, Ralph Cobey. "Very striking, rather tall and thin."

In January 1956, Bromfield became ill while on a trip to New York and was invited to recuperate at Duke Farms. "Doris was very kind to him," recalled his daughter Ellen Carson Geld. Bromfield's other daughter, Hope Stevens, said a love affair between the writer and the heiress "was possible, but he never said anything to us. Daddy may have felt he didn't want us to know. Actually, he was lonely and I would have been glad."

Cobey said the liaison was "a relationship of admiration. She used to compare him to her father, Buck Duke. They were very much taken with each other. When he'd sit in a chair and she looked at him, she'd visualize her father."

Cobey and Bromfield were frequent visitors to Duke Farms, and Doris would provide the plane tickets. "We met everybody. Cary Grant was there. She attracted a lot of people like that. So did Bromfield."

In financial trouble, Bromfield had been forced to sell acres of timberland at Malabar Farm. Doris gave him the necessary funds to buy back the land. She also contributed $30,000 to his environmental group, Friends of the Land. He was also instrumental in updating agricultural conditions at Duke Farms, which had become hopelessly outmoded. "There were also hundreds of dead elms which had been attacked by Dutch elm disease," said Rimmer. "He helped her with that."

There were rumors of an impending marriage.

"We're very fond of each other. We may get married, but it won't be right away," Bromfield told reporters.

Cobey recalled that Doris had discussed turning over Duke Farms to Bromfield's environmental group.

But Bromfield's drinking had taken a toll on his body. It was rumored that he had received a tainted blood transfusion. Doris did not think his condition serious. He returned to Mansfield from Somerville, making plans for the possible takeover of Duke Farms.

Two months later, at the age of fifty-nine, Bromfield died of liver and kidney failure as a result of hepatitis.

Years later, Doris still displayed a picture of her beloved Louie Bromfield in a silver frame next to her bed.

In gratitude for her financial support, the Friends of the Land named a tract of forest at Malabar Farm, "Doris Duke Woods."

Chapter Twelve

Lush Life

DORIS' MOODS WERE INCREASINGLY UNPREDICTABLE and her whims eccentric. "Tony Duquette designed the drawing room based around two antique screens," said Leonard Stanley. "It was really beautiful. The minute it was finished, Doris packed up the screens and sent them back to New Jersey. We never saw them again."

A list of purloined loot in a minor burglary reflected Doris' eclectic tastes: a leather camel saddle, an eight-inch silver dagger, a fifteen-inch silver hatchet, an Indian tom-tom drum, and an accordion. This is the same woman who once left $15,000 worth of jewelry in the trunk of a Manhattan taxi cab by mistake, and paid 35,700 pounds at Parke-Bernet Galleries for Renoir's "Little Girl Sewing."

There were the customary fights over the bills, and around-the-clock demands from "Miss Duke" who would arrive on the West Coast on her way to Hawaii. "I remember being there until 2 in the morning," said Stanley. "She never offered us a drink or a sandwich. There's no warmth there."

Stanley observed the volatile nature of her boyfriend, Joe Castro. "I think that's what attracted her. It intrigued her and kept her interested."

Joe and Doris commuted between Falcon's Lair and Shangri-la. "She didn't want him to work," said musician John Poole. "Doris would come looking for Joe at his apartment in Waikiki. He'd have passed out instead of going home. She'd pound on my door wanting to know where he was."

Doris thought every woman wanted what she had. Her relationship with singer Hazel Ross was one casualty of her possessiveness. "The friendship ended when Doris thought she was after Joey," said Stanley. "She has a pretty rough temper. It was weird."

During one argument, Doris hit Castro over the head with a wine bottle. Said Castro: "She was always jealous. She was a very jealous person."

Barbara Hutton met Castro and according to the musician tried to seduce him. Hutton telephoned Doris one morning and spent an hour talking to Joe. "She said, 'I'd give you more than she would,'" Castro recalled. "She said, 'If you were with me, you'd have a symphony orchestra.'"

Doris and Barbara didn't speak to each other for years. Doris complained to Castro: "She wants everything I've got." (Subsequently, Doris and Joe went to Tahiti for a vacation. In a small restaurant, they encountered Hutton. The two poor little rich girls sat across from one another at opposite ends of the room, neither one acknowledging the other's presence. "America's two wealthiest heiresses, like China and the USA, are aware of the other's existence," columnist Leonard Lyons observed, "but do not recognize each other.")

A frustrated musician, Doris was fascinated by the jazz world. John Poole, longtime drummer for jazz stylist Anita O'Day, recalled "Doris liked Anita very much. I remember parties with Duke Ellington and Buddy Rich at Shangri-la. There was a lot of Cognac, champagne and pot smoking."

O'Day, formerly lead vocalist for Gene Krupa's Big Band, was an admitted heroin junkie and had been twice jailed for drug possession. "Doris had the pad, and we hung out there," she later recalled.

Castro, who had accompanied singer June Christy, often played at the Hickory House on West Fifty-second Street, a favorite hangout of Stan Kenton and Duke Ellington. He did session work on a few albums, and played with saxophonist Teddy Edwards. He released one solo album for Atlantic, "Mood Jazz," with bassist Ed Shonk and Philly Joe Jones, a drummer who had played for many years with Miles Davis. Dave Brubeck wrote an appreciation of Castro which appeared on the liner notes, concluding that "Talent will triumph—given enough time and tenacity."

In the recording studio, "Joe was a maniac," recalled one musician. "He'd do nineteen takes on a song. He had a terrible temper. He always wanted to be the star. He wanted to be famous."

Pianist Marian McPartland met Doris through Joe at a beach party in

Aruba. "I would say he was a good pianist. But too much of a playboy to take work seriously. He didn't work at it."

As Tony Duquette put it: "He wasn't Bobby Short."

In Castro's defense, Doris' nomadic life-style and penchant for privacy did hamper his career. (She was now traveling under a new moniker: Miss Wong, leading one wag to note that the name was appropriate since she had never managed to find Mr. Right.)

"I started to get frustrated," Castro said of his derailed career. "It was a trap that I never wanted to fall into." While Castro had a press agent to get his name in the papers, Doris hired one to keep hers out.

For a job in Las Vegas, Castro and Doris rented a house in which they entertained nightly. The landlady finally served eviction papers after one particular late night bash during which someone threw a skillet of spare ribs at Castro.

There were hangers-on and the usual retinue of gurus and psychics. Doris often spoke of her belief in reincarnation. Said Castro: "She told me she was an Indian once and I was in her last life."

They traveled to Thailand and India where Doris haggled over treasures she wanted brought back to Hawaii. As tourists, they were a colorful couple. Doris and Joe arrived late one night at the Taj Mahal. "The guard would not let us in," recalled Castro. "No moonlight, no Taj. I started screaming, cursing at the man and calling him a son of a bitch." Then the piano player pulled out a thick wad of money and he and Doris were admitted.

To please Castro, Doris bought him gifts: a cashmere overcoat, a black MGB sportscar. "For Castro's birthday," said John Poole, "she took him down to a Mercedes dealer and picked out a red sportscar for him. When the salesman said he would need a check in the amount of $16,000 she merely replied, 'I'm Doris Duke.'"

The heiress was considered a celebrity in Hollywood and at that time few celebrities escaped the attention of *Confidential* magazine. The movie studios were aghast over the revelations the so-called "scandal" sheet published, but they were powerless to stop them. *Confidential*—with a circulation of 4.1 million—was the largest-selling newsstand magazine in the world. It employed a vast network of libel lawyers, private eyes, and "investigative" journalists, many of them legitimate writers moonlighting for extra cash. "Tells the Facts and Names the Names" was the magazine's motto, and those facts leaned heavily on the stars' sexual peccadillos. ("Errol Flynn and His Two-Way Mirror!")

It was no surprise that Doris Duke became the subject of an exposé. She certainly qualified, by virtue of her tempestuous affair with Castro. The magazine instead devoted a six-page spread in the May 1955 issue to "Doris Duke and Her African Prince."

Doris had befriended a fifty-four-year-old black who claimed his father was king of a tribe on Africa's Gold Coast. Prince Madupe, as he called himself, lectured on mysticism to various women's clubs in Los Angeles and came to Doris' attention. The story detailed the tobacco heiress's depressions, her "steady diet" of sleeping pills, and her well-known affection for sexual partners of "the bronze hue," as well as her friendship with the Nigerian fire-eater Samadu. (Unknown to the magazine, the fire-eater had been among Claude Marchant's group in Geneva for Doris' musical debut.)

Madupe "immediately started the tobacco tootsie on a course of involved breathing exercises, broken by sessions in African voodoo dancing," *Confidential* reported. "It must have been relaxing. Doris tossed away her sleeping pills and even redesigned her bed chamber, decorating the ceiling with ostrich plumes to go with the prince's feathered headdress, which he wore during instructions."

(One business associate later confirmed that Doris did indeed bring Madupe to social events and introduced him as "His Highness.")

The story continued: "The prince didn't draw a regular pay check. He was permitted to bring his household bills, such as groceries, gas and electric to his haughty sponsor, who paid them as the mood dictated." She also bought him a Buick Roadmaster. He in turn tried to interest her in backing him in a proposed sausage-making business in Los Angeles and when she declined he announced that he had secretly tape-recorded their sessions. He was then revealed to have lied about his royal background. The story, which already sounded like a farce, became even more farfetched when it said that Doris—who kept a network of private eyes to protect her from such clip artists—hired associates to raid Madupe's apartment and destroy the tapes and diaries. A detective was paid to take Madupe to Mexico.

(The private eye hired for the job was later identified as Robert White. "She was really on the warpath against this guy Madupe because he embarrassed the hell out of her," a former associate recalled. "Evidently he ran into some fellow musicians at a party or something. He was exposed.")

To the average magazine reader, the story was too bizarre to believe. But intimates of Doris were not surprised.

"He was there one time when I went over to the Bel Air Hotel," recalled Eleanor Hufty, Doris' colorist and personal psychic. "He was a big, heavy set fellow. He was supposed to be a prince from some African country. I never gave him much credence. I think he was a physical therapist."

Lawyer Jerry Giesler was Hollywood's premier troubleshooter at the time and his clients included Charlie Chaplin, Errol Flynn, and Lana Turner. He had also represented Barbara Hutton in her lawsuit against Count Reventlow for custody of their son, Lance. Giesler convinced the tobacco heiress that she could put the magazine out of business if she sued. He had been looking for deep pockets to help fund his legal assault, and already there were five libel cases pending against *Confidential* and its publisher, Bob Harrison. (Robert Mitchum sued for $1 million over an article alleging he disrobed at a Hollywood party.)

On behalf of Doris Duke, Giesler filed suit in July 1955, asking for $3 million in damages, claiming his client had suffered "mental anguish, shame and humiliation." The attending publicity was spearheaded by an emotional outcry from Doris' friend, syndicated columnist Inez Robb, who wrote that the heiress had "struck a blow for liberty, freedom and decency . . . against the most putrid of the so-called 'expose' magazines."

The initial publicity quickly died down, and the case was eventually dismissed on March 13, 1956, for lack of jurisdiction. The dismissal never made the news. Giesler had filed the lawsuit in Santa Monica, although it was well known that *Confidential* was published in New York.

By then, *Confidential* had changed hands, and although cash settlements were made to subjects of two articles, Doris Duke was not one of them. Nor did she put the magazine out of business. It continued publishing into the mid-1960s.

As far as striking a blow for decency, Doris' taste in reading material leaned heavily toward the type of periodical she had tried to muzzle. "She loved gossip," explained Castro. "She had every column sent to her. She loved trash."

With Nanaline Duke now an invalid, Doris moved to dispose of the Duke mansion on 78th and Fifth Avenue. Never fond of the mausoleum-like, cavernous monument to Gilded Age excess, she considered tearing it down. The New York University Institute of Fine Arts had looked longingly on the building for some time, and director Craig Hugh Smyth took the initiative. "I had heard a rumor that she had offered the house to the Metropolitan Museum of Art. I went to the Met director and asked if he were interested. After some weeks, the answer came back that the museum did not want to disburse its collection. I asked the chairman to help set up a meeting with her."

Through an old friend of Doris', Leta Morris McBean, the introduction was made. McBean thought giving the mansion to NYU was a good solution; Mrs. Duke had since moved to the Stanhope Hotel and the house had only a minimum staff.

The idea also appealed to Doris, and she gave the go-ahead, hiring a young, unknown architect from Philadelphia, Robert Venturi, to oversee the project.

It was his first commission. At a meeting, the group went over the plans for remodeling.

"Doris was always quiet, reserved and very definite when she didn't agree," recalled Smyth.

(Her one disappointment was said to be the famous elevator, which was stripped of its chandelier and mirrored walls for safety.)

In the meantime, Doris became embroiled in a bitter feud with Newport officials over her obstruction of the seaport's Cliff Walk, one of the most famous and no doubt irritating rights-of-way in America. Owners of oceanfront homes were required to keep the three-mile-long walk unobstructed under a state constitutional provision initially designed to give fishermen access to the shore. The rocky Cliff Walk was increasingly used by sightseers and nature lovers, so to discourage tourists from gawking into her windows (in reality they would have to traverse a broad expanse of lawn to get close to the house), Doris erected a heavy wire fence, thorny bushes, and a prominent No Trespassing sign.

Newport declared war on Doris, who had long since given the town the cold shoulder, arriving and departing in a black Lincoln town car with smoked windows.

That same year, in Somerville, she turned 60 acres of Duke Farms over to the Horticultural Society of New York for a national flower and plant center to be open to the public. She would call it Duke Gardens Foundation, Inc., of which she would be president. Duke Gardens was modeled after the Du Pont's famed Longwood Gardens in Delaware. She appointed Johnny Gomez in charge of supplying tropical plants, and bought control of Pittsburgh's ailing Organic Corp. of America, which was operating a new process to turn "garbage into gold" by converting it into fertilizer.

As custodian of her father's vast fortune, Doris Duke now earned more publicity than a Nobel Prize winner despite her efforts to keep a low profile. For tax purposes, the Doris Duke Foundation gave $1 million away each year to universities, including substantial grants to UCLA, Duke, and Princeton Universities for Russian studies programs.

At the University of Illinois, she endowed the James B. Duke chair of Russian Studies, which may have struck the academic world as ironic, coming from the daughter of one of the most notorious capitalists of his day.

On Thursday, April 12, 1962, Nannie Lee Holt Inman Duke, the belle of Atlanta whose unparalleled beauty won her two rich husbands, died in her apartment in New York's Stanhope Hotel on Eighty-first Street, three blocks from the old Duke mansion. She had spent the latter half of her life in isolation and was nearly blind at the end, estranged from her only daughter, and attended by a few loyal servants. Newspapers reported her age as ninety. She was actually a few months shy of her ninety-third birthday.

A week later, private funeral services were held at the Duke University chapel in Durham where Nanaline's body was interred in the family crypt alongside Washington, Ben, and James B. Duke. Contrary to gossip, Doris did attend her mother's funeral. "I know she didn't believe in funerals. She thought they were barbaric," said Susan Inman Key, the half-sister of Walker, Jr. Susan had met Doris on a few earlier occasions, and remembered feeling a sense of awe in her presence. "She was glamorous, like a movie star. And she had a way of walking which was very regal."

In her will, Nanaline left $5 million to Duke University for its Medical Center, and a fur coat to Doris. The rest of Nanaline's $40 million estate was left in trust to her orphaned eleven-year-old grandson, Walker Inman, Jr.

Nicknamed "Skipper," the boy—already the beneficiary of a sizeable trust fund left by his parents—had been staying with Caroline Lightsey, his mother Georgia's sister, and her husband Hugh on their 5,000-acre cotton and peanut farm in Brunson, South Carolina, a rural community near the Georgia border. Skipper had just completed the fourth grade of a public school and whatever chance for a normal life the family might have had ended with Nanaline's bequest. A gangly kid with close-cropped brown hair who attended Sunday school at the Baptist church, Walker had slept every night in the same bed as his uncle Hugh. Now there were reporters swarming on the front lawn, with a shotgun-wielding Lightsey keeping them at bay.

"It made him [Walker] a celebrity for no reason," recalled Susan Inman Key, who was a student at the time. (Susan is Georgia Polin's only child from a brief, first marriage.) "You have to realize Brunson was a very small town, only about 300 people. And there were no other wealthy people. I think he should not have been told. He was on the front page of the newspaper and became very spoiled after that. He could have anything he wanted. You felt so sorry for him—you didn't know who liked him for Walker, or for all that money."

According to Hugh Lightsey: "He was too young to realize. But Caroline was his guardian. She would let him do whatever he wanted to keep him happy. He started setting off firecrackers on the living room floor."

Caroline Lightsey soon developed a taste for money and social power. Hugh recalled that his wife "made herself a nervous wreck. It was too much, too soon. Skipper got wild, but Caroline let him do whatever he wanted. She wanted him to love her."

Within a year, Caroline left Brunson. Her marriage was over. "I was just a country bumpkin," Hugh Lightsey explained.

Up to now, Doris had never interfered with Caroline. After the divorce, she was successful in breaking Georgia Polin's will. According to Hugh Lightsey, Doris took custody of "Walk," as she called him. "She came to his rescue," Lightsey said.

Doris, a sophisticated, single woman of fifty, was suddenly saddled with enormous responsibility.

"It was a shock for her," Susan Inman Key said. "He was wild. It was not like he was this sweet little fellow. She put him in boarding schools. I didn't blame her. She did the best she could with Skipper. I don't think she's the kind of person to read bedtime stories."

"I was spoiled rotten, to be brutally frank," Walker himself later admitted in an interview. "A genuine, spoiled hellion."

(The poor little rich boy was eventually expelled from a string of boarding schools. He is currently on his third marriage, and was arrested, but never convicted, over the years for various offenses including drunk driving, possession of cocaine, and receiving stolen property. He makes his home on a sailboat in Australia, with "Aunt Doris" as his closest relative.)

"Walker was no great addition," recalled Joe Castro, then staying with Doris in Hawaii. "We inherited the wildest kid you ever saw in your life." The relationship between Doris and Joe grew even more tense. "I said, 'You're bringing in a child to this kind of household? I don't think this kind of thing works.' That's when I said, 'Get me out of this.'"

It was Castro who called the Honolulu fire department one balmy August evening in 1965 when two large crates of teak imported from Thailand that Doris had planned to use for her long-planned Asian Cultural Center burst into flames in the parking area of Shangri-la. Fire officials said the blaze was caused by someone playing with matches who set fire to a toy plastic car near the crates.

The loss was put at $10,000.

Said Castro, "Once I got a strap and gave it to him. I said to Doris, 'I think this boy needs a little attention.' I got him dressed up. I used to take him down to hear my band."

Joe, who had served as musical director for Tony Martin from 1961 to 1963, now worked with various bands in Honolulu and Las Vegas. "We started having problems. I was going on the road with orchestras. We felt things pulling in different directions. She might have been going through her change of life and stuff like that."

"They would fight, slam a glass or two," recalled Ed Shonk, then a young bass player. He spent hours at Shangri-la, usually joining in impromptu jam sessions with Joe and Doris. The fights, he said, were over Joe's requests for money.

Doris was now fanatical in her attempts to appear youthful.

"It was important for her to look young," said Shonk. "It looked like she had had eye tucks and chin tucks." Said Castro: "People who wanted to flatter her told her she looked like Alexis Smith."

Shonk was one of many musicians who gathered at Shangri-la. The house, he recalled, "was like a Persian dream. Doris was interested in artifacts and architectural treasures. The house was always like a museum." She had formed the Foundation for Southeast Asian Art and Culture and taken offices at 4614 Kilauea Avenue, hiring architect Howard M. Y. Wong to oversee the project. More than $1 million in art works were shipped to the island from Southeast Asia and stored in crates near the docks, including a replica of the Royal Golden Pavillion in Bangkok, used by Thai royalty for centuries. Ten other buildings were purchased outright in Southeast Asia and were dismantled and shipped to Honolulu. Two of them were teakwood dwellings reported to be over 400 years old. The center would feature a museum and Buddhist shrines and temples on eighty acres with a man-made lake.

Doris had found a decorator in Thailand who called himself San Chai and appointed him curator of the museum. She also hired the Richard Towill Corp. as engineers. Towill met with Doris and San Chai, and the group visited a remote site on the windward side of the island to discuss the proposed cultural center.

"Doris was enamored with this fellow," recalled Towill. "I thought he was just an opportunist. I felt sorry for Doris. There we were, in the brush, swatting mosquitoes. It was pitiful. She was like a little girl, trying to gain the favor of this man. Saying, 'Wouldn't this look good' . . . Obviously he wasn't interested."

At Doris' bidding, curator San Chai was dispatched back to Thailand to purchase more artifacts for the museum.

By 1963, the Duke-Castro relationship was deteriorating.

"I was in my bedroom one night," Castro said, "and she walked out of hers which was connecting with a knife in her hand. I grabbed her by both wrists." According to Castro, there was a struggle, the blade leaving a gash in the musician's arm. "Doris said, 'I suppose you're going to go to the police now.' I said, 'Don't be so corny.' Louisa Jackson brought me some bandages and I walked out the door. We never talked about it again."

While newspaper columnists on the mainland were reporting that Doris and Joe had secretly married, the love affair was winding down.

"I was resentful of her by this time," he said. "I felt like I was being used. I was half out of it myself."

Doris had employed the services of a private investigator to gather a file on Castro's activities.

Another associate recalled, "She would never go out to be seen with him in Hawaii. She didn't want to be seen with him in public unless she had a wig on or something. She would like to be seen with a prince, but not Joe Castro."

On New Year's Day 1964, Doris ordered Castro to leave Falcon's Lair.

Ten days later, he retaliated, filing an injunction barring Doris from selling the house. Castro claimed he owned one-half interest in Falcon's Lair, which he described in court papers as their "friendship house." He filed a second lawsuit in Los Angeles' Superior Court claiming he and Doris had been married on two occasions: in Providence, in 1956, and in Philadelphia, in 1960. (No marriage licenses were ever issued in those cities. Castro's attorney was hoping to prove they had lived as common-law man and wife.)

Castro won the restraining order barring Doris from disposing of any property acquired since the so-called Rhode Island marriage.

The publicity became an international scandal. In news reports, Castro was described as a thirty-six-year-old unemployed musician whose last job netted him $150 a week. Castro had also threatened to sell his story of the thrill-seeking heiress to the highest bidder.

The complaint charged cruelty, and asked for a "reasonable" amount of alimony of $5,000 a month, enough for him to live in the manner to which he had become accustomed. On January 25, Castro fired another round, filing a $150,000 lawsuit for damages, claiming in court papers that Doris had stabbed him in the arm with a butcher knife. The resulting wound, the suit claimed, left him unable to work.

Doris fled immediately to the Far East, having hired Los Angeles attorney Morton B. "Tony" Jackson to represent her. Castro was represented by R. Edward Brown, a friend of a fellow musician. Brown—banking on the fact that the publicity-shy heiress would settle rather than risk a court case—anticipated a flat payment of $2 million for his client.

Doris was adept at handling blackmailers. She hired attorney Harold Hughes—a former FBI agent—to handle Castro. Through Hughes, a private detective was dispatched to find a bogus buyer for the expose.

Peter Brooke was a freelance writer in Los Angeles when he got a call offering him $100 a day and expenses to pose as an independently wealthy journalist in search of unusual material for a recently formed publishing firm. On March 10, 1964, Brooke flew to Honolulu at Doris' expense and rented a lavish suite at the Royal Hawaiian Hotel, where he installed bugging equipment and received cash from Hughes. With the blessing of the local police department, Brooke went undercover, spending two weeks wining and dining an associate of Castro's, who was peddling the Duke-Castro story. By the end of the two weeks, Castro and his friend were bickering over the money, and the pianist eventually reconciled with Doris.

Castro's divorce suit was dismissed by the court. Doris had never been served with the papers. On May 11, 1964, Castro told a Honolulu Circuit Court judge that he never claimed to be married to Doris Duke. Castro ordered his lawyer, R. Edward Brown, to drop his lawsuits. He then claimed they were Brown's idea, not his.

In early June, Doris and Joe went to Tahiti, and stayed near Marlon Brando's home in the lush district of Paea. On their return flight to Honolulu, the tickets were issued to Mr. and Mrs. Castro.

"It was," the musician said, "a new beginning."

Doris realized that Castro, now back in the fold, was only temporarily placated. She needed something to keep him busy. At his request, she formed a record company, Clover Records, which would showcase his talents. A musical publishing company, Jo-Do (a combination of Joe and Doris), was also formed.

Doris was evidently pleased by Peter Brooke's clandestine activities. She invited him to meet her at Falcon's Lair. He was struck by this lanky, square-jawed woman who spoke in a barely audible, girlish whisper. "I do want to thank you for the way you handled things," she told him, "In whatever we may decide for you to do, as my local representative you will be accountable directly to me . . . and no one else."

Brooke said, "I felt for her. I thought she was a lost soul. I think she was so conscious of her status that it always affected her."

Doris returned to Hawaii, and resumed her relationship with Castro. She flew Brooke to the island. When he arrived at Shangri-la, Castro was shocked to see him. "Darling," she said in her faint whisper, "I suppose this must be the same Mr. Brooke you recently met yourself." She claimed mutual acquaintances recommended him to help with the new record company.

Castro never knew that Brooke had been on Doris' payroll. "It was," said Brooke, "one of the best kept secrets. Joe was totally fooled."

(Brooke's clandestine services would be requested years later when Duke attorney Tony Jackson, representing Watergate burglar Howard Hunt, offered him $25,000 to infiltrate Edmund Muskie's presidential campaign. Brooke declined.)

Peter Brooke was put in charge of Clover Records.

"I knew very little about the record business, but I knew I couldn't run it as a commercial venture. She's so paranoid about being taken advantage of all the time. I was on a short leash with her. She's terribly afraid of conspiracies within her organizations, but she courts disaster, not letting the left hand know what the right hand is doing."

Brooke encountered friction with May McFarland, secretary of the Doris Duke Foundation. "She took a dislike to me. She did everything to undermine me."

Clover offices were set up at 315 South Beverly Drive, and the first venture was a solo album by Castro, "Lush Life."

The album was pieced together from old tracks acquired from Atlantic Records, with four new songs, including "Bossa Nova All the Way" written by Castro and songwriter Joe Lubin, who was hired as musical director.

"I loved Joe's talent, but I felt sorry for what was happening in his life," Lubin recalled. "Even if he was in a position other men would envy, I don't think he liked the role he was playing. I don't think he was in command." Lubin remembered· Castro as "a very virile guy, very handsome, with beautiful hair."

One night, Lubin went up to Falcon's Lair. Castro had canceled the recording session that day, saying he had a cold. He was drinking. "I felt a little embarrassed. Doris was in the bedroom, wearing a negligee. There was antique shit all around, including a music stand which supposedly once belonged to Mozart. I opened the door and walked out onto the patio. There I was met by what seemed like a hundred Dobermans. I couldn't get out. I walked back into the room and asked Joe what was going on. He suddenly turned very aggressive. Mocking me. It was like *The Three Faces of Eve.*"

Once at home, Lubin called Peter Brooke and resigned as musical director. "Peter understood."

The album was finally mixed, and after weeks of indecision, a cover photograph of Joe chosen. "Lush Life" was delivered to 500 disk jockeys who promptly tossed it in a pile, to be forgotten. Castro was an obscure performer and Clover was an unknown company with no advertising budget or contacts. Peter Brooke was left with approximately 4,000 unsold albums.

Doris had agreed to pay Brooke a percentage of royalties from the albums, which never saw a profit. It was merely an amusement for the reclusive Doris Duke.

"When I'd pick her up at the airport, she'd look like a frump," said Brooke. "She didn't want to be recognized. She emulated Howard Hughes. They were never buddies, but I knew she had great respect for him and felt they were related in a way because of their backgrounds and the way they handled themselves.

"I ran the company. Doris didn't trust Joe with any of this. She asked me to pacify him, and make him feel like he was running it."

Doris sunk thousands of dollars into an inexperienced rock group, "The Demons." One album was recorded.

"We tried to get Anita O'Day," recalled Brooke. "She had a real problem with heroin. I used to give her checks. Doris asked me to give her money to prepare for a recording session which never came off. She'd wait for me at six in the morning at the office to get the money so she could get her fix."

Doris' own pet project was to record black singer Kitty White, who performed at the Hob Nob in Beverly Hills and always serenaded Doris with her rendition of "Happiness Is a Thing Called Joe."

"I always wanted to go to Paris," White recalled. "She knew that. She was a wonderful friend. She was very good to me. It was a period of my life when I wasn't doing a lot of music." Doris and Kitty flew to Paris where the album was recorded with the help of expatriate musicians: pianist Art Simmons, drummer Kenny Clarke, and bassist Jimmy Woode. The album cover features a smiling Kitty, coifed by Alexandre and wearing an Yves St. Laurent black leather "costume."

Meanwhile, Castro "was hopped up all the time," said Brooke. "I took him to my doctor. They said he had an enlarged liver." (Receipts from Cedars-Sinai Hospital, paid by Clover Records, show Castro was treated for liver problems.)

Brooke also became aware of Doris' nephew, Walker, Jr. He received a telephone call from Pete Cooley, then business manager of Duke Farms, who said, "'Peter, you won't believe this. They found machine guns stashed under his bed.'" Charges were ultimately dismissed.

Brooke wasn't surprised that Doris had become her nephew's guardian. "She loves people who have one foot in the grave or are in trouble with the law. I was too straightlaced for her."

As Doris' "business representative" on the West Coast, Brooke was paid $1,350 a month. "Of course, there were also expenses, but that was like pulling teeth." He became familiar with Doris' thriftiness. "I sent her a special delivery letter on some important matter to Falcon's Lair. She called and raised hell with me. She said, 'Why are you wasting office postage on this? You could have gotten in your car and brought the letter up.' I said: 'Do you know how much gas costs? And my time?' She had no concept of things like that."

Another associate recalled, "We were in an old Chrysler. She liked to drive around town in a jalopy. We stopped at a gas station and after the tank was filled, the attendant asked if we wanted green stamps. I shook my head but Doris piped up, 'Yes, the butler needs a new toaster.'"

Brooke was called upon to act as her emissary on occasion. Her foundation had donated $50,000 to UCLA for the study of American Indians. "I met with three professors from UCLA at the Bel Air Hotel. They were very surprised that I wore a business suit and tie. They were giggling about it. One said, 'The last time we got money from her she had scribbled something on the back of an envelope while on a camel in Egypt and handed it to some hippie who delivered it to us. He looked like he hadn't bathed in six months.' I said, 'Well things are changing.' But it was like that. They poked fun at her all the time.

"I was embarrassed. I knew that she was very sensitive and didn't want to be told they were phonies because she didn't want her judgment questioned. She got nasty about this guy who had the cancer machine."

Doris had befriended a man who insisted that his machine would cure cancer. "He was some quack who claimed he cured her skin cancer with his machine. She wanted me to write an article on it, to push it. She tried to have one delivered to Nat King Cole, who was then dying of cancer. She wanted him to take a cure from this machine, but he was already in the hospital dying. I was so embarrassed. She made me call him. I spoke to a man and explained that Miss Duke wanted Mr. Cole to submit himself to this treatment because she felt it might be helpful. He got back to me after he spoke with the doctors, who advised him not to interfere. It was another slap in the face for her. Of course, she blamed it on my not presenting it properly.

"I actually had the machine checked out with a doctor at UCLA who said it was like selling snake oil. I told her that and she hit the ceiling. She said, 'How dare you go to UCLA with this thing?' I answered: 'You wanted me to write an article, I've got to do some research on it.' She also wanted the Medical Center of Duke University to give him a laboratory to further his research. I met with the president of Duke."

(When Duke University declined to set up a lab for the cancer machine doctor, Doris was furious. "I almost lost my job over it," said Brooke. This was to be the final break with her father's university, which she has refused to visit since the mid-1960s.)

Another Duke associate warned Brooke that if he came to New York to work for Doris, he'd have to start wearing torn jeans, and stop shaving.

In March 1966, Doris flew to New Delhi. Castro flew to Tokyo, and stayed at the Imperial Hotel, posing as the president of Clover Records. He ran up a sizeable bill, ordering Cutty Sark and raw oysters. "She didn't want the bills going to New York, to the Foundation," said Brooke. "He used to hop around the country and charge everything to us."

Castro also used a pseudonym: Jim West.

But the record company did not satisfy him. "After having so much fun, it suddenly started getting so complicated," Castro later recalled.

Among the various musicians and artists Joe had met in Hollywood in the early 1960s was Edward Tirella, a tall, good-looking interior designer from a large Italian family in Dover, New Jersey—twenty-five miles from Somerville—who had also found work in films and was a budding singer. Tirella and Castro became close, with Castro playing piano in nightclubs while Tirella sometimes sang, his voice reminiscent of Mel Torme.

On the side, Tirella dabbled in landscape architecture and interior design. Producer Martin Ransohoff had enlisted Tirella's services for the 1965 film *The Sandpiper,* starring Elizabeth Taylor and Richard Burton. He served as advisor and consultant (he designed the bohemian artist's shack Taylor used as her oceanfront home) and appears on screen briefly in a beach scene with Taylor and Charles Bronson.

From all accounts, Tirella was immensely charming, popular, and blessed with an ingrained artistic talent. "Anything he touched," a family member later said, "something of beauty came from. He had hands of gold."

His dark good looks had earned Eddie Tirella the title of "Playboy of the Western Front" at Dover High School, where he was a cheerleader, amateur artist, and dancer. A veteran of World War II (he served in the infantry in Europe), Tirella started his career as a hat designer at Saks Fifth Avenue, selling his creations to Mae West and Hedda Hopper. As a gardener, he had worked for Peggy Lee and Alan Ladd. Along the way, he changed his name to the more European-sounding Eduardo. A free spirit and a hopeless businessman, he barely earned over $4,000 a year and, in fact, spent more than he made, often borrowing money from friends.

Tirella hosted lively jam sessions at his house, and it was there that he first met Doris Duke. He and Doris hit it off instantly, and the heiress hired him to redecorate her kitchen at Falcon's Lair. She was smitten by Tirella, and grew to rely on his judgment in matters of taste.

Like many of her intimates, he was also a homosexual. "He sensed on a couple of occasions that she wanted to have sex," said one friend. "He felt very uncomfortable. I think she got the message."

A striking figure in his turtlenecks and sporty convertible car, Tirella was known as promiscuous in the homosexual world. "He was a cupid. He loved fixing up people," recalled one friend. "But he never had any lasting relationships. They were one-night stands."

Doris enlisted Tirella to help with the refurbishing of an old hotel in Mount Washington—between Los Angeles and Pasadena—which was to serve as the main headquarters for the Self Realization Fellowship, a group of followers of the Yoginada.

Tirella was intrigued. "He liked the level on which he could spend her money," said a friend. "He did enjoy the freedom. And he liked the glamor."

While Doris took pains to avoid being photographed with Castro, she actually enjoyed being seen with Tirella. In Manhattan, they were spotted at fashion shows and photographed shopping at Ohrbach's, Doris in a three-quarter-length leopard coat made popular by First Lady Jacqueline Kennedy. With Tirella's urging, she bought copies of designer clothes for a fraction of their cost and spent $570 for five acquisitions, including a $69 faux-Balanciaga raincoat.

She also purchased a Manhattan pied-à-terre, a seven-room penthouse at 475 Park Avenue, which Tony Duquette decorated with black walls and floors and Doris' vast collection of rocks and crystals.

It was Eduardo who comforted her when she heard the news of Rubirosa's death. On July 5, 1965, the great Dominican playboy and diplomat wrapped his Ferrari around a tree after an all-night binge of nightclubbing in Paris. It was a carbon copy of the accident which had killed his friend, Aly Khan, several years earlier. He left a young widow, Odile, and scores of sobbing women at the graveside. Doris did not attend the funeral.

Eduardo and Doris became close confidantes. She began venturing out more and more. He was an amusing companion. They traveled to Europe and stayed for weeks at the Raphael Hotel in Paris. It was Tirella who would help her design the gardens at Somerville.

She also visited the home of Eduardo's friend, sculptor Edmund Kara, in Big Sur. Doris was not terribly fond of Big Sur, but Eduardo dreamed of buying a parcel of land near the coast and turning it into a park for hikers. He was trying to convince Doris to fund the project.

Meanwhile, his life-style grew more and more lavish. But since Doris never carried any cash, Eduardo was often stuck with the restaurant tabs. He grew deeper into debt, although Doris kept him on salary.

He confided to friends that working for Doris Duke was exhausting. Eduardo was expected to serve not only as a designer but as a constant source of amusement, often staying for dinner to keep her company. "He hated those nights," a close friend of Tirella's recalled. "She liked to push her food around the plate, and drink a lot of wine. He found it too fatiguing. But he was hanging in there as long as he could. He had debts, and working for Doris was lucrative. The one thing he didn't like about her was that she was abusive to the help. He thought it was medieval."

In March 1966, Doris abruptly pulled the plug on her proposed Southeast Asian Art and Culture Center in Hawaii after spending several million dollars. The priceless treasures purchased by her Thai decorator, said engineer Richard Towill, "turned out to be mostly from the flea market."

A month later, she refused to pay $147.83 for the repair of Joe Castro's car. She also balked at paying for Clover Records recording sessions. On May 20, she abruptly closed down Clover, leaving thousands of dollars of unpaid bills.

Shortly after that, Brooke was asleep when the phone rang at 3 A.M. It was a desperate, incoherent cry for help. The voice was Doris'.

Brooke threw on his clothes and rushed over to Falcon's Lair. The maid, who was hysterical, showed him to the kitchen. The room had been ransacked, broken dishes strewn on the floor. Standing in the open frame of a French window, wearing a T-shirt, though naked from the waist down, was Castro, urinating over the railing into the garden below.

As Brooke later recalled, Doris was stretched out on a blanketless bed in her room. "Her usual whisper was reduced to a muffled whimper: 'Sorry, Peter . . . for bothering you at this hour . . .' She could barely formulate the words. Her jaw had been broken. 'Please get him out of here . . . He'll listen to you . . . please just get him away from here . . .'"

Brooke spotted Nana Veary, Doris' elderly Hawaiian medium and traveling companion, seated at a small desk. She was frozen, Brooke observed, with shock and fear. Doris refused to let anyone call the police.

Brooke offered the piano player a bottle of vintage champagne from the cellar, and got him out of the house and into his car. At the intersection of Sunset and Beverly Drive, in the shadow of the pink and palm-treed Beverly Hills Hotel, Castro hurled the unopened bottle of champagne to the pavement where it exploded.

The next morning, Doris fled Hollywood for Newport, accompanied by Eduardo Tirella.

Said Joe Castro: "It was finished."

Chapter Thirteen

Money and
Madness

BUFFETED BY HURRICANES and the changing tide of the social order in the 1950s Eisenhower era, the once exclusive watering hole of Newport was now in decline.

No longer the playground of European royalty and American bluebloods, Newport had become a ghost town. Many of its gilt and marble cottages stood empty, or were donated to institutions. It was said you could buy one for a song. But who could afford the upkeep? With the dwindling servant population, inflation, and a sense that the exclusivity once so envied was now a snobbish relic of the Gilded Age, Newport would have to reinvent itself to survive.

"The whole town shut down," said one longtime resident.

Certainly, it was the end of an era; no longer would tiara-toting grandes dames dress up monkeys as princes or dinner guests dig for party favors with little gold shovels in centerpieces fashioned from piles of emerald- and diamond-studded sand.

Doris was one of the last surviving members of the original dynasty. Many of the fortunes amassed at the turn of the century were dissipated by divorce, division among heirs, investment losses, or reckless spending.

Doris had managed, according to friends and associates, to double her father's inheritance. Through shrewd investment, her stock portfolio and other funds were yielding interest of $1 million per week. It was an obscene amount of money, and with Barbara Hutton all but out of the picture, Doris was in fact, one of the wealthiest women in the world, overshadowed only by Queen Elizabeth and Queen Juliana of the Netherlands. She was also one of the most eccentric, preferring to spend her time in smoke-filled jazz clubs than the Billy Baldwin-designed drawing rooms of her peers. Like Queen Elizabeth, she had been a celebrity since the time of her birth and she lived in a world governed by her own rules and regulations, her own security force, private detectives, even her own unpasteurized milk from her own cows and her own fruits and vegetables—organically grown at Duke Farms, then flown to her dinner table, whether in Beverly Hills or Bora Bora.

After the breakup with Doris, Joey Castro returned to Honolulu. Their publishing firm, Jo-Do, was disbanded.

Joe met Loretta Haddad, an attractive singer at the Outrigger Club in early summer 1966. "It got into the papers," said Castro. A mutual friend told Doris Joe was serious this time. "Doris wanted me to make a public retraction in the newspaper about Loretta," said Castro. "I said I couldn't do that. I know that I had a very deep attachment to Doris, but another part of me knew I had to leave her. She went away with Tirella. To me, it was finished."

By the summer of 1966, four years after her mother's death, Doris' attention turned to the imposing Tudor mansion Rough Point, a gloomy white elephant. "She wanted to bring the estate back to what it had been," said Gordon King, son of the caretaker.

With Tirella, she systematically tracked down all the former furniture, tapestries, and paintings and began to assemble them at Somerville. Doris probably would not have undertaken the job without Tirella's help. The gothic castle had a sweeping view of the ocean, and the first time Eduardo Tirella stood on the wide lawn and gazed at the sea, it reminded him of the dramatic, crashing waves of Big Sur.

"It would be nothing to be up at the house and see the waves break 20 or 30 feet in the air," said Gordon King. "It was a spectacular setting. Of all the estates owned by the robber barons, it was probably the most spectacular."

Tirella had been on Doris' payroll as the chief designer of her Duke Gardens in Somerville, although workers there said it was Doris herself who did most of the work. The "Gardens of the World" display was a major accomplishment for Doris: elegant trellised greenhouses containing French, English, Italian, Chinese, and Indian gardens with hundreds of shrubs and plants, including a large white orchid developed at the farm's orchid range dubbed "The Doris." Doris and Eduardo had traveled to Europe and Asia, making sketches of various gardens they would duplicate.

Guests would be permitted to stroll through J. B. Duke's old greenhouses on weekday afternoons, by appointment only. "Eduardo would work with her in the greenhouses. They would get into arguments," recalled one former employee. "He was a nice nut. He'd take our side if she was nasty. He'd say, 'You know Miss Duke. It's the wrong time of the month.'"

"He had very effeminate gestures, and was very flamboyant," recalled the Park Manager's son, Irving Guyer. Eduardo was often visited by young men from New York who came to the house. "He had a car, and came and went as he pleased."

Said Jake Guyer: "You wouldn't see Eduardo for three or four days, he'd be in at the house. But he never bothered anyone. I thought the world of him because he was her cushion between the employees and management."

Guyer also witnessed Doris' lingering depression over the loss of her only child. "She wrote a song about that child. And she would try and sing it. We'd hear her go over it down in the theater on the piano. A horrible song. About this dead child. She was trying to publish that song."

She rarely entertained at Somerville. "She had Governor Hughes and his wife one night. Fed 'em cucumber sandwiches in her bare feet on the patio."

Guyer was responsible for clearing out the old greenhouse area. "It used to be a jungle where those gardens are. Grapevines and poison ivy. We cut poison ivy down as thick as my arm. The gardens was a big tax write off. Her business manager, Pete Cooley, had set up twenty some different foundations and she could use any of them to pay people. She also wanted the power lines detoured two and a half miles around her place."

Eduardo served on many of those foundations. He enjoyed her confidence. "He would sometimes correct her, but in a subtle way," said Irving Guyer. With his easy manner and wry sense of humor, Eduardo was well-liked by the rest of her employees. Esther Guyer, Jake's wife, once confided to Tirella that she was having a difficult time fixing up their house on the estate. "I had a couple of antiques, and I couldn't get it together because the living room was small," Esther recalled. "Eduardo came over right away. He said, 'Do this. Do that.' I said, 'What about these ugly chairs?' He said, 'Well Doris has chairs that are much uglier than that.' He made a fuss over a pair of candelabra I had, so I gave him one. We just liked him. He was a nice person."

Eduardo and Doris would often come down to the gardens at midnight. "Time meant nothing to her," said Foundation director Bob Dingwall. Often, she would want to make a change in a certain garden. One night, she and Eduardo stood there arguing. "I told them they were both talking about doing the same thing," said Dingwall. "They just stood there arguing with each other."

The regal, black iron doors to the greenhouse displayed Doris' logo: back-to-back interlocking D's, which appeared to be a royal crest. In her toreador pants and sheer blouse, Doris reigned over her estate. "Sometimes she would be good," said a former carpenter. "Sometimes she wouldn't know what she was doing. It was different moods all the time."

Doris and Tirella commuted that summer between Newport and Somerville. Johnny Gomez, her longtime majordomo from Hawaii, was called in to help.

"Doris Duke used to move the furniture around like we move our luggage," recalled Gordon King. (She also stiffed the caretaker's son for the cost of the Sunday papers, when King drove the heiress into town in her beat-up station wagon. Doris tried to pay for the two-dollar newspaper with an American Express card, which was not accepted. King handed over the money.)

"For a number of weeks, a lot of the small pieces came: armchairs, and tables," King recalled. "Some of them were gorgeous and some was ratty junk that your grandmother would have thrown away. It was a mix. Just bizarre. The tapestries came, but she didn't want them hung until she got there."

The first thing Gomez did was insist that the huge, double oak doors on the front of the house be refinished. Said King: "The doors had a gorgeous patina, aged over fifty years. The only thing we had ever done was take them down at the beginning of each summer and polish the brass hinges. Gomez looks at the doors and says, 'We've got to get all this off them.' So we took the doors down. You can't imagine how huge they are, built a temporary plywood door, set up sawhorses, and put the doors on top. We covered them with paint remover, and worked on them with steel brushes and acid." It took King and three other men two weeks to get the doors stripped. Then they were shellacked and rehung.

A week later, Doris arrived. "She just went wacky. She had this gorgeous old house with these highly varnished doors with years of patina gone. She threw a fit," recalled King. "Of course, there was nothing we could do about it."

Doris subsequently informed the staff she wanted to do all the work herself. "I guess I was 24," recalled King. "I was hired for $4 an hour to help her. We worked from nine until three in the afternoon, with no lunch. She was strong—picking up as much stuff as I could handle. But she dressed terribly. She was tall and bony, with big hands and no chest. Her hair was unkempt, pulled back. She wore no make-up and thin, baggy blouses. I always remember her as being a very homely woman, and very intimidating. She wouldn't order me around, but she was always saying, 'Move this. Move that. Let's do this.' Christ, there was some heavy stuff we moved a dozen times. She'd plop down in a chair, look around the room, jump up and decide she wanted it differently.

"There wasn't a piano in the house, so they bought one in that summer because Tirella was a piano player. All the furniture was coming back in and the house was full of workmen. We put up the chandeliers in the ballroom. Johnny Gomez was supposed to be the interior decorator. He was a bizarre bird. He used to wear leotards, and those shoes that jesters wear, with the turned-up toes."

Tirella was the opposite of Gomez: smooth, and utterly sophisticated. "He helped decorate her Beverly Hills house," recalled actress Mamie Van Doren. "He drove a navy blue Morgan, always with the top down. He wore knobby sweaters and tweedy jackets. He was really good-looking. He was also exciting, always full of good ideas. He was very close to Doris—lived with her, traveled with her everywhere."

Singer Peggy Lee was also a close friend. "Supposedly, they were the three sisters; Doris, Peggy and Eduardo," said one intimate.

In the dim, drafty Great Hall, the men had rolled out the tapestries and were waiting for instructions on where to hang them. "Some of them were great," said King. "Some of them were just old Italian tapestries, with hunting scenes.

"Johnny Gomez decided one morning that one of the tapestries would be spectacular on the floor beneath the large bay window. My father said it shouldn't go there; it wasn't a rug. Gomez said, 'No, just take the rings off. It will be beautiful here.' It's nine o'clock—we're waiting for Doris to get us started. He's standing in the middle of the tapestry with his turned-up shoes, his shirt opened to the waist and his pot belly. She comes downstairs and goes absolutely berserk because he's standing on a priceless 17th century Italian tapestry." King witnessed the full force of Miss D.D.'s temper. "The veins were standing out on her neck and she started screaming and yelling."

Tirella—ever dapper in his tweed and ascots—"didn't participate in almost any of this. He'd get up in the morning, find a book and sit in the solarium." The tall windows were lined with tree-sized coral geraniums and hanging baskets of flowers. He spent time working in the cutting garden or arranging flowers in the house. "He made the most beautiful bouquets in the world," a friend recalled. He also loved to be in the kitchen and was known as a genial and talented chef. He and Doris would pull out covered gold and silver dishes and compotes, family crystal, and magnificent porcelains for a buffet in the solarium, lit by bronze Empire candelabras flickering with seventy-five candles. While the waves crashed outside, dinner would be wheeled in through the Great Hall, hung with flags and tapestries.

Doris entertained infrequently.

"I only visited once," recalled neighbor Fitzhugh Green, who was a close friend of Doris' cousin, Tony Duke. "The night was stormy—it was like being in a medieval castle. An assistant, he was Hawaiian as I recall, helped build a fire in one of those huge, walk-in fireplaces. It was perfectly frightening."

Said Doris' former lover Tex McCrary: "It was very tacky, with all this stuff of her mother's, phony ancestors on the walls. I once said, 'Jesus Christ, you're surrounded by $3 bills.' She asked what I meant. I told her I was once the friend of a great counterfeiter who was so good at faking $2 bills, he wanted to try $3. She got the point."

Doris needed a new project every few years to ease the boredom and began discussions with Tirella involving the restoration of historic houses in Newport. Jacqueline Kennedy—who had spent summers with her mother at nearby Hammersmith Farm—knew Doris and had expressed interest in joining the effort. Doris would form the Newport Restoration Foundation and name Jackie first vice president. Jackie was drawn to the super-rich Doris the way she was drawn to Bunny Mellon and Jayne Wrightsman. Jackie and Doris were friendly, if not exactly close friends. Doris had reportedly loaned her the use of a plane to fly between Washington and Newport on occasion, and Doris' cousin Angier Biddle Duke served as the Kennedys' Chief of Protocol.

As the summer wore on, "there was some partying," said Gordon King.

"Guests would come at night. There was always a high level of energy, a lot of yelling in the house, but these people yelled and screamed all the time so you couldn't tell whether they were having fun, or it was sexual energy." Doris attended the Newport Jazz Festival and invited musicians back to the house.

Asked to describe that atmosphere, King said, "I guess I would say it was charged. A lot of highly animated conversations. Some people dressed elaborately, but they were all eccentrics."

By the end of the summer, Tirella was bored. Working for Doris Duke had lost its allure and he was anxious to return to the West Coast. Like his friend Joe Castro, he was beginning to sense that his once-brilliant career was being stymied by Doris' possessiveness and petulant demands. As his patron, Doris had been reluctant to finance any of his projects, including the Big Sur park. There were also her bouts of depression followed by the manic highs to contend with.

Producer Martin Ransohoff had offered the forty-two-year-old Tirella a job on his latest film, *Don't Make Waves*, starring Tony Curtis and Sharon Tate, and he was asked to return to Los Angeles to complete the project. Doris did not want him working on the film, and made her wishes clear. Tirella made up an excuse, saying he needed dental work. Doris offered to have her dentist treat him, but Eduardo insisted on going to Los Angeles, where he stayed with a close friend.

"He was planning to leave her employ," the friend recalled. "He was finding it far too strenuous. She was a spoiled brat who had to have everything her way. He thought she was abusive to the help and he also didn't like those endless, three-hour dinners. Doris would drink three bottles of wine and he'd have to sit there, watching her. Doris didn't want him to leave. He told me she was very angry. She kept badgering him, demanding to know what was wrong with her dentist. She was quite upset that he had come back to L.A."

In telephone conversations, Doris insisted that Tirella return East. She enticed him with hints of helping him financially, although she had previously offered little in the way of cash gifts to her friends. She had learned how money had corrupted those around her and hoped that would not be the case with Eduardo.

During that first week of October, Tirella agreed to return to Newport. "I drove him to the airport," said his friend, then an artist. "I asked him, 'What are you going back for?' He said, 'I'll get out of debt.' It seemed he owed money for taxes. It was the last time I saw him."

Tirella implied to his friend that Doris would make life difficult if he tried to leave her. After all, nobody walked out on the richest girl in the world.

On Thursday, October 6, Tirella flew east and was picked up at Newark airport by Doris. They drove to Somerville, where they spent the night. Doris was agitated not only by Tirella's perceived disloyalty, but by the telephone conversation in which she learned of Joe Castro's engagement to Loretta Haddad. On Friday morning she and Eduardo went to the greenhouses, then were driven to Newport.

Rough Point, the scene of such gay parties that summer, had grown eerily quiet. Eduardo was the only guest, aside from Johnny Gomez, in the thirty-room mansion.

Sometime before 5 P.M. on the sun-dappled afternoon of Friday, October 7, Doris and Eduardo decided to drive into town. Reports later suggested they were on their way to a dinner party at the home of Virginia Warren to discuss the Newport restoration project, but servants said the two were due back at the house by 7 P.M.

They climbed into a white station wagon, Tirella behind the wheel. The car stopped at the end of the driveway and Tirella got out, supposedly to open the padlock on the heavy iron gates which swung inward. Suddenly, the screech of burning rubber pierced the autumn afternoon and the car crashed into the fifteen-foot ornate black iron gates and shot across Bellevue Avenue, hitting a tree and coming to rest on the grassy lawn of the house directly across from Rough Point. Under the rear wheels, Tirella's body lay in a bloody mass of broken bones and torn flesh, his head smashed like a melon.

A twenty-one-year-old Naval nurse at the nearby Officer Candidate School and her visiting father had chosen that day to go sightseeing in town. "We were just taking a drive along Bellevue Avenue," recalled Judith Thomb Wartgo, "and we came across a car off the road with a blonde woman in it. I couldn't say if she braked or just hit the curb. She was in the car, about to get out. We stopped to ask if we could help. She was, I would describe it, in a state of shock. We didn't know at the time that she had run over a person."

The blonde woman was "hyper" and "agitated," Wartgo said. "I wanted her to lie down. She wasn't talking coherently. She was disoriented, but not physically injured. I don't recall her bleeding at all. She got out and started to walk back to the house. I followed her. I didn't know if she was going to pass out or drop dead, but I didn't want her to be alone. I remember going into the house. It was so large—there was a really big open staircase. I followed her upstairs. She was looking for her husband, I guess. She was calling his name: 'Eduardo.' I thought he was in the house. She was trying to get to him. I kept asking her who this person was, but I never got a coherent answer. She looked all around upstairs but wouldn't sit down. The house felt cold and uncomfortable, like a museum. I followed her back outside.

"By now, my dad could tell there was something underneath the rear of the car. It was a body that was almost in a ball."

The woman told Judith, "I hit him." She also said that she had "started to go forward and had put her foot on the gas instead of the brake. I didn't realize who Doris Duke was at the time, but I finally got her to sit down on the ground near the car." Now an ambulance rescue worker in Wisconsin, Wartgo described Doris' condition as due to "shock or alcohol or a combination."

Gordon King heard the ruckus and went up to the main house. "They said there had been an accident. There was a tremendous amount of commotion," recalled King. "My father sent two gardeners out to stop traffic. The police came right away. They called a wrecker. The body was taken away. Then the car."

As the sunlight faded, Judith and her father waited, but were told they weren't needed. "I was surprised we were allowed to leave," she recalled.

Doris was taken to the emergency room of Newport Hospital. The doctor on call that evening was Phillip McAllister, a slightly eccentric physician of dubious repute in the resort. "He was not thought highly of by any of his colleagues," recalled a fellow doctor and longtime Newport resident. "He was an opportunist and a bad doctor whose stock in trade was sedatives and other drugs. He was sort of a 'Dr. Feelgood.'"

"McAllister had never treated anyone of Doris Duke's wealth or social position before," a colleague said. "He would have done anything, given her anything she wanted. Who knew if money was passed, but he kept the police off her back. He wouldn't let anyone talk to her."

Doris was not tested for alcohol or drugs. "They just didn't want the evidence," one Newport physician familiar with the case said. The police never even asked for her driver's license. Although McAllister supposedly treated her for emotional shock, a physician in Newport at the time recalled, "I don't think she was in shock. She realized she was in a jam."

The Duke Endowment lawyers were called immediately. They supplied a list of Rhode Island attorneys. One Duke attorney recalled that the law firm had been dreading such a scandal. To her attorneys, she remained a source of constant worry, and an enigma. "She could be intelligent, humorous and on the other hand, cold as a piece of ice," one of them later said.

She stayed in a private room in the hospital until the next afternoon. Hospital personnel were the only ones allowed in the room. One of the several calls Doris made that night was to old friend, television and radio personality Tex McCrary.

"She said, 'I'm in trouble,'" he recalled. "She was panicky and incoherent. I would think it was the most shocking experience of her life. I don't think she knew what death meant, or even thought about it. She didn't care about Eduardo. She was thinking, 'How do I handle it?'"

McCrary swung into action, serving as a de facto press liaison for the Dukes. He called the editor of the *Providence Journal,* the Associated Press, and the *New York Daily News,* insisting that the mishap was a tragic accident and discounting any suggestion of foul play. She had adored Tirella, he insisted. They were such close friends. He asked that the news of the accident be downplayed, but by that time, "It was out of hand," he said.

Lawyer Wesley Fach, longtime "Mr. Fixit" for Doris, who had replaced Tom Perkins, was notified. He immediately called Duke Farms and told business manager Pete Cooley to come to Newport instantly. "Cooley called me," said Bob Dingwall, "and asked me to go up to Eduardo's room in the house to remove anything that belonged to him, all of his personal effects, in case there was an investigation." By the time Dingwall got up to the house, Tirella's belongings were already gone. "There was nothing there," the gardens director recalled.

The lawyer also asked that the switchboard be left on all night, and the phone lines kept open.

Doris sent a seaplane to Manhattan which also picked up McCrary and flew him to Newport the following day.

The headlines made the front page coast to coast. "DORIS DUKE CAR HITS, KILLS DECORATOR GUEST" and "HEIRESS' CAR KILLS FRIEND." News reports quoting McAllister claimed Doris was treated for facial cuts, despite Judith Wartgo's eyewitness account that she had suffered no injuries and there was no blood. "She was not injured," a physician at the hospital concurred. "When the police came to question her, it was almost with hat in hand. She was treated with kid gloves."

Police Chief Joseph Radice commented: "I knew her and the family, of course, since I was born here. That's quite an estate, Rough Point. She enclosed herself, like in a fortress.

"Usually, Tirella would get out and unlock the gates while she moved into the driver's seat. After she drove out the gates, he would close them and get back in the car. The day it happened, when he got out of the car it went forward, the gates flew open—we found the padlock in the bushes outside—and she drove right across the street, and struck a tree . . . The lieutenant didn't make much of an investigation during the day. When I came back the following day, Captain Paul Sullivan and I went to the home."

On Sunday, Radice went to Rough Point. "They invited us into the house and she was lying on the couch. There was an attorney there from Providence. After a while the attorney said, 'That's enough. She doesn't feel well and you can't speak to her anymore' . . . So we left."

The Q & A session lasted twenty minutes.

The following day, Radice returned to the estate. Doris—in a negligee—appeared heavily sedated. "She didn't remember anything." The police chief asked if her foot had accidentally slipped on the accelerator. "She said, 'It could have, but I don't remember.' There wasn't much more we could get from her."

Dr. McAllister was replaced by Doris' "magnito therapist," a swarthy man who arrived with crystals and prisms. "McAllister said the guy put a big magnet over her bed," a Newport physician recalled. "He was a real quack."

As news broadcasts carried the bulletin of Tirella's death, word reached California. The designer was described as Doris' "constant companion." (Other reports described Tirella as alternately her chauffeur and hairdresser.) Friends were anxious for details, but Doris Duke was not taking any calls.

Joe Castro was in Honolulu, shaving in the bathroom, when he heard the news over the radio. He shuddered. It could have been him. "I thought at first that she might have gotten nervous. That's the only thing I could think of because we went through that gate a million times."

The police "investigation" in Newport consisted of interviews with four members of the household staff. Gordon King said he was not among them. Said Radice: "I asked them if she and Tirella ever had any arguments or fights of any type and they said no, they never heard a word between 'em. They got along very well and very seldom drank."

As Gordon King recalled, "The attorneys came down from New York. The gates were painted, the car was gone. That was the last we saw of it. It was over. I mean *over*."

The station wagon was tested. The brakes were in working order. "Nothing wrong with the car," Radice said in an interview.

"The summer drifted away, and that was the end of it," King said. "I only saw her one or two times after that. And I didn't discern anything different. I'm sure the police said, 'Here's one of them killing one of their own wacky goddam people. What the hell are we supposed to do about it?'"

Judith Wartgo was never formally interviewed by the Newport police or investigators. She found that unusual. Asked now if she believes it was an accident, she replied, "I didn't know. It could have been either way. It seemed like it was never officially resolved. We were the first people on the scene and we were never interviewed."

Long lines of cars drove down the tree-lined Bellevue Avenue, the curious occupants straining to catch a glimpse of the gruesome tire marks and the grotesquely twisted wrought-iron gate as they passed the estate. Those who stopped were shooed away by a caretaker and a sleepy St. Bernard named Daisy.

In newspaper accounts, Tirella's death was the latest tragedy in the heiress' bittersweet life: her father's death, her marriage to Cromwell and the premature birth of her only child, her divorce from Rubirosa, her penchant for quacks and gurus, assumed names and disguises. "Too bad that wealth does not bring happiness," the stocky, sandy-haired Dr. McAllister told a reporter. "I'm convinced that enormous wealth brings great handicaps."

The state's attorney general, reading news accounts that claimed Doris allegedly tried to stab former boyfriend Joe Castro with a butcher knife, called Radice suggesting he send some men to Los Angeles to investigate. Radice told him he didn't have the money. "I said, 'If you want anything further you can take it up on your own.' He never did."

Tirella's funeral was held in the Sacred Heart Church in Dover, New Jersey, on October 11. A crowd of 300 curiosity seekers jammed the sidewalk. Doris did not attend. But several of her employees from Somerville and Rough Point did arrive, including Jake and Esther Guyer, bearing flowers. "He was never too busy to talk to us," one said. One of Tirella's sisters told a reporter, "I don't think it's fair that a family should lose their son, and all we hear is Doris Duke. Doris Duke. In a way, he was more important than she. He was a true artist."

Martin Ransohoff as well as Elizabeth Taylor reportedly sent flowers, although the actress, contacted recently, did not recall knowing him. An autopsy revealed that he suffered multiple skull fractures with brain hemorrhaging, a broken back, multiple fractures of the right chest with lung damage and internal bleeding, and fractures of the hip and left arm.

Four days after Tirella's death, the "investigation" was officially closed. The fatality, police said, was a freak accident. No charges would be pressed against the fifty-three-year-old heiress, who was driven back to Somerville and met by her elderly Hawaiian companion, Nana Veary.

Radice recalled how he reached his finding: "We sat down and talked about it. Everybody said, 'Fine.'"

Residents of Newport, where Rhode Island's old boy network is firmly entrenched, were not surprised at the outcome. "The police are kind of a joke," one physician said.

The records of the accident—including a reported 200-word typewritten statement from Doris Duke—are missing from the Newport police station.

Tex McCrary soon after received $50,000 from Doris to pay an income tax bill.

Chief Joseph Radice retired from the force several months after the accident.

There are still lingering doubts about how Doris Duke could have slid over in the front seat and accidentally hit the gas pedal with her foot.

Since the gates opened inward, the car would have had to stop at least fifteen feet up the driveway. As the car started forward, Tirella should have had time to escape. "It would have been easy for him to avoid. He had plenty of places to go," said Gordon King.

Doris was driving a rented 1965 Dodge. She had driven it only once before to pick up Tirella at the airport. It did not have an old-fashioned gear box which she was accustomed to, but was a new automatic and she was unfamiliar with its operation.

One scenario which the police did not consider:

Doris and Tirella pull up to the gate to exit the estate. Tirella gets out to open the gates, but realizes that the car is too close for him to swing the gates in freely. He motions for Doris to back the car up. In her haste—perhaps even having had a glass of wine or two—she forgot for a moment that the car was automatic. She slid over, shifted to what she thought was Reverse, but was actually Forward. Instead of putting her foot down on what she thought was the clutch pedal, she actually floored the gas pedal, which would account for the sudden, violent acceleration and tire marks on the driveway.

The servants at Rough Point were not surprised at the brief investigation.

"I remember my mother, who had been Mrs. Duke's maid, saying how rich people get away with everything."

Doris did not return to Newport that fall or winter. "She didn't come back for a while," Radice said.

Bob Dingwall recalled that Doris returned to the farm's greenhouses several days after the accident. "I thought she was very calm about the whole thing," he said.

Jake Guyer one afternoon agreed to drive Doris over to see a house they were renovating on the estate in Somerville. When he and Doris pulled up to the gates at the New Jersey estate in his pickup truck, he shut the truck off and took the keys with him, opening the gate, then climbing back in the truck. Doris' face was flushed with anger. "I said, 'I made you mad?' She said she thought I didn't trust her. She took offense to it, and after that our relationship wasn't the same."

At the farm, after Eduardo's death, "She just sort of stayed there and pouted," observed Guyer.

Several months later, Newport Hospital received a donation from Doris Duke in the amount of $25,000.

"She wanted to give it to McAllister," said one Newport doctor, "but he told her she could donate it to the hospital in his name, which she did." The doctor described McAllister as "slightly eccentric," and said "his prescribing pattern was not always up to the highest ethical standards. There were stories of over prescription and easy access to medications."

He and Doris Duke, said the doctor, "developed a kinship."

Two weeks after Tirella's death, Joe Castro married Loretta Haddad in Honolulu. He neither saw nor spoke to Doris for a decade. Still a talented musician he appeared in Las Vegas nightclubs and became the musical director of The Tropicana. Although he never fulfilled the early promise of his career, he is well-respected by his peers and left his turbulent past behind. Happily married, with two grown sons, he is still fond of his former patron, "Dorschka."

Doris left Somerville and flew to Los Angeles. "I picked her up at the airport," recalled Peter Brooke. "She was dressed in this black slack suit. She looked like something out of the 'Addams Family.' She was pretty shook up. She blamed it on the car." Previous Dodge models had push-button transmissions. In 1965, Dodge outfitted its cars with the new automatic transmission on the steering wheel. According to Brooke, Doris usually drove a 1954 Mercury in Los Angeles, with the transmission on the steering column. "She talked about the automatic gear shift, which she wasn't used to. She said she couldn't handle these 'new fangled' things. She said she was going to sue the car company."

In the months following the accident, Doris telephoned an artist friend of Tirella's to ask for help on a project. "She was upset that his brothers and sisters were hitting her up for money," Tirella's friend recalled. "She thought it was tacky. She felt she had no responsibility."

In conversations with friends and associates, she even put forth the theory that Tirella himself was to blame. This defense mechanism simply confirmed what the lawyers had long suspected: J. B. Duke's daughter—despite her passion for self-improvement—was simply out of touch with reality.

In December 1967, Doris was hit with a $1.25 million lawsuit filed on behalf of Tirella's five sisters and three brothers in connection with the accident. According to the suit, Doris was accused of "negligently and carelessly" operating her car so that it struck and killed Tirella. Doris marshaled her legal forces to fight the suit. She adamantly refused to settle with the family. It was the car's fault. Not hers. The case dragged on for four years; ultimately, Doris was found negligent and ordered to pay $75,000.

In the meantime, she continued her self-improvement program.

"I got a call one day from her business manager Pete Cooley," recalled Peter Brooke. "He said, 'This will go no further, will it?' I said, 'No.' He said, 'I gotta tell you. Doris is taking up belly dancing. We have to issue a check to somebody who is apparently teaching her.' I said, 'Well how is she going to use it?' He broke up and said, 'I don't know. Maybe we're gonna have some kind of harem scene here.'"

Brooke continued to field requests from Hollywood writers and producers who were anxious to interest Doris in film projects. Said Brooke, "She used to play footsie with all these people. She would drive them nuts, almost going through with backing them. But then pulling out at the last minute."

"In my case, I'm the one who pulled out," recalled Martin Ransohoff. A year earlier, Eduardo had come to Ransohoff with an intriguing idea for a film: the life of the legendary dancer Nijinsky starring Rudolph Nureyev. Doris would finance the picture, with a budget of $3 million. Edward Albee would write the screenplay with Franco Zeffirelli directing.

Ransohoff was interested. He flew to New Jersey and met with Eduardo, Doris, Pete Cooley, and attorney Wes Fach at Somerville. The subject of return on her investment was raised at the meeting. "Doris asked, 'What is customary? What is the split?'" recalled Ransohoff. "I said, 'Well it's usually 50-50.' Doris looked up. 'When I put up my money, I usually get 90-10.'" Ransohoff was amused.

"Doris," he quipped, looking around the gothic, rambling mansion built from tobacco money. "This place was built on 90-10."

She agreed to Ransohoff's terms of a 50-50 split.

The following day Ransohoff received the first installment on the estimated $3 million budget. It was a Western Union wire payment for $100,000. He flew to London to meet with the principals. Eduardo also flew over, acting as co-producer of the film. Problems usually referred to as "artistic differences" arose when Nureyev decided it would be more interesting to make a film on *his* life instead of Nijinsky's. Ransohoff decided to pull out of the project and called Doris from London. "She said, 'Fine.' I then sent her back the $100,000." Wes Fach, upon receipt of the check, was flabbergasted. Said Ransohoff with a laugh: "I may be the first guy who ever returned money to Doris Duke."

Journalist Deena Clark ran into Doris in a nightclub in New York around this time. "She was with Rudolph Nureyev. She had on a fantastic necklace. It looked like rock candy. She was all gussied up. She was either his date or at the same table."

Through actor Marlon Brando, Doris became interested in the plight of the American Indian. "Doris always liked to mingle with celebrities," said Peter Brooke. "They had dinner at her penthouse in New York. He was using her. He was a pompous ass." She invited Brando to Somerville, where he was seen jogging down the estate driveway. The two were reportedly planning a film project.

"She had given over 250 head of cattle to the Rosebud Indian tribe. There was trouble, and one of the dissidents who later wound up in the Wounded Knee incident reported that the cattle had been killed with the help of the local FBI. She decided to send me up there, posing as an investigative journalist for the *Los Angeles Times* to find out what was going on."

Brooke was wired for sound and went to the Black Hills of Dakota for two weeks. He discovered the cattle had not been slaughtered. "J. Edgar Hoover himself contacted me and sent a guy to my office here because they were afraid there was going to be a congressional investigation about the cattle disappearing."

Brooke turned over his interviews to the FBI. "Doris loved it. She just thrived on that kind of stuff. The *intrigue*."

Satisfied with his undercover caper, Doris put Brooke in charge of her Indian Oral History Research project. Started in 1965, Doris underwrote a program at various colleges, including UCLA, Utah University, Oklahoma University, and the University of South Dakota to gather the first-hand vignettes from the older members of Indian tribes. The money was disbursed from Doris' so-called "10 Percent Fund," which was not considered under the Doris Duke Foundation. The University of Arizona was given $110,000 in the form of stock. The University of Illinois was given $59,300. The University of New Mexico received $67,500. NYU's Institute of Fine Arts was given the largest grant of $200,000.

Doris had previously turned down a request from the wife of Senator Udall for a project called "Center for Arts of Indian America," but she was keenly interested in the oral history project, which continued for several years.

Brooke kept tabs on the various universities, which sent graduate students to the Indian reservations to interview elderly members of the tribes. Three decades later, Doris would indirectly contribute to Kevin Costner's Oscar-winning film on the Sioux, *Dances With Wolves*. The Doris Duke Indian Research Project is listed among the sources of historical information in the film's credits.

"She liked Hollywood," said astrologer and numerologist Sydney Omarr. "She made the rounds pretty well." Doris had become enamored with astrology and Omarr thought it would be a good idea to introduce her to author Henry Miller, who in Omarr's words, was "as usual a little short of funds." Perhaps Doris was a potential benefactress. He arranged a dinner with her and Miller. "We went to a small restaurant," recalled Omarr. "We talked about science, planets, the cycles. Of course, she was interested in her own future." The writer and the heiress sat across from one another with little in common except their interest in palmistry and the stars. She had not read any of Miller's books. Said Omarr: "He didn't take to her. I had earlier introduced him to Gloria Swanson and Kim Novak and there was a real connection. With her, it was a blank. There was no spark."

Decorators Leonard Stanley and Tony Duquette, who had worked on Falcon's Lair, were living in an old sound stage off Santa Monica Boulevard and Doris was a frequent guest. Author Brooke Hayward, then married to actor Dennis Hopper, recalled: "Tony Duquette and Dennis got on rather well. Tony was eccentric, and had entree and he appealed to Dennis. Tony decided it would be a wonderful thing to get Dennis and Doris Duke together. Tony gave a fabulous black-tie dinner. All the ladies wore their best jewelry. Well, Dennis had gone up to San Francisco for the first 'love in.' He didn't arrive in time for dinner, but he walked in after, about 10:30. Doris was quite shy, and a little awkward. Tony was very excited. He was convinced that Doris and Dennis would get along famously. Dennis arrived in his love-in outfit—filthy blue jeans, a fringed shirt and beads, not having shaved for three days—he looked ghastly. I think he had just taken his first acid. He looked like a mad animal with rabies. I don't think Tony realized how crazed Dennis was. He said, 'Dennis, will you please drive Doris home?' She got into our car, a yellow Checker taxi. Dennis drove, Doris was in the front seat. He was manic beyond belief. We were terrified."

As Hopper drove up the winding Benedict Canyon road to Falcon's Lair, he launched into "this long diatribe. He kept saying, 'The trouble with the arts is nobody subsidizes the artists. The very wealthy ought to be Medicis at heart.' He unleashed a torrent. He said communism worked better than capitalism. He was rambling, attacking rich people. Doris huddled in the front seat as close as she could to the door. Dennis kept saying if she did not finance some project, she would be considered completely worthless. It all spilled out on this wild ride." Hopper then started speculating on hocking Doris' jewelry. He pulled up Bella Drive, and overshot the mark to Doris' house. She jumped out, and ran across the road. "These enormous iron gates opened and she rushed in," recalled Hayward. "Then the gates clanged behind her. She had fled. Dennis cursed her all the way down the canyon."

Doris did strike up a friendship with actress Jennifer Jones, and singer Judy Garland who was addicted to pills and booze and was also a friend of Anita O'Day. She and Doris had a lot in common. It was Garland who once said, "I'm such a legend, why am I so lonely?" Doris reportedly helped her in the last years of her life.

She also befriended actress Sharon Tate, whom she had met through Eduardo. (The two had worked together on the film *Eye of the Devil*.) "Doris was crazy about her," said Martin Ransohoff. "She thought she was beautiful. Her low-key take on things appealed to Doris, and she was young and naive." It was not unusual for Doris to develop such "crushes" on celebrities. Ransohoff later heard that Doris had taken the twenty-two-year-old Sharon Tate shopping in Beverly Hills, buying her designer dresses, shoes, and trinkets on Rodeo Drive.

In 1967, Doris met a dashing man twelve years her junior, who was a wildlife conservationist in Africa. Peter Byrne had befriended Tony Jackson's wife Nancy in India, and been introduced to Doris through her.

(Jackson had handled the Castro caper.) "You must meet Doris Duke," Nancy told Byrne. "Her lover just left her."

Peter and Doris spent nine months together.

"I was very fond of her. She was wonderful, warm, tender and considerate. We traveled from Hawaii to New York and New Jersey." The pair showed up at a Manhattan party co-hosted by Cathy Macauley, Doris' goddaughter, honoring French actress Catherine Deneuve. "It was like a prolonged honeymoon," said Byrne. "At the end of nine months, I was tired of that. She was possessive and wanted me to stay with her, but there was no way I could work. She said if I stayed with her I'd have no more worries for the rest of my life. But the life Doris Duke was offering me was a frivolous life."

Her attempts at artistic expression, he said, were born of insecurity. "She has the nagging worry about whether she could have made it without that money."

"She could be extremely stingy," he added. "When we flew, we flew economy. She drove a battered old car. She'd get a bill from a grocery store and add it up. Every penny of it. It's a paranoia. She wasn't a happy woman; she was always lonely. When you have that much money, you never know who your friends are."

Dorothy Macauley invited Doris to Washington. "She said, 'Don't bother meeting me.' She arranged for a car to meet her at the airport but didn't find it, so she got into a cab. She rolled up in the worst possible, decrepit-looking taxi and as usual didn't have any money, and we had to run out and pay."

To avoid paying customs duty on couture dresses, she once telephoned Tex McCrary in Paris and asked him to carry home a package for her. "I made some joke about, 'Will it rattle?' She said, 'I'll have it delivered to you.' It was five or six dresses. They must have been worth $10,000 apiece. I knew customs people, but I was worried coming through."

Peter Brooke was already well-aware of Doris' parsimony. In 1968, Doris sent Brooke on a check-up tour of the universities which had received grants for the Indian research project.

"I traveled like a schmuck, really. Always third class. She held me on a tight leash, financially. It was embarrassing because I was representing Doris Duke, but when they came to pick me up I'd be staying in some fleabag. You know what she gave me for Christmas? A jar of jam. My wife was appalled. She threw it away. Meanwhile, I went out to a shop and bought her a beautiful attaché case because she always carried paper bags and I couldn't stand seeing her that way. I spent a fortune on this case and she didn't use it.

"I called Conrad Hilton at her suggestion to get her a Carte Blanche credit card. Hilton was on the board of directors. He said, 'Mr. Brooke, I'm very sorry, but like everybody else she has to go through regular channels, filing an application and submitting a financial statement.' Well, she refused to give a financial statement so I took out the card in my name. And I got stuck with the bills."

Brooke's duties were varied. They included passing along requests for money (she turned down pleas from the Eisenhower Medical Center and UCLA, which hoped to establish The Doris Duke Institute), as well as paying Doris' retinue of private investigators. More time-consuming was the job of buying a kitchen stove for Shangri-la at wholesale price and finding spare parts, long out of stock, for her old, dilapidated cars.

Although automobiles enjoyed a long and lasting relationship with Doris Duke, most people did not.

"She had a falling out with every man," said Brooke. "I knew it was coming."

According to Brooke, Doris asked him to move to New York to take over The Doris Duke Foundation. The elderly May McFarland would be eased into retirement. But in the ensuing power struggle, it was Brooke who left Doris' employ after refusing to sign a confidentiality agreement saying he would never reveal details of his work for the reclusive heiress. The Indian research project was terminated.

In the following months, Brooke was responsible for closing down Clover Enterprises, her record company. No bills were paid without Doris' personal approval, her trademark "DD OK" appearing in the bottom right-hand corner. The phone was disconnected. The rent was months overdue. Doris had embarked on a round-the-world trip, leaving no instructions on how to handle the dissolution of Clover, which was hampered by the usual confusion and lack of authority among her employees. In a letter to Doris, Brooke wrote: "I know of no single executive who can run a business or organization successfully if every one of his lieutenants has to get an okay every time he has to go to the bathroom."

(Doris called Brooke several years later when *Daddy's Duchess*, an unauthorized biography by a former employee and tabloid writer, was published. She enlisted her former clandestine operative in trying to squelch interest in any proposed movie deal.)

In New York, a new business manager was installed. "She didn't know anything about business," said Richard Kent, recalling awkward meetings held at her 30 Rockefeller Plaza offices. "She really had no business being there. It was weird. There were two accountants in the back room who looked like characters out of *David Copperfield.*" Kent suggested ways to save millions of dollars in taxes, "but she didn't go for it. She didn't try to shelter any of her income." Kent says her stock alone, in 1968, was worth $500 million.

Kent thought Doris was "a strange lady . . . One day, she invited me to lunch at Somerville. We sat on the porch, watching the Canadian geese she kept on the property. It was a tranquil, lovely setting. She said, 'Mr. Kent, do you have children?' I told her yes, that I had three daughters. 'And do they know how to cook and sew?' she asked me. I said, 'I suppose they do, Doris. Why?'" There was a pause. A look of resignation passed over her face. "'I wish I'd been taught things like that as a child.' It was sad."

Because of skin problems (Kent described her condition as basal cell carcinomas), she gave money to a Manhattan dermatologist, Dr. Norman Orentreich, and also helped finance Dr. Erno Laszlo and his line of skincare products.

Although Kent signed a five-year contract, he left after five months. "I was delighted to get out of there."

Kent was replaced by Ned Herzog of Lazard Frères, who became a trusted advisor. (Herzog has since died.) Doris also enlisted the services of Luiz C.P. Gastal, manager of La Banque Continentale, an amusing character who often served as her "walker."

In Honolulu, Doris' plans to develop Kahana Valley as a state park ended abruptly after years of costly negotiations for the 5,267-acre parcel of land. "We designed a whole Thai village complex," recalled architect Louis Persel. "It would have been a wonderful thing. At first, it was to be built on state property and the governor gave the go-ahead. But the lease could only be issued for a period of ten years. Doris said, 'I want full control. If they give a lease, they will have control.' She then tried to buy a whole valley on the other side of the island. Evidently, she objected to the commission the broker would earn. It didn't go ahead."

(In the meantime, more than $1 million in termite-infested artifacts sat rotting in crates on a state-owned pier in Honolulu. When the Coast Guard labeled the material a fire hazard, the state threatened legal action to have it moved. After paying $31,000 in storage fees, Doris had the "art works" hauled away by a truck to a warehouse west of Honolulu.)

Persel worked for Doris for seven years. "She treated me like a gardener," said the architect. "Everybody's a servant as far as she's concerned."

A former carpenter at Duke Farms put it more succinctly: "She treated people like dirt."

The architect said Doris was a stickler for details. "I've seen her up on the scaffolding, glazing tiles."

When she decided to replace the fireplace in her bedroom, she brought a photograph to Persel and asked him to draw it. "I want it like that," she demanded. She took the drawing to India and had it carved in white marble with raised sections. When it was finished, the costly mantel was shipped to Shangri-la. "She rejected it," said Persel, "and had it carved again. This would happen frequently. I would draw up things and she would say, 'You've got it all wrong.'"

Personally, she and the architect got along, despite petty concerns over the invoices. "She questioned some of my billing, but she was wrong. She's not easy with her money. She doesn't have many friends. She's a loner."

Persel met Nana Veary, Doris' Hawaiian companion, at Shangri-la. "Nana told me one day how they met. Doris went to some kind of spiritualist. Veary was there. She maintains she's clairvoyant. She said to Doris, 'I see at your place several black dogs and a table with lace covering.' Of course, everyone knew Doris had these huge dogs." Doris returned to Shangri-la and looked around. There was the Indian table with carving. "She told us to paint it white. From a slight distance, it looked like a lace tablecloth. Veary came in and said, 'That's what I envisioned.'"

Doris' watchdogs were notorious in the residential Diamond Head neighborhood. One family sued the heiress for $110,000 after their twelve-year-old son was severely bitten while walking home from school. The dogs allegedly darted out from behind the dark green wire gate topped by coils of barbed wire and attacked the boy. Caretaker Johnny Gomez settled out of court with the family for $1,000, and the suit was dropped.

(In New Jersey, another lawsuit was brought by a seventeen-year-old girl who was mauled by Doris' German shepherds while in Newport. The girl was a student in a private school there, and had been knocked down and bitten while walking down Bellevue Avenue. The suit was eventually settled.)

Writer Truman Capote was also well acquainted with Doris' dogs.

On his way to Japan, he stayed overnight at Shangri-la, and in a 1979 interview with Andy Warhol and Bob Colacello, recounted one of the most frightening experiences of his life: "It was scarcely daylight when I woke up and decided to go exploring. The room in which I slept had French doors, leading into a garden overlooking the ocean. I had been strolling in the garden perhaps half a minute when a terrifying herd of Dobermans appeared, seemingly out of nowhere; they surrounded and kept me captive within the snarling circle they made. No one had warned me that each night after Miss Duke and her guests had retired, this crowd of homicidal canines was let loose to deter, and possibly punish, unwelcome intruders.

"The dogs did not attempt to touch me; they just stood there, coldly staring at me and quivering in controlled rage. I was afraid to breathe; I felt if I moved my foot one scintilla, the beasts would spring forward to rip me apart. My hands were trembling; my legs, too. My hair was as wet as if I'd just stepped out of the ocean. There is nothing more exhausting than standing perfectly still, yet I managed to do it for over an hour. Rescue arrived in the form of a gardener who, when he saw what was happening, merely whistled and clapped his hands, and all the demon dogs rushed to greet him with friendly wagging tails."

Capote subsequently tried to publish photographs he had taken of Shangri-la for an article in *Look* magazine. Doris threatened to sue, and the magazine pulled the layout. "She didn't speak to him for a long time after that," said Peter Brooke.

Doris' habit was to give her various household staffs twenty-four hours' notice prior to her arrival. In New Jersey, the potted plants would be hastily dragged from the greenhouses to the pool, and a gardener would walk through the seemingly endless halls, carrying arm-loads of fresh, full-blown roses, placing them in wall vases. The kitchen would be readied, the staff placed on full alert.

"It was a big deal when she came," said one employee. "She was the queen and we were the serfs. It was medieval, the workers living in these thatched cottages. She drove around the estate in a white convertible wearing a scarf on her head, sunglasses and bright red lipstick with two huge German shepherds in the backseat. None of us could see what she looked like."

Doris had given money to a Newport church with a black congregation to start a museum of black history, and in New Jersey she joined the nearby predominantly black First Baptist Church of Nutley and sang in the Angelic Choir. She began traveling with the group, and sang gospel hymns incognito in the church's simple white dress, often wearing a wig. Singers Sarah Vaughan and Dionne Warwick showed up to join the choir. Doris became friendly with the Reverend Lawrence G. Roberts and several of the female black church members, who visited the farm.

That summer, another employee recalled, "She began to work on a Japanese garden. She was escorted by a woman in a nurse's uniform. I assumed she was a live-in nurse."

Doris preferred the company of the black gospel singers to the WASP contingency of the super-rich.

"She invited all these people to dinner one night in Somerville," said a former employee. "Jacqueline Kennedy and Mrs. Lyndon Johnson and all the Rockefellers. She didn't want to let Jackie's secret service men into the house. Finally, she had to or Jackie couldn't come. Before the dinner ended, she asked all her guests to leave. She just couldn't stand them anymore."

Another evening, Truman Capote and Greta Garbo arrived for dinner. Doris later told a friend, "Garbo was the most boring woman in the world."

She was a friend of Albert Einstein, and had corresponded with the scientist. On the opposite end of the spectrum, she was extremely fond of Elvis Presley, who was also a member of the Self Realization Fellowship in Los Angeles and a disciple of the Paramahansa Yogananda. Doris and Elvis had much in common: both adored soul singers, and both meditated daily, curious in their search for the spiritual meaning of life. Both also believed in reincarnation. Elvis was a world-class shopper and so was Doris.

Truman Capote attended an intimate dinner one night with the two in Las Vegas.

"Elvis went to her home in Hawaii," said another friend. "She was attracted to him."

For a woman of fifty-five, Doris' skin was surprisingly youthful, perhaps a result of plastic surgery. "I found her very attractive, very slender, and her complexion was almost girlish. There were no wrinkles on her face," recalled one employee.

The workers were also familiar with Doris' penchant for hoarding. "She saves a lot of things. Alongside a vintage 1948 Cadillac would be an old clawfoot bathtub," said the employee.

Doris at one point decided to do away with an unnecessary farm expense: toilet paper. "She had all these toilets installed," a worker said. "They were paperless toilets. A jet of water would spray your body."

Doris had also invested $6,000 in something called the Nutrition and Life Foundation, which promised a return on her investment beyond her wildest dreams. She paid its president, former health food saleswoman

Ethel Toburen, $28,000 for seventy tons of seaweed to be delivered to Somerville as mulch. The foundation also did work at Shangri-la; tying wires around the palm trees to conduct "cosmic rays" which would discourage bugs. The trees subsequently died. When Doris went to check on the foundation's "cosmic ray"-controlled tomato farm on Molokai, she was shown the flowering tomato plants and not the tomatoes in the other fields rotting with disease. The seaweed back at Duke Farms proved worthless.

Toburen was arrested previously for mislabeling drug products in New Orleans. She was found guilty of fraud and according to press accounts, sentenced to seven months in jail for the cosmic ray scheme.

"Whether it is the pigeon drop, the shell game or a con of this nature, the elements are the same," the prosecutor told the court. "The con man or woman dwells on the weakness of some individual."

In the interim, Duke University continued to appeal to their benefactor's daughter.

"When I came to Duke University," said Senator Terry Sanford, who assumed the presidency in 1970, "I decreed nobody would approach Doris for anything . . . I was tired of everybody suggesting: 'Let's get Doris Duke to do this. We only need $6 million.' Her position was quite justifiably: My father's already done all of this, why should I? I think the university played it rather badly in the way they dealt with her. I think she had been mistreated. They hadn't paid attention to her and the students felt compelled to ridicule her."

Not long after President Sanford arrived, Doris donated $500,000 for a scholarship in Dr. Wilbur Davison's name. It was matched by a grant from the Duke Endowment.

"To the best of my knowledge, it was the last time she was specifically asked to do anything."

Sanford began a quiet campaign to lure Doris back to the university "just because she belonged to Duke," not because of her financial position. Besides, Sanford added, "I didn't think we had a whole lot of influence over whether she was going to give anything or not."

One afternoon in Durham, a woman walked into Sanford's office, saying she was a friend of trumpet player Al Hirt. "She said that she was one of the world's greatest psychics," Sanford recalled. "She had a vision: in the crypt of the chapel, Mr. James B. Duke was dressed as Jesus. And Mr. Duke said, 'Go see Doris. Tell Doris that I want her to support financial efforts to find the truth about why I can be here.' In other words, psychic research."

Sanford sat at his desk, fascinated. "I said, 'What do you want me to do?'

She said, 'I want you to arrange for me to see Doris Duke.'" Sanford demurred, saying he couldn't do that. "She said, 'Well, I'll just have to use my psychic powers to arrange it.' I told her I thought that was the way to do it."

Several weeks went by. The psychic called Sanford and told him that she and Doris Duke were coming to Durham. "They were arriving on Saturday night. It was Easter weekend and they wanted to go to the chapel." At midnight, the university chancellor let the two women in. "I don't know how this woman got Doris to come, but she did."

The following day, Sanford hosted a luncheon at the university attended by Doris and her psychic. In private, the heiress told the university president that the woman wanted her to fund psychic research, but she didn't think she would. "I told her, 'No, I wouldn't do that.' I thought she was somewhat embarrassed to be there under those circumstances."

Sanford recalled he would "occasionally make some effort to see Doris, and she was always extremely cordial. But I never did say, 'Here's what I think you ought to do for Duke University.' Maybe I should have." In his estimation, Doris Duke had had "an interesting, sad, challenging, demanding life purely because she was left so much money and nobody knew how to handle that."

The last time he saw Doris, Sanford said, was at a luncheon in New York. "It was in Cordelia Robinson's apartment. She was Angie Duke's mother, Cordelia Biddle. All the people attending were good supporters of Duke. Cordelia wanted to have Doris there to hear her talk about the university. Cordelia was beginning when Angie shows up to say hello to his mother and totally changes the conversation. It broke up the luncheon. Time ran out on everybody and Angie hadn't quit talking about other, irrelevant things. It's almost as if the Lord sent him to protect Doris."

Chapter Fourteen

Forever
Young

BY THE LATE 1960s, Doris began carrying a small valet case filled with pill bottles. They contained vitamins, she said. At regular intervals, she would place the bottles on a table in front of a pulsating machine that resembled a metronome. "She said the vibrations caused the pills to get into her system," Duke Gardens Foundation head Bob Dingwall recalled. "She sat on the floor in front of the machine. She told me she didn't have to take the pills. They just entered her body."

Dingwall was just one of Doris' employees who witnessed her increasingly odd behavior.

"She looked like she'd been through the mill," said one former manager. "Every October, she'd come to the farm for two weeks to meet with Pete Cooley. Sometimes she was so bad she couldn't even attend the meetings. She wouldn't have anything to do with him."

"She'd have you walking on air one day," said a former manager, "and the next day, she'd cut your throat."

If a servant broke a glass, the cost was deducted from his or her paycheck. If a pane of glass was broken in the greenhouses, the gardener paid out of his own pocket. At other times, however, she could be amazingly benevolent.

At Duke Farms, the gas pumps were routinely used to fill up the farm vehicles. The drivers and guards—who wore a Duke insignia on one arm and an American flag on the other—were required to keep a log showing the amount of fuel pumped daily. "I don't know how she picked it up," recalled Dingwall, but Doris discovered that one of the security guards was stealing gas by entering "20 gallons" in the log, and putting half of it in his own car.

Miss Duke called the guard to the office.

"He openly admitted it," said Dingwall. The guard naturally feared for his job, but Doris looked at the middle-aged man and assumed her little girl voice. "You're a naughty boy," she said, like a child scolding a pet. "Now you won't do it again, will you?" The guard assured her he would not. "You may go now."

Doris entertained a scheme to have her milk piped underground from the dairy to the milk plant. Plans were drawn, and discussions took place. "At the last minute, she backed out," one farm manager recalled. "There was a $2,000 bill from an architect who had drawn up plans. She refused to pay it." (After the architect threatened to sue, Doris paid the bill.)

Added the manager: "At one of the residences, a pump went bad. When she got the bill she said, 'It's too much. I won't pay it.' She had the pump taken out. When the company threatened legal action, she paid it."

At one point, Doris seized on an idea to install an elaborate lighting system in the Persian garden to facilitate night tours for her private VIP guests. She wanted the lighting to simulate sunrise and sunset. She asked Dingwall what he thought it might cost. He estimated $25,000. Doris was taken aback. She thought the figure was inflated. She estimated the bill would be $4,000.

A lighting firm was hired and the work began. The bills came in at regular intervals and Dingwall sent them up to the office for Doris' okay. She authorized payment with her usual scribbled "DD OK" in the corner.

After six weeks, Doris called Dingwall to inquire how much had been spent. He replied: $18,000. She blew her stack. Dingwall pulled the file and had it sent up to the house. Later she telephoned him demanding to know how he could have predicted the job would cost what it did. "How did you know it would cost $25,000?" she demanded. Then she told her Gardens Foundation director she never authorized any payments. "I asked her if she wanted me to call in a writing expert. She hung up on me."

According to Dingwall, Doris fired the lighting company, and never paid the remaining balance.

In the mornings, Dingwall would often find Doris in the greenhouses, pulling up various shrubs and rearranging the displays. Minutes before the public tours would begin, she would scurry out the back door, not wanting anyone to catch a glimpse of her. Dingwall was left to replant the uprooted shrubbery.

She also argued with the farm manager over the tradition of giving turkeys to her employees for Thanksgiving. He suggested fresh turkeys. She wanted frozen ones; they were thirty cents a pound cheaper.

Every year, she insisted on having a Christmas party for the children on the estate. She wanted it held on Christmas Eve, a night when most families preferred to stay at home. Having no family of her own, and with her closest friends a coterie of psychics and faith healers, Doris was oblivious to most holidays and traditions. Her somewhat dated notion of indentured service led her to believe that her employees had no life of their own. For the several hundred workers on the estate, the Christmas Eve party was a command performance, and no one risked Miss Duke's wrath by not attending.

Doris would give her workers $50 to purchase a toy for each child. The gift would have to be wrapped and brought to the house where the children were made to open them in her presence. It was a bizarre scene, presided over by the awkward Dee Dee, her diamond earrings flashing. After thirty minutes, she would signal her chauffeur Stanley to have the car brought around, and then make a hasty retreat for New York leaving her guests stranded. Elderly butler Harold Sprague would take over as host, showing movies in the theater for the children and their parents, quite literally a captive audience.

"Many of them were afraid of her. She never paid well, but they were scared to leave," said Dingwall. "To her, people were to be used."

Nephew Walker Inman was learning from his aunt Doris. At regular intervals, he would descend on Somerville. "He once brought me some seeds and said they were a rare plant," recalled Dingwall. "He wanted me to plant them in the greenhouse. I discovered they were marijuana seeds."

On one occasion, he walked into the library and lit the fireplace. "Mr. Inman, would you like me to add more wood?" the butler asked. "That's your job, isn't it?" he answered. Then, Inman walked the length of the house, lighting each fireplace and watching the hapless servant scurry in with more and more wood.

Every few years, the hierarchy at Duke Farms would change. In 1968, the turmoil coincided with the arrival of the Animal Medical Center. Through her friend Leta McBean, Doris was introduced to Robert Tashjian, a Manhattan veterinarian connected with the East Sixty-second Street facility which was looking for an isolated spot to conduct experiments. Doris agreed to lease several hundred acres and a stable to Tashjian's group for one dollar a year.

The old guard and the interlopers immediately clashed. "Their purpose was to take over the whole business. She let them run rampant over the place. They got rid of several good men," recalled one former manager.

Pete Cooley, her longtime business manager, was fired. "She was very hard on Pete," a colleague recalled. "She'd scream and holler at him."

Attorney Wes Fach was also dismissed. Gardens head Dingwall knew his time was up. "Tashjian never looked at you directly," said Dingwall. The Animal Medical Center tried to convince Doris they had a scheme for making "virgin soil," which Dingwall labeled as "ludicrous." After a new rule was imposed limiting Dingwall's authority, he resigned.

The Animal Medical Center eventually elected Doris chairman of its board of directors. They would enjoy Doris' support for the next five years. But like all relationships, it came to a bitter end, resulting in a flurry of suits and countersuits amid accusations of misappropriated funds.

One evening in late 1969, Doris' friend, C. Z. Guest, arranged for a theatre party followed by a small dinner at Le Pavillon on Fifty-seventh Street. The other guests were Count Vega del Ren, a jeweler known as "Mingo" who worked for Bulgari, and a swarthy young Moroccan decorator, Leon Amar.

"Doris wouldn't talk to me the whole evening," recalled Amar. "They were all working on her. You know how people are that work on someone with money. Whether it's Jerry Zipkin or Henry Kissinger or the art goons, they all kiss her ass because of who she is and what she has. Then all of a sudden, she found out I was from Morocco and the conversation more or less turned toward me." Doris and Amar chatted about Moghul art and her passion for all things Persian. The other guests drifted off, leaving Doris and Amar. Then she suggested the two share another bottle of champagne.

"I said, 'Doris, I'm sorry but I've had enough.' She said, 'No, no, no.' I said, 'The truth is I can't afford to buy you champagne. You're drinking three star.' She said, 'Well let's go upstairs to my apartment and have a bottle.' So I walked her around the corner to the Ritz Tower at 475 Park Avenue. We sat and talked and drank."

A Sephardic Jew of Spanish-Moroccan descent, Amar was twenty-seven years younger than Doris and had emigrated to America in the 1950s. Physically, he was slight, with dark curly hair and bore a faint resemblance to Porfirio Rubirosa. Amar was also charming and well-spoken, with a knack for handling wealthy women. He had worked as an interpreter for hotels before joining the design firm Jansen, Inc., which had offices in New York and Paris, and had recently worked with Jacqueline Kennedy in her restoration of the White House.

Amar—who prided himself on his impeccable taste—was shocked at the Park Avenue penthouse. "It was tacky. The worst. Her bedroom was shimmering with chiffon, silver wallpaper and columns of inlaid multi-colored glass. The style was bordello. Fake, elaborate fur-covered sofas. A huge hunk of tree log with a glass top. The floors were black. Things were colored black and maroon, rock crystals were everywhere. Mother-of-pearl furniture. Minerals and seashells. It was just a mess." In the corner was a Bechstein piano. Amar put aside his disdain for the apartment, decorated by Hollywood designer Tony Duquette, as the two sat and chatted.

"We talked about jazz—I'm a great fan. I liked her. She was fascinating. I was very young, and from another part of the world. There was certainly a tremendous physical attraction."

Two weeks later, Doris called and invited him to Somerville along with C. Z. and Winston Guest and Charles and Jayne Wrightsman. "Doris was dazzling. She was wearing a Moghul costume and Indian jewelry. That's the night I moved in. She's an incredible woman. But her eyes are dangerous. They can be beautiful and they can be cruel."

The romance began to deteriorate shortly after it began. "Doris drank a lot. When she drank, she became violent. She was violent a couple of times with me. She threw a bottle of wine at me once and nearly killed me. It was a 1929 vintage, worth $4,000."

Friends soon became accustomed to Amar's presence at parties and gatherings. Ruth Buchanan, wife of Wiley T. Buchanan, entertained Doris at Newport. Her escort was Leon Amar. "He was a little Moroccan decorator," recalled Buchanan. "He was running around, waiting on her."

Amar said he became protective of Doris and was concerned about "the healers around her. I was very disturbed. I told her, 'I'm not trying to tell you who to give your money to, but you are making a terrible mistake.'"

Doris introduced Amar to Norbu Chen, a self-styled healer from Texas who advocated enema and grape juice treatments, and who had a wide following in the Hollywood community, including Yul Brynner and Joanne

Dru. "He conned Doris into believing that he could rejuvenate her," said Amar. "He was a scary man," recalled Tex McCrary.

Norbu Chen was the latest alias of con man Michael Lee Alexander, who used various names including Carle Clayton Johnson and Richard Michael Johnson. A small, silver-haired man who barely spoke above a whisper, his I.Q. was in the genius range. Once jailed in Kentucky for rape, he had spent time in a mental institution and was arrested in 1972 on charges of grand larceny and obtaining a credit card under a false name. At the time of his arrest, he was reportedly staying with Ed Mitchell, the Apollo 14 astronaut and sixth man to land on the moon, who had become a disciple of the healer. Mitchell was a devotee of para-psychology and met Chen at an ESP convention. He had brought his girlfriend to the healer who put her on a grape juice diet and supposedly "cured" her kidney infection. In 1974, Chen was again arrested for illegal possession of firearms.

Doris and Leon flew to Houston for treatments. "Norbu Chen locked us in separate bedrooms and fed us grape juice for three days. He said our hair was going to grow, our pains were going to disappear, and all he was looking for was a signed check."

Along with the diet, Chen performed "a kind of religious ceremony. He meditated and chanted in an Oriental language of some sort," another patient said.

"He looked like someone you'd see in Tibet," said "Love Boat" creator Geraldine Saunders, who went to Houston with astrologist Sydney Omarr. "And he had this teeny-bopper wife. People were flying in from all over the world to see him."

"He had a massive ego," recalled Omarr. "He was very arrogant about his powers." Omarr quickly deduced that the healer practiced what he described as "black magic."

In gratitude for her generous financial support, Norbu Chen named Doris to the board of directors of his Chakpori-Ling Foundation in Houston.

Amar also became familiar with Doris' concern with youth. "She was obsessed by that. One thing she tried desperately was to make her hair grow. She has very thin hair. She was also extremely frightened of diseases, of being sick. It's why she patronized these healers who were all charlatans. I saw the abuse that she tolerated. She felt she was getting something in return, while all they gave her was tea made with oregano!"

Twice a week, Amar drove Doris to her appointment with a female psychic. "Her name was Jean Houston. She was the same woman who went down to Duke University with her. Doris said, 'I'm going to tell Duke University what to teach, what to do and what academic courses should be given.' This was all because she was under the influence of this psychic, and another woman who was called 'Jean Ding-a-Ling.' These people were out of their minds.

"All kinds of kooks were popping in. Strangers, lady healers. This one was going to make her hair grow, this one was going to get rid of all the spots in her skin, this one was going to get rid of the wrinkles, this one was going to cure her liver. I remember the checks that were written."

But Amar did believe Doris "had tremendous psychic power. She's quite a healer herself. Many times I had pains and she actually meditated and through pressure points, healed me."

Ibrahim "Bobby" Farrah was a young Lebanese dancer who had met Doris and started giving her private lessons. He was also familiar with her powers. "I was studying in this dinky studio with a protégé of Katherine Dunham's. I saw this lanky lady walking bowleggedly down the steps as I was coming up. I looked at her and said to myself: 'That is somebody.'"

Bobby and Doris were introduced, and the dancer soon began instructing the heiress in Middle Eastern dance at Rudy's Rehearsal Studios on Broadway. Doris paid for two hours of private lessons daily.

Four months later, Farrah went to Lebanon where he contracted hepatitis and was detained in a hospital. When informed he was ill, Doris demanded to know the date, time, and place of his birth.

"She went through this whole ritual at the farm to cure me," said Farrah. "All I know is, I got better."

Upon his return from Lebanon, the two struck up a friendship. "She felt that the unknown or the possibility of the unknown was the answer. Doris wanted to do all the things that were dangerous to human nature and yet wanted to be healthy and have a long life."

Ruth Montgomery, who hadn't heard from Doris in years, got a telephone call "out of the clear blue. She mentioned a chapter in my book, *The Ancient Wisdom*. She was fascinated by the healer in the book, 'Mr. A,' whose real name was Bill Gray. She said she had had success healing people on her estate in New Jersey. I put her in touch with Gray. He was trying to establish a foundation. I think he felt she was rather frugal.

"I don't know Doris' method," said Montgomery, "but most healers put their hands about the head and body as if touching the aura. The universal energy comes through them to that person. She said she had remarkable results with some of the farm people."

Gradually, Leon Amar took on more authority within Doris' organizations. "She had bought all these temples and Thai houses in Bangkok many years ago. She was going to create a mini Bangkok in Hawaii, but there were too many problems. We decided to fly everything over to New Jersey." Doris and Amar assembled the treasures in an abandoned carriage house. It took three months to unpack 1,400 pieces; masks, puppet heads, carved doors, a Burmese four-poster bed and a gold-leaf Buddha. Doris appointed Amar to the boards of her various foundations and paid him a salary of $30,000 a year.

"My biggest mistake was to have worked for her," he later said. "It would have been a lot easier otherwise. The relationship might have lasted." He was named vice president of the South East Asian Art and Culture Foundation Museum, which was completed in December 1972. Doris celebrated with a party, and among the guests were Jane Engelhard, Tony Duke, Loretta Young, D. D. Ryan, Earl Blackwell, Jerry Zipkin, and Luiz Gastal.

"Thank God I got there ahead of the American army," Doris told the group, "because they cleaned it out."

Betsy Bloomingdale strolled through the museum, the shooting gallery, the theater set up with red-covered tables set with masses of flowers, taking it all in. "This evening is going to cost me money," joked her husband, Diners Club president Alfred Bloomingdale.

Amar began attending auctions, purchasing antiques for the houses. "She never wanted to pay. Everytime we went anywhere, I had to do all the haggling. And I absolutely hated it."

They went to India, where Doris bought rubies the size of pears and a sixteenth-century Indo-Isfahan carpet for $1 million. There was more: "Her 8th and 9th century Chinese bronzes, her Coramandel, her Ming furniture, the Thai houses, the temples, the Khmer collection, the Islamic collection. Plus the jewels and tapestries."

He helped redecorate the houses. "It was all revamped, restored," he said. "I also helped her with the Restoration Foundation in Newport." At Somerville, amid the Aubussons and the French antiques, Amar was enjoying his position as Doris' personal curator and guardian of her treasures.

At a dinner party one night, Doris invited Gerald Van der Kamp, the head curator of Versailles, who took Amar aside. "He said to me, 'Would you mind talking to Doris about what she's going to do with that set of furniture?' I said, 'Listen, this is the first time you've been invited to this house. You don't think I'm going to ask her that, do you?' He was trying to get it."

Amar redid the Oak Room. "It's huge, about 70 feet long and 30 feet wide. Everything was falling apart. It was drab. I restored the paintings." At Rough Point, the lampshades were worn so thin Amar could see the bare bulbs. "Everything was dirty," he recalled. "I cleaned up a lot."

He also began to revamp Doris' wardrobe.

"When I met Doris, she looked like a cheap hooker from Birdland," said Amar. "She dressed horribly. I looked in her closet. I said, 'Doris, you have Balenciagas, Balmains. What are you doing to yourself?' She wore these horrible polyester things she used to buy in Ohrbach's basement. I finally told her I was going to organize her closet. Doris would not dress without me."

Amar, who had some tailoring experience, began picking out her clothes and jewels. "I said, 'You've got to buy better clothes. You're a *grande dame du monde.*'"

Boaz Mazor, longtime assistant to designer Oscar de la Renta, recalled working in his office one day when a tall woman walked through the rear shipping door wearing a babushka on her head and carrying a paper bag. "You better take care of that woman," another assistant whispered. "Do you know who she is? Doris Duke. One of the richest people in America."

Mazor showed Doris the designer's spring collection. "She looked like a poor woman, and never took the babushka off," said Mazor. "She saw a daytime dress. It was an A-line, very Jackie. I'll never forget. It killed me. She said, 'How much is it?' I told her the wholesale price: $98.95. It would be double that in a store. She said, 'Can you do me a better price than that?' It was a sickness with her."

On various trips to Europe, Doris and Leon shopped. In Rome, a favorite spot was Millichant. "They closed the whole store. Imelda Marcos was there shopping at the same time. They both shopped for hours." Doris tried on clothes and eventually purchased $60,000 worth of goods. While waiting for Doris, Amar had picked out a $200 cashmere sweater for himself. "Doris took the bill and said in a loud voice, 'I didn't buy a cashmere sweater.' They explained it was for me. She said, 'He can pay for his own sweater.' She did this in front of all these people. It was very humiliating."

The couple went to Venice. "We were staying at the Danielli, it was a beautiful suite. It looked like a sultan's. It was my first time in Venice and I was excited. We were riding in a gondola when all of a sudden Doris broke down and started sobbing. I asked what the matter was. She said, 'I've always dreamed of coming to Venice with someone I loved.'"

Doris confided in Leon about her past. "The first time I walked into Doris' bedroom, there was a big photograph of Alec Cunningham-Reid. She said he was the only person she had ever loved in her life. The other pictures were of Eduardo Tirella and the farmer, Louis Bromfield, with a dog. She was madly in love with him. She said he was a godsend from heaven. Maybe he was a father figure, but he was also brilliant. It was because of him that she became interested in ecology.

"We were sitting in a restaurant and she pulled out a beautiful compact. It was gold, surrounded by rubies. She said it was the first gift Rubirosa ever gave her. She always spoke very highly of him; even after they were divorced they were still lovers. She never spoke highly of many other lovers. Mainly because they were violent."

Her greatest emotional problem, Amar recalled, was the deep-seated fear that psychic Eleanor Hufty had also described. When they came home at night, Doris "was so uptight that she had to lock herself in her walk-in closet for a few minutes until she locked up her jewels. I don't know why she always did that. She didn't trust anyone."

Including herself.

"The first time I went to Newport with her, we went out one night to a movie. She drove. On the way back, she stopped in front of the gate. She said, 'Don't move.' She put the car into park and turned off the ignition. She said, 'Now you can go and open the gate. I lost one friend and I'm not about to lose you.'"

On June 17, 1971, nearly five years after Tirella's death, a jury of seven women and five men was chosen in a Providence court to hear the $1.25 million wrongful death lawsuit filed by Alice Tirella Romano, Eduardo's sister, against Doris Duke. The depositions and affidavits on file shed little light on the accident. Doris was defended by Providence attorneys Aram Arabian and John Keenan.

Arabian and Keenan did not focus on her actions. They instead blamed Eduardo for not putting on the handbrake when he got out to open the gates. They also insisted that Tirella—hat designer, interior decorator, Hollywood extra, and friend of the rich and famous—spent every dime he ever made, and if the family was suing to recover future earnings, the amount would be a small sum.

Tirella became the ultimate victim. Not only was his life snuffed out, but now his character was being destroyed. It was hardly the behavior of a woman who professed to "adore" her friend and to have been shattered by his demise.

The defense demanded to examine Eduardo's tax returns. (Doris knew he filed them sporadically, if at all.)

On June 17, Doris arrived at the courthouse wearing a long blue coat, her hair pulled back in a ponytail, her chin jutting defiantly at newsmen. Her face was nearly covered by oversized black sunglasses that later became the trademark of Yoko Ono.

Doris sat impassively through the trial while the jury heard testimony from the plaintiff's lawyers on Tirella's career and were shown slides of Duke Gardens and a forty-five-minute montage of film work, including a scene from *The Sandpiper* in which Eduardo is seen drinking in a Big Sur restaurant.

"I'll be famous," he had told his family.

Then Doris took the stand. She testified that her foot was on the brake of the rented Dodge station wagon and she didn't know how the car had shot forward so violently. In fact, in answer to one of the lawyer's questions, she said she believed that a car could leap forward *without* anyone touching the accelerator.

Expert testimony revealed that there was nothing wrong with the car, and motor vehicle officials said they were barred from interviewing Doris Duke "who was in bed and under care" immediately following the accident. In his final arguments, Doris' lawyers again stressed that Tirella was a bon vivant who spent all his money and would have little future earnings.

On July 1, the jury returned their verdict: Doris was found guilty of negligence. But the damages awarded to the Tirella family were a fraction of what the family had asked for: $75,000 plus $21,000 in interest. The judge had allowed the jury to not only deduct Tirella's future lifetime personal expenses but his business expenses as well. Had Tirella continued working for Doris Duke, he certainly had little hope of reversing his downward financial slide.

The Tirella family asked for a new trial, arguing the damages were inadequate. The appeal was denied. Alice Tirella then took the case to the Supreme Court of Rhode Island, which two years later upheld the award.

By now, Barbara Hutton had married Raymond Doan, a Laotian "prince" whose title was allegedly purchased by Barbara for $50,000. He was her seventh husband. They soon divorced, and a haggard-looking Hutton took up with a twenty-four-year-old Spanish matador, Angel Tervel. It was reported that Barbara drank twenty bottles of Coca Cola a day, and was addicted to codeine, Valium, and morphine. She was frail and alarmingly thin.

As the two poor little rich girls cascaded into senior-citizen status, Doris was still being mistaken for Barbara, which infuriated her. "She couldn't stand being compared to Barbara," said Leon Amar.

"Doris was kind of jealous of Barbara," said dance instructor Bobby Farrah, who by now had a studio funded by the Doris Duke Foundation. "Doris envied her beauty. Doris didn't have the strength Barbara had in ignoring the press. While Barbara could give a damn if they said she had a new lover, it bothered Doris a lot."

Doris and Amar once arrived in Los Angeles and were met at the gate with a wheechair. 'I'm sorry, you've got the wrong one," Doris said, referring to her rival. "I'm Doris Duke. The other one's in Mexico."

Amar: "She hated being what she was. There's one thing she always said to me. 'I don't give a shit about this world. They can all kill each other to get the money when I die. I'm not leaving a will. I'm not leaving anybody a penny.' She said the only family she had was her dogs."

Attorney Sam Greenspoon said Doris was "the greatest champion of animals I've ever met." Greenspoon drew up a will in the early 1970s. In it, Doris left $1.5 million to her dogs and the rest to various charities. Duke University was not among the recipients. "She hated Duke," said Greenspoon. He revealed that at the time, Doris was worth $1 billion, and her money was invested in real estate, stocks, bonds, and treasury bills. Said the lawyer: "She's the largest holder of treasury bills in the United States outside of Salomon Brothers."

She had stopped attending meetings of the Duke Endowment, and had grown bored with the Newport Restoration project. "She didn't want to take care of her business," Amar said. "She wanted to sing and play the piano and dance. She didn't care about anything else."

"Once Brooke Astor and Babe Paley wanted to come to the Gardens. Doris said to Babe, 'You can come but you have to bring your own lunch and you have your own picnic here because I'm not going to sit here and serve you lunch.' I said, 'Doris, do you realize what you just said?' She said, 'I don't care. I have a voice lesson and a dance class. That comes first.'"

She routinely purchased the services of some of the finest instructors in the world, including Martha Graham star Peggy Lyman. "She had studied dance with everyone: classics, primitive, modern," said Bobby Farrah. "I don't think people knew how to approach her, and I don't think they took her seriously. Even if they didn't have aspirations to dig into her pocketbook for some kind of funding or grant, she was rent money."

Actress Mamie Van Doren, who had also known Eduardo Tirella, once stayed at Somerville for several weeks in 1972. Van Doren's friend was Doris' personal secretary, Lila Wisdom. "She's Brooke Shield's godmother. Doris was very upset that I was there. I think she was jealous," the actress recalled. "I came and stayed at the estate. It was gorgeous. Lots of oak floors, old Oriental rugs, cases of jade. She had her own bowling alley and a rejuvenating machine to make her feel young. She spent millions on it. She thinks it will take her back in time to when she was a young woman.

"You know, she has lost the top layer of her skin. She's lost all the pigment. She had been to everybody to try and stop it. She's completely white."

"She was very conscious of her skin problem," said Farrah. "Her arms, from elbow to hand, are all brown, with these big white spots. The rest of her skin was snow white. One part of her body, it started around the left side of her back and up one side is the same color brown. She had some of the same blotches on her legs. She was always getting some new oil or some new cream that was going to cure this. When we went to Lebanon together, she went to some quack that gave a kind of oil."

Although Doris "was not dumb like Barbara Hutton," Van Doren found her strangely gullible. "She loved trashy magazines like the *National Enquirer*," the actress recalled. "Doris was crazy about one of her cook's home-made pies. She used to fly up to Newport especially to have them. One day I was in the kitchen and found out the cook actually bought the pies. Doris thought she was getting the best pie in the world!"

The actress was impressed by the tranquil opulence of Somerville, which was made available to acquaintances as a sort of home for wayward celebrities.

"She had these wonderful mansions for you to retreat in," said Farrah. "It wasn't financial support. It was bringing you to luxurious surroundings, drying you out, feeding you nutritious food, taking walks, exercising. For a lot of people, that relief was great for a week or so, but it also became boring and that's where the trouble came in. After a while, you had enough rest."

Another visitor to the farm was former Fermata roommate Roseanna Todd. "A very odd lady, but fun. She thought she was at the Ritz in Paris," said Amar. "She would order breakfast to her bedroom. Doris called her one day and said, 'Listen, you better get off your ass and go downstairs to the kitchen and have your breakfast like everyone else. I'm the only one who has breakfast in bed.'"

"She had an animal shelter on the property, her own dairy, her own pond where turtles swam," recalled Van Doren. "They'd kill them for turtle soup. She had her own post office, her own police force and yet the richest woman in the world goes to Macy's and stands in line to buy a bathrobe on sale."

Leon Amar was all too familiar with Doris' bizarre sense of thrift. When they arrived back in New York after the shopping spree in Rome, Doris informed Amar she was not going to pay customs duty on the $60,000 worth of clothes and told the agent she had nothing to declare. When the customs agent asked Doris' occupation, she replied, "Farmer." According to Amar, the agent went through Doris' bags and found the clothes and the receipts, although attorney Sam Greenspoon disputed Amar's version, saying it was the decorator who accidentally produced the store receipts. The two were detained at John F. Kennedy International Airport for six hours. Said Amar, "I was furious."

Greenspoon eventually won the case against the U.S. Customs Department by claiming that Doris' purchases were "previously worn" clothing. After all, the attorney argued, they had certainly been tried on and modeled in Europe prior to their purchase.

"After that," said one former employee, "she'd cut the labels out of the dresses and mail them back to herself. Doris was so proud that she was screwing them. She was in the car once, laughing. 'I really got 'em,' she said."

Amar: "We once chartered a private plane. When we landed at Newark, Doris wanted to get home quickly because this black lady was coming to give her a singing lesson." Doris sent Amar to find a taxi. "She said, 'Make sure you ask the cabdriver how much he's going to charge to take us to Somerville.' I asked two drivers. One said $22, the other said $20. She made me pick the one who said $20. When the airplane cost about $8,000! That's the way she was. It was an obsession."

The black singing teacher, according to Amar, "was a funny character. She looked like Mahalia Jackson and dressed like the Duchess of Marlboro. She always arrived wearing this big flowered hat. At first she took the bus, then she demanded that Doris send the chauffeur to pick her up. He would have to go to the worst section of Newark and wait downstairs in a drug-riddled area. She'd say, 'When I come down, I want you to open the door for me.'

"The driver used to complain to me," said Amar. "He was afraid of being killed. During the lesson, the maid would look at me and start giggling because Doris sounded awful. She didn't have a very good voice. But I couldn't tell her. I loved her too much to hurt her. You had to be encouraging." Often, Amar would find her standing in front of her Louis XIV gold mirror, belting out "You Make Me Feel Like a Natural Woman." "Doris wanted to be Aretha Franklin, but her voice sounded like a rooster with laryngitis."

Bobby Farrah recalled sitting in her New York apartment one afternoon waiting for her singing lesson to end. "Sometimes after a few glasses of wine, she would sing, and tell me about the troubles she was having with her voice. I was sitting in the kitchen of her penthouse, and the maid offered me a glass of fresh tomato juice from the farm." Just as Farrah took the glass, Doris hit a high note with a loud shriek "and the glass just flew out of my hand. There we were, me and her maid, on the floor on our hands and knees, laughing hysterically as we picked up the broken glass."

At regular intervals, Doris flew to Detroit for singing lessons with Aretha Franklin's father, Reverend C. L. Franklin. "She'd come and take a dance class, leave my studio, go to La Guardia, fly to Detroit, sing, come back and call me at night while she was eating dinner," recalled Farrah.

Intimates of Doris also observed her varying moods.

"I loved her so much, and then mysteriously she would transform herself. Maybe she's just a character, playing a role," explained Amar. "She dressed up one night like Carmen, with a red wig and long skirt. She said she wanted to look like a hooker that night, and she did." (In the privacy of her room, Doris used to spend hours dressing up in costumes from "another period. Victorian things, with big skirts and all the details," a friend recalled.)

"Depending on how she acted, she was Doris Ding-a-Ling or Dolly Ditz," said Farrah. "Or she was 'Miss Duke' or she was Dorshka, or Lahi-Lahi or 'Miss Bitch.' She liked that."

Often, she reverted to Baby Doris. She accompanied Farrah to the house on Seventy-eighth Street one morning and strolled through the mansion, pointing out the rooms. "She showed me her bedroom, she showed me the stairway where she used to slide down the marble bannister." Her voice grew more child-like as the tour progressed. "Then we went down to the basement where she used to hide her toys. She said she used to go down and hide to spite her mother." Her face was distorted by anger. "It was like a movie. She completely relived this. She was seeing it all again."

· · ·

During this period, a man who captured Doris' imagination was Aristotle Onassis. "Doris loved Ari, and he was fascinated by her. He had an incredible charm and a great deal of style. He thought Doris was a kook, but fun," said Amar.

"She loved Ari," said Bobby Farrah. "She once told me, 'The man is magnetic. Don't look at his pictures. You feel it in his presence. He is so interesting and so sexy.'"

"She once hinted to me, after a couple of glasses of wine, that Ari once demonstrated more than just friendly interest in her," said Farrah. "But she knew too well the Greek mentality, and what being a wife meant. It was not something she was going to let develop.

Onassis had been crushed by the death of his son Alexander, and came to Somerville periodically to visit Doris in the spring of 1973. Ari and Leon got along well. "One night he came for dinner. It was just the two of us. Doris and I had had a fight. Jackie was too busy riding horses. He came and started to talk to me. I was ready to leave her. He was the person who put me back with her when I was fed up. That's when he invited us on the yacht."

In June 1973, Onassis sent Doris and Leon first-class tickets to Puerto Rico where they were picked up by the *Christina,* Ari's 325-foot vessel, one of the world's largest privately owned yachts. Named for his only daughter, the yacht was a garish pleasure craft outfitted with lapis-lazuli fireplaces, gold plated bathroom fixtures, and barstools upholstered in whale scrotum. They cruised to the Rockefeller resort, Caneel Bay, on the island of St. John, and then to Haiti where they would spend six days. On board were Jackie and Ari, Doris and Leon, Geraldine and Andrew Fuller, and young John F. Kennedy, Jr., with a nanny.

"Doris was always very jealous of Jackie," said Amar. "She had to dress just like Jackie. Doris was imitating her. Of course, Jackie was much younger and more beautiful." In one photograph, both women are wearing identical tan slacks, black tops, voodoo medallions, Gucci loafers, and Hermès scarves on their heads. As was her custom, Doris carried an inexpensive white, imitation leather bag, something Jackie would never have been seen with.

"Of course, as you know, Jackie likes power and money. Doris gets nothing out of Jackie except her name since she's an honorary member of Doris' Foundation, but she doesn't come to the meetings. Doesn't do a damn thing," said Amar.

Both women were obsessed with youth and had experienced tragedy. Both were private, mysterious, and headstrong. Perhaps their greatest bond was their notoriety. Jackie and Doris were two of the most celebrated women of their generations: famous for being famous. (Of course, both wore dark, oversized sunglasses which did nothing but draw attention to them.) They had both instituted a policy of making employees sign documents swearing they would never reveal details of their employment. The documents were never notarized, and the employees were too intimidated to have a lawyer examine them.

Both Jackie and Doris had a tendency to "drop" friends rather abruptly.

"I think Doris was interested to find out what made Jackie tick," said Bobby Farrah. "She wanted to get into her psyche, but I think Jackie knew how to close her out of that. Just as Doris knows how. And that was a challenge. Ari respected Doris because Doris is a connoisseur of art. And he had an insecurity that he had not purchased the right thing. One vase was wrong in the room, that kind of thing."

While in Haiti, Geraldine, Jackie, and Doris visited Port-au-Prince art galleries and each purchased several of the colorful, primitive paintings as souvenirs of the island. They decided to have an art exposition on the yacht that night after dinner. Onassis overheard their plan and before dinner gave the captain of the *Christina* money to purchase his own collection of Haitian art from the street vendors near the dock. "I'll show them what collecting art is," he told the captain, peeling off the bills.

"After dinner," recalled Geraldine Fuller, "we walked into the drawing room and there was a whole gallery of paintings. The entire room was filled with art. Jackie, Doris and I had three or four paintings each while Ari had purchased about one hundred paintings, all from street vendors." The Greek tycoon was bursting with pride. "He said, 'I'll bet I paid less for all these paintings than you did for the few you bought.'"

Leon Amar said the tension between Jackie and Ari was obvious. In the middle of the cruise, Onassis left the group and flew to Paris where he was photographed lunching with his supposed mistress, Maria Callas. When he returned, according to Amar, "All hell broke loose." (Biographer C. David Heymann later reported that Onassis allegedly asked Jackie to sign a divorce agreement on this cruise. She refused.)

Ari left the boat one day to place flowers on the grave of former dictator "Papa Doc" Duvalier, and visit his son "Baby Doc." Young John Kennedy spent the time playing backgammon with Leon Amar and raiding the refrigerator, throwing food and cartons of cigarettes overboard to the poor

Haitians who swam out to the yacht. "Onassis blew his top," recalled Amar. The group also traveled to the top of the legendary Citadel, transported over the dusty, dirt-poor regions of the country in an open Duvalier army helicopter.

The group wound up at the posh, newly opened resort L'Habitation le Clerc for a lavish dinner. Said Amar: "The bill came and Onassis went berserk. It was $8,000. There we were, circled by men with machine guns. He paid it."

In Haiti, Doris and Leon got off the yacht and flew home. The Fullers, Ari, and Jackie cruised to Puerto Rico, where Jackie got off and flew back to New York with son John. The *Christina* sailed to the Canary Islands, and later to Greece without Jackie.

In fact, the couple rarely socialized together. One Thanksgiving, Doris invited Ari and Jackie, along with daughter Christina, to have dinner at Somerville. She was excited by the prospect and ordered the staff to bring out the best silver and china. At the last minute, Jackie called and canceled. Christina also canceled. Doris was fuming. Ari alone showed up, and the two aging billionaires sat across from one another at the immense, formal table, set with priceless, gleaming silver and china. "It was pathetic," said one former employee.

Doris sent him home with one of her supposedly home-made pies and bread. A few days later, Jackie sent a note. "Ari had such a good time. I wish I had been there—Much love to you and Leon—and all thanks again, Jackie."

On March 15, 1975, Aristotle Onassis died in Paris. Jackie received a settlement of $26 million. Christina, Ari's daughter, came to a tragic end. Married four times, she died in 1988, leaving the vast Onassis fortune to her only child, daughter Athina, who was instantly crowned "The Richest Girl in the World."

However glamorous Doris' life-style appeared, she always preferred slumming it. "She used to go up to Harlem with Leon," said Sam Greenspoon, Doris' former attorney. "She was singing in some damn church. I hired a private investigative firm to send three or four people as escorts."

Another time, while driving in Manhattan with Greenspoon, "she scared the hell out of me. I was coming home with her through the worst section of New York and she jumped out and ran up some steps. I didn't know where she was going. It was some dance studio."

On one trip, she flew to Washington to see an art exhibit and stayed in the tiny apartment of Farrah's brother. Farrah didn't want to fly back to New York, so Doris insisted on accompanying him on a Greyhound bus. "There we were, traipsing into the bus station. We went into this dinky coffee shop to eat greasy scrambled eggs. We got on the bus and rode home together. She talked the whole way back, gossiping about show business and old movie stars."

She also loved the nightlife. "I used to take her to nightclubs, the Darvish, the Britannia Cafe, the Egyptian Gardens, the Port Said. Greek cabarets on Eighth Avenue," said Farrah. "She loved dancing with me. She was a great partner. She communicated. That's why I know she's an actress. She always knew you were in front of her. She would look at you and gesture with her hands. She became quite adept at that—she was graceful. She had beautiful articulation of the hands and arms and she became extremely feminine, delicate and soft."

One evening, they invited Leon Amar.

"It was like having a stuffed animal with us. He was so uptight, being, in his opinion, in such a seedy environment. At that time, I guess he wanted to be Mr. Duke. Doris was having a great time with me and she ignored him. When he said it was time to go, she said, 'By all means, go.'"

Leon departed alone.

"She called the next day. She was just like a little child, happy that she had been a mischievous girl last night. She was giggling. She said, 'We just can't take him out to places like this anymore,'" recalled Farrah. "She once told me their relationship was over a month after it began, but one of her problems was she sometimes didn't know how to get rid of somebody."

Her boredom reportedly led her to seek out unorthodox companions. Jake Guyer was delivering plants to her Manhattan apartment when he found the doorman arguing with a young black man. "He looked like a football player, he was very big. He said, 'Where's Miss Duke? I was supposed to see her at one o'clock and she ain't here yet. That bitch.' He was mad. The doorman said, 'She brings these young studs in here and they're up there fifteen or twenty minutes and then they come down. I don't know what she pays them.'"

Said Guyer, "She didn't want regular lovers. She wanted to go where she wanted and do as she pleased."

One night at 2 A.M. she called Farrah and suggested creating their own dance group. "She said she wanted to dance with us. To have the experience." The Near East Dance Group was formed, privately funded by Doris

Duke. "She wanted to be the star of her own group, like Martha Graham," said Amar. The budget was set at $8,000 to cover costumes, dancers, and musicians.

"When I first started to teach her, I thought to myself that the woman has what we call in the trade an 'anti-talent,'" said Farrah. "She was clumsy, discombobulated."

Doris, in her sixties, competed with the young female dancers. She wanted to be like them. "One day I wore a blouse to rehearsal," said one of the dancers. "It was a very plain, inexpensive, nothing blouse. She wanted to have the same thing. She asked me where I bought it. Later she went to the store and got the same blouse. It cost less than $40. I think she thought it was 'in.' I couldn't believe it."

The same woman ended up taking semi-private lessons with Doris. The young woman—who was struggling to eke out a living—always paid the instructor, as Doris never had any money.

For their performances, Doris danced in a long black wig.

Leon Amar: "She appeared on many stages in New York and no one ever knew it was her. She went under the name 'Aicha,' which is my mother's name. We gave a concert once at Cornell and they discovered it was Doris' dance company. You should have seen her hiding."

But Doris pursued her dream of a dance career.

"She was not Pavlova," said Farrah, "But she learned to keep rhythm, stay on tempo."

"She wasn't great," echoed dancer Phyllis Saretta, who performed under the name "Phaedra." "But she wasn't horrible. She tried so hard. I've never seen anybody work so hard."

"We appeared at the Armenian Culture Center on the East Side. The First Baptist Church from Nutley was performing with us. Here's Doris, incognito, wearing a long black wig," recalled Farrah. "We walked through the lobby and I heard this voice: 'My God, look! There's Sister Doris.'" Farrah took Doris to the dressing room. "She's nervous as hell. She says, 'How do I look?' I said, 'Gorgeous.' She says, 'Is the eye shadow a good color?' I said, 'Yes.' She said, 'Thank God, I hate green.' Well, her eyelids were all green," Farrah laughed.

Doris was understandably insecure about her age.

"She couldn't accept the fact that she wasn't young. To be a belly dancer, you have to be young, have a beautiful body. She could not accept the fact that she could not be the star of her own dance foundation. Doris would look at these young, gorgeous girls dancing and she would go into a rage. I'll never forget how one night she laid an egg. She fell down on the stage. It was sad."

Phyllis Saretta was her partner that night. "It was at a catering hall in Brooklyn called the Venetian Manor. We had to come out two by two. When I turned around, she was on the floor. But she got right up."

For one performance, Bobby Farrah decided to position Doris in the middle of the stage, wearing an Arabic costume and covered by a veil, playing finger cymbals.

Doris' insistence on being a star began to cause tension. During one argument, an exasperated Farrah blurted out, "You see, Doris, the scales of justice? They're not blind. You have all the money in the world and I have nothing. Look what God gave me and you're trying to buy it and you can't."

To have more control, Doris pulled the rehearsals out of Manhattan to the farm. Every day, a van would arrive to pick up the Near East Dance Group at Forty-second Street and Tenth Avenue and drive them to Somerville. The group rehearsed in her dance studio in the basement.

By now, the company had become the Near East Dance Foundation with Doris at the helm. Bobby Farrah was not happy. "I was very independent, but she wanted to play a prominent role. From a financial point of view, it was a disaster for me. I was broke."

In a confrontation, Farrah told Doris she needed discipline. There was a blow up with another female dancer. "That night, Doris was so upset," said Farrah. "She was saying, 'No one in my life has ever talked to me that way. That I have no feelings, that I'm inhuman.'

"The Foundation was dissolved. Leon called and said to return all the costumes to the farm, including a pair of boots that was made for me. I said, 'Leon, do me a favor. Tell her to put those boots under her frigging bed and I hope that all the spirits that she believes in come out and kick her in the ass like she should be kicked.'"

The dancers were given two weeks' severance pay. "Leon insisted on that. I owed them $600, so I got nothing except $75 a week unemployment," said Farrah. "They had taken out taxes, so at least we got that."

Doris fled to California, then Hawaii. "Her favorite form of retreat was always to jump into an airplane. After a month or two, Leon called me. 'She's *black ass.*' That was a term she always used when she was depressed. It was her jive expression. She was in a bad state. Leon asked me to give her a call. So I did. She was happy I called her." Once again in her good graces, Farrah became a friend and confidant, with no business ties. "When she came back, I saw her. It was very different. We started to get along much better."

To stave off boredom, Amar organized a workshop—complete with ceramic ovens—in the solarium in Newport for repairing china. At other times, Doris would be seized with a sudden desire to redesign her couture wardrobe.

"She went to her closet and started taking out these incredible Balenciaga gowns, because she wanted the collar of one coat and the cuff of another. She sat there, with a clothes ripper, tearing the clothes up and then not using them. They went into a bundle and were thrown back in the closet. She loved to do that. It made me sick."

Socially, Doris had little interest in her contemporaries.

"We were invited to go to the wedding anniversary of Jennifer Jones and Norton Simon at El Morocco," said Amar. "It was a boring dinner, and Doris sat next to Cary Grant, who she was friendly with."

(According to Farrah, Cary and Doris had enjoyed a friendship after his marriage to Barbara Hutton. "Doris, because she didn't think she was as beautiful as Barbara, wanted to show that she could get him too. But he wasn't her style. Barbara was the weak woman, the foolish woman. Doris was smart. That was her power over the beauty.")

Said Leon Amar: "Norton Simon got up and gave a long speech about how wonderful his wife was. Doris had been drinking. She started to lean over and fall asleep. Soon, she was snoring."

Farrah: "After several glasses of wine, she would get tipsy. I think she might be one of these people who just don't hold liquor very well."

Doris attended dinner parties at Brazilian banker Luiz Gastal's home. "She loved coming to his little dinners," said Eleanor Lambert. "He was vice president of La Banque Continentale on Fifth Avenue. It was a private bank, and I think she put a hunk of her money in there because he paid her so much attention and was concerned about things. They were very intimate, I know."

Gastal entertained Doris, along with several of the Du Ponts, the Egon von Furstenbergs, Cordelia Robertson, and Maggie Newhouse. Gastal would hire a numerologist to read everyone's chart.

"Doris called me one day and said she had found a shoe box at the farm full of diamonds that Mummy apparently had collected," said Gastal. "She said, 'What am I going to do with them?'" Doris had been disturbed by the riots in Newark, near her New Jersey estate. Gastal suggested she have the jewels made into a "Revolution Belt." He added, "If there's an uprising, put on a pair of jeans and the belt. Nobody will ever know they're real diamonds."

Doris had also marshalled an elite security guard force. "She hired this guy who was a soldier of fortune named Leoppard. He was really gung-ho," said former employee Nick Tanasy. "He had a 9 millimeter pistol. He didn't say much. He had come back from Cambodia and he was the chief of security."

Gastal advised Doris at one point to get married again. His choice for a groom was Tex McCrary. "I told her, 'Marry Tex. Give him a check for $20 million. If this is what you want, it will work out.' Doris never talked to me about marriage again."

The banker enjoyed a long friendship with Doris, although "As a rule, people came into Doris' life for four to six years."

By the mid-1970s, Leon Amar had lasted longer than most.

"The bottles thrown, the dishes of food hurled at me, the slaps in the face," he recalled.

"Doris would lock herself in her room for four days and nobody would see her. I knocked on the door and said, 'Please, Doris, let me in.' I walked in and she went berserk. The dogs were there and she started screaming, and took everything next to her and started throwing it. The secretaries would come running—they felt I was trying to abuse her. She was making a scene so they would believe I was doing something to her.

"The minute she opened the bottle of La Ina sherry it was going to be a rotten evening. I was always terrified. No matter what you'd say, she'd always pick a fight."

The morning after one outburst, Amar found a handwritten note from Doris pinned to his pillow. "Baby: Don't be mad at me. I'm under so much pressure right now. I'm about ready to flip! I love you!! XXXXX"

Leon would go to her room and the two would reconcile.

"I would hold her and say, 'Please, Doris, don't do that. What's wrong? What did I do?' I would practically be on my knees. An hour later, she would walk down to the garden to have lunch, looking absolutely incredible. She'd kiss me and say, 'Hi sweetheart. I'm sorry about what happened upstairs.' The secretary would come and take dictation. 'You've got to do this, you've got to do that. Call Halston.' She would call him for fittings. And Halston hated her because she was so cheap. She always bought clothes from someone else and expected him to do the alterations! That really killed him."

Doris went to Houston to visit Norbu Chen, while Amar remained in New Jersey.

"It was pouring rain. Two hours after dinner, the maid pounded on my door, saying there was some noise in Miss Duke's bedroom, which was connected to mine. I put on my bathrobe and walked out. The room was practically ransacked. One window was wide open, the door to her bedroom was forced. I think it was an inside job."

Doris' collection of priceless jade was missing.

A private detective, former FBI man Arthur Whittaker, was hired to investigate the robbery. The probe naturally focused on Leon Amar who took a lie detector test, administered at the state police headquarters. By his account and that of attorney Sam Greenspoon, he passed the test.

"I never believed there was a burglary," recalled Greenspoon.

Doris then asked Amar to disguise himself and accompany Norbu Chen to what the psychic said was a fencing operation in Manhattan. The bone-rattling, bell-ringing, chanting Norbu Chen had felt a vibration that Doris' jade was there. Amar, wearing a fake nose and a black mustache, went to the address in a seedy part of town. "Naturally, they weren't there," said Greenspoon.

Whittaker continued his investigation. "Doris thought it was an inside job. She wanted me to have everyone polygraphed," the private detective recalled. Lie detector tests were given to 114 staff members and 12 private guards. "They all came up negative." Whittaker was invited to stay at the house. "I heard her give Leon Amar the devil a few times. I thought, 'I'd hate to be him.'"

"She treated him like dirt," said maintenance man Nick Tanasy. "I used to be in the car with them and he'd be talking in French. And she would say, 'Oh quit acting stupid, Leon,' or 'Shut up, Leon.' I think Leon would have married her in a heartbeat. Leon acted like the money was his."

However unsatisfying their relationship, Doris needed a companion like Leon Amar.

"She needed someone to take care of what she called 'the shit factors' in her life," said Farrah. "Running the farm, the Newport Restoration thing. Leon was the kind of person who could keep everybody in line.

"She received stacks of mail," he recalled. "They used to bring it into her bedroom in a bowl. After her breakfast and her bath, she'd say, 'Sit at the edge of the bed. I have a present for you.' The present being the bowl of mail." Most of the correspondence consisted of what Doris termed "the gimme letters." "She'd say, 'Here. Have fun and then throw them in the garbage.'"

One of the "shit factors" that needed attention was the Animal Medical Center. By 1974, Doris had become convinced that the group was misusing her money. She had given the research center more than $2 million over the course of six years, and she was not happy with the reports coming from the farm. Fifty-five horses were infected with "swamp fever," and the conditions under which the experiments were conducted were not up to her standards. On February 1, she gave them thirty days' notice to vacate the premises. But three days later at Doris' command, Leon Amar and the security chief Leoppard stormed into the horse barn and physically removed the startled researchers, their belongings, and the animals from the premises.

The Animal Medical Center immediately filed suit for $1.7 million in damages, claiming that "armed members of the Duke Police department" illegally halted their experiments. In retaliation, Doris accused the center of fraud and demanded to examine the center's books. Doris had initially promised to donate money to the center equal to the amount lost by the research project, and she suspected they were exaggerating those losses.

Tashjian resigned his position. The New Jersey Professional Horseman's Association slapped Doris, the AMC, and the state of New Jersey with a $10 million suit, claiming the presence of the diseased horses was a threat to their livelihood. Doris filed a counterclaim against the AMC for $2.7 million. A month later, she won the right to inspect the records, which showed, according to attorney Greenspoon, that her money was indeed not put to its best use. The lawsuits were eventually dropped.

Doris and Leon went abroad. She had invited Bobby Farrah to join her. "I said I wouldn't go to India, but I would join them in Egypt. She was miserable. They fought the whole time. She kept calling me from India."

There, Leon and Doris found an unwanted guest in her hotel room. "It was a rat the size of a rabbit. Leon went nuts. She said, 'It's not bothering anybody.' He called the desk and they sent someone up with a broom. Finally, Doris said, 'Get the man and the broom out of here!' Doris later told me the rat was better company than Leon."

Farrah joined the group in Egypt. On a short trip to Morocco, Doris and Bobby Farrah rode in a taxi through the city while the driver gave a running commentary on the sights. According to Farrah, Doris leaned over and said,

"Oh, tell him to shut up." Farrah was embarrassed. "She said, 'I'm going to take a nap now and I don't want to hear you talk anymore.'"

After the tour, Farrah went to his room. The next morning, Farrah told Doris her behavior was unacceptable. "I let her have it. She suddenly acted like a little child. 'Why didn't you tell me then?' she said." Doris insisted on having the same driver that afternoon. "She pretended like the day before didn't exist," he recalled.

In Kenya, Doris took center stage and performed with an African tribal group. The picture found its way into American magazines.

Said Amar: "We were on a safari together and decided to charter a Lear jet. It was unbelievable—upholstered in black leather, the carpet all zebra skin. We flew from Nairobi to Lusaka. We arrive at the airport and out the window, we see thousands of colorful people in costume carrying flowers, a big red carpet and a band playing music. Doris froze. I said, 'Doris, I guess they're expecting you.' She put on her babushka and said, 'The minute we land, I'm gonna run. I don't want to go through this.'"

The jet landed and Doris exited out the side door and hurried across the tarmac with the pilot. "I'm carrying the bags, trying to find our driver," recalled Amar. "I'm shaking hands with various dignitaries. A photographer is taking my picture. We go inside the building to find Doris. She's hiding somewhere inside. When we locate her the driver said, 'I'm happy to meet you. We rarely see a private plane land here, but tomorrow we're expecting the king of Belgium and it gave us an opportunity to rehearse.'"

Doris burst into laughter.

By the time Doris and Leon returned from the trip, the decorator was disheartened. He had spent nearly seven years in her employ, and "I knew I wasn't going anywhere."

After one heated argument over Norbu Chen, Amar was dismissed. "I was kicked out," he said.

Doris told Nick Tanasy to go upstairs and watch Leon pack. "She said, right in front of everyone, 'After all I gave you. I bought you everything, from your toothpaste to your shaving soap.' She threw that up in his face."

The maintenance man was told to drive Amar into Manhattan. "I came here with a chauffeur and I will leave with one," Leon insisted.

Doris has not spoken to Amar since 1976. According to Greenspoon, he was offered a cash settlement of $2 million but turned it down, saying he wanted to marry Doris. Amar denied ever being offered money.

Now a decorator in Manhattan, he is still puzzled over the episode. "I thought I had built my future, but she stripped me of any credit for

Newport. Her last words to me were, 'Leon, I will make sure that you will never get ahead in life.' I remember Roy Cohn once said to me at a dinner, 'You're a fool. You should let me help you. We could sue her and get some money.' I said I couldn't live with that."

Suddenly, the designing jobs dried up. "It was like a curse put on my name. Bunny Mellon. Jane Engelhard. No one would hire me."

In 1978, he ran into Doris on the steps of Sotheby's. "I tried to talk to her. She said, 'Get out of my way. I have nothing to say to you.' I was embarrassed. There were people watching. I couldn't believe the cruelty."

Boaz Mazor, Oscar de la Renta's assistant, observed firsthand the surgical removal of Leon Amar. "He was really in the cold. People turned their backs to him. She ruined his self-esteem. Suddenly, all the people who used to seek him out turned against him. He was a victim, no doubt about it."

Chapter Fifteen

Newport Redux

EVEN THE HARSHEST CRITICS of Doris Duke gave her credit for the Newport Restoration Foundation. The Rhode Island State Senate had passed a resolution, offering "its highest commendations to her as a good citizen and benefactor of all who live in Rhode Island, with the devout wish that the good Lord will spare her many more years and that her generous and progressive deeds will long be remembered."

However, they failed to forgive her breach of etiquette when, in July 1976, she snubbed Queen Elizabeth of England who was making her Bicentennial visit to America. City officials had made repeated requests for the Queen to visit Newport. Their pleadings were bolstered by the involvement of Doris Duke and her commitment to restoring the town to its colonial glory, including the historic Trinity Church. The Queen finally consented, and rearranged her schedule to accommodate a brief stop on her way to Boston.

Cheering crowds of 3,000 spectators lined the cobblestone streets of the seaport and waited in Queen Anne's Square for the monarch to unveil a plaque. Afterwards, she would host a dinner on board the royal yacht *Britannia* with President Gerald Ford, Secretary of State Henry Kissinger, and former ambassador to Great Britain Elliot Richardson. The one guest who failed to show was Doris, scheduled to represent the Newport Restoration Foundation at the ceremonies.

Shortly before the event, officials were notified that Doris Duke would not appear. No explanation was given.

"She decided she didn't want to go," one friend recalled. "After all, she was more important than the queen, anyway. She simply snubbed her."

Later, a prominent Newport socialite who had known Doris for years invited her for lunch. The woman raised the subject of Queen Elizabeth, saying—as gently as she could—that Doris should really have attended the ceremony. Doris turned away and looked at the ocean, batting her eyes. "I wasn't feeling well that day," she said, ending the discussion.

Doris' vision and financial support had virtually changed the face of Newport. Whether it was an effort to outdo Jackie at the White House, Doris spent millions, buying up forty-seven houses, mostly colonial, in the city's oldest section. Some of the houses had been abandoned when the Navy pulled out of town, but many were inhabited by poor blacks who were virtually evicted from the eighteenth-century properties located in an area known as "The Point." The houses were snapped up at bargain prices. A 42-acre farm in nearby Portsmouth was also purchased, earmarked for a museum. Doris must have envisioned herself as a great benefactress. She had mimicked the Du Ponts, with her Longwood-like gardens, and now she was paying homage to the Rockefeller family, which had underwritten the restoration of colonial Williamsburg.

"She did a remarkable job," said former Restoration director George D. Weaver. "She focused attention on the colonial houses and helped revitalize the run-down neighborhoods. It was a complete turnaround."

Doris named herself president and treasurer of the Foundation, and established its office at 44 Pelham Street. Jacqueline Onassis was first vice president and put in charge of overseeing the collection of antiques for a museum, as she did for the White House. Doris' friend Leta McBean, as well as Virginia Warren and Duke Farms business manager Harry W. Cox, were the other officers.

The project, headed by two of America's most glamorous and wealthiest women, soon became a tourist draw. Behind the scenes, it was fraught with indecision, confusion, and second-guessing. Doris' legendary iron will became a lethal weapon.

It was decided that the unfurnished houses would be made available to tenants, who would pay standard rents. The Foundation would own the homes and maintain all control. Tenants were forbidden to install washing machines, dryers, air-conditioning, telephones, and outside television antennas without prior written permission. No pets were allowed, other than "small" dogs, birds, and cats. One tenant strung a clothesline at the side of his house. Within hours, he received a telephone call from the Foundation telling him to remove it.

Tenants were afraid to place even a historic lantern outside their home for fear they would be asked to leave. Each home was marked by a plaque, "a rubber stamp of approval" in the words of one observer.

A corps of gardeners, electricians, cabinet makers, and painters routinely descended on each newly purchased property, stripping it to the foundation and rebuilding it with new materials. According to seventy-two-year-old director Francis Comstock, Doris oversaw every detail, with a keen eye for the colors in the bathrooms and kitchens. Only fourteen exterior colors were acceptable, and twenty interior shades. Said one observer: "One couple had moved into their house and the appliances were white. Doris Duke arrived at the house and said, 'You should have brown appliances.' Well, I don't think they took her seriously, but one weekend they went away, and when they came back all the appliances in the kitchen had been replaced with ones that were brown."

"I remember a workman was in one of her renovated houses putting a fireplace in," said a former Duke employee. "She walked in the door and said, 'Move the fireplace six inches.' They had to tear the whole chimney down. It would mean nothing to her. Sometimes after a house was painted, finished and ready to go up for rent, she'd have them redo the whole thing. She wouldn't check while they were working, only when it was all done. She finally stopped when she reached 83 or 84 homes."

The project had a dramatic impact on the city. Cosmetically, it changed the run-down area and spurred other homeowners to spruce up their dwellings. It also skewed the demographics of the neighborhoods and sent property values soaring. The foundation came under fire from welfare and poverty groups distressed over the sudden disappearance of low-income housing.

Paul Goldberger of *The New York Times* noted that the Restoration Foundation was the most unusual of its kind in the country, serving as an urban renewal and housing agency at the same time. Because only private funds were involved, it was not publicly accountable for its actions which, like everything Doris did, became shrouded in secrecy.

"It can do whatever it wants," one Newport resident told Goldberger. "Since the foundation's restoration work has raised property values, no one is willing to question its operation."

The Newport project proved a welcome boost to Doris' image, tarnished after the "divorce" from Joey Castro and the death of Tirella. Glowing newspaper accounts detailed the involvement of the reclusive heiress while behind the scenes, employees were made to sign documents forbidding them to speak to the press. Their choice of tenants also remained a mystery, although one resident said, "It's easy to get in if you are a retired Navy commander."

Still, Newport was grateful for the face lift. Tourism jumped from 890,000 in 1974 to 3 million by 1977.

As a landlady, Doris was regarded as a real-life version of Walt Disney's Cruela DeVille. People who lived in the houses called themselves "DDT's"—Doris Duke Tenants. But their camaraderie was short-lived.

It seems Doris had installed custom-made storm windows in all the houses. Years after the work was completed, she sent the bills—ranging from $300 to $1,800—to the tenants who did not grasp the logic of paying for the unsolicited improvements on homes they didn't own. In some cases, the windows were installed before they had even moved in. A group of tenants formed an association to fight back. Before they had time to get a restraining order, Doris abruptly ordered her workmen to remove the windows, with the officers of the fledgling union targeted first. As one elderly woman watched her windows being ripped from their casings, she expressed the outrage of her fellow renters. "People who had never been pushed around . . . are being pushed around." A few blocks away, a retired minister watched as the storm windows on his house were taken off. Said one woman, "It's punishment. All we can do now is get down on our knees and pray. It's impossible to deal with Miss Duke on a fighting basis. She has everything on her side."

(The Restoration Foundation was comfortably in the black, with assets of nearly $12 million and liabilities of $32,444.)

A month later, Doris billed the tenants for water. (They were responsible for the other utilities.) In a final *coup de grace,* she hiked the rents by thirty percent. Not surprisingly, over half of the renters—including the officers of the now disbanded tenants group—were forced to move out.

"Who is responsible for destroying this beautiful thing?" one disappointed renter said, walking down the sunlit cobblestone street and pointing out the now vacant houses. "We all feel sad. It was a lovely memory."

Doris simply regarded her tenants as an extension of her vast network of serfs, treating both with equal disdain. One Newport resident, Jane Pickings Langley, echoed Doris' sentiment in a news account of the dwindling market for "good help." "I don't see why more people don't become domestics. It's a lovely way of life, such a nice life," the Bellevue Avenue matron said. "I let my servants have telephone calls and things of that type."

Doris had long been interested in refurbishing Queen Anne's Square, turning the area into a bucolic park. She demanded artistic freedom and full control to underwrite the work. When the project became stalled, she threatened to pull out. Officials finally gave the go-ahead. Wrapped in fur and wearing dark glasses, she personally supervised the construction, moving tons of earth, shrubbery, and fully grown trees. Bystanders watched in awe as a 16-ton boulder was moved from the rocks in front of Rough Point, and hauled through town to the square. Bulldozers whined, and at one point the massive rock was lifted to shift its position by six inches. Doris didn't like it where it was. Two historic properties were uprooted and plunked down near the square "as matter-of-factly as a householder might move the living room furniture," one reporter noted.

"I'm not sure she knows what she's doing," one bystander said, "but you can bet that if it doesn't turn out right, she'll tear it all out and start over."

A *Providence Journal* photographer happened on the scene and tried to snap a picture of Doris working in the square, which was, after all, public property. He was physically barred by a burly man who demanded that Doris stop being harassed. The newshound got off one picture before the police were called, and the incident once again put Doris in the headlines.

The police were more than willing to protect the heiress from the prying eyes of the press. After all, the mayor had just dubbed her "the sweetheart of Newport."

They had even looked the other way when she had her workers comb the beachfront, raking up the seaweed so she could truck it to New Jersey and have it ground up into fertilizer. The $5,000 it cost to ship the seaweed didn't faze her. After all, it was free. "The boys would bring us buckets of fresh seaweed," recalled Leon Amar with a laugh, "and we'd put it in the sauna, smear it on our bodies, hoping to get younger and have no wrinkles."

But Doris' garden at Queen Anne's Square proved too elaborate to maintain. Plagued by vandalism, it deteriorated in the span of two years. Officials noted it would take two full-time gardeners to care for the grounds, with the cost borne by Trinity Church. The square was redesigned at a cost of $50,000, paid for by public funds, and turned over to the city.

The mid-1970s marked a period of intense litigious activity for Doris. When private investigator Arthur Whittaker presented his $22,000 bill for five weeks of security work at the estate after the reported jade robbery, Doris refused to pay him. She thought it was an inflated amount. In retaliation, she informed authorities that Whittaker was not even licensed to practice in the state of New Jersey! He was indicted by a grand jury after the principal witness—Doris Duke—testified against him.

For the trial, Doris pulled up to the courthouse in a black Mercedes, accompanied by attorney Sam Greenspoon. She testified for fifteen minutes. The suit was dismissed, the judge ruling that the detective was hired by Miss Duke in New York where he *was* licensed to practice and therefore he was not required to be licensed in New Jersey.

A year later, a Manhattan jury deliberated for only one hour before deciding that Doris indeed owed Whittaker the $22,000 for his services and she was ordered to pay the detective. He then turned around and sued Doris for $5.5 million, charging her with malicious prosecution and making false statements about him. Doris' attorney—who was raking in hefty legal fees in the process—worked feverishly on the case, and finally succeeded in getting it dismissed.

A dispute with her Newport contractor also wound up in court. The contractor, Daryl Ford, claimed Doris never paid him for $41,000 worth of work done at Rough Point and at Prescott Farm, owned by the Restoration Foundation. An additional $54,000 was owed to him, he claimed, for construction of the restored houses. The Foundation lost the suit and was ordered to pay.

Around this time, there was a second automobile accident involving Doris' negligence. This time, it was at Somerville. "She had backed her car over some worker on the estate," said former governor Richard Hughes, who was in private practice at the time and was retained by the employee. "As I recall, he was a landscape architect or a decorator. She wouldn't pay him a settlement. We sued her in federal court of New Jersey. She had some New York lawyers. I wasn't able to get very far with her. She was a pretty good witness. We made a satisfactory settlement."

In November 1978, she filed suit in Honolulu against Hal "Aku" Lewis, a radio disc jockey, and his wife-singer Emma Veary Lewis for $94,556 she claimed they owed her. Emma is the daughter of her longtime companion, Hawaiian spiritualist Nana Veary, and Doris had loaned them money to buy a home. After the Lewises defaulted on a first note, Doris gave them a second, unaware of Hal's increasing debts.

"It was directed at him, not me," said Emma Veary. "We were getting a divorce. She didn't like Hal." It was a bitter court battle, with Lewis—the world's highest paid disc jockey—pitted against the richest girl in the world. Each accused the other of fraud. Lewis filed a counterclaim, asking for $10 million in damages, citing invasion of privacy and malicious prosecution. He and Doris, after months of unpleasant headlines, eventually dropped their legal actions and settled out of court.

Doris was now highly skilled in the art of getting rid of people. In the fall of 1978, her middle-aged field crop supervisor of nearly five years, Robert Flood, was hospitalized for gall bladder surgery. Five days after his release, he was abruptly fired and offered no severance, and given thirty days to vacate the home he had occupied on the estate. When Flood begged for more time, she demanded he pay $550 a month rent. "He was an ordinary, sympathetic, hardworking guy. Salt of the earth type," recalled his Somerville lawyer, William E. Andersen, who attempted to intervene. Abruptly, the oil deliveries were terminated, leaving the house allegedly unheated in the dead of winter. In February, she filed suit in New Jersey's Superior Court against Flood and his wife, claiming they owed her money for rent and utilities.

Before the case could be heard, she reportedly directed her farm security guards to forcibly remove Flood and his wife from the house.

One man she did not take legal action against was the prankster who in January 1980 circulated 500 commercially printed invitations to his "wedding." The flyers trumpeted "Wedding of The Year; Doris Duke and Michael Novak." The reception would be held at Duke Farms estate. "Everyone is invited for free food and beverages. Please Come All!!"

The bogus announcement—perpetrated by a New York man who was said to have a fixation on the heiress and kept a large clip file on her—was publicized across the country and even sent to Duke Endowment trustees. "At first, we were going to ignore the whole thing," said the estate's security director, "but these invitations started showing up everywhere and we started getting calls from all kinds of people."

Flowers were ordered and billed to the estate. The hoax forced guards to close the Duke Farm gardens to the public. Trespassers were threatened with arrest. "We urge the public to stay away," one guard warned. While police with guard dogs roamed the grounds, Doris found the prank amusing.

Those who knew Doris were shocked, not by the impending nuptials, but to learn that she even had 500 friends.

"Very few people ever talk as if they knew or were intimate with her," said social observer and author Cleveland Amory. "She was the J. D. Salinger of the rich set."

She often failed to respond to invitations, or accepted and then backed out at the last minute. She entertained sporadically, usually at luncheon, and without much success. "She would always try to entertain at an offbeat time, when it didn't suit other friends. That was her big thing," said one former employee. "The rich have an establishment of their own," added Amory. "And she didn't fit in. She was too hard, too outspoken, she had too many fights. She was too tough for them."

She was often invited to Cragwood, neighbor Jane Engelhard's home in Far Hills. Jane, the widow of minerals and diamond magnate Charles Engelhard, first met Doris in the late 1940s through their mutual friend, Leta Morris McBean. Mrs. Engelhard is one of the wealthiest women in the country and her invitations are among the most prized. Her daughter, Annette Reed, recently married Oscar de la Renta. Doris was often disdainful of Jane, and would complain about the presence of "all these children" at the Engelhard house. "She doesn't like children, no," Jane confirmed.

Others said Doris envied Jane's style, and her ability to keep a loyal household staff.

"I think Doris is getting better at it than when I first met her," said Jane Engelhard. "She had about eighteen trained German shepherds in the house and the guests were terrified. And you never knew what time lunch was going to be served. She'd invite me for 1 o'clock, I would arrive promptly at ten past one and lunch was sometimes at half past two. And she always had new staff. She constantly asked me, 'Where do you find your cooks?' I've had mine twenty years, my butler's been with me thirty years and my chauffeur's been with me 37 years. I take good care of them."

Leon Amar recalled a black-tie dinner party at Jane Engelhard's one evening before he and Doris parted company. "The Duchess of Windsor was there, and she was gaga. But Jane had a butler behind each chair. The service, the food, everything was impeccable. Doris had more money than Jane, but she can't do it.

"The Duchess is taking food from her plate and is feeding the dog. She said, 'This wine is ghastly.' Then all of a sudden, she turned to me and said, 'Oh, I've lost my diamond earring.' Jane winked and said, 'Leon will help you find it.'" Amar lifted the former Wallis Simpson from her chair and accompanied her upstairs to Jane Engelhard's bedroom. They searched high and low, but could not find the earring. Leon noticed the Duchess' closed fist. He asked her to open it. "You know where the earring was? In her hand. She was so out of it. After we left, Doris said, 'I can't stand that old bitch.'"

One of Doris' former chefs witnessed one of Doris' social events at the farm. "She was having a luncheon on Easter Sunday. I prepared lobster meat and pears in a special sauce. She came down that morning and watched me toss it. I made a huge, heart-shaped *coeur à la crème* which she loved. Then the phone calls started."

One by one, the guests called the Somerville office to relay their last-minute regrets to Miss Duke.

"They felt as though she had done this to them so many times, it was their way of getting back at her," the chef said. Only two of her eighteen guests showed up for the luncheon, Caroline Lynch and neighbor Malcolm Forbes, who had first met Doris when his hot air balloon "accidentally" landed on her 5,000-acre estate. Forbes, who arrived in a red, gull-winged sports car, was the leather-jacketed, motorcycle-riding publisher of *Forbes* magazine who enjoyed a heady life-style not unlike Doris'. Like most of the men who found Doris fascinating, Forbes was a homosexual. The day of the luncheon, Forbes dared not risk her wrath, although the others could afford to.

"She was furious," the cook recalled. "They all sent gifts, silver, dishes and flowers but didn't show up. I felt sorry for her."

At the luncheon, Doris posed a question to Forbes: which was finer, French or Italian art? "Doris wouldn't comment until she got Malcolm's answer," recalled butler Phil Strider, who was serving the lunch. "Forbes pondered a moment and said he had come to the conclusion that the Italians were much more creative than the French. Of course, she agreed right away."

Another frequent guest was Franco Rossellini, the nephew of Italian director Roberto Rossellini who had caused an international scandal with his affair and subsequent marriage to Ingrid Bergman. Franco had a reputation as a highly amusing Italian "walker" who served as a court jester to wealthy women, among them Philippines' First Lady Imelda Marcos.

He was fond of dramatic costumes, and often wore long black capes.

"He reminded me of a vampire," recalled attorney Sam Greenspoon. "I called him 'vamp' for short."

"Franco was there one day with his cousin Isabella, and a few friends," said Strider. Franco was suffering from laryngitis, so Doris instructed him to go to the pantry and gargle with white wine and vinegar. "Well, he was so dramatic. 'Oh Phil, do you think this is going to *keeel* me?' It was the biggest scene. But he entertained her."

Doris had made one of the guest houses at the farm available to Franco while he was working on the film *Caligula,* a joint production with *Penthouse* magazine publisher Bob Guccione. (The two had a bitter falling out over the X-rated film, and Doris supplied Franco with legal assistance.) He also elicited her sympathy by claiming evil forces in Italy were trying to kill him and his handsome bodyguard, Enso.

Franco, with his aura of Mediterranean charm, gravitated toward the super-rich. "He would say the worst things about you," said one party goer. For this reason, perhaps, he became Doris' pet. "Francoise de la Renta hated him," said Boaz Mazor. "Franco is brilliant, charming, funny and very dangerous. He loves to imitate people. He made Doris laugh."

Through Franco, Doris met Andy Warhol and the hip, young *Interview* magazine and Studio 54 crowd. Franco was a notorious gossip, and as Warhol related in his published diaries, it was he who spread the unbelievable tale about an impromptu "wedding" ceremony between Imelda Marcos and Cristina Ford.

Franco, as related by Warhol, explained: "'I only told one person and it wasn't my story anyway.' He did tell everybody in the world. It was his joke story of the week once. So now I think Imelda and Cristina are mad at him."

Franco often showed up where the glitterati gathered. When he learned President and Mrs. Reagan would be dining at Le Cirque one evening, he immediately made reservations. Warhol wrote: "Franco took the best seats and he started describing to us every little thing the presidential party was doing."

Rossellini replaced Leon Amar as Doris' constant companion. He was attentive, and showered her with flowers and gifts, usually billed to the Duke business office. She and Franco traveled to Thailand, with jet setters Sâo Schlumberger and Mercedes Kellog at the invitation of the king and queen. On the trip, Doris was "full of enthusiasm and full of vigor," recalled John Gunther Dean, then American ambassador.

Franco escorted Doris to fellow Newport resident Claus von Bulow's birthday party in 1982. Doris defended von Bulow vehemently when he was charged with the attempted murder of his wife, Sonny. "Everyone was divided about it," recalled butler Phil Strider. "They would come to lunch and discuss it. She stuck up for von Bulow. She thought the reason he gave her a shot is because she asked for it. She said von Bulow got a bad rap, that Sonny took every kind of pill she could get her hands on. She had no sympathy for Sonny."

Doris' chef, who said the weekly food bill ran to $1,700, had worked for other wealthy people, but none as bizarre as the tobacco heiress.

"There were dogs on the furniture. These beautiful couches—museum pieces—were ruined by stains. You'd think she'd have them cleaned, or change the material. She was too cheap. The animals were given the run of the house. They were more important than the help. We were not allowed to walk on the rugs, but the dogs used to urinate on them."

"My first instructions when I came to work," recalled butler Phil Strider, "were from a secretary who said, 'When Miss Duke is in residence, there's a chance she'll let Foxie and Rexie, her two German shepherds, come in. When they come in, if they should urinate or defecate on the fine Orientals, don't complain, don't get upset. Just clean it up and don't say a word and don't let her catch you yelling at the dogs.' I said, 'Yes, Ma'am.'"

Strider said "the dogs were the size of Shetland ponies and very old. They couldn't hold their water. She didn't care if they were bathed or had an odor." One employee made the mistake of threatening to kick Foxie out the back door. Doris overheard him and stormed into the room. "Let me tell you something," she hissed. "This dog lives here. *You* only work here."

"Miss Duke asked me to drive to Newport with some paintings," said Nick Tanasy, the head of maintenance at the farm. "I was also supposed to bring one of her dogs with me. The dog jumped in the backseat and its paw went right through the painting. I wanted to die. I didn't know whether to drive off a bridge or what. Miss Duke was in Newport when I got there." Tanasy nervously unpacked the car and met Doris with the bad news. "She uncovered the painting. There was a big rip in it. All she said was, 'You *naughty* dog.'"

Tanasy recalled the day Lady Bird Johnson came to the New Jersey farm for lunch.

"At first Miss Duke wouldn't let the secret service in the house, but then they were allowed to watch through the window as she and Mrs. Johnson ate on the patio. The dogs were putting their noses on the table. She was feeding them off the table." Doris had shown Mrs. Johnson the gardens at the request of Jane Engelhard, who also attended the luncheon. "I told her Mrs. Johnson didn't like animals. But Doris behaved herself that day. Lunch was more or less on time. She was impressed with having the First Lady in the house," said Mrs. Engelhard.

But Doris was not amused when Mrs. Johnson sought out Doris' chef. "She came into the house," said Tanasy. "She wanted to thank the cook personally for the food. Miss Duke didn't like that."

Servants were not allowed to speak to Miss Duke unless she spoke to them first. Maids were forbidden to run the vacuum if she was in residence because of the noise.

Each morning, she had breakfast brought to her room. If the melon was not room temperature, she refused to eat it. The cook would send the daily menu to Doris on her breakfast tray, along with faxed dispatches from her various department heads at the farm, Newport, Beverly Hills, and Honolulu. "There were daily reports of what her employees did each hour of the day," said butler Phil Strider. "How long it took a painter to paint a certain room. She would sit in her bed and read these reports."

Her menu would come down on the tray with her approval or with notes for changes. Often, the menu would not be decided until noon. Said the chef, "It was like running a restaurant for one person." If she didn't approve of one of the chosen vegetables, she crossed it out and picked another one. "She has two complete sets of identical cookbooks, one set in the kitchen and the other in the Pine Room next to her bedroom," said Strider. "Once she approves something, she knows how it's prepared because she looks in the cookbook upstairs. If the cook adds anything else as an ingredient, she'll make an issue out of it."

Doris had one consistent request. "All the fat had to be scooped out of everything. Consommés, made fresh daily from stock—if there was one little sparkle of fat she would reject it and send it back. No cholesterol. And she's been doing this for fifty years," said Strider. "She drank water from an Artesian well. Coca Cola never entered her body. She considered it impure."

Refined sugar and white flour were forbidden. Butter was allowed, but little oil. The chef recalled that every week they went through an entire case of ginsing, the herbal tea that's widely touted as an aphrodisiac. At one point, she went on a diet and ate nothing but sardines.

Visitors marveled at such a self-sufficient, private kingdom.

"You pick up the phone, you call the gardener and you tell him what you need for the day. He's there with it in thirty minutes," said Strider. "She has her own mechanic. When a car breaks down you don't call Ford Motor, you send it to her garage at the end of the driveway. She decided she wanted to generate her own electricity. She didn't want to be dependent on New

Jersey power. The change was going to cost $8.5 million. It was under consideration."

At Newport, lunch was usually served in the solarium. At night, the cook would often be made to wait until 8:30 to receive his instructions for dinner. She would take her meal—usually soup or vegetables—on a tray in the bedroom, along with a bottle of La Ina sherry. "I think, sometimes, we felt as though she really enjoyed tormenting us," the chef observed. "After all, she paid for us and that's the way it was going to be."

Florence, her maid, would wait in the hall for the bell signaling that Doris was finished with dinner, just as Nanaline had done. "One evening, Doris kept Florence waiting from 9:30 at night until 12:30 in the morning, just watching a movie and slowly having her soup," said Strider.

"It was her idea to keep you there. If she knew you were in a hurry, she'd make you wait until 5:30 for a split-second instruction about something and then let you go home," said Tanasy.

Her video tape collection was impressive. She not only collected old movies, but supposedly had every episode of the ABC hit series "Charlie's Angels." If the reception on the television was fuzzy, she called Nick Tanasy at home. He drove forty miles to adjust the set on many a Sunday afternoon.

At the age of seventy, Doris appeared remarkably youthful. She enjoyed displaying her figure, often at inappropriate moments. "There's a guard in Newport who swore that when he was on duty, she would undress in front of the window," said butler Phil Strider. "He swears it's true."

On another occasion, Nick Tanasy accompanied Doris to the tennis courts where Bob Winnegar, a carpenter, worked on the Golden Pavillon. "While telling me what work had to be done, she opened the doors to the tennis courts, and the breeze blew her housecoat open. She had nothing on underneath. She was on a balcony. There were two young men standing below her, staring. Bob saw this and told the men to get back to work. He was a very modest guy. He turned away, but she said, 'Bob, I want to talk to you.' He put his head down. The two young men were laughing. She said, 'Bob, when I'm talking to you, look at me.' He was so embarrassed."

One afternoon, Tanasy was called to Doris' room. "When I walked into the room, she had her blouse unbuttoned. I said, 'Oh, I'm sorry, Miss Duke,' and turned away. She said, 'Come back in here. What is it that you want?' She stood there, her blouse opened, not moving. For an old woman, she didn't have a bad shape."

Marveled former cook Memphis Green, "She had a figure just like a young girl."

"She'd come into the kitchen wearing a bikini before going swimming out at the point. I thought it was dangerous, but she'd climb down the rocks," said another employee.

Neighbors observed the energetic Doris in the ocean during the late fall months. "She had no fear of water," said Tex McCrary. "She only became really alive in the freezing water."

When she came in, the maid would have to scrub the sea moss from her bathing suit.

"She's not a normal woman," said Jane Engelhard. "She doesn't dress like we do. She once came for dinner wearing boots that went all the way up her thigh. Hip boots, before it was fashionable. And she's told me she's been lifted so many times I don't know how she walks. Her chin reduced, her stomach and bazooms lifted. She was telling me all about it one day and I nearly threw up.

"She likes to be outrageous, I think. To attract attention. She likes to go down to the Jersey City waterfront and see them dance at night. There are pictures of her dancing with them. She goes out there at night with her chauffeur and she gets up with the band. She'll get into trouble one day. I told her she'll get knifed or something."

But Jane Engelhard also admires Doris, calling her "a doer. I know a lot of rich, lazy women. She didn't have to do a damned thing in her life. She told me she had worked for the CIA and the OSS. The restoration of Newport. Her gardens. I think she worked every day at an office with two or three men. Fired some. Kept some. She made millions with Ned Herzog in the antique furniture business. Now why should she be interested in buying furniture?

"She certainly is a very unique person, and probably the richest woman in the world. I don't think there has been any woman like that since Catherine the Great."

Doris' personal life was run like a major corporation, with endless power struggles among her staff. "The secretaries would get rid of people if they felt threatened," said one employee.

In the mid-1980s, according to the employee, "Miss Duke was hearing things about the secretaries, the deception, the lies, the stealing, the kickbacks. She was beginning to get wind of this."

Former actress Betty Hutton arrived on the scene. The blonde, bouncy musical comedy star, who had graduated from films to her own television show in 1959, had fallen on hard times. She had reportedly been working in a rectory for several priests before Doris asked her to take over as her private secretary. "Betty was a very warm, nice person," said one staff member. "I remember they rented her old movies and watched it on the VCR." (Hutton's films included *The Miracle of Morgan's Creek, The Perils of Pauline,* and *Annie Get Your Gun.*)

The two women were close friends. Phil Strider overheard a conversation in the library at Newport. Betty, then in her mid-sixties, asked Doris what the greatest regret in her life had been. "Doris said, 'It was what a sheltered life I had.' Her biggest disappointment was not being educated at a major university. When she attended board meetings at banks and universities with very well-educated people, it intimidated her."

The other secretaries resented the arrival of Hutton. "Betty was not strong enough for the job," one employee recalled. Nick Tanasy said Hutton was "a nice person but Doris wanted her to be a bastard with the help."

After a few months, Hutton left. "I think she felt she was going to be her companion but she was treated like another member of the staff."

Tex McCrary, another old friend, was still seeing Doris. In fact, she had given him his own suite of rooms at Somerville.

"Doris had a meal for the ambassador of Morocco and Tex was there," recalled Jane Engelhard. "In the middle of the luncheon, Doris said, 'Tex, you're drinking too much. Stop drinking or leave the table.' We were all quite shocked. She said, 'You can't stay at a meal like this.' They started to have a fight right at the table. When I kicked him under the table, he said, 'Don't kick me.'"

Actor Burt Reynolds was another visitor. "One time she was having a party. She told Burt Reynolds to come, but not to bring Loni Anderson. After he declined the invitation, she finally let Loni come. Doris liked him, but just wanted to eliminate her," said a former employee.

Tom Selleck, who was a neighbor of Doris' in Hawaii, was another guest, as were Fred Astaire, Peter Duchin, young actor Henry Winkler, and TV's Gomer Pyle, Jim Nabors, another Hawaiian neighbor. "Jim was probably the biggest hit with the help because he was down to earth and he sang for them. Miss Duke came in and had a fit," said Nick Tanasy. "She said to the staff, 'You have work to do!' And Jim felt kind of embarrassed."

Most of the time, visitors were there for a purpose.

"She had visiting Israeli dignitaries," said Strider, "who wanted to borrow $25 million at 20 percent interest. At the same time, Miss Duke owns quite a bit of farmland in Nebraska. They also wanted her to store seed in underground caverns in case of nuclear annihilation. I never found out if she did it."

Martha Graham, the legendary dancer, also became a friend and beneficiary of Doris' financial support. "I was fascinated by Doris' relationship with Martha Graham," said Tex McCrary. "Because Martha didn't teach Doris to move, she taught Doris to keep moving. Doris repeatedly reached points where she wanted to stop moving and lie still, and for Doris, that was death. To lie still."

But the closest friend she had was Franco Rossellini. "He was such good entertainment," said Strider, "so she kept him around. But she didn't really have one dedicated friend. When she does zero in on somebody and extend an invitation, it's usually to people of importance or dubious character. Both get into her house."

Doris' nephew, however, was by now persona non grata.

From Hawaii, Walker had allegedly shipped a piggy bank stuffed with tablets of "Purple Haze" to the son of the parks manager, Irving Guyer. "I was supposed to hold onto it for him," Guyer said. "The tablets were ten percent LSD and ninety percent amphetamines. The police force at the estate confiscated it."

"Walker was not allowed to come to the residence," said Strider. "When he got divorced from his first wife, Doris asked for her things back. She was afraid the new wife was going to get some of the family treasures. He reluctantly packed her things up. One of the items was a portrait of Doris the size of a car. He had taken a dagger while it was hanging on the wall and thrown it at the portrait, and it struck her in the neck." Other witnesses recalled that the knife mark was directly over Doris' heart. "When the portrait came back, she had it stored downstairs in what was called the Crystal Room."

After that, "Walker was barred. She wouldn't let him in."

There were the usual coterie of gospel singers and psychics. "One day, a black female gospel singer was visiting Doris," the chef recalled. "She weighed about 300 pounds. I was there at the time. Florence the maid opened Doris' bedroom door, and there was this woman on the bed with Doris taking Polaroid pictures."

Another gospel singer, Herbert Pickard, broke his wrist after an accident in Newport. He was hospitalized after sideswiping one car, hitting two others, plowing into a tree. The station wagon he was driving was registered to the Newport Restoration Foundation. Pickard, who had met Doris through Aretha Franklin, was a guest at Rough Point. He gave her piano lessons. His album, "I Thank You Jesus," featuring his group The Pickard Singers, was about to be released.

Pickard managed to escape from the hospital, and wound up in his gown pounding on the gates of Rough Point. The maintenance men refused to admit him, and he was returned to the hospital.

Another visitor that year to Rough Point was a rather large, imposing woman who had read about Doris' interest in the paranormal in one of the supermarket tabloids and sought her out. Doris, according to former estate caretaker John Nutt, hired the woman as her personal food taster and advisor. "She had this magic wand. It looked like a flashlight with a corkscrew on the end with a little bead," said longtime caretaker Nutt, whose grandmother was a cook for the Duke family for many years. "She would run this magic wand over the plates of food. If the little screw turned clockwise, the food was fine to eat. If it turned counter clockwise, Doris wouldn't touch it. Doris invited her up to Newport to treat the dogs." Nutt was asked to go to the solarium where the woman asked him to pick up the wand and hold it over the dog. "The electricity in my body was supposedly going to the dog," Nutt recalled. But the woman didn't seem satisfied with Nutt's level of energy. She supposedly pressed her ample body against his back and commanded that he rock side to side. Doris walked in on the scene. "I'm charging John's batteries," the woman explained.

Doris and the woman decided that the caretaker had enough energy. "Now, you have to do it four times a day," Doris told him, leaving for Somerville. The caretaker asked the other servants to swear that he performed the energy-giving ritual four times each day, as Doris had requested.

"This woman even claimed she could cure the dogs from California. We had to take blood samples and express mail it to her in a baby jar. This is the stuff Doris believed in," said Nutt.

The woman was also observed chasing Florence around the house, trying to get a clipping of the maid's hair for another "energy" experiment.

Séances were held in the ballroom at Newport, where Doris was increasingly regarded as having lost touch with reality. "She comes up here and goes into a sort of trance at her mansion," said James van Alen, socially prominent tennis aficionado.

Servants repeated tales that Rough Point was haunted by a black man in a loincloth dragging a chain. It seemed that several slave ships had crashed against the rocks near Rough Point and that scores of men had drowned. Strider recalled hearing strange noises in the house "like chains being dragged down the hallway. Chills shook my entire body."

One night, he said, "the ghost of the slave came through and someone alerted Miss Duke. She got a candle, and had the guards bring in the meanest dogs. There she was in her lingerie, wandering around this enormous house on the Atlantic ocean with the wind gusting and the draperies blowing in the wind," said Strider. "The guard dogs hid their tails between their legs and started whining. She couldn't get them to go with her. They knew something was there."

Strider also recalled that the seemingly fearless Doris—who trekked through India, helicopter-safaried over Africa, and swam in treacherous seas—was afraid of lightning. "One summer night at the farm, there was a thunderstorm. There was no air-conditioning and the windows were all open. The storm came up suddenly. The lightning was furious. I was running from window to window, and French door to French door closing them. She came running down the steps in her nightgown. She and I were the only ones in the house. She was just terrified. I felt awful because it didn't bother me. I kept saying, 'Miss Duke, it's going to be all right.'"

The dinner conversation had lagged all evening, and Doris' friend Caroline Lynch watched her push her food around the plate. Doris' only question was, "Caroline, what does it mean the meek shall inherit the earth?"

To Doris, there was nothing more she could possibly want. There was a vault, known as the *Kiva,* filled with shelves containing bars of gold in the basement. (The kiva is the name of the underground chamber where the Hopi Indians held their sacred rituals.)

She had an entire Thai village stored in the indoor tennis court at the farm. "She hired Bob Winnegar to reconstruct this Golden Pavillon and then he got cancer from using the gold leaf paint. Supposedly he was the only one who knew where all the pieces went," said one employee. (When Winnegar was given six months to live, Doris at first offered to have him treated at Duke University Medical Center, but said his wife and four children could not go with him. When he declined her offer, she stopped paying his salary.)

"Anything she'd give wasn't from the heart," said Nick Tanasy. "She was always one step ahead of people. Everything she gave was like a write-off."

There was a priceless Renoir hanging in her bedroom at Newport and loose diamonds casually stored in boxes. "I saw her go out one night in a dress. You've seen the kind of belt wrestling champions wear? She had a belt that thick with all sizes of imbedded diamonds, and diamond sandals with little diamond straps across her toes. It was incredible," said Strider.

"She had things she had excavated from Egyptian tombs. They were never on the market, these little statues encased in glass all over the house. They've probably never even been photographed. I guess she had paid certain people in Egypt.

"I was told she wants to preserve her fortune because she is going to come back and use it again. She would be back, living in a new body. She had spoken to Michael Jackson, also, about cryogenics. She likes Michael Jackson a lot."

In 1984, Doris and Tex McCrary flew to Bimini where they were joined by old roommate Roseanna Todd. Doris and Tex, both in their seventies, were in search of an underwater lithium spring said to be the Fountain of Youth.

"We had to go way out, through this swamp," Todd recalled. "Doris and Tex dove down with these little bottles and filled them with water. Doris took the water back and had it tested. It really was what they considered the Fountain of Youth."

Friends recalled several conversations with Doris about the afterlife. In her view, she had no plans to expire.

"Dying," added Strider, "is not part of her thinking."

In the basement of Somerville, the cook recalled, "were all kinds of equipment including a machine to take the pain away. You'd sit on it and it would make funny noises."

Irving Guyer, the son of the park manager, recalled the machine. It had been imported from Switzerland, he said, accompanied by several men in white lab coats. The machine took up almost 20 feet at the side of the basement wall. "It was like something out of *Young Frankenstein*. There was a clear glass top, like a sarcophagus lid. She would lie on the table and pull the top over herself. An electrical charge would be sent to the table. It was a rejuvenation machine." The machine made buzzing noises, and sent arcs of light to the ceiling. "Her hair would stand straight out from her head," said Guyer. "There would be a charge, and then relaxation."

When the machine needed repairs, Irving discovered that the thick wires and 660 volts were being used to charge the "lights, bells and whistles. All she ever got was a little tingle."

"She also went to Switzerland for regular injections of cells of sheep placenta," he said.

"In the basement one day," said Strider, "I heard a little cough. I looked around and there was Miss Duke stretched out on this machine. It was supposedly pumping energy into her body. She had a sheet over her. I said, 'Miss Duke, I'm sorry. I didn't know you were here.'"

Doris glanced over. "That's all right, Phil," she said. "Just go ahead, just go ahead." When she finished, Strider recalled, she "put Foxie the dog there. It was crippled with arthritis. The machine was supposedly pumping new energy and life into the dog. A month later it died." A week after Foxie died, her other dog Rexie died. "She sent the dogs for an autopsy. I was so nervous because I was in charge of feeding them," said Strider. "She buried them by the lake on the farm, a little grave with all her pets." Other guard dogs were shipped in from Honolulu. "They were mean," said the butler. "But with her, they became like little lambs."

"She just showered them with affection," said Irving Guyer. "There were at least eight dogs. Wong, Papaya, King, Queenie. Mickey was a vicious dog. He bit one of the boys on the estate in his private parts. She also had exotic birds. Canadian geese, Chukard partridges, Tennessee red quail, California blue quail, Bobwhite quail, Chinese pheasants, Black Austrian swans. They had problems with poachers. She cried whenever a deer was killed."

There was also a hermetically sealed, heavily alarmed vault containing rare animal skins and fur coats, somewhat incongruous for a woman who claimed to be an animal lover. There was a wine cellar filled with magnums of Rothschild vintages. "There were priceless vintages," said butler Phil Strider. "Rows and rows of wines from the 1800s and early 1900s. There was a fortune down there." The temperature was kept at a constant 56 degrees, said to be better for the wine than the temperature of some of the oldest French cellars. "But they were never turned properly. There were cases and cases, though most of the wine was old and had turned to vinegar," said Guyer. (For charity, she had donated to the University of Hawaii half a dozen cases of great Sauternes from her wine cellar at Shangri-la. Included in the cache were two cases of Chateau d'Yquem 1928.)

Each of her possessions from her five residences was listed separately on a 3 by 5 index card. Her Chanel suits were hung on specially made racks. "I was there when they were putting her inventory on tape. The day it was completed, it came to one million items of personal property. She's got things stacked to the ceilings. It's money in the bank for when inflation hits," said Strider. "She has security there."

Dr. Erno Laszlo was dispatched to various auction houses to buy works of art. "He would call and say, 'Dorshka, how much do you want to pay for this?' She'd say, 'Just get it. I don't care. Just get it,'" recalled Amar. Liz

McConville, her secretary, was also given authority to bid on items brought up for auction at Parke-Bernet Galleries. "When Doris saw something she wanted, she would give Liz a limit to her bidding," said Tanasy.

"One of her secretaries removed a $14,000 classic Grecian-style sterling silver gravy boat Doris had just bought from Christie's from the locked cabinet and had it sent to Newport. They would do things like that and not inform me," he said. "And I was in charge of silver. I had to try and locate these things."

Doris made a habit of carefully inspecting her houses before she left for a trip. "She would just very quietly walk through the house and look at each item. Ashtrays, accessories. She did this in fifty-seven rooms," said the butler. "She was taking a mental inventory."

"I don't think Doris has any concept of money," said Tanasy. "She was always afraid of running out, of going broke. In her bedroom, there's a desk loaded with bank books. Piles of savings books. I guess her father taught her to save as a kid."

But her greed extended to the most minor items. When she had a favorite chocolate cake, she kept track of the pieces. "She couldn't eat all the vegetables coming in from the garden," said Tanasy, "so before they went bad, I would offer them to some of the help to take home on the weekend. Miss Duke had a fit.

"Louisa Jackson, her maid in Hawaii, came to Somerville once. Miss Duke had a picture of Louisa as a young girl in a bathing suit with long hair. Louisa asked Miss Duke, 'Could I have that picture for a keepsake because it's the only one like that?' Miss Duke told her, 'No, it's mine,' and grabbed the picture right out of her hand."

Her former chef recalled, "There were days she didn't want anyone in the house. She ate alone in her room. And she had fits. She was very erratic."

"They call rich people like her 'eccentric,'" said Jake Guyer. "But if it were you or me, we'd be in an institution."

Employees blamed her behavior on the various pills she was prescribed. "She could be lying around the house and just about make it up the stairs," said Tanasy. "Twenty minutes later, she would come flying down the steps like a new person."

The household staff were aware that drugs were present. On more than one occasion, the maintenance man was called to repair something in her bathroom. "I saw these little cocaine spoons. I left them for the maids to clean up, so the maids had to know what she was doing." He saw other drug apparatus. "Straws. She also had access to needles and to morphine. We had a dog sick with cancer who she was injecting with morphine. The veterinary hospital would give her the morphine because she had money and influence."

On Mother's Day, she invited designer Jacqueline de Ribes and Caroline Lynch for an intimate lunch. One hour before the luncheon, Doris decided she wanted the chairs on the patio to be a different color. The workmen hurriedly painted the chairs, dried them with a huge industrial blower in the basement, and set them back on the patio. "It was such a tizzy," recalled Strider. "I don't even recall what color she wanted them."

"There was a great deal of tension," he added, "in that you never knew what was coming. It could be anything."

She ordered a truck and four men to move a piano from Somerville to her Park Avenue apartment, then take the New York piano to Newport. In Newport, they were to leave the New York piano and drive the Newport piano back to Somerville.

One morning she wanted her bathtub in the New York penthouse moved to Hawaii. "The plumber had to go along," one former employee recalled. "I don't know if she had a special experience in the bathtub and thought it would happen in Hawaii, too. They had an awful time. It wouldn't fit in the elevator, and they had to put it on top with all the cables and take it down that way. It's a wonder we didn't get electrocuted."

Employees were often told to drop everything and take the next plane to Beverly Hills or Hawaii, leaving their families behind. Long stretches of boredom were punctuated by these sudden bursts of activity. "At the farm, I worked 37 straight days, 16 or 18 hour days, without a break," said Strider. (The farm had also been fined for violating state child labor laws. Among the complaints was that a minor was forced to work more than 10 hours daily.)

One overworked electrician in the greenhouse made the mistake of telling her, half in jest, "You know, Miss Duke, Lincoln freed the slaves." He was fired.

"Doris *owned* you," said Tanasy.

When Doris was in residence, the chef ended up cooking all day. The servants would have one seating. Miss Duke another. When she left, the employees would open a bottle of wine and sit talking in the darkened mansion. Said one former employee: "The guards were in the house most of the time. You couldn't let them know because that would be reported. Everything got reported."

Doris was reportedly paranoid about conspiracies within her organiza-

tion. Often, Nick Tanasy would fill in for Stanley, the chauffeur. "Sometimes she read her mail in the car, then tore it up and threw it on the floor.
Whenever I let her out of the car, I had to pick up the mail, rip it up and
distribute it in different waste baskets." Members of the household staff
were ordered to sign "loyalty oaths" promising not to reveal information
about their employer. "She was doing this to scare people. Everyone
thought they had to sign. But no one stayed with her very long," one
employee said.

After one of her employees fell on the job, Doris made an appointment to
see an insurance adjuster who arrived promptly at 4 P.M. "The guy was real
suave," recalled Tanasy. "They sat down and began talking. She started
asking questions, but he didn't have the answers. She told him to get out of
her house, that he was wasting her time. He asked to use the phone to call
his office. She said, 'You'd better come up with the answers.' The office had,
by this time, closed for the day. She said, 'Get out. I never want you back
here again. And tell your boss if he can't send someone who knows what
he's doing, I'll stop doing business with him.'"

Security guards escorted the hapless insurance man to his car. Doris
turned to her two female secretaries and flipped the back of her hair up
with both hands. "And that," she said breathily, "is how you deal with men."
She went off to the kitchen to bake cookies.

"When she wants something, she's used to having it," said another former
employee. "She doesn't understand 'No.'"

Her favorite word was "ridiculous." At one point, she wanted a particular
book flown to her house in Beverly Hills. She called a secretary and told her
to have it brought to United Airlines and have a pilot or stewardess
personally take it across country for her. The airline said packages must be
wrapped and sent by courier service or the U.S. Mail. "Ridiculous," Doris
replied. "She called somebody at United Airlines. I went down the next
morning with not only the book but more stuff she wanted, and handed it to
the pilot who took it aboard the aircraft," recalled Tanasy. "Because it was
for Doris Duke."

"She refused to make plane reservations until one hour before the
departure time," recalled Frank Como, who worked for Doris for a year in
the early 1980s. "It was fear of sabotage. They had three or four airport
accounts, so they could call at the last minute. She didn't care what the
charges were, as long as they had a plane there when she wanted. She didn't
want anyone knowing ahead of time where she was going to be. She was
worried someone would try to kill her."

She made reservations under phony names. She also purchased the entire row of seats so she wouldn't have to sit next to strangers.

Often, she rented a crop duster to fly from Somerville to Newport. "She just got in her plane and said, 'We're going.' You had to stay in a state of readiness because you didn't know what was coming up," said the former butler.

"That's all she ever did," said Tanasy. "Go from one house to another."

On commercial flights, "She traveled with no jewelry, no money, nothing on her. Just the clothes on her back and her suitcase," said another employee. "We kept her milk from her Jersey cows in boxes tied with string."

Said Strider: "She's living a whole life of fantasy. She is true American royalty."

When Nick Tanasy drove her into New York, "a lot of photographers knew Doris Duke. They used to come up to the car and say, 'Isn't that Doris Duke you're driving?' I'd say 'No.' The photographers would say, 'Aw, yes it is.'"

For years, Doris Duke kept a secret pied à terre in Manhattan. Located on East Fifty-fifth Street, off Park Avenue and within walking distance of her penthouse, it was sparsely decorated and in fact, rather shabby. There were no Moghul artifacts or Indo-Persian rugs or solid gold Buddhas. There were only her financial records. "She used to go there at 11 o'clock at night by herself," said Jane Engelhard.

Alone with her bank books, Doris would methodically scan the numbers, caressing the leather bindings.

Often she wandered the streets by herself, in an almost catatonic state. Crossing Park Avenue one day in 1984, according to Engelhard, she was hit by a cab. Naturally, she carried no wallet or identification with her. Hurt and disheveled, she was taken to a hospital. To the admitting personnel, she might well have been a homeless person suffering from dementia. "It was Bellevue or Harlem, one of the two," Jane Engelhard recalled. "In the beginning she kept saying, 'I'm Doris Duke. I'm Doris Duke.' They thought she was crazy."

Doris remained in the hospital for three days, in a state of semi-consciousness. The golden girl who had hobnobbed with princes, snubbed a queen, snake-danced as a deb across her Newport lawn, played tennis with Charlie Chaplin, been hounded and stalked by every reporter on the planet, was now a missing person. "Nobody could find her," said Engelhard. "The chauffeur had been left waiting and finally went home after five hours.

He then reported her missing to the security people. It took three days before they located her."

In truth, there was no one to contact in case of emergency. The warmth of familial relationships was missing from her life. "She thinks that's nonsense," said Engelhard. "She didn't get any affection, so she doesn't believe in it."

Doris sustained injuries from the accident. "She was in pieces," said Engelhard. "They reconstructed her whole body."

After the accident, she walked with a limp. People asked her what had happened. She told them she had fallen off a boat in Turkey.

Now more vulnerable than at any other time in her life, Doris' paranoia was now unchecked. One afternoon, her secretary had walked into the library wearing a purple quilted down raincoat. Doris looked up and said, "I've got one just like that." Minutes after the secretary left the room, Doris called her maid and asked her to go upstairs to find her purple coat. It was hanging in the closet.

Those who had not been cut off—"just like the slice of a knife," as one Newport socialite said—found her tiresome and demanding. "Doris can turn off so quickly. When she has no more use for you, she drops you like a bomb," said Honolulu secretary Violet Mimaki. Leon Amar was a good example. "I think he was very honest," said Mimaki. "I think he was a truly dedicated person. But she does not trust anybody."

Even Franco Rossellini could not be with her twenty-four hours a day, as she expected. Johnny Gomez, her former diving coach and longtime "guest in residence" at Shangri-la, remained her devoted admirer.

"Johnny and I were talking one night," said Engelhard. "I was trying to find out something about their relationship. It's so peculiar. He's ugly, he's common. He said, 'She tells everyone I'm her bodyguard, but I'm not. When she gets bored, she calls me up.'" Duty calls.

For a woman in her seventies, Doris still had a strong libido.

Taylor A. ("Tap") Pryor was the handsome, tawny-haired son of a former president of Pan Am Airways. Known as a maverick, he had once taken a schooner across the Pacific with Marlon Brando. He lived in Hawaii and created an oceanarium with seals and other sea creatures, though his financial position was always precarious. Twice divorced, he was a good-looking, strapping athlete and ecologist twenty years Doris' junior. He knew Jane Engelhard, and arranged for a meeting with Doris Duke. "I wrote to Doris," said Jane. "She said if he came to stay with me, she would see him."

Tap Pryor, Engelhard recalled, "really was a killer. The type of man who would jump out the window of his bedroom in Hawaii and land in the swimming pool. It was freezing cold here, and he went swimming in the lake every morning naked, just chopped through the ice. He went over to visit Doris one evening at six. We didn't see him again until the next day. I don't know what happened, but he wound up with a lot of Doris' money."

Newport caretaker John Nutt recalled, "She'd have a few glasses of sherry and that gleam would be in her eyes."

On May 11, 1979, at the age of sixty-six, Barbara Hutton died. The poor little rich girl came to a tragic end, addicted to a wide range of drugs and her eighty-pound body dissipated by enemas and laxatives in her quest to stay thin. She had no family, few friends, and despite her fabled millions left an estate of $3,500.

At seventy-three, Doris Duke recognized that time was running out. She sent Tex McCrary an expensive Bulgari clock with a note: "Forget the calendar; we're down to the hours." Her former best friend, Leta Morris McBean, was dying. Dee Dee and "Leat" had not spoken since the Animal Medical Center scandal. Doris felt Leta was disloyal to her in her fight with Dr. Tashjian. In the last months of her life, Leta and Doris reconciled.

Liz Whitney, horsewoman and dog lover, was also ill with cancer. Out of the blue, Doris telephoned Liz's husband but could not arrange to see her at her Virginia farm. Doris' private plane had nowhere to land.

Doris' own attempts to turn back the clock had failed.

"She took lots of enemas," said Jane Engelhard. "I took one glass of the stuff, and I promise you it made me sick. She takes six glasses a day. She does it to be thin. I asked, 'What doctor prescribed this for you?' She said, 'I don't believe in doctors. I'm my own doctor.' She takes very good care of herself, but if she continues with these enemas there won't be anything left of her."

She still traveled, although the trips were more difficult and her schedule became more rigid: winter in Hawaii, spring at the farm, summer and fall in Newport and Somerville, then back to Hawaii. Her hearing loss acceler-ated: like Nanaline, she was growing deaf. Her skin was so badly blotched from the loss of pigment, McCrary said, "When she came back from China, people thought she had AIDS."

She still took dance lessons from Martha Graham dancer Peggy Lyman, who was amazed at Doris' slim, girlish body. She also continued singing and piano playing. She installed a special synthesizer to magnify the sound. But her efforts were always frustrated. The only gift she ever wanted—talent—was one thing money could not buy. Beauty was another.

"She always had the feeling that she was ugly," said Engelhard. "She called me one night that she was going to a party at Malcolm Forbes' home. Malcolm and she had a lot in common, and she was impressed by him and his motorcycles. She asked me: 'What shall I wear? I want to look right.' I said, 'Well, you could wear a long sequined dress. I'll call Oscar de la Renta, I'll do anything.' She said, 'No. I want to arrive in boots.' I said, 'Well, I don't think it's a boot party. There will be a lot of politicians from Washington with very dreary wives.' She said, 'I feel my instinct is right.' So she wore boots. Up to her thigh, with tassels and fur. She looked totally ridiculous, like something out of the circus. She blew it. Because she thought she was going to pick up some important man that night and they were scared to death of her. They thought she was a freak, and never went near her. She was home at 11 o'clock."

Because Doris had never been able to move freely in the real world, she had been forced to create her own. Now her loneliness and isolation was unrelieved by constant travel and amusing celebrities. Flying back to Somerville from Hawaii on schedule one spring day, Doris was accompanied by her secretary, who said she must be happy to be returning home. Doris looked over at her and said, "I have no home. My home is where the dogs are."

Waste was not tolerated. If a piece of fruit was bruised, she insisted that the rotted part be removed and the rest served. "Once I took a pitcher into the kitchen after a meal," said Phil Strider. "She followed me in to make sure I hadn't poured any of the cream down the drain. A bottle of leftover red wine would stay in the refrigerator for four months and she'd drink it later. Stuff that would poison you or me."

But when it came to her animals, no expense was spared. When a nursery in Somerville was going out of business, Doris purchased $10,000 worth of azaleas and had them planted on the side of the main driveway. "The next week," said Strider, "the deer came out and ate every single one of them. $10,000 worth of azaleas. Miss Duke just said, 'Oh well, they must have been hungry.' Everybody was in shock over it."

But her dogs were no substitute for human companionship. "She was not a happy woman. She's got everything she could possibly want, but she's not a happy woman," said Frank Como.

"I think Doris desperately wanted a child," said Tex McCrary. "And a daughter, not a son."

Plagued by loneliness, she spent most of her time watching television.

"She watched an awful lot of TV. She had a satellite on the roof. She'd rent a TV in Newport and then return it when she left. She wouldn't buy one," said Como. "The help were not allowed to have TV's in their rooms. We had a TV room, and we all had to watch it downstairs."

The servants lived in dormitory-style rooms on the third floor, with a large bathroom with separate stalls. Their rooms were small, and it was a major task to have a tattered rug replaced or a shower curtain installed. "You were not allowed to have your family see you, or have any visitors," Strider recalled. "We were bored stiff."

Strider left in 1985. "The ones she trusted the most took advantage of her. It was a bad time, a turbulent time. Over a period of three months, fifteen to twenty people left. She cleaned house." For the longer-term employees, she provided pensions of $28 a month.

It is no accident that Imelda Marcos, poor little rich girl of the Third World, was drawn to Doris Duke. "She's the only woman as powerful," said Jane Engelhard. "I think power has as much to do with it as money."

Born Imelda Romualdez, she had grown up in poverty and often went barefoot. As a teenager, she blossomed into a curvaceous, upwardly mobile, dark-haired siren and beauty contest winner who wed Congressman Ferdinand Marcos. By the time he was elected president, Imelda had a well-developed taste for luxury. She soon amassed an obscene amount of worldly goods: 1,700 pairs of shoes, racks of designer gowns, and expensive furs. The family quarters of Malacanang Palace resembled a department store. She also was said to have stashed $3 billion in Swiss bank accounts, and kept a twelve-by-four-foot chest stuffed with pearls.

Imelda, who often visited Manhattan, once spent $40,000 in a single shopping spree without trying anything on. Although her husband had tried to get the Philippine National Bank to stop making cash disbursements to her—$100,000 at a time, at a rate of four or five payments per visit—he was unable to curb his wife's spending. Nothing was too extravagant. She sent a plane to Australia once to pick up a load of white sand for a Philippine beach resort. When she wanted to buy New York's gilded Fifth Avenue Crown Building for $50 million, Ferdinand nixed the real estate deal.

Imelda cried.

She got the building.

"Everything about me is ostentatious," Imelda once said. "I was born ostentatious. They will list my name in the dictionary someday. They will use 'Imeldific' to mean ostentatious extravagance."

Imelda considered herself a role model for the poor people of the Philippines. She hobnobbed with kings and presidents and countless celebrities, including George Hamilton and Gina Lollobrigida. She was fond of faith healers and psychics who frequented the palace. Her one question to them was, "Will I ever be poor again?"

Imelda also believed there were cosmic forces over the Philippines.

But there were other, more devious forces at work in the country. When her daughter Imee eloped with a man whom she violently disapproved of, he was kidnapped by the military. Political foes of her husband called her a "Dragon lady." Martial law had been declared and 1,200 political prisoners were arrested and jailed.

By 1985, Imelda was reportedly running the Philippines. Ferdinand Marcos was suffering from lupus, a disease which attacks the immune system. Imelda's clout was increasingly visible, calling cabinet meetings, screening visitors and, of course, surrounded by psychics and faith healers. *Rolling Stone* magazine described her as "crazy as a rat in a coffee can."

First introduced by Franco Rossellini, Imelda was instantly smitten with the ultra-wealthy Doris Duke and invited her to stay with her at Malacanang Palace in Manila. Imelda's hospitality was well known. If a guest happened to so much as glance at a piece of jewelry in a Manila store, it miraculously appeared on their breakfast tray the next morning.

For the first time in decades, Doris was being showered with gifts and attention by a woman as wealthy as she. "At the Palace, Doris was so happy," recalled Rossellini. "She said, 'How can we pay her back?'"

While Imelda and Doris differed on many issues, they had much in common: both were frustrated singers, and devotees of mediums and clairvoyants. Both loved off-color jokes, salty language, and X-rated movies.

Both were also out of touch with reality.

In California on a visit, Doris was invited to lunch by a man said to be worth $60 million. When she and her companion left his estate, Doris said, "I just can't believe how far the middle class has come."

Imelda convinced Doris not to feel ashamed of her wealth, to enjoy her position. Imelda also flattered Doris, as she did most American guests.

"I went to Manila once on business," recalled Tex McCrary who was met at the airport by one of the Marcoses' assistants and invited to the palace. "We were standing there nervously in the Great Hall of Heroes and suddenly I heard the *tap tap tap* of high heels echoing through the palace, and in walks Imelda followed by fifteen ladies all dressed in blue. The Blue Ladies. We were introduced and got into a freight elevator and rode to the top of the palace where she had her disco. I was on Imelda's right and Saudi arms dealer Adnan Khashoggi was on her left. She found out what songs I liked: 'Me and My Shadow,' 'Has Anybody Seen My Gal?' She was going to sing all the songs from my youth. Khashoggi was there swapping oil for sugar and I think that's how Doris met Khashoggi. Through Imelda."

"The only photograph Doris had everywhere was Imelda," said Tex McCrary. Their close friendship led to gossip.

"I don't know at what point Doris was bored with men. No question that Imelda was," recalled McCrary.

Chapter Sixteen

Daughter Dearest

BY THE MID-1970s, the north shore of the Hawaiian island of Oahu became a magnet for a new breed of vagabonds: flower children, social dropouts and devotees of various spiritual movements. Among the influx was Charlene Gail Heffner, a young girl from a suburb of Baltimore. At five-four, and one hundred twenty pounds, she was pretty and slightly plump, with waist-length brown hair. In 1971, she graduated from a private Catholic girls school, Notre Dame Academy. Charlene had grown up with two younger sisters, Claudia and Holly, in a middle-class household in an area known as Spring Lake. Her father, William J. Heffner, was an attorney and bank vice president, her mother Barbara ("Bunny") was a surgical nurse.

Charlene had been known as a recluse and a loner. "She was tough," said a former classmate. She was remembered primarily for her aloofness. "She was a real hippie," recalled one classmate. "She had a tattoo on her arm. She got into all this weird stuff." Said another Notre Dame student, "She was odd, no question."

"Charlene was a bizarre girl," recalled classmate Mary Gamberdella. "Not too many people knew her well." In her torn jeans and loose, Indian blouses, she was swept up in the post-1960s counter culture and left home, first settling in California before heading further west. She arrived in Hawaii in 1972 with a female companion named Faith, and the two wandered onto a small farm owned by local horseman Jimmy Reynolds. In exchange for grooming and exercising his horses, Charlene and Faith were given room and board. They lived in Reynolds' tack room for about eighteen months. "They were two flower children as gentle as could be," he recalled. "They were very young and had gotten involved with meditation and chanting. As the Hare Krishnas would do. Charlene was interested in riding. They both seemed very happy. Very spiritual. They were not into material things." Reynolds also observed they weren't interested in men. "They didn't seem to ever want to date."

The two women left in early 1973. At some point, Charlene met Gary Winslow McElroy, then one of the top lieutenants of the Hare Krishna organization. McElroy had come to Hawaii from San Francisco with his wife Bobbie in 1968 with orders to set up a Krishna temple. A native of San Antonio and a former University of Texas art student (he never graduated), McElroy reportedly organized temples at Kaaawa and on McKinley Street in Manoa.

Soon after they met, Charlene and Gary, eight years her senior, moved to the Big Island where they rented five acres of land adjacent to Kolopa State Park from a local rancher, George L. Ferreira. Faith was also living with them, and the two women often wore the distinctive poppy-colored Krishna saris and veils. The group, all vegetarians, formed a commune.

"There were nine of them, more men than women, as I recall, living together in this dirty shack. Part of the floor was just dirt," said Ferreira, who lived in his own home just up the road. "Gary was a priest. They got some lumber and built a temple with an altar where they held services. They stayed there for thirteen years."

The rent on the property was $180 a month. "She always claimed she was broke," said Ferreira, who was not particularly fond of Heffner. "She was moody. She always talked back to me. Even if she was wrong, she kept arguing. Sometimes she owed me money. They left rubbish around, even old, abandoned trucks on the property."

In 1977, Gary and Charlene went to India to meet the spiritual master of the International Society for Krishna Consciousness, A. C. Bhaktivedanta Swami Prabhupada. It was the guru who christened Heffner "Chandi," a Sanskrit name meaning "female energy personified." She and McElroy were reportedly married in a Krishna ceremony in India.

In 1979, the group offered to buy Ferreira's land for $60,000. Gary's name was put on the deed. They began making monthly mortgage payments to Ferreira.

By the early 1980s, Chandi had a few horses on the property. "There were a couple more girls living there," said Ferreira. But Chandi Heffner had eventually grown tired of the commune and made frequent trips to Oahu where she was spotted at polo matches. Jimmy Reynolds was surprised to see his old stable girl, who had developed a sudden interest in wealthy Hawaiians and their pursuits.

Coincidentally, she also developed a sudden interest in Doris Duke's passion: bellydancing. On a trip back East to visit her sister, Claudia, Chandi sought out Bobby Farrah's Eastern-inspired dance company, the same company once funded by Doris Duke.

"I first met Chandi in 1984," recalled Doris' former teacher, Phyllis Saretta, who performed under the name "Phaedra." "She knew about Doris. She said she knew a friend of Doris, but had never met her. I remembered her saying something about Imelda Marcos. That she had met her once through this guy who lived near Doris who also knew Imelda. Chandi said, 'I would love to see Doris' home.'"

Saretta also met Gary McElroy. "He was very non-descript, light-haired, very American. They had been married in India, or that's what they said."

Chandi told Phyllis she was from a wealthy family that disapproved of her life-style and had cut off her trust fund. "I remember saying, 'Well, it's no fun being poor.' You better think about that trust fund.'" Phyllis learned that Chandi's younger sister Claudia, who had done some modeling, had married Nelson Peltz. Peltz, the president of a small copper wire and vending machine company, New York's Triangle Industries, had made news with his recent takeover of the more powerful National Can. The takeover was leveraged by junk bonds raised by Drexel's notorious Michael Milken. Peltz appointed his father-in-law William J. Heffner to the board of directors.

"They arrived one day in her sister's limousine," Phyllis Saretta said. "Chandi was overwhelmed when Claudia married Nelson Peltz. He had all this money."

Farrah remembered Chandi as "a poor rag doll of a girl" when she came to his studio on Eighth Avenue and Forty-seventh Street. "The other girls always felt sorry for her. Her sister would try to buy her expensive clothes." Phyllis began receiving ingratiating letters from Chandi. "She wrote and said things like, 'I couldn't get my mind off of you.'"

Like Doris, she also displayed a fondness for animals. "She kept a pet baby pig. She was feeding this pig with a baby bottle. She just loved animals."

"I remember there was this group of people who called themselves 'Breatharians.' They lived on air," said Saretta. "Those were the kind of people Chandi hung out with."

But Heffner displayed a keen intellect. "She was a hippie," said Saretta, "but a sharp hippie. She seemed to be hiding something."

In early 1985, Chandi arranged for Phyllis and Bobby to conduct a dance seminar in Hawaii. "Chandi came to the seminar with a cast all the way up her leg," said Saretta. Heffner had shattered her leg against the railing of a race track during a riding mishap. "She seemed quite troubled."

Bobby Farrah, now editing *Arabesque* dance magazine, contacted Doris in Honolulu. "I'd been out of touch with Doris, but I called her. She had just come back from the Philippines. She said, 'I got bored there. I'm so glad you're here.' She was there with Franco and she sent him off. She got bored with him, too. She thought Imelda was froufrou. And she didn't care for The Palace. She told me it was like Chinese food, all mixed up. Beautiful objects hidden beneath all this other stuff. And the evening's entertainment consisted of Imelda singing. Then she proceeded to imitate Imelda for me."

The night before his departure, Farrah—who had been spending his free time at Shangri-la—planned to have dinner with Chandi Heffner. He asked her to meet him at Doris' estate, but to wait outside the gate. Bobby told Doris that a friend would be picking him up. Shortly before 8 P.M., as Bobby and Doris were saying goodbye, Johnny Gomez suddenly arrived at the door with a visitor: Chandi Heffner. She had ignored his instructions and walked into Shangri-la on her own.

The three went to a side room and Doris asked for a glass of La Ina sherry. Chandi asked for mint tea. Said Farrah: "We had a conversation. Doris told Chandi about this Japanese doctor she was seeing, and told her she shouldn't have a leg operation, she should go to him. When we left, they exchanged phone numbers."

On the way to dinner, Chandi was giddy over the meeting. "She was just giggling all the way. Telling me, 'Oh Bob, she's human. She's pretty nice.' Then she said to me, 'Why doesn't she help you with the magazine?' I said, 'That's why we're friends. Because we're not in business.'"

A week later, Farrah called Doris to thank her for her hospitality in Hawaii. "Doris said, 'By the way, guess who's coming for lunch tomorrow. Chandi.'"

Shortly afterward, Phyllis Serrata recalled, "The phone rang. It was Doris. She said, 'I don't know what Chandi is doing. One of you make her call me. She says she's having trouble with her husband, and I need to speak to her.' I had no idea they had become so friendly. In fact, Bobby and I were both shocked."

That week, Chandi flew back to the Big Island and left the commune. "When she left, everybody left," said landlord George Ferreira. "She was the backbone."

In February 1986, Ferdinand and Imelda Marcos were ousted from power after a military-civilian revolt catapulted Corazon Aquino to the presidency. The Marcoses' twenty-year reign of terror, greed, and corruption had come to an end. To avoid bloodshed, the Reagan administration convinced Marcos that he must leave the country. Marcos asked that he be allowed to spend a few days at Ilocos Norte, his native province. The new government refused, and Marcos and Imelda—warbling "New York, New York"—were flown to Guam, and then on to Hawaii.

Photographs of Malacanang Palace featured Imelda's bulging closets and customized shelves filled with more than 1,700 pairs of shoes, including a set of spike heels with blinking disco lights. Observers also found Imelda's bullet-proof bra. There was no doubt that Imelda Marcos was a world-class shopper.

When the deposed dictator and his wife landed in Honolulu, Washington, D.C., attorney Richard A. Hibey, a tall, circumspect former prosecutor now in private practice, was on the first plane to Hawaii. He would head Ferdinand Marcos' legal team. At first, the Marcoses were under the impression that their troubles could be "fixed" in America as they once had been in the Philippines.

As for Imelda, the first person she turned to in Honolulu was the ultra-wealthy tobacco heiress Doris Duke, now ensconced at Shangri-la with Chandi Heffner.

With their Swiss bank accounts frozen, Imelda and Ferdinand Marcos were suddenly dependent on the financial support of friends and political allies. Their legal bills would be costly. Imelda began to see Doris as her personal piggybank.

Coincidentally, so did Chandi Heffner who had just that month called George Ferreira and said she was going to pay off the mortgage for the land that she and Gary McElroy had lived on in Kolopa. "I couldn't understand where she suddenly got this money," said Ferreira. She reportedly paid McElroy $33,760 for his share of the land.

A few weeks later, Heffner telephoned landowner Anna Perry-Fiske, and offered her $1.5 million for a 290-acre ranch in the Kohala Mountains on

the Big Island. Perry-Fiske said Heffner was extremely anxious and determined to buy the property, which had not even been listed. But it wasn't her
money. "Doris Duke bought it, and put it in the girl's name," said Perry-
Fiske. The transaction was made in cash.

After the sale, Doris began telephoning Perry-Fiske, saying, "The car is
coming to take you to lunch." But Perry-Fiske usually had other plans, and
did not comply with the command performances. "She's very demanding,"
said Perry-Fiske. "She called a number of times. Even when I was in
Honolulu. I'm very busy. I finally had to say, 'Don't bother me.'" Perry-Fiske
believed that Doris was desperately lonely.

In Kohala, Doris and Chandi stayed together at the ranch, rarely seeing
anyone. There was no telephone. "Doris was living there with the girl. She
never left her," recalled Perry-Fiske.

It was on the ranch that Chandi and Doris experienced their first
"channeling" sessions, recalling the spirits of the dead as she had once done
with Nana Veary. In one of those sessions, Chandi convinced Doris that she
was the reincarnation of her daughter who had died shortly after birth in
1940 in Honolulu.

For Doris, the discovery was better than the Fountain of Youth. Arden
had returned to her.

By mid-1986, Chandi and Doris were openly living together. "From the
beginning, I saw something strange," recalled Franco Rossellini. "Chandi
said she was a millionaire. But Doris is so naive. Chandi talked about her
rich family. She said she hated them."

Jane Engelhard hosted a dinner party to which Doris brought her new
companion. "When she first came in as the *jeune fille,* she curtsied to me. I
thought, 'Well, well.' I put her next to Malcolm Forbes because he was
quite smart in detecting people. I explained to him who she was. Afterwards, he told me, 'Boy, is she a dangerous woman.' Another man who was
sitting across from her that evening said, 'She's sexy that girl.' I didn't see it
at all. She reminded me of a little Filipino maid."

"In the beginning, Chandi was like a carpet. You could walk on her," said
Rossellini. "She was the perfect slave."

"She appeared to be a devoted companion," agreed Doris' Newport
security chief Stephen Scott.

As her relationship with Doris solidified, Chandi assumed more authority within the Duke organization. Said Nick Tanasy, "She was getting more

powerful. She started giving orders, dealing with the household help, firing people. We went through so many butlers and maids."

Lawyer Sam Greenspoon first met Chandi in 1986 at Doris' apartment at 475 Park Avenue. "Doris was sitting there barefoot," said Greenspoon. Doris introduced Chandi to the lawyer as her friend. "They seemed to be affectionate. They held hands."

Reports began to circulate of Chandi's growing intimacy with Doris. Violet Mimaki recalled the morning she walked into Doris' bedroom in Hawaii. "They were both under the covers. When I came in, Chandi said, 'We're meditating.'"

A female secretary in Somerville during this period entered Doris' bedroom at the farm and discovered the two women in bed. According to Chandi, they had just given each other injections of sheep's cell placenta, a rejuvenating substance.

"They were shooting up six or seven times a day," said another employee. "It was supposed to be something to make her and Doris young."

John Nutt, the Newport caretaker, walked into the solarium one afternoon in 1986 and found the two women seated side by side on a sofa. "Doris and Chandi were caressing each other," Nutt said. He was "mortified" because it appeared that Chandi was partially undressed. Two months later, Nutt was fired abruptly, and is reportedly still owed $18,000 in back wages.

As Chandi began running Doris' affairs, many Duke employees began to wonder. Who was this girl?

"Chandi was supposed to have money. She had a big horse farm in Hawaii. Then she said she was related to Hugh Hefner," said Nick Tanasy, who drove her back and forth to the business office at the farm. "She was telling people different stories. She told me she raised horses. Everybody knew that Chandi was conning her."

Tanasy quit shortly after Chandi arrived.

In Hawaii, personal secretary Violet Mimaki became more and more alarmed at Chandi's behavior. One afternoon, Chandi stood in the mosaic Indo-Persian room, surrounded by priceless antiques, looking out at the swimming pool, tennis courts, and acres of lush land. "Someday," she said, "this will all be mine."

Chandi asked for a meeting with attorney Sam Greenspoon. "Doris had this half-assed pension plan for the workers at Somerville," said Greenspoon. "Chandi said, 'Is it true that Doris can terminate the pension plan?' I said, 'Yes.' Chandi asked, 'She can legally terminate it?' I said, 'Yes, why do you ask?' 'Well, we might want to save some money.' She didn't say Doris, she said 'we.'"

At Chandi's direction, the Duke Farms pension plan was canceled.

Doris and Chandi applied to the state of New Jersey to have her 2,700-acre estate made a part of the Farmland Preservation Program. When township elders piped up and said it had other plans for a ten-acre piece of her property—a road-widening project—Doris and Chandi threatened to turn the land over to an AIDS hospice or an amusement park instead, suggestions meant to strike terror in the hearts of local officials.

"Chandi was interfering and asking very oddball questions," said Greenspoon, who was replaced as Doris' lawyer.

One Duke associate who became an ally was Newark attorney Donald Robinson, who had first handled Doris' legal affairs with the Animal Medical Center. Robinson found Chandi to be, in the words of one observer, "a brilliant woman" with a curious mind who would serve as a trusted companion and mouthpiece for Doris.

But Doris' employees saw a different side to Chandi. She was increasingly difficult, even with Doris. She became petulant and demanding, especially about money. "All hell was breaking loose," said Violet Mimaki, "She and Chandi were fighting day and night. When Mrs. Marcos came, she would lock herself in her room. Things were a bit rocky."

Mimaki was fired after serving Doris for twenty years. "She was fired on the spot. I mean that day, they told her: 'Get out,'" said one observer.

Chandi seemed delirious with her unlimited purchasing power. "She was buying everything," said Rossellini. Purchases included jewelry, guitars, and a $20,000 black Ford Bronco. She became a familiar figure at the Chanel and Ralph Lauren Polo boutiques and during lingerie sprees, purchased a dozen bras at a time.

"They were great shoppers," said a former employee. "They would order things by phone." Doris was partial to velour sweatsuits in every color, while Chandi became addicted to Chanel fashions. She even began sporting skimpy Chanel tennis dresses around the house, although she never actually played the game.

In Manhattan, they bought luggage, clothes, expensive horse saddles, and shoes. When Doris read that a store in Manhattan sold one-of-a-kind saris, she made a special trip. "She came in one afternoon. We didn't know who she was," recalled Bina Ramani, owner of Once Upon a Time Boutique. "She had difficulty walking. She was trying to keep her balance with a walking stick. She picked out the best jacket we had. It was $600. She had no money with her and no checkbook. She just said she was Doris Duke, and to send the bill to Duke Farms."

By 1987, Doris had hired a private pilot to fly her and Chandi back and forth between Somerville and Hawaii in chartered planes. "Chandi told me her father started Triangle Industries. She had gone to finishing schools. Her sister, Claudia, had her own plane. A 727. Chandi wanted something bigger," recalled Ken DeWitt, a former pilot who worked for Doris for nearly three years.

Through Imelda, a plane was located. It was a gleaming white Boeing 737 outfitted for nineteen passengers with a price tag of $25 million. DeWitt said the plane was registered in the Cayman Islands, having belonged to a Kuwaiti who was supposedly delivering the plane to Imelda's friend, Saudi arms merchant Adnan Khashoggi.

On November 10, the plane was flown from the Caymans to Arizona. When DeWitt inspected the plane in Tucson, the engines had not been "run up." The pilot suggested Doris keep $2 million in escrow, in case there were mechanical problems they were unaware of.

But Doris and Chandi did not want to wait. In lieu of the $2 million, Chandi asked for two Mongolian humpback camels and a polo cap with a Saudi Arabian insignia.

On the sale papers, the aircraft was registered to Duke Farms. Attorney Donald Robinson signed the papers and listed himself as vice president. According to Violet Mimaki, Imelda Marcos received a ten-percent commission from the sale. "We called her Madame Ten Percent," said Violet Mimaki.

Both Doris and Chandi were required to have photo identification cards as members of the flight crew. Chandi listed her occupation as vice president of Flight Operations for Duke Farms. Doris, who supplied a head shot taken in the 1950s, was listed as president of Duke Farms. She gave her birthdate as November 22, 1922, shaving ten years off her age. Her once firm signature appeared frail and wobbly.

Bernard Lafferty was also issued a flight card. The young Irish butler who wore an earring and ponytail (and doubled as a "flight attendant") had previously been employed by Claudia Peltz before Chandi hired him.

Soon after the two camels arrived, they were given a "coming-out" tea party at Rough Point. As the fog rolled in over the wide lawn, a small group of Newport friends, including Senator Claiborne Pell, his wife Nuella, Noreen Drexel, and Oatsie Charles, joined Chandi and Doris in toasting the latest and most amusing addition to the Duke menagerie. The camels were named "Princess" and "Baby" and given a large pink and white striped tent. They tended to annoy people by spitting. On many days, they had free roam of the spacious house where servants were expected to scoop up the camel dung. "The camels trashed the place," said security head Stephen Scott.

"They were these unbelievable animals wearing pink hibiscus," observed Charles, of their coming-out party. "It was mind bogglingly humorous."

The camels became another exotic affectation of Doris Duke, who was said to enjoy riding them at times. "It is extraordinary to see camels walk in your dining room," said Jane Engelhard. "But nothing surprises me there anymore."

On Easter Sunday, 1988, Christopher Duffy, a former Peace Corps volunteer and actor, was hired to manage Doris' Hawaiian estate, which he described as in "disarray."

He signed a document, saying he would be fired if he spoke of his employment. His first impression of Doris Duke was that of "an elderly woman trying not to appear elderly." She wore a bikini ("a scary sight") and shoulder-length hair. Chandi, her young companion, ran the house.

"She told me she had come from money and had it all her life." In retrospect, he said, talking with members of the Hawaiian blueblood set, "Chandi had an itinerary to get hooked up with someone rich."

Doris slept in the Moroccan room on the ground floor, with its white marble and private garden. Her quarters were strictly off-limits to the staff. Chandi occupied the Damascus room at the top of the stairs. Doris swam every day in her pool, which she shared with her dogs who used the step ladders, and played the piano while Chandi did her Hare Krishna chanting. "Both were fond of Retin A. They were looking into whatever it took to maintain youth," said Duffy.

He often witnessed tension between the two women. "Chandi threatened to leave Doris a number of times," said Duffy, who began to feel sorry for the heiress. "I think Doris really wanted to have someone to love. She was so lonely and wanted someone to share her life with."

But the two women fought often. "The whole house reverberated when the two of them were screaming," said Duffy. Chandi's behavior was troubling to the new estate manager. "She was yelling at everyone. There wasn't one day she didn't reduce someone to tears." The first thing Chandi instructed Duffy to do was fire longtime majordomo Johnny Gomez. "She wanted me to do her dirty work. But I refused to fire this 80-year-old man. He was harmless."

Gomez had decided to replace the worn-out cushions on the patio furniture. When Doris—through Chandi—learned of the unauthorized expenditure, "Johnny Gomez ended up having to pay for them himself," said Duffy.

Doris, in a handwritten note, told Gomez, "John, this is my house and you are a guest in this house—guests do not go around giving orders and making purchases without my permission— . . . if you are unwilling to abide by these rules, we will have to part." Said Duffy: "Johnny Gomez would have died if I had fired him. He had no purpose except to serve Miss Duke."

Imelda was a frequent visitor. The servants learned one thing about the former First Lady: she was always late. "Doris would sometimes start lunch without her. Imelda had difficulty not being the focus of attention," said Duffy. "She's a very insecure, frightened person." Once hospitalized for manic depression in New York, Imelda Marcos displayed a flamboyance that was in sharp contrast to Doris' stinginess. Imelda gave expensive gifts to Doris' help: gold money clips with $100 bills, designer watch for the butler, a $500 tip to the maid.

"I think Imelda and Chandi got along very well. They would often lie together getting massages. Chandi became a close advisor of Imelda," said Duffy.

In faxed memos between Hawaii attorney Ron Oldenburg and Newark attorney Donald Robinson, Chandi and Doris are described as Imelda's "two closest advisors." Oldenburg, an immigration lawyer hired by Doris and Chandi to secure green cards for the servants, kept Robinson informed on the local situation. "Another chapter in the continuing saga of Imelda Faces Life," began one missive. "The major problem is to try to distinguish where the TV soap ends and reality sets in."

Chandi was now driving a new white XJS Jaguar and imitating the extravagance of the former First Lady. "Chandi wanted to enjoy her position as the richest little girl," said Duffy. "I think Chandi prodded Doris to get more involved with Imelda than she would have."

Imelda's rented home in exile on Makiki Heights Drive was not far from Doris'. The 4,500-square-foot residence (worth $2 million) was filled with religious statues and fresh flowers, although yellow ones were not acceptable. She converted a toolshed into a tissue-paper and tin-foiled chapel. Imelda's staff included a hairdresser, priest, and piano player, and expenses were said to run $80,000 a month, paid for by supporters and friends. She confided to one reporter that the Marcoses were "wealthy beyond belief," but the nagging question remained: where was all the money?

While publicly claiming she was penniless, her groceries were paid for with crisp new $100 bills. She was a frequent shopper at the upscale Liberty House department store where she would buy twelve outfits at a time and then return them for cash refunds. Several of the salesgirls refused to wait on her.

In a single visit to a Honolulu mall, she purchased $8,000 worth of shoes.

Once the "Steel Butterfly" back in the Philippines, fifty-nine-year-old Imelda refused to believe that her life in exile was any different from her days in Manila when she would gaze into the mirror and say to herself, "Imelda, there is nothing in the world that you cannot buy."

Everything about her was ostentatious, as she once boasted. *Time* magazine dubbed her "the generalissimo of glamour."

Chandi kept Imelda informed on the legal case through daily faxes. "Imelda and Chandi were very similar. They created a fantasy life for themselves," said Duffy.

The Marcoses, who allegedly used the Philippine national treasury as their private bank account, were under criminal investigation for looting their country of $103 million in government funds, then soaking U.S. banks for $165 million in secret purchases of four Manhattan buildings. Marcos himself had bragged of hoarding $14 billion in gold somewhere in his country.

With the assistance of Adnan Khashoggi, they allegedly continued their corruption after accepting asylum in Hawaii, using various front men to disguise their activities.

On October 21, 1988, the Marcoses were indicted on fraud and racketeering charges and ordered to travel to New York for the arraignment. If convicted, the Marcoses faced fifty years in prison and fines totalling $1 million. Khashoggi was also indicted for allegedly helping to conceal the Marcoses' Manhattan real estate interests. He was reported to be in hiding somewhere in Europe.

Ferdinand Marcos, at seventy-one, was said to be too ill to travel. His lawyers, Richard Hibey and John Bartko, would handle Imelda's case. Imelda was said to distrust Hibey, an imposing, no-nonsense lawyer who does not suffer fools. Imelda secretly worried that he was Ferdinand's advocate, not hers. She wanted someone more flamboyant. Someone who could *fix* things.

Doris was in New Jersey, and at Chandi's urging, she had Ken DeWitt fly her plane to pick up Imelda in Honolulu and bring her East for the arraignment.

"She was emotional during the ten-hour flight," recalled DeWitt. "I would say a little bit teary. Worried and concerned. She had her entourage of bodyguards and a priest who said mass over the Pacific. She kept talking about her 'best friend' Doris." Clutching her rosary beads, she silently prayed as a member of her entourage videotaped her performance.

The plane stopped in California to pick up attorney John Bartko, and Imelda's daughter, Irene Araneta, and later arrived at Newark International Airport. The aircraft was met by a horde of reporters and television crews. Imelda's three-limousine convoy motored into New York.

The arraignment was an Oscar-winning performance.

The former beauty queen and First Lady arrived at the courthouse in a turquoise silk, floor-length *terno,* the Philippine national dress, carrying rosary beads and accompanied by an entourage of nearly two dozen bodyguards. She was lined up for mug shots and fingerprinted. Imelda the "Angel of Asia" was now Imelda the martyr. "I came here with beautiful, clean hands, now you dirtied them," she told the lawmen. She wept silently and pled not guilty to the charges. The judge imposed a bail of $5 million. Imelda claimed she was indigent. As she walked through a crowd of demonstrators outside the courthouse holding signs deriding the Marcoses as "bloodsuckers," Imelda said she felt strange "pinpricks" and feared she was infected with the AIDS virus.

"It was one of the most bizarre scenes you've ever seen in the twentieth century," said Bartko. "It made 'Bonfire of the Vanities' look tame. They were rocking the car, shouting and jeering. It was physically threatening."

At the arraignment, the government convinced the court that Imelda might flee the country. Bail was set at $5 million. Hibey and Bartko were taken aback by the amount. They had forty-eight hours to come up with the money.

Back at the Waldorf Hotel, Imelda immediately got on the telephone. She called Chandi and Doris. They told her to come to the penthouse apartment at 475 Park Avenue.

The thought of Imelda in the bowels of the New York Correctional system prompted Doris to call Donald Robinson, who arrived at the apartment and immediately summoned Hibey and Bartko from the Waldorf Hotel. The lawyers met at Doris' penthouse that evening to discuss the case. At a dining room table, surrounded by Doris' collection of crystals and sea shells, the attorneys hammered out details of the bailout. At the head of the table was an empty chair, alternately occupied by Chandi and Doris, who asked the lawyers to explain the situation. Chandi was animated in her desire "to do what's best for Imelda." Franco Rossellini was also present, with his bodyguard, Enso. Doris—dressed in clothes appropriate for a twenty-year-old and barefoot—was businesslike, caring less for the nuances of the case than the exact amount of money the bailout would require.

On November 2, word leaked that the reclusive tobacco heiress Doris Duke had posted $5.3 million in municipal bonds as bail for Imelda Marcos, saying she believed in "loyalty to friends."

"Doris Duke has saved my faith in America," Imelda trilled.

Few people knew that Doris and Imelda were friends. They were also surprised that she would risk the glare of publicity after maintaining such a low profile. And the loan of $5 million in bail from the notoriously stingy Miss Duke? It was so unlike her.

"I am disgusted, embarrassed and ashamed of my country's mistreatment of Imelda and her ailing husband," Doris was quoted as saying.

The following day, Doris showed up at Carolina Herrera's fashion show in Manhattan and sat next to writer Fran Lebowitz. "She [Doris] looked like a bag lady," said *Newsday* gossip columnist James Revson.

"I'm not a recluse. I'm a loose wreck," she joked.

The bailout landed Doris once again in the headlines: A DUKE SAVES A QUEEN, trumpeted the front page of the *New York Daily News*. "DORIS' DUKES ARE UP OVER IMELDA." Quipped Revson, "I don't think anyone thought Doris Duke had any friends."

(Doris evidently beat Libyan leader Colonel Muammar Qaddafi to the bank. He said he would have put up the $5 million for Imelda.)

Doris also reportedly picked up the tab for Imelda's stay in the $1,800-a-night suite at the Waldorf. One of the first calls of congratulations to Imelda came from Ronald and Nancy Reagan, who had publicly distanced themselves from the Marcoses to avoid any political fallout in the Republican party as vice president George Bush headed into the final days of his presidential campaign.

Imelda wanted to celebrate her freedom in Manhattan with friends, but Doris insisted that she and her daughter come to Somerville for the weekend. Imelda balked. Associates were shocked at her display of ungratefulness. "She had to be persuaded to show gratitude," recalled one.

Finally, she relented and with her daughter, attorneys, and entourage drove out to the New Jersey countryside.

Many bluebloods, aware of Doris' maverick standing, were nevertheless outraged by her show of support for the Marcoses. "From my point of view it was mind-boggling," said Newport socialite Eileen Slocum. "It was a very poor use of her money. I hate to see one American dollar go to someone charged with fraud and racketeering."

The *Durham Morning Herald* published a cartoon showing "The New Women of Duke Calendar" featuring Doris and Imelda galloping together on the backs of two camels: "Princess" and "Baby."

That Sunday, November 6, Jane Engelhard had planned a lunch at her Far Hills estate. Houseguest Sister Parish, Gianni and Marella Agnelli, Douglas and Susan Dillon, Jane's daughter Annette Reed, and Oscar de la Renta were also invited. Unknown to the guests, Doris Duke had telephoned Jane that morning and asked if she could bring a party of six, including Imelda. Jane had written Doris a note, expressing her support for her act of generosity.

On that sun-dappled autumn afternoon, the guests arrived shortly after one o'clock in a festive mood. Jane admitted they were waiting for someone, but wouldn't say who. The guests were intrigued. After all, Jane had previously hosted a lunch for neighbor Mike Tyson and his bride Robin Givens before their public break-up, so the spectre of another celebrity was enticing. Malcolm Forbes pulled up in his huge Land-Rover-type Lamborghini. The tension was mounting.

Finally, Jane admitted that she was doing a favor for an old friend. "But who is coming?" said the guests. Without batting an eye, Jane said, "Doris is bringing Imelda Marcos." Some were amused, others were shocked. "Shall we all take off our shoes and line them in the hallway to make her feel at home?" quipped one.

The sound of a motorcycle interrupted the conversation and Imelda Marcos made her entrance. "Imelda entered like a star," said one of the guests. "It was a ham actress' performance."

She was regal and radiant in a black wool dress, with an aquamarine cashmere scarf draped over her shoulders, her bodice accented by two long strands of perfect pearls, one black, one white. She wore sheer black stockings and black suede pumps.

Doris, wearing a nondescript outfit, faded into the background while Imelda took center stage.

With her broad face and flawless, porcelain skin, Imelda's presence was commanding. The guests moved into the large, sunny dining room where two round tables had been covered in yellow cloths. Imelda was seated at one table, flanked by Gianni Agnelli and Malcolm Forbes. Oscar de la Renta, Susan Dillon, Franco Rossellini, decorator Sister Parish and two other guests were also seated. At the second table, Doris sat with Douglas Dillon, Marella Angelli, and the rest of the party, including Chandi Heffner and Imelda's daughter Irene.

Said Jane Engelhard: "Malcolm didn't talk too much to Mrs. Marcos. I was amazed that day how quiet he was. I thought he was going to be more of a showoff, talking a lot to Mrs. Marcos and asking questions, and it turned into a very serious business conversation about military bases on the Philippines."

Rossellini turned to his partner and reeled off his somewhat inflated accomplishments as a film producer. He said a room had been named for him at the Film Institute. He was currently working on a film about Karl Marx. Franco droned on, and brought up Cory Aquino or "That Woman," as he referred to her. "Who could possibly think That Woman could run anything?" Franco said. When the Marcoses were airlifted from Manila, they thought they were being taken to a nearby island in the Philippines and were shocked to learn that Hawaii was their destination, Franco said heatedly. Doris, an old friend, thought they had been shabbily treated and when they were ordered to appear in court, she naturally made her Boeing 737 available to them.

Imelda may have had cause to feel betrayed. For decades, the Marcoses were supported by the American government and hailed as bulwarks against communism.

As she nibbled her lunch, Imelda launched into a tirade against her accuser. "The United States had no right to take me, a head of state, and try me in their courts. People seem to forget that the president was a very rich man before he came to serve his country." All they wanted was to return to their country. The president was a very sick man and even if they returned in a box, they wanted to go home.

Imelda gestured dramatically, pointing her manicured fingers with the delicate white tips and moons. No one could compete with her monologue.

"Someone asked me as I came out of the courthouse, 'How would I feel if I were put in jail.' Jail? We are in jail. We can go nowhere. We have nothing. Everything has been taken from us. Your beautiful Hawaiian paradise is a jail for us. Worse than Alcatraz. At least there they give you free room and board."

Malcolm Forbes tried to change the subject, asking how the guests would vote in the election. "Of course, George Bush must win," Imelda interjected. "He has been your ambassador to China. He knows, as I do, that China is the real peril for the U.S. He understands the Chinese. I understand the Chinese. After all, as Mao once said to me, the Chinese are the oldest civilization in the world and will survive all."

Conversation at the other table had virtually stopped. "Mrs. Marcos was 'on,'" said another guest. "She controlled the luncheon. Her monologue had obviously been rehearsed. Doris was absolutely a mouse." Dinner and luncheon partners had long known that to sit next to Doris was a chore. She never made much of an effort, and her partners had to work hard to amuse her. But her behavior that day was different. She seemed noticeably subdued, almost catatonic. Her face lacked expression, her eyes appeared without a spark of recognition as she was introduced to Douglas Dillon, whom she had known for years. She was silent and remote throughout the meal.

Observed Jane Engelhard: "Doris never opened her mouth. I thought she was doped."

The entourage finally left, and the convoy motored to Morristown Airport. Ken DeWitt had arranged for the plane to be parked on the far side of the tarmac to allow the group to avoid going through the airport and being besieged by reporters. "But when we got there, Imelda insisted on walking straight through. The press were all there. I had been trying to avoid a scene, but she liked it."

Chandi and Doris returned to Newport. Bobby Farrah spoke to Doris that weekend. "She called me from Newport and said she wasn't feeling well. She said she wanted to see me."

Four days later, on Thursday, November 10, Doris' limousine pulled up to the Somerville courthouse at 4 P.M., minutes before closing time. Penny Stabile, a clerk, was called from her office by Judge Wilfred Diana to witness a proceeding in the family court. The adoption papers had already been typed up.

"There was no advance warning. They just arrived," Stabile recalled. She learned that it was Doris Duke, the tobacco heiress, accompanied by Chandi Heffner and attorney Donald Robinson. "She wore a scarf covering her face, and sunglasses. The younger woman seemed thin, and very solicitous of her. Doris had trouble walking. She was walking slowly, haltingly."

The group went upstairs to an empty courthouse and Judge Diana presided. "Doris appeared to be vague. Out of it," said Stabile. "When the judge asked Doris to spell her name she misunderstood. It had to be repeated." While Chandi seemed impatient, Doris acted confused. "She seemed to appear as if it wasn't what she wanted. She looked like she didn't know what was going on. It was as if she wasn't sure where she was or what she was doing."

The hearing took less than ten minutes. Afterwards, the group left the courthouse in the limousine, and immediately boarded the Boeing 737 for the ten-hour flight to Hawaii.

The adoption papers, prepared by Robinson, said the two women had known each other since 1981. Heffner said she had been estranged from her parents for seventeen years and had been living with Doris since 1985 as the "devoted and loving companion" to Doris, who in turn provided "love, guidance and support to Charlene Heffner as if she were Doris Duke's own daughter."

The two decided on the adoption "to participate in the kind of fulfilling and intimate relationship that only a daughter and her legal mother can enjoy."

Doris further attested that the adoption "is not requested whatsoever for the sole or primary purpose of conferring property interests upon Charlene Heffner."

"She has treated me like the mother I never really had," Heffner said in her separate petition. But the two women had confronted experiences "where outsiders refuse to treat us as such. For example when Doris was hospitalized, I was denied access to her because I was not her blood relative, even though she wanted me at her bedside. This kind of scenario has caused us great embarrassment and frustration."

Heffner said she owned the 300-acre ranch in North Kahala, with a value of $3 million, plus the six acres in Kalopa, valued at $200,000. Her checking account with the Bank of Hawaii had a balance of $30,000, and another with Citibank in New York had $30,000. She also listed among her assets eighteen horses, three guitars, and personal jewelry valued at $10,000.

What she neglected to mention was that Doris had provided her with these assets.

Judge Diana entered the judgment of adoption, including the fact that

Heffner had legally changed her name to "Chandi Duke Heffner." The relationship was now valid in the eyes of the law, "the same as if Chandi Duke Heffner had been born to Doris Duke in lawful wedlock, including the right to take and inherit intestate, personal and real property from and through each other."

The following day, newspapers carried the story that the childless Doris Duke, at seventy-five, had legally adopted a mysterious thirty-five-year-old "conservationist." "Miss Heffner in no way needs any economic advantage," lawyer Donald Robinson told a reporter, adding that Heffner owned "extensive property in Hawaii."

Chandi said that she and Doris were involved in botanical tissue culture research at the University of Hawaii to save the endangered sandalwood trees. (A spokesman for the university denied any knowledge of Duke or Heffner.) A spokesman for Playboy enterprises similarly denied that Chandi was related to Hugh Heffner, well-known publisher, as she had told Doris' employees.

Lawyer Sam Greenspoon was aghast. He questioned whether Doris had received proper advice. "He had to think Chandi was pushing this for money. A single woman adopting a girl in her mid-30s? Why?"

(Although considered highly unusual, the adoption of grown adults was not unheard of among the rich rich. In one of Newport's most celebrated attachments, Mrs. Hamilton Fish Webster legally adopted as her son a fifty-seven-year-old retired Brigadier General.)

Of course, adoption was Chandi's only legal recourse since in New Jersey two women cannot be married. Chandi Duke Heffner was now Doris' rightful heir and next of kin. She was made a vice president of Doris' Newport Restoration Foundation.

Although Doris could not have cared what the reaction was, Newport socialites like Mrs. John Drexel took the high road, at least for the record. "I think she's a wonderful girl. I think she'll bring a lot of happiness to Doris."

Family members privately wondered if the adoption was done primarily to "screw Duke University." Had Doris left no legal heir, her money would eventually revert to the college.

There had already been a test of the Doris Duke Foundation when in October 1986, Doris had tried unsuccessfully to restructure the $100 million trust set up in 1917 by her father, which she shares with cousins and other relatives. In court papers she said the trust—which generated $5 million of income each year and was held at Citibank—was set up "solely to provide for her support, maintenance and education, and for that of her children and descendants." At her age, she said she had no children and did not plan to have any and therefore should be legally entitled to take over the trust.

She lost the fight.

However, there was precedent for Doris to have an additional beneficiary added to the trust. Tony Duke, Jr., won a fight to have his adopted son, Todd, be included in the list of trust beneficiaries. Todd Duke was ruled eligible as a rightful heir. "It gave her a legal opening," said one family member.

Nervous trustees of The Duke Endowment immediately launched an investigation to determine if Chandi Duke Heffner would qualify as Doris' lineal descendant.

Meanwhile Duke University was still hopeful that she would somehow be drawn back into the fold. Angier Biddle Duke became the main intermediary, as he began plans to form the Duke Family Association. In October 1988, he wrote to Doris, reminding her of the "genius" of her father and inviting her to a Founders Day ceremony at the university, even though he knew the school "may turn you off these days."

"Angie" was the only family member who still had Doris' ear. His brother Tony had been rebuked by Doris years earlier when he approached her for a donation to his Boy's Harbor charity in New York and made the mistake of mentioning a specific figure he hoped she would give. He was coldly denied.

Whatever he may privately have thought, Angie wrote a gushing letter to Doris, expressing his support for the bailout of Imelda and his pride in Doris' public remarks regarding the betrayal of the Marcoses. On November 15, Doris telephoned to thank him. A week later, he struggled over a note to Doris on the adoption. It was not easy to compose. He nevertheless congratulated her on the surprise adoption, and enclosed a separate letter to Chandi (misspelled as "Chandy Hefner"), the newest member of the Duke family. Angie told Chandi he hoped their paths would cross soon. "It is good to see us multiply and just great for Doris to have a new daughter." It was signed, "Your new cousin, Angie."

In Honolulu, Imelda Marcos began to spend more and more time at Doris' home. "She wanted to decorate Doris' room with flowers. I had to call Doris and say, 'She's determined to go in your room and decorate,'" said estate manager Duffy. "She overwhelmed the place with plants."

When Doris returned to Hawaii, Ferdinand Marcos had been hospitalized for congestive heart failure. As he lay in St. Francis Hospital, he was visited almost daily by the heiress, who brushed his hair and tried to "heal" the deposed president of the Philippines by massaging his feet.

"It was quite a sight," said one observer. "I walked in one day and there was Doris leaning over the end of the bed, rubbing Marcos' bare feet. I think the president tolerated her for the good of their financial situation."

On those mornings, the sleek white Jaguar pulled up to the hospital entrance and a slack-jawed Doris—wearing polyester pants, a blouse from K-mart, and a yellow plastic digital watch—would be escorted inside, trailed a few yards behind by the dark-haired Heffner, carrying a cellular phone. Walking with a pronounced limp, Doris shuffled through the hallway, her eyes downcast, and her lifeless blonde hair appearing thin and unwashed.

"Doris inspires the president," Imelda said. "She is an angel from heaven." Imelda set up a round-the-clock vigil and began tasting his food and medication, fearful of an attempt on his life. "I'm watching him like a hawk," she said. "Nothing is secure and safe anymore."

Doris and Imelda were literally feeding off one another; Imelda offered the kind of intrigue Doris thrived on, and of course, Doris offered the financial support Imelda needed. (One plan proposed that Imelda "sell" Doris her diamond engagement ring, worth $1 million, and then have the former First Lady repurchase it in time, but apparently Doris didn't agree.) Imelda began receiving her official correspondence—faxes and cables—at Doris' home. She thought she was being bugged.

Doris also, in a pique, had her New York accountant Irwin Bloom (hired by Chandi) write to three Swiss banks requesting that her gold deposits—reportedly four tons—be transferred to other European banks as a result of the Swiss government's cooperation with the Philippines in the investigation of the Marcoses' assets.

Chandi also helped rearrange Doris' massive stock portfolio. "Chandi got Doris to get rid of stock in any company that did anything to animals or the environment," said Duffy. She was also, in the last days of the Reagan presidency, bringing pressure to bear on the administration to pardon the Marcoses. Close Reagan advisor, former Nevada Senator Paul Laxalt was contacted by Donald Robinson, who flew to Washington to meet with Hibey and Laxalt on the Marcoses' behalf.

In December, Ralph Wolfe Cowan, a well-known "royal" portrait painter from Palm Beach who specializes in highly idealized lifesize paintings of the rich and famous, received a telephone call from old friend Imelda Marcos. Eleven of his paintings were hung in Malacanang Palace. Other clients included Ronald and Nancy Reagan, the Royal family of Monaco, King Fahd of Saudi Arabia, King Hassan II of Morocco, and the Sultan of Brunei, who had paid $600,000 for a series of portraits.

"Mrs. Marcos always calls me at 2 or 3 in the morning. She only sleeps three or four hours. She's always on the phone to somewhere in the world. She said, 'I would love for you to paint one of your large masterpieces of my friend Doris Duke.'" Cowan asked Imelda if she had any pictures of Doris. "Imelda said, 'I will get you some.'"

Cowan called his sources, but could only find three vintage photographs.

"Her most glamorous period was late 1930s and early 1940s. She wouldn't allow anyone to photograph her now, so we had to rely on those pictures. I decided to paint her in a white fur, sort of a Harlow look. Mrs. Marcos kept saying, 'Now she's very tall. When you paint her, paint her as the Statue of Liberty.'"

When the portrait was finished, Cowan and his assistant flew to Hawaii to deliver it. They first went to Imelda's home, where the painting was rolled out on a table.

"It's magnificent," Imelda said, "except I don't really care for the shoes."

Cowan, unable to suppress a laugh, said he could fix them.

The next day, Cowan was given the password to Shangri-la and told to sneak the painting in so Doris wouldn't see. "We were met by eight screaming Doberman attack dogs. All the servants were running around. They were excited because new people were there. Doris had become so reclusive that they didn't see anybody except Mrs. Marcos."

When Doris walked in, she was barefoot in white slacks. "I couldn't believe it. For a woman over seventy she still had a sexy look," said Cowan. "She had very fair skin, an exquisite nose and no chin. I had seen pictures of her with a very prominent chin. I don't know what she had done over the years to her face."

Doris looked up at her dreamlike image, in the white fur with upswept hair, the vista of Somerville and two camels in the background.

Said Cowan: "She just stood there and stared for a second with a perplexed look on her face, then said, 'I'm overwhelmed.'"

They sat down for drinks. Cowan showed Doris his books of portraits: George Hamilton, Robert Redford, Donald Trump, Marilyn Monroe, Barbra Streisand, and Elvis Presley. "She made comments about different people. She came to the Elvis Presley portrait, and out of all the people she looked at, she stuck on him." Doris stared at the image for what seemed like an inordinate amount of time. "She said she had liked him."

"She was madly in love with Elvis," recalled Leon Amar. "Elvis gave a lot of money to the Self Realization Fellowship. Doris did too. She tried to convert Elvis. She pushed the whole issue to him."

Cowan mentioned his futile search for photographs of the heiress. "My whole life had been destroyed by photographers," she said in her breathy voice. "Everywhere I went they were flashing bulbs. They always picked out the ugliest pictures." Cowan said Doris "went on for a long time. She had tears in her eyes. I tried to change the subject. When I told her she was beautiful and still had sex appeal, she giggled a little."

The subject of Ferdinand Marcos came up. "Imelda had told us Doris was going to the hospital and healing him. Doris said, 'It's just a little healing thing that I can do with my fingers. I learned it when I was young. But because he is so frail, I can't give him a rough massage.'"

Then Chandi came in. "Imelda had explained she was the Uniroyal heiress and was worth $900 million. They live together because they are two of the richest women in the world and they share the same interest in animals. Mrs. Marcos told me that she had arranged for her to adopt this girl so they would have their fortunes combined."

Chandi's eyes were red. "She had been crying," said Cowan. It seemed the local government would not allow her to bring humpback camels Baby and Princess to Hawaii unless they were quarantined. When Imelda came in, "Doris' eyes lit up. As if she was such a close friend. They admired the portrait. Then Imelda looked at Doris and said, 'Isn't she beautiful?' Mrs. Marcos mentioned that father always called Doris the ugly duckling."

Now that the portrait was done, Imelda wanted a picture of her standing next to Cowan's masterpiece. She whispered to Doris, "Can I just get a Polaroid of your face?" Said Cowan: "Doris never poses for photographs, but Imelda said, 'I can talk her into it.' We got a picture. Doris does whatever Mrs. Marcos asks her to do."

Cowan's assistant, Mark Deren, observed Imelda "sort of leading Doris around." When they left Shangri-la, "Doris was visibly nervous. She said, 'Where are you going? Are you leaving?' She didn't want Imelda to leave."

The portrait was subsequently disposed of. "I was there when the painting arrived," recalled estate manager Duffy. "Imelda thought it was a work of art. The biggest challenge was to keep a straight face. Doris hated the painting. I think she donated it to Duke University."

By now, Chandi and Doris had developed an aversion to walking through airports. Chandi and Doris asked the Honolulu Airport for permission for her cars to pull directly onto restricted areas of the tarmac. After the arrangements were made, Doris paid $118 for six detachable magnetic "Duke Farms" signs which were affixed to the sides of her vehicles.

They used the private Boeing 737 frequently. On April 1, 1989, Doris, Chandi and Imelda were flown to the Big Island where they attended the Merrie Monarch Festival, a show featuring ancient Hawaiian hula dancing. While Imelda thrived on the attention from reporters, Doris kept her face hidden by a program booklet.

In the meantime, Chandi's health became a subject of concern as she succumbed to various mysterious ailments.

"Her illnesses were very selective. They were ways of getting sympathy," said Duffy. "Chandi was an ace manipulator. Very calculating. There wasn't anything Chandi wouldn't do."

She was also unconcerned with modesty. In meetings with Imelda's attorneys, Chandi would frequently expose her breasts as she gave herself injections of what she said was penicillin for a so-called "heart infection."

There was also a trip with Honolulu friend Jim Nabors to Bangkok and Bali. "I think Jim felt sorry for Doris," said one Duke employee, explaining the friendship. "Because she was so lonely." However, it was Doris who was now ill. "Miss Duke was not feeling well. In fact, she was quite sick in Delhi," said pilot Ken DeWitt. Chandi rode horses while Doris stayed in her room. The pilot was familiar with the unstructured itineraries of Doris' trips. "We never had a schedule. Whenever she has a whim, we leave. Jim Nabors had come along on the trip. He got sick and tired of it and left. I think it was the boredom."

Nabors had also brought Paul Reubens to lunch one day at Shangri-la. Reubens, a thirty-seven-year-old comedian and actor, had started his career in the Los Angeles-based improvisational comedy group The Groundlings, and had created the wildly successful alter ego Pee-wee Herman. The mischievous, enchanting boy-child who owed much of his sensibilities to campy 1950s kid shows and who had laced his routines with sexual innuendos, had starred in a Saturday morning television show, "Pee-wee's Playhouse," as well as feature films. Reubens and his writing partner and close companion, another male, had rented a beach house from Nabors. "Reubens' friend was obviously the person behind the star," recalled Duffy. "They had shared a house in Los Angeles and were collaborators."

But there was a troubled side to Reubens, born Paul Rubenfeld. Something of a recluse, he had grown restless with the Pee-wee character, feeling he was too old to continue the role, and was anxious to branch out. He also had a history of drug use. In 1971, he had been arrested in Sarasota, Florida, for marijuana possession, and had also been arrested in 1983 for loitering outside an adult peep show/bookstore. Both charges were dropped.)

Chandi took an instant liking to Reubens, known as a voracious shopper. "She and Paul Reubens were like brother and sister," recalled Duffy. "They went out shopping together. They'd go to 'The Sharper Image' and play with all the toys. She shopped and shopped." Reubens became a frequent guest at Shangri-la when he came to Hawaii. "He would call Chandi and talk for hours on end," recalled Franco Rossellini. "He was a sleazy person." Said Duffy: "It was all very grand to come to the Duke estate. Reubens joked all the time to Chandi, 'Maybe your mother would like to adopt a son.'"

Reubens loved to drop names, and boasted of his relationships with "celebrities." On one visit to Newport, Chandi asked Stephen Scott for a Duke security uniform. She wanted to give it to Reubens as a Christmas gift.

In the spring of 1989, while Doris was on the mainland, Chandi orchestrated a spontaneous celebration. "I had a day's notice to get the flowers and leis," said Duffy. "Apparently, Paul Reubens and his boyfriend were going to get 'married.'" In a side room, which boasts a replica of a Moslem altar, Duffy placed the flowers. The "wedding" took place with a few selected guests. "Chandi was there. Imelda Marcos and Jim Nabors both sang at the wedding."

Although Chandi preferred Hawaii, she was a familiar presence in Doris' other homes. Former Duke Gardens head Robert Dingwall received a call from Doris asking him to return to Somerville and help her with the farm. "Everything was so disorganized," he said. Employees were asked to fill out time cards and report cards. Chandi Heffner was in charge. "She didn't like my presence there. It was quite obvious." Dingwall also observed that Doris and Chandi were not getting along. "I thought the two were gonna have a fight right there."

"Miss Heffner didn't like the old employees in the house," said Doris' personal maid. "She wanted to be number one. And she hated me because I would wait on Miss Duke first."

"She would routinely stay up until four or five in the morning," said Newport security head Stephen Scott. "She would talk on the phone until all hours. She rarely woke up before noon, and some days she would stay inside all day. No one heard from her." One maid recalled she slept with three or four dogs in the room at one time.

At Chandi's direction, Doris' Christmas list was pared to only a few select friends. "It all stopped after Chandi got adopted," said Duffy.

Doris also abruptly ceased her visits to a Park Avenue chiropractor, Dr. Joseph Mirto. "She had been coming to me for degenerative kneecaps. She was in a weak condition and her immunity seemed low. Chandi and I did not get along. She didn't like me. She didn't want Doris to see me," said Mirto.

"If you got too close to Miss Duke, Chandi didn't like it," said Denise Winkler, former maintenance head at Somerville. "She was very, very tough."

Chandi ordered that Doris' German shepherds be put on a vegetarian diet. "All the dogs died," said Duffy. The directive was extended to the employees. "Chandi wouldn't let the staff eat meat," Duffy recalled. "So the employees started hoarding meat in their rooms which led to a severe rodent problem at the estate."

Chandi instructed Duffy to hire a Krishna monk as the chef. The menus were limited to the Krishna Consciousness cookbook, and the choices were narrowed to five menus. Chandi also installed a young woman whose husband had been a member of her Krishna commune as the housekeeper. She eventually became Chandi's personal maid.

In Newport, socialites were alerted that Chandi Duke Heffner did not eat meat. Said one: "I was asked to provide nuts and berries for her when she came once with Doris."

"I didn't particularly like Chandi," said artist Richard Banks, a longtime Newport friend of Doris. "She was supposed to be on these health foods, but when I invited them to dinner and asked Doris what to serve her, Doris said, 'Oh just give her a pizza. That's all she eats anyway.'"

In February 1989, Pandora Biddle, Nicholas Biddle's daughter and Angie's niece, flew to Hawaii on her honeymoon. She telephoned Doris and went over to the house. She was curious to meet Doris' new daughter. "There were rumors surrounding their relationship. I was expecting to see a little minion," she recalled, "but Chandi was very pretty, dark-haired, and quite exotic-looking. She had had some operation, she said, for an embolism in the lungs. Doris had been at her side the whole time. She had been through the mill with Chandi."

Although appearing "fragile," Doris "looked pretty darn good. She and

Chandi were both barefoot. Chandi stayed for the first half hour, protecting her. There was a butler wearing a diamond earring, and a lot of Saint Bernard dogs."

That fall, Chandi wanted to go to Ireland. She convinced Doris to lease a large estate. "She got Doris to rent Lismore Castle. Jim Nabors and Honolulu businessman Bob Magoon came along for the trip," said pilot Ken DeWitt. "Nobody was getting along with Chandi. She'd flare up and jump at people." Chandi ordered DeWitt to telephone her at the castle every hour on the hour from his hotel room. "Those were her orders. It's not a case of agreeing. You couldn't talk to Miss Duke. You just played the game." After Chandi engaged in an altercation with the chef, Nabors and Magoon left and flew home to Hawaii.

On the return flight to America, Ken DeWitt recalled, "Chandi was looking for a calculator and opened every overhead compartment and dumping things on the floor. She was supposedly taking 56 different prescriptions, plus smoking marijuana. She was out of it." DeWitt managed to keep the door to the cabin locked. "I didn't want her in the cockpit."

As for his employer, Doris Duke, "She went along with everything Chandi wanted to do. I think it was fear. Especially when she was violent."

The supercilious young girl had turned into the daughter from hell. "She turned very bad," observed Cristina Ford. "I think she was greedy."

"There was a lot more screaming and hollering going on after the adoption," confirmed Duffy. "Chandi was so ungrateful. She out-Leona Helmsleyed Leona Helmsley. Nothing was good enough for her."

Doris routinely overlooked Chandi's tirades. According to witnesses, she would merely lower her eyes. Perhaps the relationship mimicked her own unhappy one with Nanaline. She once told Duffy, "Mothers and daughters never get along." Said Duffy: "Doris really was convinced that mothers and daughters act like that."

But friends who had previously professed their support for Chandi began to criticize her.

"Chandi was a bitch. She became too big for her britches," said Ford. "She thought she *was* Doris Duke."

At Christmas, Chandi and Doris invited Tex McCrary to Hawaii for a holiday dinner. "I stepped into this snake pit. At the table was a St. Bernard bigger than I am, a guy who was running this channelling group and a girl who wanted to run Doris' life." He was uneasy about the Hare Krishna guests.

Aware of her disdain for Duke University, Tex had been working quietly to have Rutgers University set up a biotechnical institute in Doris' name. That night he became concerned for Doris. "There were all sorts of crazy people there." Doris went into a trance, trying to recall the spirits of the dead. "Her father and Rubirosa were at the top of her list."

Tex hurriedly left the dinner party. Several months later he received a cable from Doris, warning him to immediately stop using her name in conversations about the biotechnical institute with anyone. He suspected Chandi was behind the break. "I think she thought this project at Rutgers was diverting the money she was going to get. It blew my mind."

Tex began to suspect that the Hare Krishna group would be the main beneficiary of Doris Duke's millions.

"A lot of Chandi's Hare Krishna people were coming around," recalled one employee. "They will do anything to get money."

Chandi was convinced that one of Doris' ex-employees wanted to kill her. She hired a bodyguard, James Burns, a karate expert who also worked as a bouncer at the Hard Rock Cafe.

"He looked like a Chippendale's dancer," said Ken DeWitt, referring to the all-male strip tease revue.

DeWitt was, by now, tiring of Doris and Chandi's strange sense of thrift. The wealthy Doris Duke still insisted on renting televisions for the various estates. She thought it was cheaper than buying them. Once DeWitt flew Chandi and Doris from New Jersey to Newport. After he dropped the women off, he returned the plane to Morristown Airport. He then got a call from Chandi to return to Newport to pick up a sofa and take it to Somerville. But he was not permitted to use the plane. Chandi ordered DeWitt to get a truck and drive it to Rhode Island. He arrived at 6 A.M., after driving all night. Chandi had left orders for him to wait until she awoke. She did so at lunchtime, then refused to see him.

In Hawaii, "I'd be constantly flying people back and forth to the Big Island. Some of them were Hare Krishna. They would go out on the street, beating pots and pans and begging for money."

Even Doris was having doubts about Chandi.

"I don't know what to do with that girl," she confided to Jane Engelhard one afternoon in Far Hills while Chandi was outside waiting in the limousine. "I need her. I want her. She's good for me." Said Engelhard: "I think Doris was a little bit scared of Chandi."

Oatsie Charles noticed a distinct change in Chandi's attitude. "She was not as considerate."

By this time, Chandi's mysterious illness had landed her in a Honolulu hospital. A former high school classmate, Anne Mueller Baker, who was living in Hawaii, was a friend of Christopher Duffy's. He happened to mention Chandi and her illness. Anne went to the hospital to visit her. "Chandi was not happy seeing someone from her past. I don't think she liked that at all," said Duffy, who learned that Chandi had grown up in a Catholic, middle-class household. There was no trust fund. "I knew she was living a lie."

Chandi ordered Duffy to resign.

Pilot Ernie Betz was also fired. "We went through nine pilots in a year," said DeWitt. "It got to be a joke."

DeWitt resigned in October 1989, and in his letter, a copy of which was sent to the Federal Aviation Administration, he cited the "unwarranted abuse and slander directed at me," and told the FAA Heffner's behavior seriously impaired the safety of the Boeing 737 and had endangered lives.

In August of 1989, several of Doris' Newport staff quit simultaneously. "Miss Heffner was fighting with the cook. I left in the morning," said Doris' former maid. "The cook left in the afternoon." Doris was heard to bemoan: "I'm the richest woman in the world. Why can't I find anyone to work for me?" Chandi was growing more desperate in her attempts to alienate Doris' friends. Even Imelda Marcos came under fire. "Chandi got on the telephone and told Imelda, 'You are a bitch,'" said Franco Rossellini. "Mrs. Marcos almost passed out."

"Chandi decided she didn't like Imelda," recalled pilot Ken DeWitt. "She thought she was a pain."

Amid her mounting legal problems, Imelda was talking openly of an escape plan for herself and her ailing husband. She said Doris had made her plane available, and it could be outfitted with the necessary medical equipment for Marcos. "We would leave in the middle of the night. And once we're off the ground, American officials will just say good riddance and let us go." The FBI kept a close watch on Doris' plane as a result, and began boarding it prior to each take-off to make sure Imelda was not stowed away. They even looked in the overhead compartments.

And what of the $5 million bail? "She told me to forget about it," Imelda said. The return party would include a small entourage, and the media in the Philippines would be alerted. "Oh, what an entrance I will make," she said. "I did it at the federal courthouse in New York. And I'll do it in Manila."

Despite Doris' healing efforts, on September 28, 1989, Ferdinand Marcos died of cardiac arrest before the plan could be carried out. He was seventy-two. He had ruled longer than any other Philippine president, but had ended his days in disgrace, leaving behind a shattered economy and a nation described as the "sick man of Asia." He and his wife, the former Imelda Romualdez, were suspected of misappropriating $10 billion in funds.

Now that Ferdinand was dead, Imelda stepped up her efforts to have Richard Hibey taken off the case. She concluded that he didn't have enough political "clout" and disagreed with him over strategy. Chandi and Imelda had wanted him to file a writ of habeas corpus to allow the Marcoses to return to the Philippines. Hibey refused. Chandi and Imelda suggested Ferdinand's medical bills be paid for by the Veteran's Administration, as he was entitled to VA benefits. Hibey felt it was a cheap publicity stunt. Imelda—who had sold most of her jewelry to pay her bills—believed the United States government should be liable for her living expenses, as she was "kidnapped" and brought to the country. Hibey explained that the government was not liable. Behind the scenes, Chandi and Hawaii immigration attorney Ron Oldenburg also lobbied for his dismissal. More importantly, it became clear that Doris would not foot the bill for Hibey, and resented his flying to the island first class and staying at the posh Kahala Hilton. Chandi and Oldenburg met with Philippines consul Gomez to try and work out a deal. Before his death, Marcos had offered to repay the Aquino government $5 billion, petty cash considering the country's national debt of $28 billion. This arrangement was rejected.

Imelda considered defending herself, or asking the court to appoint a public defender. By now, the taciturn Hibey was convinced that Imelda had no credibility with the American public. In February 1990, six weeks before the trial, Doris suddenly hired flamboyant trial attorney Gerald Spence to defend Imelda and promised to pay his bill, which eventually topped $5 million. He asked Hibey to be his second chair. Hibey declined. (Reportedly, Hibey is still owed several million dollars in unpaid legal fees.) John Bartko remained on the defense team.

Imelda arrived in New York on Doris' plane. Accused of using $222 million allegedly stolen from the Philippine treasury to secretly buy artwork, jewelry, and four Manhattan skyscrapers, her defense rested on the claim that she never knew where her husband's money came from. When she arrived in Manhattan, she was escorted to a rented condominium on

East Forty-seventh Street by men wearing jackets bearing the insignia: Duke Farms Security.

Imelda clutched rosary beads throughout most of the three-month trial and wore blood pressure and heart monitors. Spence—in a case laid out by Hibey and Bartko—admitted that Marcos was a "world-class shopper," but said she never knew the source of her husband's wealth. Like Doris, Imelda was a woman who had never written a check in her life or paid a bill.

Imelda collapsed three times during the trial, the third time coughing up blood. It was a dramatic performance, perhaps her finest. She was diagnosed with gastritis, inflammation of the stomach lining. There were rumors that Doris would attend the trial, but she never did. Unknown to all but a few, Doris and Imelda had experienced a falling-out and were not speaking. Doris was disgusted with Spence and wanted to fire him three weeks before the end of the trial. "She wanted to recover her $5 million and claim fraud," said one insider.

In the end, Spence won Imelda's acquittal. The jurors later said the government simply failed to make their case and many questioned the propriety of bringing her to trial in Manhattan. *New York Post* columnist Pete Hamill seemed to echo their feelings: "She was part Lucretia Borgia, part Evita Peron, part Madame Nhu," he wrote, "generous to her lackeys, ruthless with her enemies, and utterly ruled by her baroque vanities." But he still could not understand "why this is any business of the United States. Clearly, this is a trial that should be held in the Philippines . . . Essentially, Imelda Marcos is being prosecuted for shopping."

Imelda and Doris eventually effected a truce. "Their relationship was like a roller coaster," said John Bartko. It seemed that Doris had tired of Imelda's plea of poverty. The tension was also fueled by Chandi, who had grown bored with the former Philippine First Lady.

Franco Rossellini had gone to Tokyo for business. When he returned, he was told by Imelda that Doris was not well. "She said, 'This girl is a real problem.' I told Doris she'd better open her eyes."

By now, most of Doris' friends had been alienated by Chandi, or like Malcolm Forbes had recently died. "He found out he had AIDS and committed suicide," said one close friend.

Despite the heavy and often garish make-up Chandi would regularly apply to Doris' face and the blonde hair dye she used to lighten Doris' gray roots, the heiress was said to be increasingly frail and unable to come to the phone. "I would call her in Newport and Chandi would get on the phone and say, 'No, she's not here,'" said Richard Banks, who was concerned for Doris' welfare. "It was like *Whatever Happened to Baby Jane?* Chandi could easily declare Doris incapacitated. You could feel she was evil."

"Doris was always sick. She never had any energy and spent a lot of time in bed. Chandi was constantly bringing her sherry," recalled Rossellini.

"Miss Duke didn't have enough concentration to read the newspaper," said her personal maid in Newport.

That summer, security head Stephen Scott was summoned to the front gate at Rough Point where an ambulance from the Newport Fire Department pulled up. "Miss Duke had apparently fallen in her bathroom. There was blood all over the floor. They took her to the hospital, and Chandi rode with her in the rescue wagon."

Doris returned home several days later. "After that," he said, "I noticed her doctor coming up more than he had in the past."

In New Jersey, Jane Engelhard became alarmed at the reports coming from the farm.

Doris had literally not been seen for months.

Chandi and James Burns, according to household staff, became increasingly close. "He seemed like more of a boyfriend from what I saw," said security head Stephen Scott.

By late 1990, butler Bernard Lafferty was alarmed enough to call Rossellini for advice. The butler told Franco: "This is a monster. How do we get rid of her?"

According to one source, James Burns had reportedly convinced Doris to spend thousands of dollars on new security systems for her houses. After a confrontation, he left Doris' employ. Chandi defended him, and she and Doris quarreled. According to one witness, "Miss Duke told Chandi she had to choose; it was either her or James. Chandi told Miss Duke she wanted a family." "She was in love with him," said one observer. The gates to Shangri-la clanged shut.

In February 1991, the Boeing 737 was made ready. Unknown to Chandi, Doris had secretly made plans to leave Honolulu. As she was reaching cruising altitude, her adopted daughter returned home and was met by Duke security guards at the head of the driveway. The gate was locked. She was instructed to leave the property at once. "They told her to get out," recalled Franco, "under penalty of jail."

Staffers at the other residences received a faxed memo, saying Chandi

Duke Heffner, vice president of Duke Farms Inc., was "persona non grata." In Newport, "we packed up all her belongings: books, clothes, cosmetics and magazines, and a truck came up from New Jersey to take them away," said Stephen Scott. "The word was, she was out."

Attorney Sam Greenspoon now believes that Heffner came "within a hair" of inheriting one of the largest fortunes in the history of America.

Even after her exit, many of Chandi's former cohorts were still close to Doris. On July 26, 1991, Paul Reubens—known professionally as Pee-wee Herman—was arrested at a Sarasota pornographic theater after undercover police observed him masturbating. He was charged with indecent exposure. The arrest sent shock waves through the entertainment world, and his career was pronounced over. CBS immediately canceled reruns of his children's television show, "Pee-wee's Playhouse."

One of the first persons Reubens telephoned was Doris, who immediately offered him sanctuary in the Imelda Marcos suite at her New Jersey estate. She had come to his rescue just as she had done for notorious orphans of the past. Like many of his predecessors, Reubens was reported in the press as being petulant and demanding to Doris' staff. The misdemeanor carried a penalty of sixty days in jail and a $500 fine. Reubens pleaded no contest to the charge and agreed to perform fifty hours of community service.

Gradually, Doris began to reach out to others, trying to make amends. Johnny Gomez telephoned a number of former employees. In Newport, John Nutt was asked by Gomez if he might be interested in working again for Miss Duke. He declined.

"There was a message from Doris on my tape," said Bobby Farrah. "It was sad. Her voice had the sound of a sick woman. It was weak. 'Robert? This is Dolly Ditz. Do you remember me? Please call me.'" Farrah had not spoken to Doris for six years. "When I spoke to her, she said she knew for sure that something was being slipped to her. She feared for her life. She said she had begun to hear the stories that Chandi told people describing her as always getting drunk. Doris said it wasn't true. It was she who wanted to go out, not Chandi. But she was intimidated by her."

Farrah began to piece together the puzzle. "Doris told me she had first met Chandi through Imelda Marcos, but they weren't really friends until Chandi started taking my dance classes and I brought her to the house. I think Chandi had something to do with this cultivation of Imelda. They must have used her somehow. I think this all happened in a very very vulnerable point in Doris' life."

"I think it was a conspiracy between them," said one former Duke employee. "Doris eventually felt Imelda was using her."

Farrah had seen the best and the worst of Doris Duke. He is reluctant to judge her, because, as he put it, "Who knows how I would have handled being born into all that money? I think Doris has been a woman in search of happiness from the time she could think for herself. Looking for a life she wanted and never finding it."

Doris told Farrah the ordeal with Chandi had been "a nightmare," and that the adoption was "'the greatest mistake I ever made in my life.'"

There were rumors that Chandi Duke Heffner had hired a Philadelphia law firm to seek a financial settlement with Doris. "If Chandi tried to do anything legally, Doris will be her most spiteful," said Farrah. "The times she is attacked are the times she doesn't give a damn. If she has to dip in for ten million more to fight it, she will. And Doris will win."

On a late August afternoon, as the deadly force of Hurricane Bob made its way up the Eastern seaboard, Doris ordered her staff to remove all the furniture from her solarium in Newport. Her two camels were then ushered inside the glass-paned room, and remained there throughout the storm, attended by their glassy-eyed mistress who stared out to the storm-tossed Atlantic stroking the animals lovingly.

Epilogue

ON NOVEMBER 4, 1991, Imelda Marcos returned to the Philippines after nearly six years in exile to face tax-fraud and other charges. The widow of the late dictator took up residence in a $2,000-a-day suite at the Westin-Philippine Plaza. After four weeks, she was evicted from the hotel, and forced to move to a modest, two-story concrete house.

Chandi Heffner is reported to be living on the Big Island of Hawaii.

Doris Duke, at seventy-nine, is thriving. She has returned to her old chiropractor, Dr. Mirto, and is building an indoor swimming pool at Rough Point, in Newport. She has become interested in saving Greyhound dogs.

She has also resumed friendships with many of those she had alienated over the past two decades.

One night she was spotted at a Broadway show, *The Will Rogers Follies.* Her presence was duly noted in a New York gossip column.

Bibliography

Amory, Cleveland. *The Last Resorts*. New York: Harper & Brothers, 1948.
——— *Who Killed Society?* New York: Harper & Brothers, 1960.
Anger, Kenneth. *Hollywood Babylon*. San Francisco: Straight Arrow Books, 1975.
Auchincloss, Louis. *The Vanderbilt Era, Profiles of a Gilded Age*. New York: Macmillan Company, 1989.
Beebe, Lucius M. *The Big Spenders*. Garden City, N.Y.: Doubleday, 1966.
Birmingham, Stephen. *The Grandes Dames*. New York: Simon & Schuster, 1982.
Blumenson, Martin. *The Patton Papers 1940–1945*. Boston: Houghton Mifflin Co., 1974.
Brown, Eve. *Champagne Cholly, The Life and Times of Maury Paul*. New York: E. F. Dutton, 1947.
Burt, Nathaniel. *The Perennial Philadelphians*. Boston: Little, Brown & Co., 1963.
Cable, Mary. *Top Drawer: American High Society From The Gilded Age to The Roaring Twenties*. New York: Atheneum, 1984.
Camuti, Louis. *All My Patients Are Under the Bed*. New York: Simon & Schuster, 1980.
Clase, Pablo, hijo. *Rubi: La vida de Porfirio Rubirosa*. Santo Domingo, Dominican Republic: Publicaciones America, 1983.
Colacello, Bob. *Holy Terror: Andy Warhol Close Up*. New York: Harper-Collins, 1990.
Cunningham-Reid, Alec. *Planes & Personalities*. London: 1920.
Davies, Marion. *The Times We Had*. Edited by Pamela Pfau and Kenneth S. Marx. Indianapolis: Bobbs-Merrill, 1975.
Durden, Robert F. *The Dukes of Durham, 1865–1929*. Durham, N.C.: Duke University Press, 1975.

Ellison, Katherine. *Imelda: Steel Butterfly of the Philippines.* New York: McGraw-Hill, 1988.

Epstein, Edward Z. *Notorious Divorces.* Secaucus, N.J.: Lyle Stuart, 1976.

Flynn, John T. *The Roosevelt Myth.* New York: Devin-Adair Company, 1948.

Frank, Gerold. *Zsa Zsa Gabor: My Story.* Cleveland: World Publishing Co., 1960.

Gavan, Terrence. *The Barons of Newport, A Guide to The Gilded Age.* Newport: Pineapple Publications, 1988.

Gifford, James F. *The Evolution of a Medical Center. A History of Medicine at Duke University to 1941.* Durham: Duke University Press, 1972.

Goldsmith, Barbara. *Little Gloria . . . Happy At Last.* New York: Knopf, 1980.

Goldston, Robert. *The Great Depression: The United States in the Thirties.* New York: Bobbs-Merrill, 1968.

Graham, Sheila. *How to Marry Super Rich: or Love, Money and the Morning After.* New York: Grosset & Dunlap, 1974.

Granger, Stewart. *Sparks Fly Upward.* New York: G. P. Putnam's Sons, 1981.

Guiles, Fred Lawrence. *Marion Davies.* New York: McGraw-Hill, 1972.

Hackett, Pat. *The Andy Warhol Diaries.* New York: Warner Books, 1989.

Heymann, C. David. *Poor Little Rich Girl.* New York: Lyle Stuart, 1984.

———*A Woman Named Jackie.* New York: Lyle Stuart, 1989.

Higham, Charles. *Errol Flynn: The Untold Story.* Garden City, N.Y.: Doubleday, 1980.

Holloway, Betsy. *Heaven For Beginners.* Orlando: Persimmon Press, 1986.

Hubner, John and Gruson, Lindsey. *Monkey on A Stick: Murder, Madness and the Hare Krishnas.* New York: Harcourt, Brace, Jovanovich, 1988.

Jenkins, Alan. *The Rich Rich: The Story of the Big Spenders.* New York: G. P. Putnam's Sons, 1978.

Jenkins, John Wilbur. *James B. Duke, Master Builder.* New York: George H. Doran Co., 1927.

Jennings, Dean. *Barbara Hutton: A Candid Biography.* New York: Frederick Fell, 1968.

Josephson, Matthew. *The Robber Barons.* New York: Harcourt, Brace, 1934.

Kirstein, George G. *The Rich: Are They Different?* Boston: Houghton Mifflin Co., 1968.

Knight, James A. *For the Love of Money, Human Behavior & Money.* New York: J.P. Lippincott Company, 1968.

Konolige, Kit. *The Richest Women In the World.* New York: Macmillan Co., 1985.

Latham, Caroline and Agresta, David. *Dodge Dynasty, the Car and the Family That Rocked Detroit.* New York: Harcourt, Brace. 1989.

McAllister, Ward. *Society As I Have Found It.* New York: Cassell, 1890.

McLean, Evalyn Walsh. *Father Struck It Rich.* Boston: Little, Brown, 1936.

Maher, James T. *Twilight of Splendor.* Boston: Little, Brown, 1975.

Maxwell, Elsa. *The Celebrity Circus.* New York: Appleton-Century, 1963.

———— *R.S.V.P.: Elsa Maxwell's Own Story.* Boston: Little, Brown, 1954.

Meller, William Bancroft. *Patton; Fighting Man.* New York; G. P. Putnam's Sons, 1946.

Moats, Alice Leone. *The Million Dollar Studs.* New York: Delacorte, 1958.

Montgomery, Ruth. *Hail to the Chiefs: My Life and Times With Six Presidents.* New York: Coward-McCann, Inc., 1970.

Nielson, Waldemar A. *The Big Foundations.* New York: Columbia University Press, 1972.

O'Day, Anita with George Eells. *High Times Hard Times.* New York: Limelight Editions, 1981.

Pearson, Drew. *Diaries 1949–1959.* New York: Holt, Rhinehart & Winston, 1974.

Perkerson, Medora. *White Columns in Georgia.* New York: Rhinehart & Company, Inc., 1952.

Rasponi, Lanfranco. *The International Nomads.* New York: G. P. Putnam's Sons, 1966.

Reynolds, Patrick and Shachtman, Tom. *The Gilded Leaf: Triumph, Tragedy, and Tobacco.* Boston: Little, Brown & Company, 1989.

Snow, Carmel and Aswell, Mary Louise. *The World of Carmel Snow.* New York: McGraw-Hill, 1962.

Tebbel, John. *The Life and Good Times of William Randolph Hearst.* New York; E. P. Dutton & Company Inc., 1952.

Thompson, Jacqueline. *The Very Rich Book.* New York: Morrow, 1981.

Thorndike, Joseph, Jr. *The Very Rich; A History of Wealth.* New York: American Heritage, 1976.

Tilley, Nannie M. *The Bright Tobacco Industry, 1860–1929.* Chapel Hill: University of North Carolina Press, 1948.

Veary, Nana. *Change We Must, My Spiritual Journey.* Honolulu: Institute of Zen Studies, 1989.

Winkler, John K. *Tobacco Tycoon, The Story of James Buchanan Duke.* New York: Random House, 1942.

Wright, Cobina. *I Never Grew Up.* New York: Prentice-Hall, 1952.

Index